W9-BIS-939

TRADITIONAL and MODERN APPROACHES
to the ENVIRONMENT on the PACIFIC RIM

TRADITIONAL and MODERN APPROACHES to the ENVIRONMENT on the PACIFIC RIM

Tensions and Values

edited by
HAROLD COWARD

with a foreword by
MAURICE STRONG

STATE UNIVERSITY OF NEW YORK PRESS

Published by
State University of New York Press

© 1998 State Univeristy of New York

For information, address the State University of New York Press,
State University Plaza, Albany, NY 12246

Marketing by Nancy Farrell
Production by Bernadine Dawes

Library of Congress Cataloging-in-Publication Data

Traditional and modern approaches to the environment on the Pacific Rim:
    tensions and values / edited by Harold Coward; with a foreword by
    Maurice Strong.
          p.   cm.
    Includes index.
    ISBN 0-7914-3845-7 (hardcover: alk. paper). — ISBN 0-7914-3846-5
pbk.: alk. paper)
        1. Economic development—Environmental aspects—Pacific Area.
        2. Pacific Area—Economic conditions. 3. Pacific Area—Environmental
    conditions. 4. Environmental policy—Pacific Area.
        I. Coward, Harold G.
    HC681.3.E5T7   1998
    333.7'099—dc21   98-9800

CONTENTS

FOREWORD

Growing international concern for the environment led to the convening in 1972 in Stockholm, Sweden, of the United Nations Conference on the Human Environment, which put the environment firmly on the global agenda. Twenty years later, in response to evidence that despite progress environmental deterioration was continuing, an unprecedented number of world leaders, representatives of civil society, and the media assembled in Rio de Janeiro, Brazil, in June 1992, for the United Nations Conference on Environment and Development, best known as the Earth Summit. The conference produced agreement on a set of principles, the Declaration of Rio, and a comprehensive action program, Agenda 21, to give effect to them, as well as historic Conventions on Climate Change and Biodiversity, and established the negotiating process that has since led to agreement on a Convention on Desertification. Notwithstanding lack of agreement on some key issues, the results of the Earth Summit provide the most authoritative blueprint ever adopted by governments for the global transition to development that is sustainable in environmental and social as well as economic terms.

This book examines the apparent dichotomy contained in the Rio commitments to, at the same time, preserve the Earth's environment and engage in the economic development of the Earth's natural resources. Can these two goals be compatible or do they embody a fundamental clash of values? This question is examined in depth by focusing on activities on the

Pacific Rim. In the summer of 1995 some ten scientists, social scientists, humanists, and researchers from the private sector gathered at the University of Victoria's Centre for Studies in Religion and Society on Vancouver Island in British Columbia, Canada. They came from countries surrounding the Pacific Ocean: the United States, Canada, Russia, Japan, China, and Australia.

These scholars and scientists studied the tensions between traditional and modern approaches to environment and development. Their results are important not only for what we have done in the past but equally for what we should do in the future. Unlike most books on the environment that tend to highlight only scientific and economic issues, this book concentrates on the underlying values that can lead to conflict between economic development policy and the values of Aboriginal and traditional religions. However, society is now experiencing radical changes, which is producing a historic convergence between our traditional perceptions of relationships, between the practical aspects of human life and its moral and spiritual dimensions. We are learning that the way we treat each other and treat the Earth must be motivated by a new sense of cooperative stewardship rooted in our deepest ethical, moral, and spiritual traditions, as well as in our common interests and responsibilities.

In this book the thematic surveys of the Pacific region range from case studies of the Colorado River, the forests of Western Canada, to energy in Siberia, and urban growth in the Pearl River Delta of southern China. These chapters offer fresh insights into the various tensions between traditional and modern environment and development values in the Pacific. The broad interdisciplinary nature of this study makes it a unique and important contribution to both scholars and those who make policy decisions in both government and the private sector.

Maurice Strong
20 July 1996

PREFACE

This book is the result of an interdisciplinary team research project of the Centre for Studies in Religion and Society, University of Victoria, Canada. Scholars from such diverse areas as law, geography, anthropology, economics, theology, religion, environmental studies, and Asian studies combined to focus on "Tensions Between Traditional and Modern Approaches to the Environment in the Pacific." Criticism of draft chapters was offered by scientists, politicians, and private sector representatives.

Thanks are due to the Canadian Global Change Program, MacMillan Bloedel, Canadian Forest Products, and Dr David Strong, President, University of Victoria, for funding the research. The idea for the project was provided by the "Costing Values" series of studies of the Institute for Advanced Studies in the Humanities, University of Edinburgh.

Ludgard De Decker of our Centre staff prepared the manuscript for publication. Lois Patton and her staff at the State University of New York Press are to be thanked for the care and attention which they gave to the publication of the volume.

HAROLD COWARD

Introduction

The most vigorously developing economies and largest markets today are located on the Pacific Rim. The United States and Japan are superpowers in the global market economy. China is rapidly industrializing and, with the addition of Hong Kong, will be a major player. Then one must add Canada, Mexico, Taiwan, the Philippines, Indonesia, Thailand, Malaysia, Australia, and New Zealand as lesser but strongly developing economies. There is every reason to suggest that the economic "center of gravity" is shifting from the shores of the North Atlantic to the rim of the Pacific Basin.

But the Pacific is also the location of much of the earth's most spectacular natural beauty. Europeans continue to be enchanted by South Sea islands like Hawaii, Fiji, or Tahiti. Traditional Aboriginal societies still thrive on islands such as Tonga, the Queen Charlottes, and along the coasts of British Columbia and Siberia. Classical civilizations are challenged by modernization in Thailand, Cambodia, Viet Nam, China, and Japan. Cities like Bangkok and Mexico City, once famed for the beauty of their waterways, are now suffocated by smog and snarled with traffic on the filled and paved canals. The natural beauty of the Pacific Basin and the Aboriginal and Classical peoples who have made that environment their home are today confronting the forces of modern development. The result is a tension between traditional and modern approaches to the environment that forms the focus of this book—a book written by an interdis-

1

ciplinary team of scientists, social scientists, and humanists, all of whom focus on the environmental values that the rapid development of the Pacific Basin is placing in question.

Chapter 1 engages the issue from a global historical perspective—the context out of which the development around the Pacific Rim is arising. Ivan Head, Professor of Law and former head of the International Development Research Centre of Canada, surveys historical forces at work in the industrial development of the North and their current impact on the economies of the Pacific. He sees the challenges facing the Pacific Basin governments today as twofold: (a) to accommodate the activity of human development to the constraints of nature; and (b) to manage the multiplying populations and increasingly pluralistic societies. How? By shifting from material and consumption goals that have typified qualitative GNP-type measures to development approaches that give priority to environmental values and humanistic goals. Such a new qualitative approach, Head argues, is in line with the 1995 UN Copenhagen World Summit for Social Development, which called for economic growth that is not an end in itself but that supports social and environmental values. He points out that current practices of the developed economies and the World Bank in Washington send contradictory messages to developing economies—they ask them to adhere to environmentally sustainable practices while at the same time telling them to measure success on the basis of traditional measures of aggregate economic growth (e.g., balance of payments and GNP), which, as the developed countries well know, are usually maximized by ignoring social and environmental values. Pacific Rim leaders from the South such as Prime Minister Mahathir Mohamad of Malaysia point out the inconsistency and hypocrisy of such policies. Such inconsistencies in policy and practice need resolution if wholesome social life and a sustainable natural environment are to be preserved in the Pacific of the future.

Issues surrounding the impact of population and consumption after the Rio Earth Summit are examined by a geographer, Art Hanson, in chapter 2. Hanson observes that the Pacific Rim countries, especially those of Asia, had the most to gain from Rio. He notes that most of the world's biological diversity is found within Pacific countries and points out that the energy choices and consumption patterns of China have enormous environmental implications for the entire globe.

The conflict between rich and poor peoples and the tension between forest or fish exploitation and the ecologically based lifestyles of Aborigi-

nal people is common throughout the Pacific. Since Rio, however, a combination of NGO activism and electronic communication ensures world
attention. Rio marked the opening of UN negotiations to a wider range of
peoples' inputs—a trend that has continued up to the present including
the 1995 Beijing Women's Conference. Since Rio, any cultural or Aboriginal group experiencing government oppression or ecological damage to
traditional lands has a very active global environmental and human rights
network to call upon. Hanson catalogues the successes and failures of
Pacific countries post-Rio and offers assessments for the future in this
postmodern age when all traditional values are questioned. Traditional
values tend not to promote materialism while industrial development
does. Trade, investment, and tourism patterns post-Rio are examined with
an eye for their future impact upon the environment in the Pacific. Here
the possible effects of eco-labeling and the global development of environmental management systems standards for certifying businesses are
discussed. The greatly enhanced capacity of NGO organizations throughout the Pacific to monitor and report on environmental and social abuses
(via the electronic information networks) is seen by Hanson as one of the
very positive results produced by the Rio Earth Summit. Finally, urban
expansion and the very large "environmental footprint" needed to sustain
cities such as Tokyo or Bangkok along with the ecological debt their pollution creates are very real causes of concern for the future. A lesson at Rio
from North American Aboriginal people is that the seventh generation in
the future is the reference point for sustainable development. If current
trends continue, says Hanson, it is clear that the next ten to twenty years
will bring a great increase in pollution and in conflict between modern and
traditional values in the Pacific. Yet there are also signs of a resurgence of
spiritual beliefs that are skeptical of technological excesses and instead
turn to traditional holistic values.

A critical assessment of networking as a means for promoting positive
change in the Pacific Basin is offered in chapter 3 by Jan Walls, a Communications Professor at Simon Fraser University. He begins by identifying historically embedded Asian mindsets which are obstacles to forming
networks fostering environmental action. They include: viewing nature as
a place of truth for social dropouts to return to; taking one's primary
group as one's only concern; placing personal prosperity before environmental concern; and believing that "big company" and "big brother" are
unbeatable. However, Walls proposes various networking strategies to

overcome these obstacles. Use of the Internet allows small grassroots groups to link with others around the world who are like-minded. Walls describes many such groups that have formed in Japan, China, Taiwan, and Korea. The EnviroLink network on the World Wide Web already has links to more than 180 environmental organizations. Internet communication, says Walls, is fostering communication that supports the ancient Asian traditions of awareness and respect for Nature. The Internet also fosters action groups, both local and international, that offer alternatives to the old obstructing mindsets. The old spiritual values regarding Nature plus economical access to global electronic networks by local pro-environment groups and eco-village networks offer the hope of somehow harmonizing industry and ecology so that development can be sustainable in the Pacific. The Eco village Network is offered as an example.

Having outlined the major tensions between traditional and modern values in broad strokes in part I, part II offers an examination of specific issues in more detail. In chapter 4, Elizabeth A. Wilman and R. Douglas Burch, Canadian environmental economists, examine the problem of the commons (those parts of the environment no one owns, e.g., the atmosphere or the oceans and their fish). They seek an answer to the question, how can we get people to take care of commonly owned environmental resources? Self-interest alone will not protect the commons—indeed, it will lead to what has been called the tragedy of the commons. As Adam Smith, the founder of economics observed, the invisible hand of morals, religion, and tradition is also needed. The market works within a social contract where we agree to restrain ourselves on the condition that everyone else will agree to restrain themselves. The question is how to make this happen. The authors review the way traditional societies in the Pacific have interacted with the commons. They find practices that ensure the minimization of waste and foster conservation. These practices formed a part of the religion of traditional societies. The commons as a part of Nature were with a respect that placed a control on individual self-interest. Institutional arrangements to avoid depletion of commonly owned fishstocks are intricately interwoven into the traditional society's social fabric and are based on detailed observational knowledge of what happens in nature, but little knowledge of why. The authors suggest that rather than disrupting fragile traditional approaches, the way forward is to help traditional societies develop more scientific understanding of the natural systems. From traditional societies, the rest of the world should learn that social, cultural, and religious norms can be effective in controlling self-interested exploitation of the commons.

The role of religion is examined in chapter 5 by the eco-feminist theologian Rosemary Radford Ruether. She examines the causes behind the current treatment of women and the environment in the Pacific and finds them to be rooted in the hierarchical attitudes adopted by patriarchal Christianity. She argues that patriarchal Western culture sees women as identified with Nature, with both being open to domination and exploitation by male-dominated Christian culture. Arising in Mediterranean Europe, this worldview was carried to the Pacific by colonizing Christian missionaries. After demonstrating how it was that women came to be identified with Nature and males with culture, Ruether goes on to show that this situation was made worse with the arrival of plow agriculture and in the modem period by the Western scientific industrial Revolution—taking the domination of women and nature to new heights. In the history of Christian thought, early Christianity affirmed the Hebrew Biblical view of Nature and body as God's good creation while Greek and Latin Christianity increasingly incorporated the Platonic view of the body and Nature as the locus of sin that needed to be transcended for eternal spiritual life. The Medieval fascination with the Greek view of Nature as possessing demonic power to be tamed by male-dominated religion and culture was given further support in the Reformation by Calvin who saw Nature as totally depraved with no residue of divine presence in it. While the Scientific revolution at first exorcised Calvinistic demonic powers from Nature so as to see Nature as a manifestation of divine reason, the natural science of the seventeenth and eighteenth centuries secularized Nature so that it came to be viewed as nothing but dead matter in motion. As Ruether puts it, with no life or soul of its own, Nature could be safely expropriated by the male elite of science and industry and used to augment their wealth and power. European colonialism from the sixteenth to the twentieth centuries carried this exploitative attitude to Nature and women to the Americas, Africa, and the Asian peoples of the Pacific. Ruether's powerful and penetrating analysis is intended to make us question the negative images of women and Nature that still operate in the Pacific Basin. But she cautions against swinging the pendulum too far in the opposite direction to a romantic idealization of Nature and women. Both of these extremes need to be rejected and replaced with a view that women are neither inferior nor superior to men and that Nature is neither mindless, spiritless matter nor the idealized "ever-loving mother." Nature is to be recognized as the complex matrix of all life in which humans, male and female, are rooted as one species among others. Asian women of the Pacific Basin, says Ruether, have a special role to play in the contemporary debate—they are less likely than Euro-American women to forget that the baseline domination of women and of Nature is the impoverishment of themselves, their children, and the sea or land.

The spiritual perspective of Pacific North American First or Native Peoples is examined by Nancy Turner, an ethnobotanist, and Richard Atleo, himself a Hereditary Chief, in chapter 6. Using discussions with First Nations Elders as well as ethnographic accounts, the authors characterize the values and interaction with the environment of the Pacific First Peoples and draw contrasts with the approach of the prevailing Eurocanadian culture. Their analysis is based upon experience gained from serving on an important recent British Columbia panel, "The Scientific Panel for Sustainable Forest Practices in Clayoquot Sound," composed of both environmental scientists and Elders. The panel's review of government forest practices showed that there are major differences between traditional Aboriginal values and the values of the dominant society. While both views perceive the earth to have resources, Aboriginal values imbue these resources with sacred life and personhood in contrast to the values of the dominant society which see these same resources as having impersonal economic value. In an attempt to overcome this tension, the authors propose ways in which some Aboriginal values can be incorporated into mainstream society. Their six proposals are of special interest because they have been put forth by a panel of Elders and contemporary scientists. As of this writing these proposals have been adopted by the British Columbia government as a basis for public policy decision making and members of the forest industry have also indicated their support. The six proposals respecting forest practices in Clayoquot Sound are of broad general interest in that they place ecological relationships before development objectives while recognizing that environmental protection and economic development are mutually dependent. What this chapter offers is a unique success story where Pacific First Peoples, environmental scientists, government officials, and the public have found an ethic and practice in which Aboriginal and economic values coexist.

Against the backdrop of the rapid industrialization now racing through China and the environmental degradation such development has visited upon Taiwan, chapter 7 reviews the traditional wisdom of China and Japan as to how humans are to live in harmony with Nature. Kunihiro and Walls tell Shinto, Taoist, Buddhist, and Confucian stories illustrating how human development is to interact with Nature in a sustainable fashion. Traditional Chinese and Japanese thought is shown to contain indigenous foundations for an effective environmental ethic. Warnings are offered against imposing too much civilization upon Nature, and humans are urged to follow the Taoist *wú-wéi* principle of exploiting Nature without destroying its regenerative capacity. The private landscape garden of China and Japan attempts to recreate and maintain a piece of unspoiled Nature in an urban setting to serve as a microcosmic retreat after a hard day at the office. The idea is that one should preserve the virtue of the natural environment by "doing without overdoing." The principle of the interconnectedness of everything is examined in the Japanese awareness of the ecological link between woods, river, and sea. Reforestation on land is found to nurture seaweed in the ocean and make possible the return of fish to coasts that had become barren. This has led fishermen, foresters, and the general public to come together in a unified environmental effort. In Asian fashion this ecological truth may be stated as "fish may be found by planting trees."

In Australia, development has demanded immigration and, from the viewpoint of the Aboriginal peoples, each wave of immigration has damaged their environment irreparably. It is this tension between immigration, environment, and public policy in Australia that Fazal Rizvi examines in chapter 8. Immigration to developed countries like Australia has demonstrated that population growth and its associated degradation of the environment is not just a Third World problem. Historically, Aboriginals took from the land only those foods and materials upon which their livelihood depended. The European settlers, however, not only produced what they needed to consume but also what they could sell abroad. This latter approach has resulted in environmental damage and caused tension between the Aboriginals and the British settlers. A further point dealt with in the chapter is the Australian attempt to keep Asians out. This restrictive immigration policy was justified on environmental grounds. Asians, it was said, were either incapable of surviving in the harsh Australian climate or else were not able to look after its fragile environment. Recent debates over the future of Sydney have re-evoked the historical tendency in Australia to link environmental degradation with what are called inappropriate immigration policies—a coded way of referring to issues of race, especially Asian immigration. Other causes of environmental degradation having to do with the structure of the Australian economy and poor urban planning are examined.

The final section of the volume looks at case studies from around the Pacific Rim of attempts to reconcile traditional and modern approaches to the environment. In chapter 9, Stephen Owen and David Greer describe an innovative approach to forest management that has been developed in British Columbia—one that attempts to balance economic, environmental, and social interests so that a sustainable result is achieved. Special attention is given to the role of public participation, especially from the Aboriginal communities, in developing government forestry policy. As a result there has been a shift in the past decade away from a pattern of conflict with separate treatment of economic and environmental issues to a model based upon consensus with respect for and the accommodation of a broad range of values including both the traditional and the modern. This new approach is seen to be applicable to other Pacific Rim countries.

In chapter 10, David Getches offers a careful reading of the developmental history of the United States Columbia River Basin. Aboriginals respected and interacted with the natural processes of the river. To them the salmon offered the basis for a permanent, flourishing, and sustainable society. For them the ultimate value lay in protecting the health of the Columbia River so as to ensure the return of the salmon. By contrast, European settlers exploited water as the essential ingredient for the development of flourishing economies and the immediate satisfaction of human demands. This approach has resulted in dams and irrigation systems that have radically altered the natural flows of the river and the life cycle of the salmon—an environmental change not only for the United States and its Aboriginal population but also one that has an impact upon other Pacific peoples. Against the baseline lifestyle of the Northwest Indians who lived in a balanced interdependence with the river and its salmon, Getches charts the conflict of values that comes with European expansion into the region. Irrigation and hydroelectric projects have turned what was once the richest salmon river in the world into a series of slack water ponds and reservoirs in which few Pacific salmon survive. Policy issues such as the transfer of water from a public to a private resource are shown to have had a serious negative environmental impact on the Indians, the white coastal fisherman, and the river itself. Various remedial approaches now being tried are given critical examination. A combination of dam modification and removal along with court decisions favoring Aboriginal values over irrigation are fostering a new approach aimed at reestablishing the salmon and ensuring the survival of the tribal fisheries. The overall aim is a return to the idea of sustainability or permanence as a value for the river, its fish, and its people.

Chapter 11 shifts the focus from the United States across the Pacific to the Russian Pacific regions. Vassily Sokolov notes that these areas contain both large numbers of Aboriginals and a high percentage of Russia's rich energy resources. Projects to develop these resources have seriously disrupted the traditional Aboriginal ethic of conservation and sustainable use of natural resources. Government policies relating to both economic development and the administration of Aboriginals are reviewed and their impact upon the environment identified. Not only has severe degradation of the environment occurred but the Aboriginal populations have been reduced to a state of poverty. This is especially seen to be the case in the dynamics surrounding the development of energy systems—particularly nuclear power plants and hydroelectric dams. In recent developments, some scientists support the idea of Aboriginals being given the responsibility and power to manage their own resources. Administrative changes since the mid-1980s had resulted in the development of political activities by Aboriginal groups. But at the same time pushes by the government to exploit the vast gas reserves of the region place increased Aboriginal control over their own ecology in question.

The final chapter shifts the focus to one of the most rapidly developing economies of the Pacific Basin—the Pearl River Delta region of China. Graham E. Johnson and Yuen-fong Woon examine the uniquely Chinese pattern of making social and environmental values coexist with rapid industrial development. They demonstrate that peasant communities are not necessarily victims of industrialization and the global market economy. Instead, the Pearl River Delta Region's economic reform and open door policy from 1978 have allowed for local economic decision making in both rural and urban areas that has resulted in dynamic growth and the preservation of traditional ways of responding to and protecting the environment. Field studies by the authors offer a detailed analysis of how this is happening at four sites in the Pearl River Delta region. These vary from Dongguan Shi, next to Hong Kong, which the authors characterize as "Fully Open to the World" to the "Sustainable Development" of

Shunde Shi in the Central delta and the impact of the "Overseas Chinese Links" of the Taishan Shi communities of the Western Delta. The 1994 policy of setting up agricultural reserves has helped to prevent the push to urbanized industrial development from going beyond the point of no return. But social values derived from neo-Confucian philosophy, especially among overseas Chinese, have led them to be investors in and protectors of their ancestral environments rather than exploiters of it. This attitude together with the social values of local peoples and the policy of the central state to preserve farm land has protected the rural landscape from being eaten up by urban sprawl at a time of extremely rapid economic growth. This Chinese solution to tensions between traditional values and modern development may have valuable lessons for other Pacific peoples.

All around the Pacific Basin the struggle to resolve the tension between traditional values, modern development, and concern over the environment occupies center stage. These chapters offer insights from both thematic and case study analyses of the battle between environmental and developmental values in the Pacific.

PART I

TENSIONS BETWEEN TRADITIONS
AND MODERN DEVELOPMENT

IVAN HEAD

1. Roots and Values Inherent in Modern Development*

The Pacific Basin is an immense geographic feature: a body of water of 181 million square kilometers, circumscribed by a littoral—and dotted with islands—home to more than two billion persons. Any search for common values or shared experience must begin with an awareness of the widely scattered and disparate nature of these communities, of their distinctive histories and cultural practices, and of the broad range of economic performances found throughout this sprawling sector of the Earth's surface. From this region in ages past emerged one of the world's great religions, from it came as well some of the earliest scientific and technological accomplishments, still important to contemporary human endeavor. Within this single basin are located today examples of human activity that are among the most accomplished in the world and others so basic as to be pre-literate in character. In these lands and waters there is no single standard of environmental wholesomeness, and no common root, indeed no common definition, of development. Nevertheless, in the current period of rapid transportation and instant communications, certain industrial techniques have become increasingly widespread, as some economic indicators have gained acceptance in most countries. In these

---

*This chapter includes some thoughts first expressed by the author in the course of an address to a Conference on the Public Service and the Needs of Changing Societies held at Montebello, Quebec, September 1988.

13

circumstances, a better understanding of the tensions between traditional values and modern development may shed some light upon the current search for environmentally sustainable practices and regulatory processes.

I

Any discussion of the environmental impact of development in the Pacific or elsewhere necessarily embraces social and political structures as well as development theories and activities.[1] Since 1945, the very concept of development has been marked worldwide by several fundamental shifts and discontinuities as efforts to stimulate development in the South initially mimicked earlier successful practices in the North and then, in light of results that were either indifferent or contradictory, shifted emphasis considerably.

The major financial institutions, and those units of the United Nations dedicated to international development issues, began with the premise that economic growth was the principal necessary element. Over the years, that emphasis on growth has fluctuated, giving way to meeting "basic human needs" during the influential McNamara years at the World Bank, and more recently made subject to the strictures of "structural adjustment" policies. Throughout, however, these institutional practitioners have never varied far from the economic growth imperative, overwhelming the voices of those who have argued that development is first and foremost a social, not an economic, process and goal. These latter regard the key development factors to be the fostering of human competence and the engagement of public participation. Their influence has tended to be marginal, however, a factor that may well have contributed to environmental indifference by many decisionmakers.

In its original sense, "development" possessed a holistic meaning quite distinct from the narrow, economic interpretation still so dominant. According to Partridge,[2] the word "develop" is derived from the same old-French, middle-French root as is "envelope," and is prompted by that word. In that sense, it suggests "rolling up" or "enveloping," "enclosing"; a process much more coherent and encompassing than simple economic stimulus, especially when the latter is designed as a "trickle-down," or "rising tide" phenomenon. How, then, did the more narrowly focused interpretation come about? It is helpful to an understanding of where we are if we trace the path followed, even if it is possible to do so only by means of a series of snapshots. That path, and properly, leads through several sectors of human activity: anthropologic, economic, cultural, scientific, and political.

The origin of development is surely found in those first successes of human beings in enhancing their own physical effectiveness through the utilization of tools—one of two factors that distinguish the species from all others (the second factor being the ability to record). These two functions, tool maker and chronicler, combined with the miracles of bread wheat and other staples—rice, maize, potatoes—to permit humans to transform themselves from nomads to settlers. From the beginning of sedentary agriculture some 10,000 years ago in the fertile crescent of the Middle East, humans would become architects and engineers, shipbuilders and navigators. Technologies became more sophisticated and structures more complex. Yet there was always a limiting factor in the scale of activity and accomplishment—energy conversion. So long as human or animal labor was multiplied only by the inefficient employment of wind, water, or combustion, human activity remained essentially local, of a modest scale, and of virtually no cumulative effect upon the environment.

Not until the early eighteenth century did more robust energy transformations appear, first in the form of water wheels, then, in England, in 1769, Watt's steam engine. Now inventive humans were in command of powerful means to drive ever more complicated and effective machines. Products were manufactured that multiplied human dominance over Nature—weatherproof housing and clothing—and diminished the influence of distance—steam powered locomotives and ships. By mid-century, the industrial revolution was under way. This was the machine age, with a sudden immense increase in productivity. The initial impact was felt in the English countryside, for this revolution was a conversion of cottage industry to factories, of individual activity to groups. The result was a transformation of the English economy but, as well, of the pastoral environment.

These early assaults upon the environment did not pass without critical notice. From the perspective of a late-twentieth-century commentator, it was as if the discovery of machines and the discovery of Nature had occurred simultaneously. There was a human quality to the initial environmental commentators, one approached in this century by only a few, perhaps most notably Rachel Carson[3] and E. F. Schumacher.[4] In comparison with the shrill and often vulgar invective employed by many contemporary critics of the causes of environmental degradation, the gracious yet spirited observations of their forebears of centuries past shine like a beacon of reason and spirituality. In Britain, Ruskin; in America, Thoreau; in Europe, Goethe and Rousseau. In the period of intense literary accomplishment two centuries ago, poets joined philosophers in defense of Nature and the joys it represented to the human spirit. It was an age of immense disparities in wealth and station between the privileged and the masses, yet poetry was often able to express the feelings of all humans, as it continued to do into the nineteenth century:

> . . . on every side
> Imagination's limitless domain
> Displayed a wealth of wondrous sounds and sights.[5]

The Romantics,[6] as had the original captains of industry such as Josiah Wedgwood or Matthew Boulton, displayed a well-honed social consciousness, a deeply felt sense of social responsibility, and an intuitive awareness of the essential worth of nature. There was a decency apparent in many of these influential persons, an apparent respect for and relationship with the poverty-stricken masses, and with Nature itself, that one senses is all too often absent in the board rooms of today's powerful corporations. Where such earlier industrialists as Wedgwood and Henry Ford understood that material goods were a means to a better life, not an expression of it, the same principle expressed now by a Thomas Bata is a rare exception to the much more general and dispiriting message of materialism that influences twentieth-century society. From the graceful and uplifting language of William Wordsworth we have passed to the mindless repetitions of Barry Manilow; from a wholesome reverence for the natural countryside we are witnesses to a hypnotic dedication to urban shopping malls; in the graphic arts, Calder is preferred to Constable.

"Postmodern" tendencies are evident in one form or another throughout the entire Pacific Basin and exert considerable influence on development theory and practice even in the absence of any clearly definable Pacific community. Communal phenomena there are, of course, lending credence to some sort of amorphous society, all of them of recent origin: (i) an immensely enhanced ability to travel and communicate; (ii) the overwhelming importance that attaches everywhere to economic activity; (iii) a vague sense of commonalties and vulnerabilities—demographic, cultural, environmental, societal, political—called "security" issues by traditionalists, called "community" by the new realists. These impressions, in turn, bring to bear considerable influence on our daily lifestyles and practices. In the result, the universal desire for enhanced living standards has placed much more emphasis on economic well-being than on environmental wholesomeness. For that reason, it may be argued that environmental sustainability as an attainable goal will be achieved much less as a result of a society's choices of economic activity than it will upon the sense of value its inhabitants attach to the integrity and beauty of their natural surroundings. If this is a defensible thesis, sustainable development practices will be a product of value priorities much more than they will be the result of new technological accomplishment or improved industrial processes. Unless peoples throughout the Pacific Basin believe deeply in the significance of their natural habitat, not simply for its pharmaceutical potential or its agricultural prospects, but as the rich tapestry that lends focus and perspective to the role of the human species on its journey through life, environmental quality will without question continue to deteriorate. Only such insights and understandings of purpose will determine the limits to be imposed upon wholesale, destructive development, no matter how contributive that development might temporarily be to national accounts or to personal incomes.

The choice is not between absolutes, but it does demand a coupling of economic and spiritual requirements. It is ironic in this respect that one of the most powerful reasons why the present generation hesitates to accept the possibility of global warming, or tropical forest destruction, or species depletion, is its simple, atavistic belief in the power and resiliency of natural systems.[7] We are not yet prepared as individuals to acknowledge that the human species has been so successful in harnessing sources of power to mechanical devices that Nature is now subject to the vicissitudes of humans, and no longer the reverse. The immense strength of that false belief, combined with a narrow sense that material well-being is an ultimate human goal, represents a formula for environmental degradation of global and absolute proportions. If humankind is to curtail the propensity for destructiveness that these beliefs represent, societies everywhere must cease, in the words once employed by Dr. Lewis Thomas, to look upon this planet as nothing more than a combination of restaurant, playground, and zoo.[8]

These attitudinal factors are among those that have led to a lack of consensus on the precise goals being sought in developmental activities, and have in turn fomented disagreement on the criteria for measurement of overall success. Developmental indicators thus become vitally important for they assume a normative character and have a formative value. If delivery of electric power is the sole, measurable purpose of a hydroelectric facility, little heed need be paid to the physical effect upon the dam's catchment basin or to the numbers of persons in that area forced to relocate. If increased foreign exchange earnings are to be paramount, then it is acceptable to convert thousands of tiny, sustainable family farms into one or two giant plantations growing monocultured, exotic crops for export. If manufacturing costs and profit margins are the only standard of success, then hazardous working conditions and uncontrolled discharge of toxic effluents are not regarded as significant. When development is viewed and gauged exclusively in quantitative terms, utilizing only classical economic indicators as measurements of success, then qualitative criteria are reduced to the level of metaphor, if considered at all. Quantitative measurements by their very nature are mathematical and rational, Cartesian in their purity. They become subject as a result to the criticism of Jacques Maritain:

> Cartesian evidence goes straight to mechanism. It mechanizes nature; it does violence to it; it annihilates everything which causes things to symbolize with the spirit, to partake of the genius of the Creator, to speak to us. The universe becomes dumb.[9]

And, the evidence reveals, the natural environment suffers.

II

Rational measurements may well be most closely associated with development activities in the post-1945 period, but there is little reason to excuse earlier excesses because of their then absence. Subject only to the limitations of technology, the colonial era a century and more ago offered ample illustration of most of the currently destructive types of activities even if the motivating factor was not always the same as now. Concern, however, was contained more locally in earlier centuries and for several reasons. For one, awareness of conditions in remote parts of the world was much lower and, conditioned by the arrogance of imperialism, populations in countries of the North were largely insensitive to the plight and circumstances of far-away peoples and the lands where they dwelled. Second, the relative inefficiencies of many forms of developmental activity contained the scale of the effects. Limitations of access, machinery, markets, and overall endeavor meant that the magnitude of influence was considerably more confined than in more recent times. Third, the discipline of the social sciences had not attained the threshold of acceptance and influence that has since occurred. Thus the modern concept of social measurements was unknown; criticism of the consequence of this or that economic activity was expressed only in philosophic or religious, not scientific, terms. Finally, calculations of environmental degradation were either fragmentary or suspect. Credible data bases of the impact of human activity were simply nonexistent.

All of this, of course, has changed considerably in the past half-century. Satellites convey transmissions in real time from the most remote locations on the planet; the power and scope of modern machinery and technologies permits destruction on a massive, sometimes permanent, scale; the qualitative measurement of development and developmental activities is the subject of active work by scientifically trained scholars; considerable knowledge and innovative techniques have evolved with respect to the detrimental aspects of environmental deterioration. There is now a widespread concern that developmental efforts are in all too many instances neither benign nor effective. In the result, there is broad skepticism about development, which often makes more difficult any efforts to achieve a moderate and sustainable balance.

One explanation is found in the fact that this skepticism is not an isolated phenomenon, but part of a broad withdrawal of public confidence in governance institutions and processes of all kinds. The withdrawal, in turn, is unquestionably a reflection of the speed and dimension of the applications of modern science and technology. These latter have not only changed much more rapidly than have social organizations, they have forced social change. This, by itself, should not be surprising; technology, after all, is the greatest change agent in the history of humankind, and has been so from the first application of flint against stone to ignite fuel, from the shaping of a plow to introduce the practice of sedentary agriculture, through the steam engine, the wireless, and the electric lamp, to the manufacture of pharmaceutical marvels to preserve human life and the manufacture of weapons of mass destruction to destroy it. Societies may resist the introduction of new technologies, but in that struggle disequilibria evolve which can be more destabilizing than the changes that are opposed. The relationship between technology and governance needs to be addressed honestly, however, if modern development and its impact upon the environment is to be understood and constructively addressed.

As part of such an examination, it must be understood that there is still another element of change in this sequence. It is science. Sometime this century, science irreversibly moved ahead of technology as the initial ingredient in the duality. No longer does technology precede the scientific understanding of the underlying concept, as was the case for millennia. The principle of the lever followed by centuries its initial applications in the valleys of the Tigris and Euphrates. Thomas Edison and Alexander Graham Bell, arguably two of the most prolific innovators of all time, were inventors, not scientists. In contrast, today's technologies, without exception, are the application of scientific discoveries first evolved in laboratories, not in workshops. Thus has been increased the distance between originator and end user, making even more mysterious the processes of change and the change agents themselves, steadily eroding public confidence in the ability of public and private sector governance systems alike to manage effectively.

Equally important, one must recognize that what has changed least of all in the past 200 years is the form of government. In this age of a single biosphere, of a global economy, and of a surging population, human societies govern themselves today as they have for two centuries. Adequate as were these techniques in the age of Locke or Rousseau, their ineffectiveness in the face of nuclear holocaust, of militant terrorism, of the pandemic of AIDS, of widespread environmental degradation, and of rising social expectations is well known to peoples worldwide. Yet there is no shared agreement as to why those techniques are now inadequate, even as it is realized that there is urgency to reform them because the present momentum of technological change is irreversible and, in the nuclear age, error can be irremedial.

One of the reasons why governance seems now to be so irrelevant to the quantum and kind of problems faced in all our societies may well be rooted in the apparent inability of governors to reflect accurately the physical and natural world in which we live. This schism is much more profound than it first appears.

Those giants of political and economic constructionism to whom we have all owed so much for hundreds of years, Thomas Hobbes, John Locke, Jean Jacques Rousseau, Adam Smith, Friedrich Engels, Karl Marx, were either contemporaries or inheritors of the period of brilliant scientific accomplishment marked most significantly by the work of Sir Isaac Newton. Newton's *Principia*, published in 1687, was the most far-reaching and definitive account of the natural order of things in the history of humankind. His theories built upon the work of Copernicus and Galileo, and extended the principles of universality and consistency to all physical behavior. The laws of Nature, wrote Newton, were quantifiable, were subject to measurement and to arithmetic explanation. This concept led naturally to the presumption that the universe was predictable.

Following on the Protestant Reformation of the sixteenth century, political philosophers such as Locke and Rousseau were given the opportunity to postulate a concept of the social order not dissimilar to Newton's analysis of the natural order. Nor should it be surprising to us that they did so in a period when Newtonian ideas permeated all sectors of human activity. Astute observers such as Kidder, Kevles, and Cohen have described the phenomena thus: if the physical laws of the universe were discoverable, why should not social and political laws also be subject to experimentation and proof.[10] And so did intellectuals believe this to be the case. According to these and other scholars, there can be traced a clear relationship between the scientific revolution of Newtonianism and the social and political developments of the eighteenth century. In the same sense, it may be observed that the ongoing twentieth-century technological revolution has influenced considerably contemporary societal and political attitudes and circumstances.

Common attributes that have long appealed to scientists, to religious leaders, and to secular politicians almost everywhere have been orderliness and predictability. Governments thus came to be organized as universities had been for centuries, in carefully constructed compartments. The independent pursuit of specific scientific disciplines, the parallel tracks of a dozen or so ministries of government, the presence of often-impermeable jurisdictional membranes to separate the activities of otherwise overlapping actors—these became the norm. So was the expectation that it could all fit together if only the process were well designed. The model was available and well tested—the age-old pyramidical command and control structure of the military. Responsibility upward, authority downward. In the result, specialists proliferated; middle managers prospered. Enterprises of all kinds adopted the model: government, church, business. In Eastern societies where cultural and religious attitudes and practices were much different, many of these Western principles of governance and constructs of organization nevertheless were either introduced or consolidated.

And they seemed to work. Perhaps not always efficiently, but generally effectively. Variations there were from place to place and time to time: federal systems and unitary systems, monarchies and republics, responsible governments and those with separation of powers. But the universal popularity of the British TV series, *Yes, Minister*, is evidence of the familiarity of it all. Bureaucracy had become as universal, and some might argue as predictable, as Newton's physical principles.

Should this be surprising? No, it should not. But it will be intellectually unforgivable if we fail to understand the implications of Newton's impact upon political science and political economy, or if social scientists continue to pursue theories based upon the premise that Newtonian principles remain correct. Environmental and governance realities alike make it necessary that we accept the influence of the physical world upon our societal structures and processes, or suffer the consequences of increasing political turbulence and spreading environmental degradation.

It is not a coincidence that the now-familiar challenges to government began to emerge as Max Planck, Albert Einstein, Niels Bohr, and Werner Heisenberg revealed the shortcomings of Newton's principles of universal determinism. The first, with his quantum theory, and the second, with his theory of relativity, ushered in the modern age of physics. What was once orderly, predictable, and subject to classification had now been shown to be none of these. In the age of quantum mechanics, lack of clarity is the norm, probability has replaced certainty, and tolerance for the vaguely understood has become a necessity.

These changes in theory have profound implications, yet to date their impact has attracted much more attention from physical scientists than from political scientists. Disciplines such as anthropology and ecology are now held in high regard by scientists precisely because they are *inter*disciplinary, because they attempt to study a complex system as a whole and not break it into isolated components, as physicists for so many centuries did and as governmental administrators still tend to do.

There is irony here, for the contemporary social order is in many

respects fuzzy, somewhat out of focus, much less predictable than in earlier eras. Whether comforted or not by that knowledge, governors must
nevertheless adapt, they must accept that truth and understanding and
effectiveness depend now upon wholeness and completeness, not upon
fragmentation and simplicity. Humanity, no less than the physical universe, is organized into complex systems. Governors, to be effective, need
to acknowledge and reflect that complexity, perhaps especially so when
drafting environmental regulations and development criteria.

III

What are the challenges facing Pacific Basin governments today? They fall
broadly, in my judgment, into two categories. The first is the accommodation of human activity to the natural constraints of the planetary biosphere.
The second is the management of a rapidly multiplying and increasingly
pluralistic global society. Neither of these circumstances can be dealt with
in isolation from the other any more than can apparently discrete issues and
problems within either category. If our human reach is limited, as it is, and
our human understanding less than perfect, as it must be, our response as
individuals and governments must be one of more—not less—humility.

A beginning point in the expression of humility is to shift attention
from materialist concepts and consumption goals. One immediate effect
of doing so would be the embrace of a broad range of considerations when
considering the practice of "development," some of which are environmentally, as well as humanistically, positive. If this thesis is sustainable,
developmental practices should respond constructively. In the position
paper prepared by UNESCO for the Copenhagen World Summit for
Social Development in March 1995, for example, the Director General
argued that development is a comprehensive process: "Beyond economic
growth, which is an engine and not an end in itself, development is first
and foremost social; it is also intimately linked to peace, human rights,
democratic governance, environment, and last but not least, the culture
and lifestyles of the people."[11]

Pursuing such a comprehensive catalogue of developmental factors
may or may not result in more environmentally sustainable policies and
practices. More effective, perhaps, in diminishing the overwhelming
weight still given to economic factors are likely to be the arguments

mounted by Professor Ignacy Sachs who for years has contended that the long-adhered-to development measurement—per capita GNP—is not only incomplete and misleading but gives rise to meaningless comparisons of the "progress" or "success" of one society or another.[12] Without some means of calculating Purchasing Power Parity (PPP), or Net Human Benefit (NHB),[13] current classification endeavors are misleading at best, disingenuous at worst. In this respect, much more is involved than calculations with respect to exchange rates and per capita incomes. Lifestyles and consumption practices are of the greatest importance, as UNDP's Human Development Report persuasively argues.

Any discussion of social indicators, of course, leads inexorably to the contradiction so often apparent in value exhortations and political practices, even within a single society. In this respect, the North seems incapable of understanding that it is sending entirely contradictory signals to the South when it implores on the one hand that environmentally sustainable practices be adhered to (as in timber harvesting), yet measures success, and designs borrowing and investment incentives, on the basis of aggregate economic growth—balance of payments, GNP, public accounts surpluses, and the like. Much more negative in effect than the obvious hypocrisy of expecting the South to abandon the very sort of development policies and practices still so common in the North, are these "success" criteria designed in and imposed by Northern-dominated institutions.

Not surprisingly, leaders such as Prime Minister Mahathir Mohamad of Malaysia have become outspoken critics of what they call neo-imperialistic social policies projected from the North. Lee Xuan Yew, for example, has emphasized unceasingly the inherent inconsistency of many Northern policies. In one relevant instance, Japan advocates sustainable forest management practices to the nations of Southeast Asia and extends financial assistance to that end, while coincidentally proffering that assistance in the form of repayable loans (instead of grants). All the while, Japan offers to these countries a seemingly insatiable domestic market for tropical forest products at prices that do not reflect the cost of environmentally sound extraction techniques. In the result, the South may be excused for bewildered and incoherent responses. Thus are contradictions revealed between values and practices. The knowledge and cultural preferences of indigenous peoples in Sarawak have little chance of prevailing over the policies set by the Ministry of Finance in Kuala Lumpur in response to directives from the World Bank in Washington, D.C.

IV

Can the world continue to tolerate these shortsighted, fundamentally flawed policies and practices? The evidence is mounting that it cannot. The combination of human activities collectively described as development has now reached a level of such actual and potential environmental destruction as to induce disruption of natural systems. The primary reason, quite clearly and ever more ominously, is scale. From a relatively recent record of human transformation of energy and materials that was minuscule in comparison with the extent of natural planetary resources and systems, human activities are now in many instances of a scale equal to fundamental natural processes. In such circumstances there have emerged complex, possibly irreversible syndromes of environmental destruction.[14]

To overcome these grave imbalances, the human species must undertake attitudinal and behavioral changes of at least similar scale, and likely as large as at any time in recorded history. These changes cannot be accomplished simply, and certainly not only through the introduction of new technologies or new accounting practices. Nor, with a world population rapidly approaching six billion on its way to ten billion or more in the following few decades, can the North on its own affect the necessary adjustments. With a South-North population spread of 80–20 now, to be 90–10 soon, the policies and practices of the South are critical. The frightening reality is that the immense current South–North imbalances in well-being and participation guarantee a continuation and an acceleration of these environmentally destructive phenomena unless major structural and systemic alterations are made in the international community as a whole. The rate of that acceleration and the magnitude of impact give us precious little time to make the massive adjustments necessary.[15]

The negotiation of the necessary transition, with the redesign of so much with which we are familiar, demands a demonstration of wisdom much in excess of any that is presently evident anywhere in this vast Pacific Basin. The current sense of failure of governance, as one example, is a reflection of basic design flaws. The increasing diminishment of the effectiveness of sovereign states has not yet given way either to adequate international institutions and processes, or to broad national understandings of why such are necessary.

Centuries ago, in the age of innocence, when certainty was assumed and Nature was dominant, all notions of community were local and most decisions were driven by faith. Development at that time was shaped not so much by technological prowess as by the holistic concept of the term and the process. In the age of reason and of geographic discovery, which has been dominant for some 300 years, our sense of community has failed to evolve with equal coherence. We acknowledge the proximity of societies from one side of the world to the other, and understand the increasing ease of communication and travel, yet reject the necessary community elements of shared responsibility and sense of common cause. The massive increase in information flow has not evolved into a concept of neighborhood, one that engages natural, as well as human, phenomena; one that recognizes that otherwise rational individual decisions are often not only destructive of the common good, but of the long-term private good as well.

The value we must address is much more salient than that of a wholesome environment; it is as basic as human survival. That value, surely, is more than a "Pactfic" value; it is respected universally. If conscientiously adhered to, and reflected in sensitive, realistic governance practices, it might reduce current tensions and restore the quality of humility necessary for environmentally sustainable and equitable development—not just throughout the Pacific Basin, but worldwide. Ironically, yet constructively, we shall have rediscovered the holistic root structure of sustainable development coincidental with renewed respect for the majesty of the natural environment.

NOTES

1. In this text, the term "development" will be employed primarily in the context of "the developing countries," that large number of often recently independent states located in Africa, Asia, Latin America, and the island states of the Caribbean and the South Pacific, collectively referred to as "the South." Other development circumstances will be examined, but always identified.

2. Eric Partridge, *Origins; The Encyclopedia of Words* (New York: Macmillan, 1958).

3. Rachel Carson, *The Silent Spring* (Boston: Houghton Mifflin, 1962).

4. E. F. Schumacher, *Small is Beautiful; Economics as if People Mattered* (New York: Perennial Library, 1975).

5. Robert Browning, "Parlayings with Certain Peoples of Importance," in *The Complete Works of Robert Browning*, ed. Charlotte Porter and Helen A. Clarke (New York: Florentine, 1910).

6. i.e., those writers and painters in Britain and Europe associated with the Romantic Movement, which took place roughly between 1770 and 1850. Among them were Wordsworth, Coleridge, Goethe, Rousseau, Byron, Shelley, Keats, and the English painter J.M.W. Turner. "The Romantics saw and felt things brilliantly afresh.... They were strenuous walkers, hill-climbers, sea-bathers, or river-lovers. They had a new intuition for the primal power of the wild landscape, the spiritual correspondence between Man and Nature, and the aesthetic principle of 'organic' form...." *(The Oxford Companion to English Literature*, 5th ed., ed. Margaret Drabble [New York: Oxford University Press, 1985], pp. 842–43).

7. Another is an unwillingness to accept as credible either the assessment or the prescription of governments in diverse sectors, the environment among them, as discussed later.

8. Then chancellor of Memorial Sloan-Kettering Cancer Center. This phrase was employed by him on public speaking occasions, such as at a dinner in his honor organized by The Aspen Institute for Humanistic Studies in New York City, November 1984.

9. Jacques Maritain, *The Dream of Descartes* (London: 1946), quoted in E. F. Schumacher, *A Guide for the Perplexed* (New York: Harper and Row, 1977).

10. Rushworth M. Kidder, Daniel J. Kevles, I. Bernard Cohen.

11. Paris, UNESCO, 29 July 1974.

12. See, for example, Ignacy Sachs, *Environment and Development: A New Rationale for Domestic Policy Formulation and International Cooperation Strategies* (Ottawa: Environment Canada, 1977).

13. A term first proposed by Prime Minister Pierre Elliott Trudeau of Canada in 1969.

14. See, in this respect, Jim MacNeill, Pieter Winsemius, Taizo Yakushiji, *Beyond Interdependence; The Meshing of the World's Economy and the Earth's Ecology* (New York: Oxford University Press, 1991).

15. We live on what I have called "A Hinge of History," See *On a Hinge of History; the Mutual Vulnerability of South and North* (Toronto: University of Toronto Press, 1991).

ARTHUR HANSON

2. The Pacific after Rio: Population, Consumption, and the Environment

THE DOWNWARD SPIRAL

The 1992 Earth Summit in Rio de Janeiro linked political leaders from the South and North in unprecedented agreement on an "Agenda for the twenty-first century" (Ramphal 1992). Countries such as Malaysia, China, Japan, Canada, and Costa Rica played a very prominent role during two preparatory years of negotiations that focused on sustainable development. The purpose of sustainable development is to link concerns of environmental integrity, economic development, and the well-being of people (World Bank 1992). This must be done in a fashion that protects options for future generations as well as meeting present needs. If successful it would reduce the current tension between traditional and modern approaches to the environment.

Pacific Rim countries, especially those of Asia, had the most to gain from Rio (ADB 1990; ECLAC 1991; ESCAP 1990; UNDP 1994; Seager 1995). Most of the world's people share this vast basin. It is the region with the most rapid rates of economic growth; the new foundry of the industrial age; and, simultaneously, the centre of the information economy. Countries such as Japan and the United States cast a gigantic ecological shadow throughout the entire Pacific Rim through their import of raw materials and their export of polluting industries to offshore sites. Most of the world's biological diversity is found within Pacific countries, particu-

29

larly the "megadiversity" countries such as Indonesia, China, and Australia (McNeely et al. 1990). The significance of energy choices and future consumption patterns within China, in particular, and other parts of Asia has enormous implications for the entire globe (CCICED 1995).

The Pacific includes vociferous small island states concerned about rising sea levels if global warming occurs; it includes tropical timber producers such as Malaysia and Indonesia that fear non-tariff, environmental trade barriers for their products; and it includes "Ecotopia," the thin band of land stretching from Alaska through British Columbia to California, where values and decisions are now shaped by environmental as much as other considerations. The Pacific countries, which have sought to wrestle the production base of the world from the United States, Western Europe, and Japan, with few exceptions (e.g., Singapore) have not come to grips with the complex relationship of environment and economy. The "Little Dragons," China, and Mexico continue to build a substantial ecological debt. It will be decades before their environmental problems can be fully addressed. And, on the supply side of raw resources, the ecologically destructive role of Siberia as a supplier of low cost materials to the Pacific Rim economies is becoming a matter of regional, even global concern. As Vassily Sokolov makes clear in chapter 11, the impact of Siberian energy development upon the native peoples there has been disastrous.

Culture and religion have been, are, and will continue to be important to environment and social conditions in the Pacific. Even with the migration of people away from the land into huge cities, rich traditions remain. Layering of beliefs presents complexity. For example, Javanese culture layers animist belief with Hindu and Buddhist concepts and subscribes to Muslim religion. The mosaic of culture within countries like Indonesia and China, or within the indigenous cultures of the mountainous regions of western Canada and Latin America at the best of times has spread the seed of conflict. Yet these levels of conflict frequently were confined to very local areas before colonial times. Indeed, it was the colonial powers that brought about much of the early environment and development conflict and systemic violence, even while documenting the fantastic resource base of the Pacific region (Ponting 1991, Grove 1995). Later, the massive influence of World War II and the follow-up Cold War conflicts throughout the Pacific introduced a new level of violence against humanity and civil society, but also produced ecological damage on an unprecedented scale. Wars set the stage for technological incursions into the remotest corners; and for the switch from colonial political regions to the range of democratic to authoritarian systems now in place.

Regrettably, conflict still continues. Now it has a blatantly ecological as well as social identity. This is most dramatically seen in the situation of aboriginal/indigenous/First Nations' peoples who base their economy on healthy ecosystems (Durning 1993). The plight of forest-dependent people in Sabah, British Columbia, and the western Amazon is remarkably similar. Where conflict is based upon religious differences, for example in Mindanao's secession-minded Muslims, the national response is frequently resource-based destruction. People without a forest are no longer a forest people. They are impoverished and controllable. This sad strategy has been played out all too often with the active assistance of governments. Now, at least, there is better opportunity for the world to know and act when these transgressions occur. For in the post-Rio period, information flow is swifter, thanks to the combination of NGO activism and electronic communication (Hall and Hanson 1992).

The conflict of rich and poor is common throughout the Pacific and rarely does it not involve either fierce competition for land and resources or insidious environmental degradation. The case of El Salvador is one of the most depressing and, possibly, a harbinger of stories to come within parts of the Pacific region. The absolute concentration of the highest quality land within a small number of families left little for most of the country's population to farm. The combination of intensive use of the most marginal lands and decades of civil conflict have reduced the ecological carrying capacity very significantly.

While there may be some recovery of landscapes in El Salvador, it will be measured in decades or even centuries. This is the bleak dilemma facing much of the Pacific. Population levels are now at such a level that civil wars, or other disturbances, have tremendous potential to destroy the ecological base of a country. Consider the effects of the drug war in Latin America, the impact of a breakup of a country as vast as China or Indonesia. It is not surprising that global and regional security are now being measured in ecological as well as social and more conventional military terms.

In no country within the Pacific is there an adequate relationship, or harmony, between environment and development. The relationships of population, consumption, and environment are in complex transitions. It is important to recognize that the situation is bad within countries such as

Canada, Australia, Japan, and the United States. It is wrong to point fingers at Mexico, China, and Indonesia, or expect higher performance on their part, without fundamental changes in the higher income nations of the Pacific.

At Rio, and in follow-up global meetings such as the 1994 Cairo Conference on Population and Development, much time was spent on considering whether the most important impacts on environment are those of population pressure or consumption patterns, especially those of the richer nations. The distinction is blurring for some nations such as China. Not only is it the most populous, but it is also becoming the manufacturing center for the world. Thus, it is assuming the pollution load of a huge range of exported products. At the same time, its population is in transition to becoming a consumer society. Can there be a more difficult environmental management situation in the world? Yet, as chapter 12 demonstrates, there are some unique solutions being pioneered in China's Pearl River Delta—at the heart of its industrialization.

This introduction has focused on some of the more serious problems of poverty, economic growth, conflict, and environment in the Pacific. The critical issue, of course, is to identify workable solutions, including the institutional arrangements, capacity building, and new international relations that will help bring about these solutions. This was the purpose of the Earth Summit. The question now is whether change in the Pacific is progressing toward a more sustainable pathway of development. And whether any new pathway will present a reduction of the tensions between traditional and modern approaches.

THE RIO AGENDA AND PACIFIC VIEWS

In the preparations for Rio, extensive regional consultations took place, for example via ESCAP and its Latin American equivalent. There was no trans-Pacific grouping. Western Europe, the United States, and Canada collaborated among themselves much more than with developing nations. Views presented in Rio represented coalitions around specific economic cultures, geographic groupings, and sectoral themes for example, forests, where Malaysia and Canada were leaders, the association of small island states worldwide, and Aboriginal peoples, especially from the Americas, Asia, and the Pacific.

It is perhaps not surprising that the resulting documents were complex (Grubb et al. 1993; Johnson 1993; Keating 1993): Agenda 21, the blueprint of future sustainable development initiatives; the Global Conventions on Biodiversity and Climate Change; the bothersome (because of inconsistencies) Rio Declaration; and more specialized outputs such as the Forestry Principles, the preparations for a Convention on Desertification, the agreements for a Conference on Small Island Management, and for Convention negotiations on Straddling Fish Stocks on the High Seas. It was not an unreasonable outcome. In fact, one could hardly have expected more from a global consensus-seeking effort.

Compared to some other parts of the world, many Pacific nations have developed quite sophisticated approaches to environmental matters. Russia could learn much from the experience of Indonesia or other Southeast Asian nations on environmental pollution control. The pursuit of integrated agricultural systems is very advanced in East and Southeast Asia compared to almost anywhere else. The pursuit of fish culture while intensifying rice and other cropping systems stands as an example. Yet nations attending the Rio Summit by and large were not particularly interested in this level of exchange. The interest of all governments was focused on financial flows, but there were special interests as well: access to Western markets on the part of developing nations, and concern for tropical and subtropical biodiversity protection on the part of richer nations.

It was left to the NGOs to press concerns related to the ecological and social damages faced by indigenous peoples, the need for change in the ethics of consumption, and many other topics important in building values for sustainable development. Rio, for the first time, opened UN negotiations to this broader range of peoples' inputs. It was an important milestone in global regional democratization. This trend has continued right up to the present, including the Beijing Women's Conference in September 1995. No cultural group need feel quite so isolated in the face of government oppression or ecological damage to traditional lands in the post-Rio period. There is now a very active network that is not only Trans-Pacific, but also global for most environment and development concerns including those related to human rights. This is a lasting outcome catalyzed by the intense period of preparations leading up to Rio.

Three Pacific nations stand above all others in their impact on these issues. China, Japan, and the United States can "queer the deal" (as the

United States tried at Rio); be "wooed" (China in the post-Rio period); or "buy influence" (Japan's efforts to bolster environmental development assistance throughout the region). It is, however, far too simplistic to categorize these notions so imply, or to ignore the importance of leadership of other Pacific nations. Tiny Costa Rica is now building its economy on sustainability principles, for example by commitment to responsibility-based ecological tourism. China has, on paper at least, perhaps the world's best national response to Agenda 21 (PRC State Council 1994).

Indeed, it is tempting to pick "winners and losers" in the post-UNCED period. It is difficult to do so because it truly is a multivariate game. China, which achieved a certain level of inspiration and direction from Rio, at the same time is moving into a phase of economic growth that will lead to a short-term downward spiral in environmental quality. Whether the wealth creation will lead to longer-term investment for environmental protection is uncertain. Also uncertain is whether there can be long-term political stability and expression of human rights necessary for sustainable development.

In the case of Japan the situation is different. While fostering domestic environmental quality (it is the most forested nation on earth by some measures), its destructive ecological influence throughout the Pacific is still uncorrected. Japanese corporations play one region against another to ensure ready access to low cost timber, minerals, and other resources. Their role in Pacific fisheries is predatory. They have moved "dirty" industries such as smelters offshore to locations such as Sumatra.

And the United States continues to hold back progress in important areas such as energy pricing, agricultural subsidies that influence use of marginal lands, and in its general antipathy toward constructive action on the Climate Change and Biodiversity Conventions. No Pacific nation is tackling the issues of sustainable development with the fervor of a few West European nations such as Germany, Norway, the Netherlands, and Denmark. Ironically, some of the positive action in Europe reflects negatively on parts of the Pacific. The stringent recycling laws within the EU countries have led to a diversion of wastes to Asia.

Thus, it is difficult to point to any single nation in the Pacific region that can be classified as an overall "leader" in environment and development without reference to specific elements of the post-Rio agenda. We must also consider those with special interests and concerns, and those that, for one reason or another, stand to lose mightily through accumulated environmental debts. Undoubtedly it is China that will gain the most attention in the years to come.

THE CLASH OF TRADITIONAL AND MODERN VALUES IN THE SEARCH FOR SUSTAINABILITY

As the new millennium approaches, it is difficult to focus exclusively on either traditional or modern values. We live in a time when "postmodern" values and assumptions have become important, even essential, for notions such as intergenerational equity. Yet we cannot fully define what it is that will be of most material comfort to our children's children. Nor can we fully predict within nations whether assimilation or multicultural strategies will be the wave of the future. The rapidly expanding flow of people; global communications via satellite broadcasting, fax machines, and the Internet; and the penetration of international trade and multinational corporations are powerful forces that would seem to break down traditional values.

We certainly can find examples where this breakdown is the case. Yet we must also consider how these values can reassert themselves, especially as societies enter their postindustrial or postmodern phase. As an example, the Haida nation, traditional inhabitants of the European-named Queen Charlotte Islands. Reduced earlier this century to a population in the hundreds, they are recovering, are still prolific in their native art, and are dependent for their cultural values on access to 700-year-old cedar forests. They have successfully resisted the logging of traditional lands. Now, in 1995, they are co-managers of a park reserve that is ecologically regarded as the "Galapagos of the North." They are in the vanguard of aboriginal nations seeking to reestablish traditional values and settle land and resource claims. The Haida nation is sharing these values with rapidly expanding numbers of sea kayakers and others who are adding new forms of sustainable economic activity. These new activities, as often as not, are linked to low impact, low consumption approaches that seek reconciliation of spiritual, cultural, and material values.

Unfortunately, this example is more the exception than the rule. In Chiapas, Mexico; the Western Amazon; the jungles of Sabah and Sarawak; Irian Jaya; and in many of the coastal fishing communities of Asia and the Americas, there is unrelenting pressure and violence against the resource base and the original inhabitants. At best, traditional knowledge and management approaches are lost. At worst, people become environmental refugees, forced to flee for their lives or their livelihoods.

There is some hope that such acts may be curbed. After Rio, international agencies, such as the World Bank and the Asian Development Bank, have become far less likely to support poorly conceived, highly subsidized land development and other ecologically destructive projects (World Bank Environment Department 1995). Systems of recourse are starting to emerge. One of the most effective routes to start the process is through NGO information channels working between developed and developing countries. Transnational corporations are vulnerable in their home countries if they are perceived by NGOs to be affecting traditional values and ecosystems elsewhere. Within the Pacific, this counterpressure works with transnational corporations from Europe and North America. In the past five years particularly, many now apply the same stringent standards to a plant in Taiwan that they would in the United States.

On the other hand, companies originating in Japan, or in countries such as Taiwan, Korea, or Hong Kong, or those in Thailand and Indonesia have far fewer domestic pressures to ensure that they will adhere to high standards internationally.

Traditional values in many Pacific societies focus on a holistic appreciation of Nature (often with deep spiritual connections), with stewardship rather than ownership, and with community-based sharing. While these values may be robust in isolated settings, they can quickly disintegrate in the face of imposed, outside values; or in the face of technological interventions such as new harvesting techniques. It is only within the past decade that a reasonable appreciation of the worth of traditional knowledge is gaining ascendancy in natural resource scientific and decisionmaking circles. This is at a time when there is widespread concern about the inadequacies of resource management models promoted by organizations such as FAO. The failure of foresters to consider biodiversity, the failure of "managed" fisheries, including the impact on marine mammals of Pacific driftnets and other gear, and the erosion of plant crop genetic diversity as a result of green revolution introductions are shaping the search for models that do incorporate traditional knowledge and values.

Traditional values tend not to promote materialism, certainly not on the scale found in countries such as Australia or the United States. With consumption levels further reduced by community-based recycling in low income areas, consumption levels seem almost inconsequential until multiplied by enormous population numbers. The arithmetic of China in relation to almost any type of consumption is a case in point (Ryan and Flavin 1995).

As people migrate into cities and achieve a higher level of income we can expect to see much greater levels of per capita consumption. At Rio the celebrated argument was the impact of having a refrigerator in every Chinese household: effects on the ozone layer, energy consumption, etc. Surely there will be a day when every Chinese family does have this essential complement of Western living. What will those on the other side of the Pacific have to give up for this to happen? On the other hand, the Chinese may well develop a higher per capita consumption of wheat products, beef, or other imported products that will affect land use and ecology of the North American Great Plains. What should be the response of Canada and the United States in such a situation?

In the post-Rio period it is now common to discuss "sustainable consumption." To apply this term with any sense of equivalency for a tribal member in New Guinea and a suburban householder in California, or a middle-class resident of Jakarta, is very difficult.

TRADE AND INVESTMENT

Pacific countries will attract the bulk of the world's investment in the decade to come. This continues a trend that is, of course, the most significant source of change for developing nations. It is said that international currency flows respect no national boundaries, have no moral or ethical underpinning and provide the most striking and effective commentary on a country's fiscal management. Countries in Asia have tended to carry out their own structural adjustments, acting along lines that the IMF would find very gratifying, in order to make their economies more open to investors. Investors are interested not only in the potential of cheaper labor for the production of expert-oriented goods, but also in creating mass markets within populous countries. When annual paper consumption is still at a level of two to four kg/person compared to hundreds of kg in the United States, market opportunity beckons.

Investment rules should be designed to take into account both environmental and social impacts of foreign projects. Indeed, the donor agencies and international development banks now try to do so, although imperfectly. But most development investment no longer flows through these channels. It is private sector investment that is the engine of economic growth in the Pacific countries. Since the time of Rio this trend has shifted even more. Development assistance is waning in terms of overall amount. It is certainly not sufficient to meet the expanding demands for global and regional initiatives such as those related to climate change (Najman and d'Orville 1995). Proportional to the rate of private sector investment growth, the decline is even more dramatic. Thus, just at a time when they are most needed to address the relationship of environment and development, development organizations are curtailing activities drastically.

There are many case studies of how investments (national and international) have disrupted the ways of traditional peoples within the Pacific. Standard textbook views on economic development suggest this as a normal course of events—not the exception. Governments routinely use regional investment strategies as a means to convert traditional and secessionist views to national views (Southern Thailand, many parts of Indonesia) as part of a strategy for exerting rights of lent and resource ownership (East Malaysian forestry practices) and as a means to fill the national treasury (offshore oil development in Vietnam and other countries). More nefarious are strategies of investment directly intended to destroy tribalism and local culture. The examples pertaining to aboriginal peoples are numerous and depressing since it is clear that they continue despite international campaigns and local resistance. They can also be invidious, for example, the effects of tourism on road building and economic agendas on the hill tribes of Thailand. The increased recruitment of young hill tribe women as prostitutes, and the breakdown of local value systems are examples of impacts. These effects are intensifying rather than decreasing in the post-Rio period.

How governments perceive existing and potential impacts of investment depends in part on the rate of economic growth. Most countries are now aware of past environmental and social impacts. One of the powerful arguments for rapid economic investment and growth is to use this wealth creation process to address major problems. Indeed, it is a central argument of the Brundtland Commission's 1987 report, "Our Common Future," that such growth is essential if we are to solve world development problems (WCED 1987).

The powerful elixir promoted by countries is a combination of access to basic health and family planning services; education (after the 1994 Cairo Conference on Population and Development especially with attention to access for women); basic infrastructure; rural credit at reasonable interest rates, and investments promoting local industries and/or natural "development". Many Pacific countries look to the success of South Korea as an example. It is now a "graduate" of the World Bank, an entrant to the OECD pack, and a country that produced a contender to lead the new World Trade Organization. It is also a country that has maintained many of its traditions, but that is not known for sensitive treatment of either environment or cultures in its worldwide project engineering dominance. Korea has not addressed its own environmental problems thoroughly, but in the post-Rio climate it is beginning to demonstrate some leadership internationally. Most significantly, Korea more than many other Asia-Pacific nations recognizes the potential economic benefit of being a leader in the sale of environmental technologies, and the danger of losing markets as a result of green consumerism.

An approach that is pragmatic and quite widely followed now is to place more emphasis on regulating new industrial and other projects differentially from activities already in place. The rationale is threefold: rapid economic growth diminishes the significance of existing activities in comparison to the new; hard-to-deal-with small and medium scale enterprises may be exempted from costly pollution control legislation or receive other special treatments; concentration of limited enforcement capacity can be directed to high profile situations including those involving multinationals. China is the leading example of the first case. When economic growth rates of more than ten to fifteen percent per year are compounded over even a few years, it is easy to understand how significant it is to get the decisions right for any new investment.

It is much easier to take this approach for the so-called "brown" environmental concerns—those related to pollution and to the built environment, including urban environmental quality. It is much more difficult to adequately address biodiversity and rural social impacts via this approach. Throughout the Pacific Rim these impacts are felt as the cumulative result of a plethora of projects interacting with local resource use that is also affected by rapid population growth and increasing access of local markets to international trade. Sorting out cause and effect can be difficult, but insidious environmental and social change over periods of time is the end result.

Sometimes these changes eventually manifest themselves in dramatic ways, such as the 1988 landslides in Southern Thailand (Royal Thai Government and USAID 1989). This major environmental disaster resulted from decades of poor upland use, in part to serve foreign rubber markets, and left 400 people dead and a dreadful legacy for future generations to deal with. This legacy includes rivers clogged with debris and prime agricultural areas reduced to rock gardens. The impact was nationwide since forest cutting was then banned throughout Thailand. There are impacts on traditional peoples in neighboring countries such as Cambodia and Myanmar. Because Thailand is now a log importer these people suffer loss of forest biodiversity and face further disruptions in their way of life.

The Thailand example illustrates the post-Rio dilemma. There now exist global, and therefore also regional agendas to deal with environment and development concerns. A sufficient amount of rhetoric and agreement in principle among nations exists to cover major problems, including biodiversity and the eradication of poverty (formally agreed to by Heads of State at the Social Summit in Copenhagen, March 1995). Yet these agreements either fly in the face of actual performance within countries, or of the behavior of Pacific nations toward their neighbors, or globally, as the lack of progress at the 1995 Berlin Conference of Parties on Climate Change demonstrated.

How can trade and investment help to safeguard local cultures, respect traditional rights, and protect biodiversity? This is a tall order, and one of the most important new themes to merge since 1992 (Anderson and Blackhurst 1992; IISD 1994; Guevara 1995). Completion of the Uruguay Round of GATT did little to advance the cause directly, but in the process much greater interest emerged in the use of trade-related measures to ensure that goods are being produced in an "environmentally and socially sustainable fashion," that harmful substances are not offloaded into nations ill-equipped to handle them, and that endangered species not be traded internationally. Some of these matters are at least partly dealt with through the Basel Convention on Transport of Hazardous Goods, and the earlier, pathbreaking Convention on International Trade in Endangered Species (CITES) (Andersson et al. 1995).

Action has focused on what may be accomplished through the new World Trade Organization (WTO) and via various regional agreements such as NAFTA, and within regional organizations such as ASEAN and

APEC. Somewhat predictably, there is potential for a major North–South split. Nations such as Malaysia fear a new Northern-inspired conditionality on market access, unaccompanied by new offers of financial support for biodiversity maintenance or environmental technology sharing (a major concern of China).

There is enough progress being made to predict that within the next three to five years trade agreements will routinely incorporate environmental conditions. These may have both positive and negative impacts on traditional peoples and the areas they inhabit. The negative may occur if some of their tradable products are indiscriminately incorporated into lists of contentious goods. Some forest products such as rattan come to mind. On the other hand, through the international trading systems there is a powerful means to create accountability about how goods are produced. Whether the issue is harsh child labor practices, destruction of tribal lands, or biodiversity production, there may be channels for at least dialogue, and possibly action.

A complementary approach that is coming together rapidly is the creation of voluntary certification standards nationally, or internationally via the International Organization for Standardization (ISO). In particular, rapid progress has been made on the development of environmental management systems standards (ISO 14 000), by which a business can be certified as adopting an acceptable approach to environmental matters in its overall operations. This certification may, in the future, be demanded by manufacturers and others in North America, Japan, and Europe, from suppliers, including those in developed nations. It is worth noting that the approach emerged in Europe, in response to new EU regulations, not in the Asia-Pacific region. But it will affect producers in this region and could be one of the routes for new environmental action.

There is a related approach that is emerging within several developing countries such as Indonesia, as well as in countries such as Canada, and via the ISO. This is eco-labeling: the acknowledgment by a national or international standards group that a good is produced according to some environmentally and socially acceptable criteria. The problems with eco-labeling are that criteria may not be internationally acceptable, or that the process may be "green wash" marketing, or that the effort to make a proper system work may be simply overwhelming. This approach, however, offers consumers some needed information to broaden their choices.

Green consumerism is still largely the province of the North American and European marketplaces, but the situation is changing, as the world-wide Consumers International organization can attest. Eventually, within all major Pacific Rim cities, eco-labeling will have a following among local consumers.

Finally, a small but important counter to the homogenization of products and locally negative impacts of trade is the role of "alternative trade networks" drawing upon products created by traditional peoples, and products harvested on a sustainable basis from the forest and seas of tropical regions. The stimulus for this trade comes from numerous sources, including groups active within developed countries of the Pacific. Whether it is "Amos and Andes" sweaters from Ecuador or wood carvings from villages in Bali, the imported products are intended to support rather than destroy local culture. Hopefully, this type of trade will continue to expand, and be linked to locally defined development initiatives. Yet it is always likely to be a tiny fraction of global trade.

More significant in terms of impact is the role of tourism as a component of international trade. As any regular user of airports within the Pacific Basin will attest, growth is exponential. The impacts on traditional culture and religion are undeniably major, although not always negative. The strength of Balinese culture and religion in the face of ever-increasing tourism is one of the best examples. The case of Northern hill tribes in Thailand is among the worst. Many more cases lie in between. Eco-tourism has emerged in the post-Rio period as the most rapidly growing segment of the tourist industry. There is genuine opportunity here for reconciliation of traditional, modern, and postmodern influences, although the task is not easy. The image of Pacific tourism is still dominated by middle-class travelers sampling a safe array of sights, shopping, and seashore; the Japanese tour group; the ubiquitous North American or European student backpacker (who is not necessarily an innocent in terms of creating cultural change); and sex-seekers inhabiting resort centers and cities such as Bangkok.

This overview of the significance of trade and investment as a dominant factor creating change in the Pacific only scratches the surface of issues. And to complete the picture it is necessary to introduce the complex subject of electronic communications, and the impact instant information transfer can have on both new and traditional forms of development.

NETWORKS AND INSTANT COMMUNICATION

The crisis of confidence suffered by Mexico early in 1995 was the direct result of international currency tracers' judgment on events within the country, including uprisings in Chiapas as well as national fiscal policy. The repercussions were felt throughout national capitals in the Pacific, for no nation could feel immune. As another example, when the Japanese yen strengthens, the debt repayment load of countries such as Indonesia is significantly increased, resulting in more rapid exploitation of natural resources (the values of which do not increase proportionately) such as forest and sea products, with impacts on local peoples. This cycle is not new, but it is increasing in impact in part because the electronic linking of world currency trading centers has created a reality that these traders (including speculators) can upset national desires and plans virtually overnight.

On the more positive side of the communications revolution is the growing NGO-based capacity to report on progress in negotiations and on potential environmental and social impacts before they occur, and to access information such as the performance of companies in various parts of the world (for a description of key NGO organizations and their roles see Bergesen and Parmann 1995). This electronic interface between technology and traditionalism allows for accurate documentation of impact (video camera); relatively low cost, and therefore more frequent communication among groups; instant information transmittal on serious environmental and human rights concerns from isolated communities to the rest of the world (fax and now E-mail); and, for the future, possibilities that relate to distance education (with all the pluses and minuses related to who sets curricula). The main point is that it is becoming increasingly difficult for governments to control information flow. Much of the panic within the Chinese government regarding the NGO aspect of the 1995 Beijing Women's Conference was related to this new reality.

It may be argued that communications phenomena promote the global rather than regional level of networking. To some extent this is true. Perhaps most likely is that communications channels reinforce existing linkages even as they open new corridors: Indonesia with the Netherlands; Central America with other Latin American countries and the United States; or communications among the Pacific islands. However, Rio spawned or strengthened some very specific networks; small island states concerned about subjects such as coastal fisheries' sustainability and rising sea levels; indigenous peoples' networks (generally not pan-Pacific in focus); Forest Action Networks; and a cottage industry attached to the multiple concerns arising from the Montreal Protocol Agreement, the Climate Change Convention, and the Biodiversity Convention.

How well all of these, plus many other topic-specific and sectoral networks are actually performing to create a more satisfactory relationship between modernization and traditional approaches is still very much an open question. They are, after all, creations of modern technological approaches and even the most ardent defenders of traditional ways may change views as the result of what is in effect an ongoing, sometimes very intense exchange of views, and both informal and formal negotiations. We can assume that the tendency to move what were once viewed as strictly local concerns into the broader domain of international negotiation will continue. Therefore effective NGO networks are essential.

An important test case is the current focus on forest land use and forestry practices. The most active points of conflict over forest use are now mainly around the Pacific Rim (including the Amazon if the long-discussed western access route becomes a reality). Japan, China, and the other industrial powerhouse of East Asia can readily adapt to the use of tropical hardwoods, Siberian or British Columbian softwoods. As well, the competition for regional and world markets in pulp and paper is being felt throughout the region. Fast-growing plantations in Chile and Indonesia provide what is perceived to be competitive advantage over producers in other areas. This focus on increasing production is driven not only by Western markets but also by demand within Asian cities and other centers of economic growth. We can expect to see another decade of extreme demand on traditional land use patterns and stewardship. If problems are not resolved over this time frame, there will be a very significant loss of biodiversity and local rights among the widespread local regions already engaged in rearguard action.

Organizations such as SUAN (Indonesia) and the Western Wilderness Committee (B.C.), to name but two of dozens, have a more or less common agenda that is being played out with local and national governments, and with international bodies such as the Commission on Sustainable Development, which is seeking the basis for a world accord on forests. Interestingly, it is Canada and Malaysia that have hosted critical meetings, despite their own significant differences of views and the many unresolved issues of forest land use and ownership with their forest-dwelling indigenous peoples and other forest-dependent communities. There is now also an independent World Commission of Forests, co-chaired by an Indonesian, Dr. Emil Salim, and with several members from the Pacific region. The strength of networking to ensure that traditional views are well represented in these processes will certainly be tested. It is a critical test because forest use must always be reconciled to local needs, responsibilities and rights. Chapter 9 offers a useful case study in this regard.

URBAN EXPANSION

Anyone who has observed the transformation of Tokyo, Hong Kong, or Singapore over the past thirty years will understand that the leading edge of modernization, including education, sophisticated health care, commerce and industry, and pollution control is found mainly within the population centers of Asia. These massive urban "magnets" are globally significant in terms of their innovation and cast a broad ecological shadow in terms of their use of others' resources. Singapore is considered a world-class city of the twenty-first century, where people of various religious beliefs live in relative harmony, in an environment that is clean and well maintained, and with excellent economic prospects. The basic three pillars of sustainable development appear to have been achieved. Many would argue, however, that a high price is being paid: lack of political freedom, erosion of many aspects of traditional culture, and continued exploitation of resources from surrounding countries in order to support Singaporean wealth.

Whether it is Jakarta, Shanghai, or Santiago, urban development in the Pacific will be the key settlement trend of the foreseeable future. The first UN Habitat Conference (1976) took place in Vancouver. The next such meeting is outside the Pacific Rim (in Turkey, June 1996), but it is clear that most of the world's urban population will live within the Pacific, and therefore, the cities of this region will be setting much of the agenda. Increasingly, the agenda is driven by environmental quality concerns, not only by the more standard agenda of housing, transportation, safety, plus education and health.

While Pacific cities are powerful agents of modernization, their role in nurturing cultural and religious beliefs and in promoting national environmental quality is significant. With wealth creation comes an interest in investments to preserve and protect traditional ways. Sometimes this is also expressed in very political ways (e.g., some Sikh organizations in Canada); but it also is expressed via eco-tourism of Southeast Asian urban dwellers, who visit and support new national parks in Indonesia, or via urban neighborhoods that are homogeneous centers for specific cultural groups.

There are numerous problems arising from rural-urban contact. One is the episodic migration of rural people into cities to take advantage of the urban marketplace, or jobs. The issues surrounding such migration range from systematic recruitment of young women and men into prostitution (N.E. Thailand to Bangkok) to separation from families and culture of the many construction workers building urban infrastructure, political destabilization created by rural migrants unable to find reasonable employment (China), and substandard living conditions (Manila, Mexico City, among many others).

The environmental footprint from major cities is large and growing. It can be expressed as the cause of downstream pollution on fishing communities, or the destruction of agricultural and aquacultural lands to support major airports, weekend cottages, suburban residential and industrial developments. The high energy and water consumption of cities with populations in excess of two to ten million means that many ties are quite distant, via aqueducts and hydroelectric lines. These impacts may involve the international community as well, since bodies such as the World Bank are major investors in urban infrastructure.

Another perspective on the link between modern Pacific cities and more traditional rural cultures is that the rising demand for food and other products within the cities helps maintain the value of traditional lands in the countryside. The mainstay of poverty alleviation may be healthy urban markets. This can be dramatically demonstrated in the highlands of Java, which are visibly more prosperous as a consequence of high urban demand for fresh, temperate-zone fruits and vegetables (onions, carrots, cabbage, apples). This wealth comes with a price tag. To supply high quality vegetables, a very high level of pesticide use is required. From a cultural perspective, however, the Hindu-based Tenggarese mountain people of East Java are probably more able to support their own cultural traditions as a consequence of being able to sell tremendous quantities of produce to the coastal city of Surabaya, Indonesia's second largest.

Urban agendas will drive much, perhaps most, of the future Pacific economic investment. Few cities feel confident that they are actually in control of the situation (Singapore is an exception; Jakarta and Vancouver are perhaps more typical). National governments and regional authorities should be providing many of the safeguards to ensure rational approaches to land use, to conduct environmental and social impact analyses to protect rural people affected by urban demands, and to address the vital links to international interests such as reduction in carbon dioxide arising from urban energy consumption. It is reasonable to expect continuing leadership by best example to come from innovative urban centers in the Pacific region. But we may also experience some of the worst-case scenarios in the future of this region as a consequence of earthquakes (Pacific "ring of fire" and "faults"), urban terrorism, and poor management of development (e.g., Bangkok transportation networks and vehicle control).

ADDRESSING POVERTY ALLEVIATION

East Asia is now cited as the "development miracle" by the World Bank (World Bank 1993). It is the region that has been most successful within the Pacific in terms of building export-driven economic growth with redistribution of the wealth through industrial development, maintenance of high quality agriculture, creation of extremely large service sectors, and attention to education and other social needs. It is now apparent that a considerable ecological debt has accrued, of which only a part can ever be settled. Pollution control can and likely will be addressed, as it has been in Japan, and is now being tackled in other rich places such as South Korea and Taiwan. But the impacts of cultural change and loss of tropical forest are much more permanent and damaging, as are changes that result from major hydroelectric dams and the loss of productive estuarine wetlands.

In the 1990s, the remaining very large number of situations for poverty alleviation within the Pacific may be more intractable and even more closely tied to cultural change. The context for poverty alleviation is a combination of macropolicy (trade, proper currency exchange rates, fair environmental rules) and locally based resilience/adaptation in the face of merging development and market pressures and opportunities. It is apparent that aboriginal/indigenous peoples throughout the Pacific face some of the greatest challenges. The market-based models of export products bear very limited relevance to their approach. And even where this approach is significant (e.g., fur trappers in Canada), there can be problems in maintaining markets. The protection afforded these people and their culture in the post-Rio period is still very limited, as we have seen. Within their own countries, aboriginal peoples are threatened by the combination of a lack of understanding of their ways and special needs and by efforts to ensure they are powerless in the face of demands on their lands and resources. While this situation is changing through negotiated settlements, the trend is still downhill in most parts of the Pacific.

Numerically, it is the small landholders and rural landless of Asia and Latin America that form the largest body of poor people in the Pacific (Jazairy et al. 1992). There is some optimism about their future, despite rapid population growth and the enormous need for job creation Although there is much discussion about what the phrase "sustainable livelihood" means in the cities and countryside of Asia and the Pacific, it is becoming recognized that employment strategies should not be promoted in ways that lead to massive environmental destruction. For a country such as China, however, the transition will be very, very difficult. Not only are the numbers of rural job seekers staggering, but also the competition among local authorities for new industrial plants is intense. Thus, environment may occupy a very limited place in actual development decisions, despite excellent national government rhetoric.

Finally, it is important to mention the growing concern for poverty alleviation needs in the postmodern economics of the Pacific, and for the eastern part of Russia. While it is difficult to lump these together, there are certain common defining characteristics. One is that these are situations of decline—where culture and community sense is weakened; where there is a slide from some level of "middle class" prosperity; and where drug and alcohol abuse may be prevalent. Large North American cities present a prime case where poverty is on the increase and where the division between rich and poor is becoming more rather than less apparent. The degree to which religion and cultural roots can help to tackle overwhelming problems is an important, if unanswered, question. For countries like Japan, there is a need to learn what to avoid from North American experience, since it would be highly desirable not to see a spread of this sense of hopelessness that now permeates perhaps fifteen to twenty percent of the population marginalized within large North American cities.

In summary, poverty alleviation, modernization, and erosion of environmental quality and traditional ways are linked in a complex fashion. The emergence of religious values can be part of the response (Buddhist revival in China, black Muslim populations in North America), and strength of culture can be a significant part of the resilient local response for poverty alleviation. In general, those concerned with development do not give very much attention to culture and religion in poverty alleviation strategies. This has been particularly true within the East and Southeast Asian settings where the major emphasis continues to be on export-driven economic growth. Hence, valuable traditional knowledge and respect for local needs is lost. Aboriginal peoples have the most to lose since their traditions are furthest from the dominant growth model.

LOOKING TO THE TWENTY-FIRST CENTURY

What can we conclude about the future tensions of traditional and modern views and environmental change in the Pacific? One of the lessons of Rio was from North American aboriginal people who speak of the Seventh Generation as their reference point for sustainable development. This is the generation with which we can have only indirect contact through our care of the environment and by passing on our knowledge base. It is a view consistent with ancient traditions and religious beliefs that guide Asian and other Pacific cultures. When we apply today's reference points to a time span stretching seven generations into the future, it is very clear that major reconciliation of population, consumption, and environment will have to take place—not within seven generations but, at most, two or three. Otherwise the Pacific will be a culturally and biologically dead place of degraded countrysides and communities, perhaps unable to feed its population or to have the type of civil societies where strong values can flourish. Certainly biodiversity is likely to be much reduced under even the most optimistic of scenarios over this time span.

The agreements in Rio have provided a start for the global framework and a strong stimulus for regional action that could make the difference between this potentially dismal outcome and situations where there is indeed better harmony of religion, culture, and environment than currently exists. We should not be satisfied always with seeking the status quo relationship of these variables. Culture and the natural environment have always been dynamic features. We need to explore and understand levels of resilience if we are to have adequate reconciliation.

The economy and societies of the Pacific in the next century will be based upon complex information technologies that we can only begin to imagine now. Based upon the actual experience of the past decade, we can assume that penetration of these technologies into rural areas and traditional communities will be rapid. Indeed, the new approaches have certain similarities to the oral traditions that characterize these societies, therefore it is not surprising that there has been acceptance of information technologies such as VCRs in villages.

The increasing access to education, longer life spans, and the growing access (in real financial terms as well as presence on store shelves) to consumer goods are central considerations for future economic trends in the Pacific. In the short run (ten to twenty years), there will be a great increase in the level of pollution, and in the conflict between traditional and modern values. While this trend would appear to fly in the face of every aspect of the Earth Summit accords, it is a reality dictated by the current level of population and the trends toward a Western lifestyle documented throughout the region (population and consumption trends worldwide are carefully discussed in WRI/UNEP 1994 and for developing regions in Harrison 1992).

Hope is in the seeds now being sown, not only within the postmodern lifestyles now emerging within North America and Europe, but also within the individual, governmental, and corporate circles throughout the Pacific. It is becoming fashionable in some trend-setting organizations to seriously discuss the recommendations of the "Factor 10 Club." That is, to seek reduction in material and energy use by a factor of ten in production processes. In the postmodern societies cultural and biological diversity are again becoming highly valued. In societies where services and information are among the highest economic performers, these forms of diversity take on new meaning as sources of livelihoods. And finally, we are witnessing a redefinition of spiritual belief on the part of people who value science but are skeptical of technological excesses, and who turn to traditional beliefs for their holistic value. This is a trend in North America today, but arguably, it has long been a way of dealing with the reconciliation of clashing ideas in Asia and elsewhere in the Pacific.

In closing, it is essential to underscore how important it is to continue growing the roots and stem now, if we are to have full flowering of new approaches by 2020 or 2030. We are still in the earliest stages of the post-Rio transformation to sustainable development in the Pacific. The next decade will be the most dramatic in terms of the pathways actually taken.

REFERENCES

Anderson, Kym, and Richard Blackhurst. 1992. *The Greening of World Trade Issues.* Hertfordshire, England: Harvester Wheatsheaf.

Andersson, Thomas, C. Folke, and S. Nyström. 1995. *Trading with the Environment—Ecology, Economics, Institutions and Policy.* London: Earthscan Publications Limited.

Asian Development Bank (ADB). 1990. *Economic Policies for Sustainable Development.* Manila: Asian Development Bank.

China Council for International Cooperation on Environment and Development (CCICED). 1995. *Proceedings—The Third Meeting of China Council for International Cooperation on Environment and Development.* Beijing: China Environment Science Press.

Durning, Alan. 1993. "Supporting Indigenous Peoples." In Lester Brown, et al. *State of the World 1993—A Worldwatch Institute Report on Progress Toward a Sustainable Society.* New York: W. W. Norton & Company, Inc.

ECLAC. 1991. *Sustainable Development: Changing Production Patterns, Social Equity and the Environment.* Santiago (Chile): Economic Commission for Latin America and the Caribbean.

ESCAP. 1992. *State of the Environment in Asia and the Pacific 1990.* Bangkok: Economic and Social Commission for Asia and the Pacific.

Fridtjof Nansen Institute, The. 1995. *Green Globe Yearbook of International Co-operation on Environment and Development 1995.* New York: Oxford University Press Inc.

Grove, Richard H. 1995. *Green Imperialism—Colonial Expansion, Tropical Island Edens and the Origin of Environmentalism, 1600–1860.* Cambridge: Cambridge University Press.

Grubb, Michael, M. Koch, A. Munson, F. Sullivan, K. Thomson. 1993. *The Earth Summit Agreement—A Guide and Assessment.* London:

Earthscan Publications Limited and The Royal Institute of International Affairs.

Guevera, Mana Isolda P. 1995. *Trade, Sustainable Development, and the Environment: A Bibliography.* Ottawa: Centre for Trade Policy and Law, and the International Institute for Sustainable Development.

Hall, June D., and Arthur J. Hanson. 1992. *A New Kind of Sharing—Why We Can't Ignore Global Environmental Change.* Ottawa: International Development Research Centre.

Harrison, Paul. 1992. *The Third Revolution—Environment, Population and a Sustainable World.* London: I. B. Taurus & Co. Ltd.

International Institute for Sustainable Development. 1994. *Trade and Sustainable Development Principles.* Winnipeg: International Institute for Sustainable Development.

Jazairy, Idress, M. Alamgir, and T. Panuccio. 1992. *The State of the World Rural Poverty.* London: Intermediate Technology Publications.

Johnson, Stanley P. 1995. *The Earth Summit: The United Nations Conference on Environment and Development (UNCED).* London: Graham & Trotman Limited.

Keating, Michael. 1993. *The Earth Summit's Agenda for Change—A plain language version of Agenda 21 and the other Rio Agreements.* Geneva: Centre for Our Common Future.

McNeely, Jeffrey A., K. R. Miller, W. V. Reid, R. Mittermeier, T. B. Werner. 1990. *Conserving the World's Biological Diversity.* Washington, D.C.: IUCN, WRI, CI, WWF-US and the World Bank.

Najman Dragoljub and Hans d'Orville. 1995. *Towards a New Multilateralism: Funding Global Priorities—Innovative Financing Mechanisms for Internationally Agreed Programmes.* New York: Independent Commission on Population and Quality of Life.

Ponting, Clive. 1994. *A Green History of the World.* London: Sinclair-Stevenson Limited.

PRC State Council. 1994. China's Agenda 21—White Paper on China's Population, Environment, and Development in the 21st Century. Beijing: China Environmental Science Press.

Ramphal, Shridath. 1992. *Our Country the Planet—Forging a Partnership for Survival.* Washington, D.C.: Island Press.

Royal Thai Government and USAID. 1989. *Safeguarding the Future—Restoration and Sustainable Development in the South of Thailand.* Bangkok: National Economic and Social Development Board.

Ryan, Megan and C. Flavin. 1995. *Facing China's Limits.* In Lester Brown et al. *State of the World 1995—A Worldwatch Institute Report on Progress Toward a Sustainable Society.* New York: W. W. Norton & Company, Inc.

Seager, Joni. 1995. *The New State of the Earth Atlas, 2nd Edition—A Concise Survey of the Environment Through Full-color International Maps.* New York: Touchstone, Simon & Schuster, Inc.

UNDP. 1993. *Pacific Human Development Report.* Suva, Fiji: United Nations Development Programme.

World Bank. 1993. *The East Asian Miracle—Economic Growth and Public Policy.* New York: Oxford University Press, Inc.

World Bank. 1992. *World Development Report 1992—Development and the Environment.* New York: Oxford University Press, Inc.

World Bank Environment Department. 1995. *Mainstreaming the Environment—The World Bank Group and the Environment Since the Rio Earth Summit—Fiscal 1995.* Washington, D.C.: World Bank.

World Resources Institute, The United Nations Environment Programme and the United Nations Development Programme. 1994. *World Resources 1994–95—People and the Environment.* New York: Oxford University Press, Inc.

JAN WALLS

3. Modern Communications and Opportunities for Pro-Environmental Networking in East Asia

This chapter will examine some of the factors of traditional East Asian culture that should be conducive to environmental activism, then consider some traditional and modern cultural constraints upon effective pro-environmental social movements, and conclude by considering new opportunities and recent experiences in global networking that allow people in Asia to "link and think globally and regionally; link, think, and act locally."

PRO-ENVIRONMENTAL TRADITIONS IN EAST ASIA

Nearly everyone in China has read or heard the allegorical tale from the Taoist philosopher *Zhuang Zi* (ca. fourth century B.C.), about the dangers of imposing too much civilization on primal nature:

> The God of the South Sea was called *Shu* (Swift), and the God of the North Sea was named *Hu* (Sudden). They often paid each other visits and over time became very close. Whenever they visited each other, they had to pass over the domain of the God of the Centre. This primordial God was called *Hundun* (Chaos), and he was very tolerant, never interfering with Shu and Hu's travels back and forth through his territory.
> One day Shu and Hu were visiting again, and when the topic

55

of conversation turned to Hundun, they agreed that they owed him a debt of gratitude for allowing their trespasses, and wanted to repay him for his kindness. After much discussion, they came up with a clever idea: they would take it upon themselves to create the seven apertures for Hundun so that he might have eyes, ears, nostrils and mouth to see, hear, smell and eat like everyone else.

Without even asking him, they started to create apertures on Hundun, one of them holding a big chisel, the other swinging an iron hammer. They pounded away, working on him every day. Their work progressed smoothly at first, and they completed a new aperture in his head every day. On the seventh day, however, all seven of Hundun's apertures started bleeding, and he died. (Walls 1982)

The allegory is unmistakable, and might just as easily have been written yesterday as in the fourth century B.C. At the most general level, people must respect the wilderness ("Nature" in its "natural" state), or risk destroying her in their well-intentioned efforts to improve upon her. More specifically, we might even interpret the message that it is good to have undeveloped spaces between the developed spaces of civilization. The point is this: every educated Chinese knows this as a powerful allegorical statement by one of China's greatest philosophers.

Making do without overdoing (wu wei er we)

Something else known by every educated Chinese is the famous and most fundamental Taoist concept known as " *wu-wei*" (variously translated as "non-assertion," "non-intervention," "non-ado," "non-action," etc.), its environmental implications being that society may need to exploit its natural environment, but should try to do so without destroying its regenerative capacity. In the words of the great philosophy scholar Wing-tsit Chan:

Lao Tzu taught the strange doctrine of *wu-wei*, generally interpreted as "inaction." But it is a mistake to think of *wu-wei* as anything suggesting complete inactivity, renunciation, or the cult of unconsciousness. It is, rather, a peculiar way, or, more exactly, the natural way, of behavior. "The sage manages affairs without action, and spreads doctrines without words." The natural way is to "support all things in their natural state" and thus allow them to "transform spontaneously." In this manner, "The Way invariably takes no action, and yet there is nothing left undone." (Chan 1963)

A famous allegorical Chinese proverb advises against "tugging the sprouts to speed up their growth," referring to the tale of a farmer who tried to speed up the natural growth process by tugging on his rice sprouts, and lost the whole crop, of course (Walls 1982, 51).

Translated into policy guidelines for practical living, the implications of Taoist non-ado could not be clearer: Do not overexploit Nature, "practice doing without overdoing, and nothing will be left undone." The important thing to remember here is that the examples presented above are conventional wisdom, known and quoted by everyone in China, and appreciated by students and scholars in Korea and Japan as part of their traditional education.

The pastoral and Eremitic traditions: Farming as the ideal life and Nature as the source of truth

In the traditional East Asian view, Nature is regarded not only as the original and ultimate source of Truth, but as the place where a gentleman repairs when fed up with life in the grimy "red dust" (Chinese *hong-chen*) of human society. One turns to the mountains and rivers to regain the perspective that is lost in the hustle and bustle of political and social life. When official corruption, or the blind pursuit of wealth, power, and influence came to dominate life in the political or social spheres, it was customary for the Chinese, Korean, or Japanese gentleman either to repair to the hills (perhaps to take up temporary residence in a mountain temple) in imitation of the hermit's life, or to return to the family acreage in the countryside. We recall that in the traditional Confucianist hierarchies of China, Korea, and Japan, the farmer was second only to the scholar-official, and ranked above the craftsman and the merchant. (Reischauer and Fairbank 1960, 55). This amounts to culturally institutionalized acknowledgment of the importance of Nature as *the* source of Truth, and agricultural activity as the most respectable of non-governmental economic activities.

Every Chinese, Korean, and Japanese knows of the legendary "Peach Blossom Spring" fable, which tells of a Chinese who rowed his boat upriver to its source, and discovered a rural Shangri La. When he paddled through a mountain cave to emerge on the other side, he found himself in an idyllic land where villagers had been unspoiled by the ravages of history—the centuries of turmoil and rising and falling dynasties and civilizations. Farmers, fishermen, and kindling cutters pursued their work at peace with Nature and the world. When he returned home he told others of his discovery, but no one has been able to retrace his amazing journey since (Giles 1964, 104–105). This is a fundamental and unchallenged notion that peace, tranquillity, and "the good life" are to be found in the pursuits of farming and fishing. It is an image of people living in harmony among themselves, and in harmony with Nature. It is also an acknowledgment that such harmony may lie in an irretrievably lost, nostalgic past.

Landscape garden as idealized natural environment

The private landscape garden in China and Japan has been for centuries an urban embodiment of the natural countryside, which serves as a microcosmic retreat into True Nature after "a hard day at the office." One contemplates the balanced images of light and dark, hard and soft, patterned and plain, young and old, smooth and rough, dry and wet, high and low, regular and irregular shapes, and sees in them the greater and lesser truths that are to be found only in unspoiled Nature (Morris 1983, 77). Such gardens are embodiments of the Taoistic ideal of "design without design" to recreate and maintain a piece of unspoiled Nature in an urban setting. (Itoh 1984, 32).

The point is this: that East Asian peoples have long been aware that the farther we remove ourselves from the forests, rivers, and farmlands, the more estranged we become from Nature, which is the overpowering standard for Truth, and to whom we must return to regain perspective that is inevitably lost in the workaday world. While living in urban settings, the least we can do is to create a garden microcosm of unspoiled Nature, to whom we can turn after work to regain lost perspective, and to whom we should look for reminders of how life should be lived.

There is, in the great traditions of East Asia, ample philosophical and cultural grounding in the virtue of the unspoiled natural state of the universe. This, complemented by the notion of "doing without overdoing, with nothing left undone," would seem to provide a cultural shield against environmental degradation. Yet, as we have noted, five of the seven most polluted cities in the world are in Asia, and environmental degradation seems to have been accepted as the price one must pay for economic development. Several of the "dragons" have been spoiling their own nests. What are the constraints on environmental protection that have allowed this to happen?

CONSTRAINTS ON PRO-ENVIRONMENTAL NETWORKING

Constraint #1: Return to Nature seen as dropping out of social networks

The East Asian view of Nature as the original and ultimate source of Truth, unfortunately, has created in many people's minds an "either-or" vision of society and Nature, wherein one must choose between destructive social activities in cities, and the "natural" (good) life of the farmer, the fisherman, the kindling gatherer, or the hermit in the countryside and in the mountains (Liu 1966, 63). This attitude has been strengthened by the historical experience that the spoilers of large systems are usually powerful and determined people, who often are merciless in their treatment of those who would challenge their right to exploit the system. This assumption is more than enough to convince most people that withdrawal is safer than engagement.

The often quoted Chinese line, "When the Cang-lang River runs clear, I wash my official cap in it; when the Cang-lang River runs muddy, I wash my bare feet in it," is an allegorical affirmation of the True Gentleman's attitude toward the worldly life: "When the socio-political system runs well, I will participate in it; when it runs poorly, I will withdraw from it." This is not the attitude of an engaged citizen. It is the mindset of one who would rather "run away, and live to serve another day."

Constraint #2: "My primary group" regarded as "my only concern"

In China, Korea and Japan, individuals usually see themselves, and are seen by others, as identified with and responsible to their primary organization (family, school, or company), and have difficulty identifying with causes that originate outside their primary affiliation. Many will first have to be convinced that a threat exists to one of their primary social groups, and only then will they be moved to action in concert with others who are not primary affiliates. This, of course, is not conducive to the "goal-oriented networking mentality," which has characterized successful environmental protection movements in recent years.

China:
Prosperity concerns supersede environmental concerns

Having lived through so many decades of life driven by communist ideology, in which the proletariat struggles simultaneously against Nature and against enemies of the working class, most people in China today are more concerned with keeping ahead of inflation than with the very real danger of environmental collapse. For the first time in recent history, they have an opportunity to participate in the actual quadrupling of China's GNP, which means a significant improvement in the lives of most Chinese people—never mind that the quadrupled intensity in exploitation of an already overexploited environment may not be sustainable for many years. The result has been that most Chinese citizens, while interested in both increased productivity and environmental protection, will be willing to put environmental concerns on the back burner for the time being, in order to achieve the national goals of becoming a "moderately well-off society" *(xiaokang shehui)* by the early twenty-first century

Korea and Japan:
Big company and big brother are unbeatable

Most Korean and Japanese citizens are convinced that the major industrial polluters and the pro-industry government bureaucracy support each other, both on specific public issues and on general policy matters. After all, one of the factors in the success of the "East Asian Dragons" has been the positivistic coordination between the needs and policies of major corporate alliances *(chaebol* in Korea, *keiretsu* in Japan) and government as administered through the bureaucracies in Japan and Korea. The resulting attitude among the people of Japan has been one that accepts the unpleasant reality of *"kanson minpi"* ("respect for the establishment, disdain for the people") (Griffith 1990, 94–95). The resulting popular apathy, even cynicism, toward the possibility of reining in the government-industry establishment when their collaboration appears to be harmful to the environment, is not conducive to popular proactive movement.

These mindsets—viewing Nature as a place of eternal Truth for dropouts to return to; regarding my primary group as my only concern; placing prosperity before environmental protection; and believing that "big company" and "big brother" are unbeatable—are deeply imbedded in the belief systems of most East Asian peoples, and are among the most significant impediments to positivistic networking and coordination of pro-environmentalist activity in Asia, even to this day.

ENVIRONMENTAL INFORMATION AND INTERNET-WORKING

Environment-focused global Internet-working

The appearance and dramatic spread of electronically linked desktop computers, themselves networked with other networks, culminating in the Internet (international network of networks), has opened the door for international, intercultural, intersectoral, and even interlingual consultation and cooperation on matters of shared interest and commitment (Walls 1993, 163–65). Recent years have seen the development of EcoNet in the United States, GreenNet in England, and similar networks in Sweden, Canada, Brazil, Nicaragua, and Australia.

> This led in 1990 to the founding of the Association for Progressive Communications (APC) to coordinate this global operation. Today, more than 15,000 subscribers in ninety countries are fully interconnected through low-cost personal computers. APC members are fond of saying that they "dial locally and act globally." Today there are APC partner networks in the United States, Nicaragua, Brazil, Russia, Australia, the United Kingdom, Canada, Sweden and Germany and affiliated systems in Uruguay, Costa Rica, Czechoslovakia, Bolivia, Kenya, and many other countries. (Frederick 1993, 289–90)

Individual users who are members of these various Internet-worked groups need only make a local phone call to connect to their host computer to send and receive E-mail, including "mail lists" that distribute any member's message to all members of a particular group, team, or task force, and download or upload postings on electronic conferences or electronic bulletin boards. This relatively inexpensive, user-friendly, and highly efficient electronic networking technology would seem to offer great promise for linking locally based environmental protection and sustainable development groups, and for allowing national and international collaboration and coordination for local activities.

Information technologies and East Asian networking

When it comes to environmental protection or improvement, there seems to be an endemic distrust of big government and big business in the minds of most East Asian peoples with local concerns. There are traditions, however, of local people organizing themselves to pressure governments and/or industries to address their concerns. In Japan, for instance, there are single-issue neighborhood groups composed of a few dedicated individuals who produce handwritten and photocopied newsletters. One scholar estimates that there are hundreds, perhaps even thousands of these small groups in Japan,

> [A]rising in reaction to the relentless pressure of pro-development forces—real-estate developers, construction companies and their natural allies, the members of prefectural civil engineering departments, who hate to let their expertise remain unappreciated for very long. Activities include rousing public opinion with slide shows, writing articles for the local media, leafleting, holding marches, and lobbying local government officials connected (sometimes altogether too closely) with the project. (Griffith 1990, 92)

In addition to the above small grassroots organizations, there are several international non-governmental organizations (INGOs) active in Japan. They include: the Worldwide Fund for Nature-Japan (WWF-J); Greenpeace Japan; Friends of the Earth Japan (FOE-J); the Japan Tropical Forest Action Network (JATAN), and the Japan Environmental Exchange

(JEE). These organizations, large and small, national and neighborhood, currently communicate through face-to-face, print, phone or fax-based technologies. With the continuing increase in accessibility of low cost, user-friendly computers and modems, it stands to reason that these Japanese pro-environmental organizations, along with their counterparts in Taiwan and Korea, would be able to work with much greater efficiency and effectiveness through Internet-working, which would allow them to "link globally, and act locally." The Appendix presents a list of well-known Japanese Environmental Organizations, with brief descriptions of their activities.

Increasingly, it is becoming possible for environmentalists in China, especially if they are attached to a major university, to gain access to the Internet. Academics may now gain access through CERNET (China Education and Research Network) via the State Education Commission. Many Chinese university personnel now have an E-mail address printed on their business cards, and this practice is expected to spread to other sectors of society. Besides universities, other organizations may now obtain Internet access through a handful of public service providers, and most recent developments include the approval for an alternative, non-governmental carrier to enter into competition with the Chinese Ministry of Posts and Telecommunications. This would seem to augur well for the future strengthening of environmental protection organizations and networks in China.

Internet opportunities for Asian environmental networking

The Internet has already proven itself to be a very hospitable medium for pro-environmental groups who benefit from local access to global experience with similar issues.

Outside of Asia, we can already point to a number of successful projects linking environmentalists and students internationally and interculturally. Students in Canada, for example, have been able to access information on "Weather Patterns and the Greenhouse Effect" in communication with Australia and the United States (Riel 1993, 229).

The United Nations Development Program (UNDP) recently has authorized and supported the creation of "Sustainable Development Networks" around the world. SDNs combine electronic communication, face-to-face meetings, and other means of communication to link sources and users of information on sustainable development in government, research, non-governmental organizations, grassroots and entrepreneurial organizations on a global scale.

> The SDN is more than an information network. SDNs foster informed dialogue and communications to empower stakeholders—those who stand to be directly affected by development—to become more active participants in the development process. Round table processes as well as public or community participation in decision making are examples of the type of consultation that a SDN encourages and becomes involved with. (Document accessed through Internet, ftp: FF121 .undp.org)

Currently there is an ongoing feasibility study to set up an SDN within China's Agenda 21 secretariat, with hopes of the system being operational within four months (personal E-mail message from Chuck Lankester, UNDP, 24 July 1995).

Another approach to using the Internet for local purposes originates in Halifax, Nova Scotia. It is called the Sustainable Communities Network. The mandate of the SCN is to promote a vision of resilient communities that are "environment and people friendly." In this vision,

> communities have a healthy and diverse economic, social and cultural life, and a measure of self-reliance. The SCN promotes this vision by facilitating information exchange, educational opportunities and cooperation among groups and individuals with an interest in sustainable livelihoods and communities. Sustainable community development links issues of environment, health, culture and economics through a democratic community process. Accessing tools and resources, and hearing of other's successes is a valuable part of that process. (Description downloaded from Internet, 26 July 1995)

Such holistic ideals, attitudes, and visions are so perfectly compatible with the spirit of grassroots neighborhood groups in East Asia, that one can only hope the electronic connections, with the help of local translators as required, may be set up to link Asian groups into the web.

A Hong Kong example for East Asia: EarthCare

There exists in Hong Kong a very interesting example of how the environmentalist's commitment may harness electronic communication technologies to create education and action-oriented global networks to better address local and regional environmental protection goals. The organization is called EarthCare. EarthCare is an independent, not-for-profit NGO, founded in February 1993 by a group of local Chinese enthusiasts. Their members combine considerable experience in animal welfare, ecology, education, and administration. They were granted the status of charity in 1994. During the past several years, EarthCare has seen a number of achievements in its programs to promote green education, animal welfare, and sustainable development. The basic aims of the organization (as advertised on their World Wide Web site) are to:

- Educate children about anti-cruelty issues.

- Help reforestation and conservation in China through close cooperation with environmental and animal groups worldwide.

- Promote the use of herbal medicines as alternatives to animal derivatives in order to save endangered species and prevent animal cruelty.

- Promote humane education to our children and teach them to live in harmony with Nature and animals.

- Promote sustainable, organic vegetarian farming and eco-friendly lifestyles like vegetarianism for a sustainable future society based on environmentally sound development.

EarthCare has been advising the authorities in Guizhou, a Chinese province with a severe water problem, on water recycling systems and on reforestation and reconstruction of the ecosystem. In 1993 and 1994, in cooperation with the world renowned Environmental Investigation Agency (EIA), they conducted an investigation into the trafficking and illegal sales of rhinoceros horns in China, which prompted the Chinese Government to take immediate action to combat these large-scale criminal activities.

To address their local and regional goals, EarthCare currently networks with 340 environmental and animal protection organizations in more than thirty-nine countries to bring the most up-to-date scientific research and information to Hong Kong and China on a regular basis. EarthCare's practice is a classic example of what could be called "linking and thinking globally and regionally; linking, thinking, and acting locally."

They utilize electronic communications media to draw upon international and regional sources of information, expertise, and organizational support to achieve local and regional goals, both short-term and long-term. Their short-term goals include the systematic exposure of instances of environmental (including endangered animal species) abuse. Long-term goals are addressed through vigorous public education activities. All of these activities are made possible and made more effective through "linking and thinking globally and regionally; linking, thinking, and acting locally."

Another textbook example of local-regional-global networking for local pro-environmental activity is the Hong Kong EcoNet. EcoNet is linked to the Federation of Engineering Institutions in Southeast Asia and the Pacific (FEISEAP), which represents the national engineering institutions of twelve nations in the region. FEISEAP, in turn, is a link in the larger global network. Thus EcoNet is able to focus on local pro-environmental goals in a regionally sensitive context, drawing upon global information and resources (cf. EcoNet Web Page: www.hk.super.net/~hkie_env/hkeconet.htm).

CONCLUSION

I began this chapter by referring to ancient Asian beliefs and practices. Let me end it by sharing the inspired vision of a contemporary Japanese thinker:

> Globalism is not the preserve of state leaders and seasoned diplomats posturing at superpower summits or holding forth at Group of Seven meetings. The "grass-roots globalism" of which I speak embraces a fairly high level of exchange, unlike the approach taken by existing nongovernmental organizations, and it offers a basis for an alternative framework for international relations. I believe that Asia's new international order will evolve from the

multidimensional intertwining of such forums for exchange. (Nakajima 1993, 44)

This spirit, based upon the indigenous traditions of awareness and respect for Nature, and supplemented by the new and economical access to national, regional, and global electronic networks for communication and coordination of local pro-environment groups, would appear to offer hope of overcoming the enormous obstacles to harmonizing industry and ecology, with the hope of achieving sustainable development in East Asia. With the growth of the notions of legitimacy, importance, and efficacy of non-profit-seeking non-governmental organizations committed to the betterment of local community development in East Asia, we could now witness a historic convergence of awareness, commitment, organizational competence, and technological access that results in an unprecedented empowerment and growth of locally based, regionally conscious, internationally networked pro-environmental groups.

APPENDIX: Japanese Environmental Organizations (From *Whole Earth Review*, Winter 1990, p. 96)

Citizens' Alliance Saving the Atmosphere
As the name indicates they are particularly active in atmosphere issues, but also do education and public outreach on other issues. Affiliated with Osaka branch of *Shodanren*, a consumer cooperative.

Consumers' Union of Japan
Active regarding golf course development problems, synthetic detergents, water pollution, nuclear power. Twelve full-time staff members. Newsletter: *Shohisha Rippo* three times monthly (in Japanese); *Japan Resources*, bimonthly (in English).

Friends of the Earth, Japan
Current focus is on ODA, World Bank reform, tropical forests, global warming. Four to five full-time staffers.

Greenpeace Japan
Six full-time Japanese campaigners on traditional Greenpeace issues:

ocean ecology, atmosphere, marine mammals, nuclear power, Antarctica. Working hard to overcome antipathy among many Japanese resulting from Greenpeace's history of direct action, opposition to whaling (both of which being very uncool in Japan). Newsletter: *Greenpeace* (in Japanese).

Japan Environmental Exchange
Focus on public awareness-raising. Main issues: recycling, tropical forests, environmental education. All-volunteer project of Earth Island Institute. Newsletter: *JEE Bulletin*, monthly (Japanese and English).

Japan Tropical Forest Action Network
Current focus is on the Sarawak campaign, mangrove protection in Indonesia and, increasingly, temperate-forest issues. Two to three full-time staffers. Newsletter *JATAN News* (in Japanese only).

Nature Conservation Society of Japan
Domestic focus. Administers specific funds for research and conservation of primeval forests, coral reefs, wild rivers, and wild animals. Fourteen full-time staffers, plus six naturalist guides working in national parks. Magazine: *Conservation of Nature*, monthly (Japanese, with English index).

Seikatsu Club
Involved mainly in agricultural pesticides, recycling, nuclear power issues, as well as the promotion of workers' cooperatives, grassroots democracy. Newsletter: *Seikatsu to Jiji*, monthly (in Japanese).

Worldwide Fund for Nature
One sometimes hears grumbling about WWF-J's conservatism, and it is closely connected to the Japanese establishment, but it does fund a good deal of useful research on a wide variety of wildlife-related issues, and gives financial assistance to many other groups. Newsletter: *Yasei Seibutsu*, ten times/year (in Japanese).

REFERENCES AND FURTHER READINGS

Chan, Wing-tsit. 1963. *A Source Book in Chinese Philosophy*. Princeton: Princeton University Press.

Frederick, Howard. 1993. "Computer Networks and the Emergence of Global Civil Society." in Linda Harasim, ed. *Global Networks: Computers and International Communication.* Cambridge, Mass.: The MIT Press, pp. 283–95.

Giles, Herbert A. 1964. *Gems of Chinese Literature.* Shanghai: New York: Paragon.

Griffith, Jim. 1990. "The Environmental Movement in Japan." *Whole Earth Review* No. 69 (Winter): 90–96.

Howard, Michael C., ed. 1993. *Asia's Environmental Crisis.* Boulder: Westview Press.

Ishii, Hiroshi. 1990. "Cross-Cultural Communication & Computer-Supported Cooperative Work." *Whole Earth Review* No. 69 (Winter): 48–52.

Itoh, Teiji. 1984. *The Gardens of Japan.* Tokyo: Kodansha International.

Kodansha International, ed. 1994. *Japan: Profile of a Nation.* New York: Kodansha International Ltd.

Kumon, Shumpei. 1990. "Toward Co-Emulation: Japan and the United States in the Information Age." *Whole Earth Review* No. 69 (Winter): 54–62.

Lacy, Colin, and Roy Williams, eds. 1987. *Education, Ecology and Development: the case for an education network.* London: Kogan Page.

Liu, Wu-chi. 1966. *An Introduction to Chinese Literature.* Bloomington: Indiana University Press.

Morris, Edwin T. 1983. *The Gardens of China.* New York: Charles Scribner's Sons.

Nakajima, Mineo. 1993. "The Three Chinas in Asia's New Order." *Japan Echo* Volume XX Special Issue. 38–44.

Ofreneo, Rene E. 1993. "Japan and the Environmental Degradation of the Philippines." Michael C. Howard, ed, *Asia's Environmental Crisis.* Boulder: Westview Press. pp. 201–220.

Qu, Geping and Li Jinchang. 1994. *Population and the Environment in China.* Translated by Jiang Baozhong and Gu Ran; English language edition edited by Robert B. Boardman. Boulder, Colo.: L. Rienner Publishers.

Reischauer, Edwin O., and John K. Fairbank. 1960. *East Asia: The Great Tradition.* Boston: Houghton Mifflin Company.

Riel, Margaret. 1993. "Global Education through Learning Circles." Linda Harasim, ed. *Global Networks: Computers and International Com-*

munication. Cambridge, Mass.: The MIT Press. 221–36.

Shapard, Jeffrey. 1990. "Observations on Cross-Cultural Electronic Networking." *Whole Earth Review* No. 69 (Winter): 32–35.

Smil, Vaclav. 1993. *China's Environmental Crisis: an inquiry into the limits of national development*. Armonk, N.Y.: M. E. Sharpe.

Smil, Vaclav. 1984. *The Bad Earth: environmental degradation in China*. Armonk, N.Y.: M. E.Sharpe.

Walls, Jan. 1993. "Global Networking for Local Development: Task Focus and Relationship Focus in Cross-Cultural Communication." Linda Harasim, ed. *Global Networks: Computers and International Communication*. Cambridge, Mass.: The MIT Press, pp. 153–65.

Walls, Jan, and Yvonne Li Walls. 1982. *100 Allegorical Tales from Traditional China* (ed., with critical Introduction, Notes, Type Index, and Source List). Hong Kong: Joint Publishing Co.

Youth Sourcebook on Sustainable Development. Winnipeg: IISD, 1995 (Accessible through Internet at http://iisd1.iisd.ca/youth/).

PART II

BELIEF SYSTEMS, INSTITUTIONS, AND THE ENVIRONMENT

ELIZABETH A. WILMAN and
R. DOUGLAS BURCH

4. Traditional and Modern Institutions and the Commons

A valuable resource for students of environmental economics is the collection of seminal essays edited by Dorfman and Dorfman, *Economics of the Environment*.[1] The first paper in this collection is Garrett Hardin's 1968 *Science* classic, "The Tragedy of the Commons."[2] While the idea that common property can be the precursor to a lack of care bestowed upon that property was not original to Hardin, he certainly recognized that many environmental resources have characteristics that make common ownership the norm. This recognition leads to the central question of environmental economics: How can we oblige users, including ourselves, to take adequate care of commonly owned environmental resources?

Environmental problems that can be characterized as stemming from a lack of care for common property range from local issues to global dilemmas. The potential solutions to these problems also cover a wide range of possibilities. At one extreme there is the creation of private property rights. At the other there is formal regulation by the state. Between, there are many types of collective organization and behavior.

This next section of this chapter will look at the explanation for the behavior that can lead to the tragedy of commons. Also, it will look at the general nature of solutions that can avoid the tragedy. Section II will look at examples of commons' failures and successes in traditional societies. Section III will consider some lessons to be learned from the examples of the previous section. Finally, in section IV, some comparisons with current environment problems, and approaches to solutions, are presented.

I. PRIVATE CHOICE AND PUBLIC INTEREST

A simple model that economists use to describe the tragedy of commons problem is the "prisoners' dilemma" game. Two partners in crime, Bonnie and Clyde, are apprehended and imprisoned separately. The maximum sentence is ten years. Each is independently presented with the following options. If you confess and your partner does not, your sentence will be reduced from the maximum by nine years; you will be incarcerated for one year. If you do not confess, but your partner does, you will receive no reduction. If you both confess you will have five years subtracted from your sentence, and if neither confesses you will receive an eight-year reduction. The figure below shows the payoff matrix for the game. In each cell, Bonnie's reduction is the first number, and Clyde's the second.

As the figure indicates, Bonnie will receive a greater reduction by confessing, regardless of whether Clyde confesses. The same is true for Clyde. Hence, confessing is a dominant strategy for both. This leads to both confessing, and both get five years. Had neither confessed they could both have had lighter sentences. The difficulty is how to achieve that result.

To translate this problem into a more familiar economic setting, think of Bonnie and Clyde as owners of cattle that graze a common pasture. The payoffs are the long-term returns each receives from the cattle that graze the common pasture. The decision options are: graze ten cattle (confess) or graze five cattle (don't confess). Long-term returns from the pasture are reduced if excessive grazing occurs. If Bonnie independently pursues her own self-interest, she will graze ten cattle. Facing the same circumstance, Clyde will make the same decision. They would both be better off if a binding agreement, to limit the number of cattle to five each, could be achieved. If the agreement cannot be made a binding one, then it is unlikely to be made at all, and if it is made it is likely to break down.

THE PRISONERS' DILEMMA

Sentence Reduction:	*Clyde confesses*	*Clyde doesn't confess*
Bonnie confesses	Bonnie: 5 years Clyde: 5 years	Bonnie: 9 years Clyde: 0 years
Bonnie doesn't confess	Bonnie: 0 years Clyde: 9 years	Bonnie: 8 years Clyde: 8 years

The science of economics was launched two centuries ago by Adam Smith, who showed that individuals pursuing their self-interest could serve the interests of all. This insight was termed the "invisible hand." Much of economics since then has been devoted to the refinement, quantification, and application of this insight, and most economists share a faith in the ability of the invisible hand to allocate resources in a way that produces the greatest total benefit.

In fact, Adam Smith's view of the working of the invisible hand was not that of unrestrained independent pursuit of self-interest. The invisible hand was aided by the restraint to the pursuit of self-interest derived from "morals, religion, custom, and education."[3] Hirsch suggests religion was "a behavioral standard supporting collective action and cooperative relationship."[4]

The ways in which human society has dealt with the need to act collectively, to achieve greater benefit for individuals, are many and diverse. As Thomas Schelling put it:

> A good part of social organization—of what we call society—consists of institutional arrangements to overcome these divergencies between perceived individual interest and some larger collective bargain. Some of it is market-oriented ownership, contracts, damage suits, patents and copyrights promissory notes, rental agreements and a variety of communications and information systems. Some have to do with government—taxes to cover public services, protection of persons, a weather bureau if weather information is not otherwise marketable, one-way streets, laws against littering, wrecking crews to clear away the wreckage in the southbound lane and policemen to wave us on in the northbound lane. More selective groupings—the union, the club, the neighborhood—can try to organize incentive systems or regulations to help people to do what individually they wouldn't, but collectively may wish to do.[5]

The main point is that it has always been recognized that there must be some restraints on the pursuit of self-interest. These restraints may be voluntarily undertaken, in the sense that we agree to restrain ourselves, on the condition that everyone else will agree to restrain themselves. This is the social contract. The market can only work within the set of formal and informal rules that define the social contract.

As the above quotation from Schelling suggests, there are a number of ways of reconciling private choice with public interest. Some of them involve changes in the property rights structure within which the market operates, some involve contracts among affected parties, some involve the formation of organizations of private individuals (clubs), some involve government intervention. Which is appropriate depends upon the particular situation.

Government regulation has been the form of collective action most frequently proposed by economists and others. However, there is another school of thought, whose proponents argue for the extension of private property rights, private market contracts, and damage suits, in an environment in which the government acts as a defender of property rights and an adjudicator of conflicts.[6] It is also sometimes argued that conservation organizations that collect money from their members to purchase land in the market to preserve it in its natural state provide vehicles through which collective action to preserve environmental resources can take place.[7] In addition, it is pointed out that politicians and government bureaucrats are not ideal social planners. Stroup and Baden point out that what we think of as a market failure may indeed be a "government failure."[8]

Although, as the example in the Prisoners' Dilemma figure shows, there is a gain to be had from restraining the independent pursuit of self-interest in the commons, different institutional arrangements may distribute this gain differently. Voluntary cooperation is predicated on an expectation of a share of the gain. But in many cases cooperation may be voluntary only in the sense that the individual has no recourse to other action. One of the keys to the success of institutional arrangements to limit access to the use of a common property resource is the ability to exclude. It is often the case that some users of an open-access resource are completely excluded when institutional arrangements to restrict use are agreed upon. The Game Laws of England, from 1671 until the nineteenth century, are a well-documented example. Access to wild game was reserved to wealthy land owners, and severe penalties were imposed on poachers. Similar arrangements applied to inland fisheries.[9] Even within the participating group it need not be the case that all have equal access to the use of a resource. This of course brings up questions of fairness. Different institutional approaches to the commons have different fairness implications.

The privatization of wildlife habitat in Europe may have preserved wildlife populations and their habitat, but this came at the expense of the poor, who were denied access to the resources owned by the wealthy. The exclusion of commoners was not entirely successful. It was widely regarded as unfair, and poaching was common.[10]

II. TRADITIONAL SOCIETIES AND COMMONS

Sometimes it is argued that traditional societies managed their natural environment in a more sustainable way than do modern societies. A variety of arguments have been made to support this hypothesis, and these will be investigated. But it is useful to look first at three conditions that must exist for the tragedy of commons to occur. Paraphrasing Berkes:

1. The resource must be freely open to any user (open access).
2. An individual user must have no incentive or constraint that limits his independent pursuit of self-interest.
3. The resource must be used so intensively as to cause individuals' private choices to interfere with one another.[11]

Prehistoric extinctions

One need not look only within the period of recorded history to find possible examples of the tragedy of commons. The hypothesis, that overhunting by prehistoric man was a contributing cause in widespread late-Pleistocene megafaunal extinctions, has supporting evidence.[12] Although there is also evidence that climate played a role, the arrival of prehistoric human hunters is the most widespread known common factor.

There is evidence of efficient hunting in artifacts of the period, such as Clovis and Folsom projectiles. As Smith points out, the combination of efficient hunting, megafaunal prey that exhibit slow population growth (small numbers of offspring, and long gestation period), and open access is a recipe for extinction.[13]

Nor are Pleistocene terrestrial megafauna the only prey to which the overhunting hypothesis has been applied. Hunters on the Oregon coast between 2000 and 1000 B.C. may have overhunted local seal and sea lion rookeries.[14]

In the above examples, there is archeological evidence of what prehistoric hunters did. But there is no evidence regarding their understanding or beliefs about the effects of their actions.

More recent examples

If we move forward in time, it is possible to investigate the understanding
and beliefs of traditional societies, as well as their actions. Common to traditional societies are an intimate knowledge of, and a reverence for, the
natural environments in which they lived.

Intimate knowledge of the natural environment was essential for survival. Writing about the Plains Indian, Mails states:

> [W]hile the Indian did believe that the Almighty gave each of His
> creations some particular grace or power, and that these favors, at
> least in part, might be obtained from them, by him, he knew he
> could only acquire them if he studied their possessors' habits and
> then copied them to the limit of his own ability. . . . Accordingly,
> . . . he acquired abilities for scouting, hunting and wise living far
> beyond those of many other peoples.[15]

Like that of most traditional societies, the Plains Indian's understanding
of Nature came from studying until he was part of it. His understanding
was not scientific but bound up with his religion, his way of life, and his
survival.

There is a question of whether there existed within traditional societies a knowledge of animal population dynamics. There are examples of
beliefs that imply an absence of such knowledge. Brightman cites the
belief, of the Boreal Forest Algonquins, that animals killed by hunters
spontaneously regenerate after death. Ritual procedures for disposing of
animal bones were believed to encourage reincarnation. When killed,
consumed, and disposed of with respect (according to ritual procedures),
the animals, which were believed to regenerate according to the numbers
killed, would continue to "give" themselves to hunters when needed.[16]

Another example is provided by Sillitoe in his study of the Wola people of the Southern Highland Province of Papua New Guinea, who
believe that demon spirits inhabit the forests of their region. Sillitoe suggests that this should not be interpreted as institutionalized forest conser-

vation: don't destroy the forest, or you will offend a demon. The Wola do destroy forest, as part of their shifting cultivation, but clearing has been gradual and restrained. Often, secondary growth is cleared for new gardens. In any case, the forest is too vast for the Wola to conceive of its complete destruction. The demon image perhaps provides a mild restraint on excessive clearing, but it does not make the Wola innate conservationists.[17]

The Ponam Islanders of Papua New Guinea believed that ancestors and, after exposure to Christianity, God (the ultimate ancestor) controlled the resources they used. If sea turtles were going to die out, it was God's will, and they could do little to prevent it. When the Ponam shell beds began to fail, due to overexploitation of the source of shell money, Ponam disrespect for the group that controlled the production of shell money caused God to relocate the shell bed (Carrier 1990). Another aspect of Ponam society was that property rights in marine resources were valuable because these could be used to create a reputation of generosity. Although generosity in allowing others to fish in your waters might result in overfishing, it would create an obligation for others to be generous toward you and your patrilineage.[18]

A Ponam Islander's reputation for generosity was a kind of insurance against the vagaries of Nature. This insurance aspect is also found in other societies. Asiatic Eskimos, who hunted sea mammals, sometimes harvested up to double their own consumption requirements. The surplus was used for trading with tundra pastoralists. In a year when the marine mammals did not appear, trade with the pastoralists allowed the coastal hunters to survive.[19]

The idea of animals giving themselves to knowledgeable and respectful humans is a common theme among North American aboriginal people. Gottesfeld documents similar beliefs among the Gitksan and Wet'suwet'en people of northwestern British Columbia. The Gitksan people believe that all edible parts of a fish must be consumed, and that all fish remains must be returned to the water, to ensure reincarnation. Wasting fish by allowing them to rot will cause the waster to be spoken of badly by community members, who fear that the salmon may not give themselves in the future.[20]

The first key feature in these beliefs and rituals seems to be the minimization of waste. In no case is there a prohibition on hunting, fishing, or clearing. Indeed, the harvest may include a surplus for giving or trading to reduce risk. But there are disincentives to harvest more than necessary. Second, they are for the most part culture specific, indirect ways of achieving conservation, and quite fragile in the face of outside influences. The European demand for furs, and introduction of European harvesting technology, were forces that pushed the Boreal Forest Algonquins toward depletion of the furbearing and game animal populations. Under aboriginal conditions, killing a large enough number of animals to deplete the population would have required a very large amount of effort, and would not have been considered worthwhile. However, the new demand for furs, and the introduction of more efficient hunting technology in the form of steel traps, guns, and poison bait, changed the convention of killing as many animals as possible from a benign to a disastrous behavior. The common hunting society practice, of moving on when game becomes scarce, did not help. The inability to control incursions into one's hunting lands would have rendered any conservation efforts on those lands disadvantageous.

For the Gitksan and the Wet'suwet'en, a crucial factor in preventing overfishing was the way in which traditional beliefs interacted with the allocation of fishing sites and smokehouse space. The Gitksan use a kinship system of allocation. The lineage to which a fishing site belongs has right of first place in the allocation of fishing time and smokehouse space. After its needs are met, more distant relatives and friends may have a turn, if there are any fish left. The limiting constraint was smokehouse space. This constraint combined with the abhorrence of waste to regulate fishing effort.

Practices more congenial to conservation did eventually develop among the boreal Algonquins. It became possible partly because increased sedentism gave greater freedom from trespass. According to Brightman, conservation techniques may have been influenced by Hudson's Bay Company policies.[21] In any case the concept of "waste" seems to have become more effective. Overhunting came to be regarded as "wasteful" and offensive to animal spirits. An offended spirit would interfere with the harvests of those who had "wastefully" overhunted.

What seems to be indicated by the above examples is that traditional societies can incorporate conservation strategies into their behavior through their cultural and religious beliefs. Two of the prerequisites for developing conservation-oriented beliefs and behaviors are: their necessity to survival, and ability to exclude outsiders. Whether the boreal Algonquins' initial failure to conserve furbearing and game resources was due to the absence of exclusive territories or the failure of cultural mores and religious beliefs to adapt quickly enough is difficult to speculate.

McGrath et al. provide an example in which a traditional society was able to respond rapidly to threatened fisheries. Until recently the lake fisheries of the Amazonian floodplain *(varzea)* were generally regarded as inexhaustible because of limited ability of the floodplain inhabitants *(varzeiros)* to capture and preserve fish. The economy has been integrated into the regional economy for almost three centuries. Many plant and animal products have been the focus of economic activity, including cacao, turtles and turtle eggs, manatee, and jute. When the commercial value of a species was high it was heavily exploited, driving local populations to the brink of extinction. Until now there has not been much local concern about the depletion of *varzea* resources. McGrath et al. suggest that this is because none was critical to the subsistence system.[22]

With few remaining options many local *varzeiros* have turned to fishing. At the same time commercial fishing has intensified. Although they have engaged in overuse of their resources in the past, the *varzeiros* now seem aware that they must act now to protect the lake fisheries, if they are to maintain their way of life. Various lake communities (defined by the ownership of property surrounding the lake) succeeded in asserting control over local lakes and excluding fishers from outside the community, establishing informal lake reserves and community management. Enforcing the exclusion of outsiders is costly, and there are many conflicts. Community management takes the form of restrictions on gear and on the sale of fish outside the community. In one case, the use of ice is prohibited, so fishers must salt their catch to preserve. The need to salt the fish quickly is intended to limit the amount of fish that can be taken at any one time.

Community management is not always successful. In Nigeria, community management was based in a land tenure system in which community leaders hold the land and its living resources in trust for the entire community. This meant that all wild plants and animals of cultural and economic value to the community were under the strict control of the community. But increased population pressure, new technologies, political forces, and changes in the beliefs in which community management is based have led to a breakdown of the community management system. With nothing to replace this system, local people are being excluded, and have become the opponents of biodiversity preservation. This attitude is similar to that of the lower and middle classes excluded by the English Game Laws. Exclusion that violates widely held views of fairness is likely to be difficult to enforce. Wild biotic resources are being overharvested and their habitat is being lost.

In Botswana, access to dry season water was often privately controlled, although access to grazing land was not. The limited access to water limited the number of cattle on the common pasture. A government program, of sinking new boreholes to increase water availability to pastoralists, increased the number of cattle and led to overgrazing. The government program effectively removed the constraint that had limited grazing.

III. LESSONS FROM TRADITIONAL SOCIETIES

What can be learned from examples of how traditional societies succeeded or failed in developing institutions to manage common property resources? The task of these institutions is to encourage the individual to restrain his pursuit of self-interest for the good of the community. In most cases a system of norms and conventions, enforced by the desire of the individual to gain and hold the approbation of his fellows in the community, was used.

Such an approach works well when the community and the commonly owned resource are easily identified. This requires that individuals outside the community can be excluded. Individuals within the community must clearly understand the behavior that is required of them. It is also desirable that members of the community are able to monitor the behavior of their fellows, and the state of the resource. As economists often point out in other contexts, there is a tradeoff between the probability of detecting inappropriate behavior and the punishment for such behavior. If inappropriate behavior is hard to detect, the penalty if it is detected is likely to be more severe. Low and Ridley suggest that when cooperation evolves, it is often of a tit-for-tat variety. In prisoners' dilemma terms, a player will cooperate as long as other players cooperate, but will retaliate when others do not cooperate (e.g., shunning, speaking badly of the offender, etc.). At minimum, an offender will lose respect in the community.

For many North American aboriginal societies, the appropriate behavior with respect to common property resources was part of their religion. Nature was viewed as having the ability to bestow gifts. However, these gifts could only be obtained via the development of an intimate knowledge of, and a respect for, Nature. A lack of knowledge or respect would offend animal spirits, who would withhold their gifts, to the detriment of the community.

The general idea of the natural world as a bestower or withholder of gifts is common to many traditional societies. However, the behavior required to show respect varied according to how crucial it was to restrain individuals from excessive exploitation. If technology prevented human predation from having any significant effect on the prey population, or if exclusion of those outside the community was not possible, there would not likely be very effective restraints on excessive use. This is exemplified by early observations of beliefs and behavior of the boreal forest Algonquin. The beliefs and behavior of the Wola of Papua New Guinea are similarly not too restraining. The entire forest is not in danger of being destroyed. The Wola are not engaged in reckless destruction of the forest, but neither are they innate conservationists. The religious beliefs or social norms that traditional communities develop to manage their commons seem tailored very specifically to the particular circumstances of the community and the resource.

Because they are not clearly linked to scientific facts, the cultural and religious beliefs that govern resource management in traditional societies change more slowly than other influences on the resource and its use. The new hunting technology introduced by the fur trade increased hunting pressure and severely reduced prey populations. Although they did eventually happen, the changes in social and religious institutions necessary to reduce hunting pressure were slow to develop.

Even if they are not intimately bound up in religious beliefs, the institutions or constraints that have prevented overuse of the commons by traditional societies may not be all that obvious. Ensminger and Rutten's example of the Botswanan government's bore hole program shows the ease with which effectively operating institutional constraints can be rendered ineffective.

Osemeobo's Nigerian example points to the need to be concerned about exclusions that are widely regarded as unfair. In Nigeria, outside forces have led to a breakdown of a community management system for common property biotic resources. Ownership of land is being privatized, and many local people are being excluded. This makes them opponents of conservation, and many of Nigeria's plant and animal species are in danger of loss of habitat or overharvesting. In Nigeria, as in most developing countries, successful conservation of common property resources requires that local communities see some gain from participating in the conservation of wild plants and animals.

When the stakes are high, communities that were previously unable to exercise effective exclusion of outsiders or restrict activities of their members may be able to do so. The more recent experience of the boreal forest Algonquins illustrates this, as do the initiatives of the lake communities of the Amazon floodplain, who have been willing to incur significant costs to exclude outsiders.

In a time when the forces of globalization are increasingly exposing traditional societies to the markets and formal property rights structures of modern societies, the way in which the interaction between modern and traditional occurs is important to social stability and environmental management. It is overly simplistic to think that traditional societies will move easily toward the formal property rights structure of modern societies. How communities solve potential conflicts internally depends crucially upon attitudes developed within the history and culture of that society. These are not quickly or easily changed. One solution is for state governments working side by side with traditional leaders to negotiate ways of achieving appropriate resource management.

This idea is reminiscent of a what has been called co-management. While the term is not well defined, it implies a collaboration between traditional communities and state governments in managing local resources. Part of the idea is to take advantage of the knowledge that exists in traditional communities. Whether it implies that the state will provide an infrastructure within which traditional communities can take full responsibility for management of their resources is difficult to say. While many of the above examples indicate that traditional systems do not adapt quickly to changes in outside influences, there is also some evidence that when the stakes are high, and the local community truly wishes to protect its traditional way of life, community management can work.

Whether or not co-management achieves its objective is likely to depend on how committed the state is and how high the stakes are for the traditional community. The state has to avoid regulations that undermine community management. This means taking traditional knowledge and the practices that stem from them seriously. Had the British Columbia government made an exception to its fire suppression policy for Gitksan berry patches, the Gitskan might have continued to manage productive berry patches.

For their part, traditional societies may have to incorporate more scientific information on animal population dynamics into their knowledge and beliefs. They must be very serious about the objective of maintaining their traditional lifestyle. Sale of harvested resources or harvesting rights to outsiders is widely deemed to be inappropriate by other citizens of the state. The traditional community must be a cohesive unit that can be strengthened by successful co-management.

On the international front, non-governmental organizations have begun to fill the institutional role of developing complex contracts to preserve biodiversity. Developing countries have claimed sovereign rights to genetic resources under the Biodiversity Convention. A further definition of property rights for genetic resources has not occurred, and would be unlikely to yield a fair outcome or efficient incentives. Contracts such as that developed by the National Biodiversity Institute of Costa Rica (INBio) provide an alternative. INBio operates under a cooperative arrangement with Costa Rica's Ministry of the Environment. INBio's contract with Merck Chemical and Co. provides samples of genetic material to Merck in return for investments in the human and natural capital of Costa Rica. Whether the INBio model will be widely repeated is difficult to say, but it does provide an example of a new type of institution which can exist beside a traditional system and promote an economically efficient and fair allocation of resources.

IV. CONCLUSION

In traditional societies, institutional arrangements to overcome or avoid depletion of commonly owned resource stocks are often intricately woven into the society's cultural fabric. They are based on a very detailed knowledge of what happens in Nature, but little knowledge of why it happens.[31] Hence, the belief arose that animal spirits controlled events, and that, according to whether they were pleased or offended, they could give or withhold favors. Through trial and error, heuristic systems of rules that suit the particular situation have evolved. But rules developed through a process of trial and error, with no real understanding of the dynamics of the natural system, are not easily adjusted when there is a shock to the system. With the introduction of a new technology, or an institutional change imposed from outside the community, the process of trial and error must begin again. The success of any particular set of rules in controlling overuse is fragile.

The lessons to be learned include a recognition of the fragility of traditional institutions. Rather than trying directly to change traditional institutions, it would be desirable for the state to help traditional communities develop a more scientific understanding of the natural system. This has to be done in a way that melds traditional and scientific knowledge to make the result understandable at the community level.

More generally, the institutions developed by traditional societies remind us that social and cultural norms can be effective ways of enforcing restraint on the pursuit of self-interest. They are likely to have low transaction costs, conform to the community view of fairness and promote a more efficient allocation of resources than would otherwise be possible. While, in general, the impersonal nature of many relationships in modern society is not conducive to the use of social norms to enforce the restraint of self-interest, there may be some situations in which they can at least support other more formal methods of enforcement. For example, if the public were to take an active role in reporting violations of pollution regulations, substantial government funds might be saved through a reduction in the level of government monitoring activities.

In developing countries, where traditional systems still hold sway, it will generally be more productive to work with those systems than to try to replace them. The development of new forms of institutional arrangements, such as the biodiversity contract, provide ways to integrate modern and traditional approaches to resource management, without destroying the traditional approach.

NOTES

1. Robert Dorfman and Nancy S. Dorfman, *Economics of the Environment: Selected Readings*, (New York: W. W. Norton and Company, Inc., 1993).

2. Garrett Hardin, "The Tragedy of the Commons," *Science* 162 (1968): 1243–48.

3. Fred Hirsch, *Social Limits to Growth* (Cambridge: Harvard University Press, 1976), p. 137.

4. Fred Hirsch, *Social Limits to Growth*, p. 141.

5. Thomas Schelling, "On the Ecology of Micromotives," *The Corporate Society*, R. Marris, ed. (London: The Macmillan Press Ltd., 1974), p. 28.

6. John Baden and Richard Stroup, "Natural Resource Scarcity, Entrepreneurship and the Economy of Hope," *Economics and the Environment: A Reconciliation*, W. E. Block, ed. (The Fraser Institute, Vancouver, B.C., 1990), pp. 117–36.

7. Terry Anderson, "The Market Process and Environmental Amenities," *Economics and the Environment: A Reconciliation*, pp. 137–58.

8. John Baden and Richard Stroup, "Natural Resource Scarcity and the Economy of Hope," p. 134.

9. Bonnie J. McCay, "The Culture of the Commoners: Historical Observations on New and Old World Fisheries," *The Question of the Commons*, B. J. McCay and J. M. Acheson, eds. (Tucson: The University of Arizona Press, 1990), pp. 195–216.

10. As McCay points out, an "underground law" developed among the poor, and to some extent the middle class, that game and fish were not properly the subject of the discriminatory game laws. Hence, a poaching culture developed. Taylor reports a case in which the fishermen of Teelin rejected the opportunity to purchase the fishing rights to the salmon fishery of the Glen River and Teelin Bay, so they would be able to better control poaching. The fishermen preferred the existing institutional structure in which they were not required to enforce poaching restrictions on their friends and neighbors. See Bonnie J. McCay, "The Culture of the Commoners," and Lawrence Taylor, "'The River Would Run Red with Blood': Community and Common Property in an Irish Fishing Settlement, "The Question of the Commons, pp. 290–310.

11. Fikret Berkes, "Common Property Resource Management and Cree Indian Fisheries in Subarctic Canada," *The Question of the Commons*, p. 67.

12. P. S. Martin and H. E. Wright, Jr., *Pleistocene Extinctions: the Search for a Cause* (New Haven: Yale University Press, 1967).

13. Vernon L. Smith, "The Primitive Hunter Culture, Pleistocene Extinction and the Rise of Agriculture," *Journal of Political Economy* 83 (1975): 727–55. It has been pointed out by Slaughter that a long gestation period can also mean a decreased ability to adjust to changes in climate. See Bob H. Slaughter, "Animal Ranges as a Clue to Late-Pleistocene Extinction," *Pleistocene Extinctions: the Search for a Cause*, P. S. Martin and H. E. Wright, Jr., eds. (New Haven: Yale University Press, 1967), pp. 155–67.

14. See R. Lee Lyman, "Subsistence Change and Pinniped Hunting," *Human Predators and Prey Mortality*, M. C. Stiner, ed. (Boulder: Westview Press. 1991) and Terry L. Jones and Wm. R. Hildebrandt, "Reasserting a Prehistoric

Tragedy of the Commons: Reply to Lyman," *Journal of Anthropological Archaeology* 14 (1995): 78–98.

15. Thomas E. Mails, *The Mystic Warriors of the Plains* (New York: Mallard Press, 1991), p. 94.

16. Robert A. Brightman, "Conservation and Resource Depletion: The Case of the Boreal Forest Algonquins," *The Question of the Commons*, pp. 121–41.

17. Paul Sillitoe, "Forest Demons in the Papua New Guinea Highlands," *The Australian Journal of Anthropology* 4.1 (1993): 220–31.

18. James G. Carrier, "Marine Tenure in Papua New Guinea: Problems in Interpretation," *The Question of the Commons.* pp. 142–70.

19. Igor Krupnik, *Arctic Adaptations: Native Whalers and Reindeer Herders of Northern Eurasia* (Hanover, New Hampshire: University Press of New England, 1993), pp. 185–215.

20. Leslie M. Johnson Gottesfeld, "Conservation, Territory, and Traditional Beliefs: An Analysis of Gitksan and Wet'suwet'en Subsistence, Northwest British Columbia, Canada," *Human Ecology* 22.4 (1994): 443–62.

21. Robert A. Brightman, "Conservation and Resource Depletion: The Case of the Boreal Forest Algonquins," pp. 121–41.

22. David G. McGrath, Fabio de Castro, Celia Fotemma, Benedito Domiques, and Juliana Calabria, "Fisheries and the Evolution of Resource Management on the Lower Amazon Floodplain," *Human Ecology* 221. 2 (1993): 167–95.

ROSEMARY RADFORD RUETHER

5. Ecofeminism, Religion, Gender, Hierarchy, and Environment

The term "ecofeminism" is a recent coinage from the 1970s, but it has become an international idea. Asian women particularly have been quick to connect concerns of the poverty and oppression of women and the impoverishment of the earth. Thus gender is an important aspect of traditional and modern approaches to the environment. The Indian ecofeminist Vandana Shiva has long made this connection in her writings. Filipino and Korean women, such as Victoria Tauli-Corpuz and Sun Ai Lee Park, are also exploring the connection between women and environment. Latin American women are also making this connection. Brazilian theologian Ivone Gebara has made ecofeminism the defining term of her critical and reconstructive work.[1]

In this chapter I will explore the relation between Christianity and gender hierarchy. Most of this study will not be in a Pacific context, but rather will take the issues back to Christian origins and development in the Mediterranean and European worlds. But I wish to state at the outset that this issue is not only a Christian or Western one. Particularly as Christianity became global with modern colonialism and missionary work after the sixteenth and especially the nineteenth century, Western patterns of both culture and economic exploitation have made the connection between Christianity and the treatment of women and the environment one which women and men throughout the world, including the Pacific Basin, are exploring today.

I wish to start by examining the presuppositions contained in the word "ecofeminism." What is ecofeminism? Ecofeminism represents the union of the radical ecology movement, or what has been called "deep ecology," and feminism. The word "ecology" emerges from the biological science of natural environmental systems. It examines how these natural communities function to sustain a healthy web of life and how they become disrupted, causing death to plant and animal life. Human intervention is obviously one of the main causes of such disruption. Thus, ecology emerged as a combined socioeconomic and biological study in the late sixties to examine how human use of Nature is causing pollution of soil, air, and water, and destruction of the natural systems of plants and animals, threatening the base of life on which the human community itself depends.

Deep ecology takes this study of social ecology another step. It examines the symbolic, psychological, and ethical patterns of destructive relations of humans with Nature and determines how to replace this with a life-affirming culture.[2]

Feminism also is a complex movement with many layers. It can be defined only as a movement within the liberal democratic societies for the full inclusion of women in political rights and economic access to employment. It can be defined more radically in a socialist and liberation tradition as a transformation of the patriarchal socioeconomic system, in which male domination of women is the foundation of all socioeconomic hierarchies.[3] Feminism can be also studied in terms of culture and consciousness, charting the symbolic, psychological, and ethical connections of domination of women and male monopolization of resources and controlling power. This third level of feminist analysis connects closely with deep ecology. Some would say that feminism is the primary expression of deep ecology.[4]

Although many feminists make a verbal connection between domination of women and domination of Nature, the in-depth exploration of what this means is just beginning. There are two levels on which this relationship between sexism and ecological exploitation can be made: the cultural-symbolic level and the socioeconomic level. Feminist cultural historians, particularly in the West, are beginning to chart the complex ways in which patriarchal culture has identified women as being "closer to Nature" or as belonging on the Nature side of the culture-Nature split.

Even less explored are the socioeconomic underpinnings of this identification of women with Nature.[5] How have women as a gender group, their bodies and their work, been colonized by patriarchy as a legal, economic, social, and political system, and how does this colonization of women's bodies and work function as the invisible substructure for the exploitation of Nature? How does this positioning of women as the caretakers of small children, the gardeners, weavers, cooks, cleaners, and waste managers for men both denigrate this work and serve to identify women with the sub-human? Some Third World ecofeminists, such as Vandana Shiva in India, are beginning to surface these concrete relationships between the symbolism of woman as Nature-like and women's concrete roles in the agricultural and domestic work.

It seems to me essential not simply to explore the connection of women's domination and that of Nature on a cultural-symbolic level but to detail its socioeconomic underpinnings, if we are to think of how this relationship can be changed in the way that really transforms these substructures of the culture. Such an exploration goes beyond the expertise of any one person. It calls for the collaboration of cultural historians, feminist scientists, and economists, as well as social organizers. It also demands a cross-class and cross-cultural perspective today, seeing this relationship as it has been constructed as a world-wide system of exploitation of women and the natural world across social classes within and between nations.

In this chapter I wish to look at the history of the cultural-symbolic connections between domination of women and domination of Nature in Western Christianity with its roots in the Ancient Near Eastern, Hebrew, and Greek cultures and the continuation of those patterns of women's roles today. This discussion will lay the basis for exploring how these cultural-symbolic patterns of our religious culture that uphold the system of domination might be changed to incarnate more life-giving relations in our cultural consciousness and in our social system.

PREHISTORIC ROOTS

Anthropological studies have suggested that the identification of women with Nature and males with culture is both ancient and widespread.[6] This cultural pattern itself expresses a monopolizing of the definition of culture by males. The very word "Nature" in this formula is part of the problem, because it defines "Nature" as a reality below and separated from "man," rather than one nexus in which humanity itself is inseparably embedded. It is, in fact, human beings who cannot live apart from the rest of Nature as our life-sustaining context, while the community of plants and animal both can and, for billions of years, did exist without humans. The concept of humans outside of Nature is a cultural reversal of natural reality.

How did this reversal take place in our cultural consciousness? One key element of this identification of women with non-human Nature lies in the early human social patterns in which women's reproductive role as childbearer was tied to making women the primary productive and main-tenance workers. Women did most of the work associated with child care, food production and preparation, production of clothing, baskets, and other artifacts of daily life, cleanup and waste disposal.[7]

Although there is considerable variation of these patterns cross-cul-turally, generally males situated themselves in work that was both more prestigious and more occasional, demanding bursts of energy, such as hunting larger animals, waging war, and clearing fields, but allowing them more space for leisure. This is the primary social base for the male monopolization of culture, by which men reinforced their privileges of leisure, the superior prestige of their activities, and the inferiority of the activities associated with women.

Perhaps, for much of human history, women ignored or discounted these male claims to superiority, being entirely too busy with the tasks of daily life, and expressing among themselves their assumptions about the obvious importance of their own work as the primary producers and reproducers.[8] But, by stages, this female consciousness and culture was sunk underneath the growing male power to define the culture for the whole society, socializing both males and females into this male-defined point of view.

It is from the perspective of this male monopoly of culture that the work of women in maintaining the material basis of daily life is defined as an inferior realm. The material world itself is then seen as something sep-arated from males and symbolically linked with women. The earth, as the place from which plant and animal life arises, becomes linked with the bodies of women from which babies emerge.

The development of plow agriculture and human slavery very likely took this connection of woman and Nature another step. Both are seen as a realm, not on which men depend, but that men dominate and rule over with coercive power. Wild animals that are hunted retain their autonomy and freedom. Domesticated animals become an extension of the human family. But animals yoked and put to the plow, driven under the whip, are now in the new relation to humans. They are enslaved and coerced for their labor.

Plow agriculture generally involves a gender shift in agricultural production. While women monopolize food gathering and gardening, men monopolize food production done with plow animals. With this shift to men as agriculturalists comes a new sense of land as owned by the male family head, passed down through a male line of descent, rather than communal landholding and matrilineal descent that is often found in hunting-gathering and gardening societies.[9]

The conquest and enslavement of other tribal groups created another category of humans, beneath the familiar community, owned by it, whose labor is coerced. Enslavement of other people through military conquest typically takes the form of killing the males and enslaving the women and their children for labor and sexual service. Women's work becomes identified with slave work.[10] The women of the family are defined as a higher-type slave over a lower category of slaves drawn from conquered people. In patriarchal law, possession of women, slaves, animals, and land are all symbolically and socially linked together. All are species of property and instruments of labor, owned and controlled by a male heads of family as a ruling class.[11]

As we look at the mythologies of the Ancient Near Eastern, Hebrew, Greek, and early Christian cultures, one can see a shifting symbolization of women and Nature as spheres to be conquered, ruled over and, finally, repudiated altogether. In the Babylonian Creation story, which goes back to the third millennium B.C., Marduk, the warrior champion of the gods of the city states, is seen as creating the cosmos by conquering the Mother Goddess Tiamat, pictured as a monstrous female animal. Marduk kills her, treads her body underfoot and then splits it in half, using one half to fashion the starry firmament of the skies, and the other half to constitute the earth below.[12] The elemental mother is literally turned into the matter out of which the cosmos is fashioned (not accidentally, the words "mother" and "matter" have the same etymological root). She can be used as matter only by being killed; that is, by destroying her as "wild," autonomous life, making her life-giving body into "stuff" possessed and controlled by the architect of a male-defined cosmos.

THE HEBRAIC WORLD

The view of Nature found in Hebrew scripture has several cultural layers. But the overall tendency is to see the natural world, together with human society, as something created, shaped, and controlled by God, a God imaged after the patriarchal ruling class. The patriarchal male is entrusted with being the steward and caretaker of Nature, but under God, who remains its ultimate creator and Lord. This also means that Nature remains partly an uncontrollable realm that can confront human society in destructive droughts and storms. These experiences of Nature that transcend human control, bringing destruction to human work, are seen as divine judgment against human sin and unfaithfulness to God.[13]

God acts in the droughts and the storms to bring human work to naught, to punish humans for sin, but also to call humans (that is, Israel) back to faithfulness to God. When Israel learns obedience to God, Nature in turn will become benign and fruitful, a source of reliable blessings rather than unreliable destruction. Nature remains ultimately in God's hands, and only secondarily, and through becoming servants of God, in male hands. Yet the symbolization of God as a patriarchal male, and Israel as wife, son, and servant of God, creates a basic analogy of woman and Nature. God is the ultimate patriarchal Lord under whom the human patriarchal lord rules over woman, children, slaves, and land.

The image of God as single, male, and transcendent, prior to Nature, also shifts the symbolic relation of male consciousness to material life. Marduk was a young male god, who was produced out of a process of theogony and cosmogony: He conquers and shapes the cosmos out of the body of an older Goddess that existed prior to himself, within which he himself stands. The Hebrew God exists above and prior to the cosmos, shaping it out of a chaos that is under his control. Genesis 2 gives us a parallel view of the male, not as the child of woman, but as the source of woman. She arises out of him, with the help of the male God, and is handed over to him as her Master.[14]

THE GREEK WORLD

When we turn to Greek philosophical myth, the link between mother and matter is made explicit. Plato, in his creation myth, the *Timaeus*, speaks of primal, unformed matter as the receptacle and "nurse."[15] He imagines a disembodied male mind as divine architect or Demiurgos, shaping this matter into the cosmos by fashioning it after the intellectual blueprint of the Eternal Ideas. These Eternal Ideas exist in an immaterial, transcendent world of Mind, separate from and above the material stuff that he is fashioning into the visible cosmos.

The World Soul is also created by the Demiurgos, by mixing together dynamics of antithetical relations (the Same and the Other). This world soul is infused into the body of the cosmos in order to make it move in harmonic motion. The remnants of this world soul are divided into bits to create the souls of humans. These souls are first placed in the stars, so that human souls will gain knowledge of the eternal ideas. Then the souls are sown in the bodies of humans on earth. The task of the soul is to govern the unruly passions that arise from the body.

If the soul succeeds in this task, it will return at death to its native star and there live a life of leisured contemplation. If not, the soul will be reincarnated into the body of a woman or an animal. It will then have to work its way back into the form of an (elite) male and finally escape from bodily reincarnation altogether, to return to its original disincarnate form in the starry realm above.[16] Plato takes for granted an ontological hierarchy of being, the immaterial intellectual world over material cosmos, and, within this ontological hierarchy, the descending hierarchy of male, female, and animal.

In the Greco-Roman era, a sense of pessimism about the possibility of blessing and well-being within the bodily, historical world deepened in Eastern Mediterranean culture, expressing itself in apocalypticism and gnosticism. In apocalypticism God is seen as intervening in history to destroy the present sinful and finite world of human society and Nature and to create a new heaven and earth freed from both sin and death.[17] In gnosticism mystical philosophies chart the path to salvation by way of withdrawal of the soul from the body and its passions and its return to an immaterial realm outside of and above the visible cosmos.[18]

CHRISTIANITY

Early Christianity was shaped by both the Hebraic and Greek traditions, including their alienated forms in apocalypticism and gnosticism. Second-century Christianity struggled against gnosticism, reaffirming the Hebraic view of Nature and body as God's good creation. The second-century Christian theologian Irenaeus sought to combat gnostic anticosmism and to synthesize apocalypticism and Hebraic creationalism. He imaged the whole cosmos as a bodying forth of the Word and Spirit of God, as the sacramental embodiment of the invisible God.

Sin arises through a human denial of this relation to God. But salvific grace, dispensed progressively through the Hebrew and Christian revelations, allows humanity to heal its relation to God. The cosmos, in turn, grows into being a blessed and immortalized manifestation of the divine Word and Spirit which is its ground of being.[19]

However, Greek and Latin Christianity, increasingly influenced by neo-Platonism, found this materialism distasteful. They deeply imbibed the Platonic eschatology of the escape of the soul from the body and its return to a transcendent world outside the Earth. The Earth and the body must be left behind in order to ascend to another, heavenly world of disembodied life. Even though the Hebrew idea of resurrection of the body was retained, increasingly this notion was envisioned as a vehicle of immortal light for the soul, not the material body in all its distasteful physical processes, which they saw as the very essence of sin as mortal corruptibilty.[20]

The view of women in this ascetic Christian system was profoundly ambivalent. A part of ascetic Christianity imagined women becoming freed from subordination, freed both for equality in salvation and to act as agents of Christian preaching and teaching. But this freedom was based on woman rejecting her sexuality and reproductive role and becoming symbolically male. The classic Christian "good news" to woman as equal to man in Christ was rooted in a misogynist view of female sexuality and reproduction as the essence of sinful and mortal, corruptible life.[21]

But for most male ascetic Christians, even ascetic women, who had rejected their sexuality and reproductive role, were too dangerously sexual. Ascetic women were increasingly deprived of their minor roles in public ministry, such as deaconesses, and locked away in convents where obedience to God was to be expressed in total obedience to male ecclesiastical authority. Sexual woman, drawing male seminal power into herself, her womb swelling with new life, became the very essence of sin, corruptibility, and death, from which the male ascetic fled. Eternal life was disembodied male soul, freed from all material underpinnings in the mortal bodily life, represented by woman and Nature.

Medieval Latin Christianity was also deeply ambivalent about its view of Nature. One side of Medieval thought retained something of Irenaeus's sacramental cosmos, which becomes the icon of God through feeding on the redemptive power of Christ in the sacraments of bread and wine. The redeemed cosmos as resurrected body, united with God, is possible only by freeing the body of its sexuality and mortality. Mary, the virgin Mother of Christ, assumed into heaven to reign by the side of her son, was the representative of this redeemed body of the cosmos, the resurrected body of the Church.[22]

But the dark side of Medieval thought saw Nature as possessed by demonic powers that draw us down to sin and death through sexual temptation. Women, particularly old crones with sagging breasts and bellies, still perversely retaining their sexual appetites, are the vehicles of the demonic power of Nature. They are the witches who sell their souls to the Devil in a satanic parody of the Christian sacraments.[23]

THE REFORMATION AND THE SCIENTIFIC REVOLUTION

The Calvinist Reformation and the Scientific Revolution in England in the late sixteenth and seventeenth centuries represent key turning points in the Western concept of Nature. In these two movements the Medieval struggle between the sacramental and the demonic views of Nature was recast. Calvinism dismembered the Medieval sacramental sense of Nature. For Calvinism Nature was totally depraved. There was no residue of divine presence in it that could sustain a natural knowledge or relation to God. Saving knowledge of God descends from on high, beyond Nature, in the revealed Word available only in Scripture, as preached by the Reformers.

Populist Calvinism was notable for its iconoclastic hostility toward visual art. Stained glass, statues, and carvings were smashed, and the churches stripped of all visible imagery. Only the disembodied word, descending from the preacher to the ear of the listener, together with music, could be bearers of divine presence. Nothing one could see, touch, taste, or smell was trustworthy as bearer of the divine. Even the bread and wine was no longer seen as the physical embodiment of Christ, but as symbolic reminders of the message of Christ's salvific act enacted in the past.

Calvinism dismantled the sacramental world of Medieval Christianity, but it maintained and reinforced its demonic universe. The fallen world, especially physical Nature and other human groups outside of the control of the Calvinist church, lay in the grip of the Devil. All that were labeled pagan, whether Catholics or Indians and Africans, were the playground of demonic powers. But, even within the Calvinist church, women were the gateway of the devil. If women were completely obedient to their fathers, husbands, ministers, and magistrates, they might be redeemed as goodwives. But in any independence of women lurked heresy and witchcraft. Among Protestants, Calvinists were the primary witchhunters.[24] Dominicans were the main witchhunters among Catholics.

The Scientific Revolution at first moved in a different direction, exorcising the demonic powers from Nature in order to reclaim it as an icon of divine reason manifest in natural law.[25] But in the seventeenth and eighteenth centuries, the more animist natural science that unified material and spiritual lost out to a strict dualism of transcendent intellect and dead matter. Nature was secularized. It was no longer the scene of a struggle between Christ and the Devil. Both divine and demonic spirits were driven out of it. In Cartesian dualism and Newtonian physics it becomes matter in motion, dead stuff moving obediently according to mathematical laws knowable to a new male elite of scientists. With no life or soul of its own, Nature could be safely expropriated by this male elite and infinitely reconstructed to augment their wealth and power.

In Western society the application of science to technological control over Nature marched side by side with colonialism. From the sixteenth to the twentieth centuries, Western Europeans would appropriate the lands of the Americas, Asia, and Africa, and reduce their human populations to servitude. The wealth accrued by this vast expropriation of land and labor would fuel new levels of technological development, transforming material resources into new forms of energy and mechanical work, control of disease, increasing speed of communication and travel. Western elites grew increasingly optimistic, imagining that this technological way of life would gradually conquer all problems of material scarcity and even push back the limits of human mortality. The Christian dream of immortal blessedness, freed from finite limits, was translated into scientific technological terms and exported to the Pacific Basin where it played a major role in producing the tensions focused on in this book.

ECOLOGICAL CRISIS

However, in a short three-quarters of a century this dream of infinite progress has been turned into a nightmare. The medical conquest of disease, lessening infant mortality and doubling the life span of the affluent, insufficiently matched by birth limitation, especially among the poor, has created a population explosion that is rapidly outrunning the food supply. Every year ten million children die of malnutrition.[27] The gap between rich and poor, between the wealthy elites of the industrialized sector and the impoverished masses, especially in the colonized continents of Latin America, Asia, and Africa,[28] grows ever wider.

Women among the poor, as well as the children that depend primarily on women for their sustenance, are the greatest victims of this polarization of wealth for the few and poverty for the majority. As jobs shrink, it is women who are the first to be dropped from jobs. When the World Bank imposes structural adjustment demands on poor countries to pay their debts by cutting government investment in health, education, and welfare, it is women who pick up the extra load of caring for the sick and the elderly, growing food and seeking medicinal herbs to replace what society is no longer providing, inventing means of survival for themselves and their children in the informal economy outside the dominant economic system. It is women who walk long hours to fetch wood and water for households without modern systems of lighting, heat, or water. When all other sources of income fail, it is women who sell their own bodies to feed their families.[29]

This modern scientific, industrial revolution has been built on injustice from its beginnings. It has been based on the takeover of the land, its agricultural, metallic, and mineral wealth appropriated through the exploitation of the labor of the indigenous people, with a doubled exploitation of women among the colonized, including throughout the Pacific Basin. This wealth has flowed back to enrich the West, with some for local elites, while the laboring people, men and, even more, women, of these lands grew poorer. This system of global affluence, based on exploitation of the land and labor of the many for the benefit of the few, with its high consumption of energy and waste, cannot be expanded to include the poor without destroying the basis of life of the planet itself. We are literally destroying the air, water, and soil upon which human life and planetary life depends.

In order to preserve the unjust monopoly on material resources from the growing protests of the poor, the world became more and more militarized. Most nations have been using the lion's share of their state budgets for weapons, both to guard against each other and to control their own poor. Weapons have also become one of the major exports of wealthy nations to poor nations. Poor nations grew increasingly indebted to wealthy nations while buying weapons to repress their own impoverished masses. In the 1990s, as the rationale for military spending has faded somewhat with the end of the Cold War between the capitalist and communist systems, the patterns of exploitation have grown more directly economic, and focused more explicitly on the North-South relation between the wealthier industrialized nations and the poor areas of former colonization. World trade agreements and world banking agencies fix in place an even more draconian system of extraction of wealth through low-paid labor, low-priced commodities, and servicing of debt, the net effect of which is to transfer wealth from the poor to the rich. Despite some rhetoric about the need for environmental protection, in fact the right to pollute the lands, waters, and air where poor people live is an integral part of this system of global wealth extraction and is evident in many Pacific Rim countries.

Can this global system be changed and is it useful to focus particularly on the woman-Nature connection in our struggle against it? Many concerned with ecological disaster see any special concern for women's exploitation in this system as trivial or a marginal component at best. A glance at the establishment forms of ecological analysis found, for example, in Vice President Gore's book or even more socially radical ecological think tanks such as the World Watch Institute will show how marginal concern for women is to such male ecological analyses. Women, when mentioned at all, tend to be recognized primarily in terms of curbing population explosion, and here more as objects rather than as subjects of population control.

Some feminists look at ecofeminism with suspicion also because it seems to ratify patriarchal thought patterns in which women are identified with Nature and hence with the nonrational and somatic side of the human-Nature split. If women are to be liberated we must affirm women's full humanity. This means affirming women's equal capacity for rationality and agency, not by continuing to identify women with the nonhuman. I think we need to take this challenge to ecofeminism seriously.

It is important to realize that patriarchal culture does not merely denigrate women and Nature as inferior or evil, but it also idealizes both women and Nature. We have in our cultures two images of woman as Nature in complementary tension: woman as evil Nature, associated with sin, sex, and death; and woman as bountiful, ever-nurturing Nature, Nature as paradise. Ecofeminists, while repudiating the first stereotype of woman and Nature, often uncritically take over the second stereotype.

Much ecofeminist spirituality imagines an original time before the rise of patriarchy when woman ruled and the whole earth was a paradise of loving relations and natural bounty. They see a transformation of culture to worship of a feminine earth-deity as key to restoring such as paradisal Nature and society. Nature as a place of hard struggle for survival, as finite and tragic, is banished from consciousness as a patriarchal bad dream or as only the fruit of unjust social exploitation. I think an ecofeminism that is grounded in the realities of earth and earth history needs to come to terms with the cruel and the tragic faces of Nature and to eschew the romanticized concept of Nature which one can only hold if one looks at it through a plate-glass window.

We need to question both the negative images of women and Nature as inferior, as the source of sex, sin, and death, and also Nature as paradise, as ever-bountiful mother. The connections the patriarchal tradition has drawn between women and Nature can be used to surface both the symbolic and the socioeconomic connections between these interlocking exploitations. But we should draw upon this interconnection, not to perpetuate the romantic image of either woman or Nature, but to explode both of these images. Women are not inferior to men, ethically or intellectually, but they are also not morally superior and naturally loving. They, like men, are complex human beings who seek their whole humanity in struggle as well as in mutuality with others.

Likewise Nature is neither to be reduced to mindless, spiritless matter nor idealized as ever-loving mother, but recognized as the complex matrix of all life in which humans are rooted as one species among others. We need a much deeper deconstruction of the binary dualisms of woman as Nature/men as culture that deconstructs all sides of this false division, if we are to begin to figure out both the real context of our lives as earth creatures and how to integrate our own aspirations into these realities in a way that can better sustain all our lives together.

Third World women, Asian women in particular, have much to contribute to the development of a more adequate paradigm of ecofeminism.

Asian ecofeminists are concerned with many of the same themes as Euro-Americans, but in their own historical and cultural contexts. Many are analyzing the masculine-feminine dualism and its effects on views of women and Nature both in their own religious and cultural heritages and in terms of the patterns brought by Christianity and Western colonialism. Many Asian women also see a special link of women to Nature, both because of the roles played by women in the family economy and in a psycho-physical sense of ways in which women are more in tune with natural rhythms of life than men. Filipino, Korean, and Indian women are also keenly interested in reaching back to pre-colonial and even to pre-patriarchal patterns in their own cultures to reclaim a sacral spirituality of Nature imaged as feminine.

But there are two important differences when these themes are contextualized by Asian-Pacific women. First, women from Asia are much less likely to forget, as Euro-American women are, that the base line of domination of women and of Nature is impoverishment, impoverishment of the majority of their people, particularly women and children, and of the land. This poverty is not an abstract theory expressed in statistics, but is present in concrete realities that one lives and observes every day. Deforestation means women walk twice as far to gather wood. Drought means women walk twice as far seeking water. Pollution means a struggle for clean water that directly affects the health and survival of one's family.

Secondly, although many Asian women are interested in exploring patterns of sacrality of Nature as feminine in ancient pre-patriarchal cultures, these cultures belong to their own indigenous roots. These indigenous roots are still present in their world today, although they have been partly silenced and shattered by modernization. Korean women look to Shaman practices of their own mothers. Filipino women explore the indigenous spiritualities of their rural roots. Thus, there are more real roots as well as reality checks in such explorations for Asian women, than is the case with Euro-American women who have long been cut off from such indigenous cultures.[30]

Asian-Pacific people also are seldom interested in simply jettisoning modern developments, including Christianity, if they have become Christian, for an idealized pre-modern culture, even as they search for integrate their own Asian cultures with these new developments. Rather, they are seeking to be creatively multilingual, able to speak both a prophetic language that came to them from the Bible and a language of sacral cosmology from their Asian roots. Dialogue between Euro-American and Asian women and men on ecofeminism can stimulate us all, on both sides of the Pacific basin, to reject what is oppressive and integrate what is liberating and life-giving in both our ancient and modern cultures, creating a new synthesis for the global society of the twenty-first century.

NOTES

1. See Rosemary R. Ruether, ed., *Women Healing Earth: Third World Women on Ecology, Feminism and Religion* (Maryknoll, N.Y.: Orbis Press, 1996).

2. Paul R. Ehrlich et al., *Human Ecology: Problems and Solutions* (San Francisco: W. H. Freeman, Co., 1973). Bill Devall and George Sessions, *Deep Ecology: Living as if Nature Mattered* (Salt Lake City: Peregrine Smith Books, 1985).

3. Zillah Eisenstein, ed., *Capitalist Patriarchy and the Case for Socialist Feminism* (New York: Monthly Review Press, 1979).

4. For example, see Sharon Doribiago's essay, "Mama Coyote Talks to the Boys," in Judith Plant, *Healing the Wounds: The Promise of Ecofeminism* (Philadelphia: New Society Publishers, 1989), pp. 40–44.

5. Plant, ibid.

6. Sherry Ortner, "Is Female to Male as Nature is to Culture?" in Michelle Z. Rosaldo and Louise Lamphere, *Woman, Culture, and Society* (Stanford: Stanford University Press, 1974), pp. 67–88.

7. See Marilyn French, "The Long View Back: Matricentry," in her *Beyond Power: On Women, Men, and Morals* (New York: Summit Books, 1985), pp. 25–64.

8. Yolanda and Robert Murphy, *Women of the Forest* (New York: Columbia University Press, 1974), pp. 111–41.

9. M. Kay Martin and Barbara Voorhies, *Female of the Species* (New York: Columbia University Press, 1975), pp. 276–332.

10. Gerda Lerner, *The Creation of Patriarchy* (New York: Oxford University Press, 1986), chapter 4.

11. On the Roman family in late antiquity, see David Herlihy, *Medieval Households* (Cambridge: Harvard University Press, 1988), pp. 1–28.

12. "The Creation Epic," in Isaac Mendelsohn, ed., *Religion in the Ancient Near East* (New York: Liberal Arts Press, 1955), pp. 17–46.

13. For example, Isaiah, chapter 24.

14. Phyllis Trible views the story of Eve's creation from Adam as essentially egalitarian: "Depatriarchalizing in Biblical Interpretation," *Journal of the American Academy of Religion* 41 no. 1 (March, 1973): 29–48. For an alternative view from the Jewish tradition, see Theodor Reik, *The Creation of Woman* (New York: McGraw-Hill, 1960).

15. Plato, *Timaeus* (49), from *The Dialogues of Plato*, vol. 2, B. Jowett, ed. (New York: Random House, 1937), p. 29.

16. Ibid. (42), 23.

17. For the major writings of inter-testamental apocalyptic, see R. H. Charles, *The Pseudepigrapha of the Old Testament* (Oxford: Clarendon Press, 1913).

18. For the major gnostic literature, see James M. Robinson, ed. *The Nag Hammadi Library* (San Francisco: Harper and Row, 1977).

19. Irenaeus, *Adv. Haer*, from *Early Christian Fathers*, Cyril Richardson, ed. (Philadelphia: Westminster Press, 1953), vol. 1, pp. 387–98.

20. Origen, *On First Principles*, G. W. Butterworth, ed. (New York: Harper and Row, 1966), Bk. II, ch. 3, pp. 83–94. Also Gregory Nyssa, *On the Soul and the Resurrection*, in *Nicene and Post-Nicene Fathers*, second series, vol. 5 (New York: Parker, 1893), pp. 464–65.

21. See Kari Vogt, "Becoming Male: A Gnostic and Early Christian Metaphor," in Kari Borresen, ed. *Image of God and Gender Models in Judaeo-Christian Tradition* (Oslo: Solum Forlag, 1990).

22. See Otto Semmelroth, *Mary: Archetype of the Church* (New York: Sheed and Ward, 1963), pp. 166–68.

23. *Malleus Maleficarum*, Montague Summers, ed. (London: J. Rodker, 1928).

24. William Perkins, *Christian Oeconomie* (London, 1590); also his *A Discourse on the Damned Art of Witchcraft* (London: 1596). See also Carol F. Carlsen, *The Devil in the Shape of a Woman: The Witch in 17th Century New England*. Ph.D. Diss: Yale University, 1980.

25. Brian Easlea, *Witchhunting, Magic and the New Philosophy* (Highlands, N.J.: Humanities Press, 1980).

26. Antoine-Nicholas de Condorcet, *Sketch for a Historical Picture of the Progress of the Human Mind* (1794).

27. Cited in talk in London, 29 May 1989, by Dr. Nafis Sadik, head of the United Nations Fund for Population Activities; see David Broder, *Chicago Tribune*, 31 May 1989, sec. 1, 17.

28. Francis Wilson and Mamphela Ramphele, *Uprooting Poverty: The South African Challenge* (Capetown: David Philip, 1989).

29. Rosemary Radford Ruether, "Women, First and Last Colony," in *Humboldt Journal of Social Relations* 19:2 (1993), pp. 391–416.

30. See essays by Asian women, Vandana Shiva, Victoria Tauli-Corpuz, Gabriele Dietrich, and Sun Ai Lee Park in Rosemary Ruether, *Women Healing Earth* (op. cit., note 1)

NANCY TURNER and RICHARD ATLEO

6. Pacific North American First Peoples and the Environment

Because human behavior and practices are guided by human values, they can have a profound influence on people's interactions with the environment at both individual and societal levels. Differences in values, leading to divergent, sometimes contrary, approaches and practices relating to the environment have resulted in many strong and ongoing tensions between indigenous peoples and mainstream society in northwestern North America. Even within and between different indigenous communities are tensions that relate to varying interpretations of traditional and modern values and practices, and how these should be played out in the context of modern society and its approach to the environment.

In this chapter we identify and characterize important traditional values of the First Peoples[1] of northwestern North America, based on discussions with First Nations Elders and specialists in traditional knowledge, and on historic and ethnographic accounts. We then discuss ways in which these values are reflected in traditional lifestyles and attitudes toward the environment. These values, lifestyles, and attitudes are then contrasted with those of prevailing Eurocanadian culture. Finally, we propose ways in which some aspects of Aboriginal values can be incorporated into mainstream society.

Many authors[2] have observed that while there are many variations within and among Aboriginal cultural and linguistic groups throughout

105

the Americas, there are also many commonalities. Joseph Epes Brown, for example, noted that:

> [T]his common binding thread is found in beliefs and attitudes held by the people in the quality of their relationships to the natural environment. All American Indian peoples possessed what has been called a metaphysic of Nature; and manifest a reverence for the myriad forms and forces of the natural world specific to their immediate environment; and for all, their rich complexes of rites and ceremonies are expressed in terms which have reference to or utilize the forms of the natural world.[3]

However, not all Aboriginal people today espouse traditional views and values. Many who have been educated and raised in mainstream institutions may share the same worldviews as those of the dominant society. Daisy Sewid-Smith, a Kwagiulh historian and language specialist, explains:

> When we're talking about Kwakwaka'wakw people, there are two types, the traditionalists, and the people who are, I guess you would call "Euro-Kwagiulhs" because they are more inclined to [be like], they are not different from Europeans. But traditionalists are very close to their environment, and they know that to survive in this world, you have to have respect for your environment, because without the environment you cannot live, and they knew this.[4]

Recently (from 1993 to 1995), our work on the Scientific Panel for Sustainable Forest Practices in Clayoquot Sound (hereafter referred to as "the Panel") has given us a unique opportunity to focus upon traditional knowledge and to learn about potential value conflicts between the First Peoples and others in society. In addition to the fifteen scientists appointed to the Panel, four First Nations Nuu-Chah-Nulth,[5] including three elders and one academic (ERA), were also appointed and these provided the tension between the traditional and modern approaches to the environment.

The Panel's review of government forest practices documents showed clearly that there are major differences between traditional aboriginal values and the values of the dominant society. While both perceive the Earth to have resources, traditional aboriginal values imbue these resources with sacred life and personhood in contrast to the values of the dominant society which imbue these same resources with impersonal economic value. Our chapter will address some of these differences, some of the tensions between traditional and modern approaches. In so doing, it is hoped that the Panel's work may serve as an example of possibilities for the resolution of, and reconciliation between, these tensions. (See chapters 9, 10, and 11 for case studies of such tensions.)

TRADITIONAL VALUES OF THE FIRST PEOPLES OF NORTHWESTERN NORTH AMERICA

It appears reasonable to assume that human values arise from belief systems. What people believe determines what values are held and practiced. People who do not believe in the spiritual realm may hold different values from people who believe in God or Creator. Science, through its technological marvels, is one belief system that leads to strong individual values because the essence of science is a search for isolated variables that can be proven to be related. When variables are shown not to be related, as is often the case, then reality may be assumed to be characterized by fragmentation. Reality in this belief system is made up of *individual* fragments. In contrast, traditional beliefs are based upon the notion of a Creator who is One, indivisible, with all of creation. Reality in this belief system is group oriented. The belief system from which traditional aboriginal values arise can be articulated as follows:

> *The Creator made all things one.*
> *All things are related and interconnected.*
> *All things are sacred.*
> *All things are therefore to be respected.*[6]

The first fundamental concept of traditional belief systems is a Creator who not only created all things but also, in holistic fashion, has a continuing association in and through all creation. The universe, therefore, both personal and impersonal, physical and metaphysical, embodies the characteristics of the Creator who is one, indivisible whole. Reality is characterized by the Creator, and the Creator characterizes reality. All things are one, all things are related, and all things are interconnected. This traditional assumption about the nature of reality directly impacts upon the best of traditional values and practices. If the Creator is One, then the people are also one. In the words of Lame Deer, "We aren't divided up into separate, neat little families. . . . The whole damn tribe is one big family; that's our kind of reality."[7]

Consider, for example, the following quotations related to the first two concepts of oneness and relatedness:

The Creator made all things one.
All things are related and interconnected.

> We should understand well that all things are the works of the Great Spirit. We should know that He is within all things; the trees, the grasses, the rivers, the mountains and all the four-legged animals, and the winged peoples; and even more important, we should understand that He is also above all these things and peoples. (Frank Black Elk, Oglala, Sioux) [8]

> A long time ago, the Creator, He gave us what we call the Three Sisters, and it's the beans, corn and squash. They were our sustainers of life. The Corn Spirit was so thrilled at being one of the sustainers of life, she asked the Creator if there was anything more she could do for her people. . . . (Maisie Shenandoah, Oneida) [9]

> You give thanks before you even receive your gifts from the Creator. When you ask, you give thanks. Your prayers are thanksgivings for everything—the sun, the moon, the snow, the water, the fire, the rocks. You see them as being alive, having a life of their own. A tree has its own life. . . . (Vickie Downey, Tewa) [10]

What is apparent is that traditional First Nations people do not separate the spiritual dimension from the physical. The coincidence of these two dimensions is so complete that everything, including all matter, is alive. There is an absence of inert matter. What is also apparent is that the spiritual dimension is considered the source of the physical dimension. That is why deliberate interaction with the spiritual realm is thought necessary to ensure the maintenance and continuation of necessary provisions. This is the reason "You give thanks."

All things are sacred.

> We regard all created beings as sacred and important, for everything has a wochangi, or influence, which can be given to us, through which we may gain a little more understanding if we are attentive. (Frank Black Elk, Oglala, Sioux)[11]

> We believe that all life, whether it be animal, plant or marine is sacred and is as important as human life. We are but one small part of the big picture and our food gathering practices and ceremonies remind us of that [Kwagiulh]. (Kim Recalma-Clutesi, Kwagiulh)[12]

> Underlying and interconnecting the phenomena of Hopi experience is the sacred. The sacred—that is, basic reality—is known by several Hopi terms. . . .[13] Asked why they pray, the Hopi almost always respond that they do so for rain, crops, health, and long life. . . . Prayer creates life, and life evokes experience of the sacred. . . . (Hopi)[14]

> Everything was sacred with our people. . . . How sacred it was to them when spring came and the new ground was being broken. New things emerging from the ground, and all celebrated the strawberries and the beans and the corn and the coming of the fall and the medicine and stuff. . . . (Cecelia Mitchell, Mohawk)[15]

All things are therefore to be respected.

> Respect is the very core of our traditions, culture and existence. It is very basic to all we encounter in life. . . . Respect for Nature

requires a healthy state of stewardship with a healthy attitude. It is wise to respect Nature. Respect the Spiritual. . . . It is not human to waste food. It is inhuman to overexploit. "Protect and Conserve" are key values in respect of Nature and natural food sources. Never harm or kill for sport. It is degrading to your honour. . . . It challenges your integrity and accountability. Nature has that shield or protective barrier [that], once broken, will hit back at you. (Roy Haiyupis, Nuu-Chah-Nulth)[16]

The Sliammon hunter treated the dead bear with a great deal of respect and sang a special song to it, asking for luck.[17]

Don't ever forget what I am going to tell you. During your lifetime do as I do—respect all the animals, don't ever make them suffer before you kill them, don't ever waste anything by killing more than you need, and don't ever try to keep an animal in captivity because the animals are necessary for the survival of future generations. (A dying Innu man to his grandson)[18]

Respect does not preclude pride of accomplishment since the ceremony of cutting and transforming a giant cedar tree into a magnificent whaling canoe may be admired and applauded by the most severe critics. In traditional values, respect also has deep roots into the origins of life and into a homeland bestowed upon First Peoples by the Creator. Initially, everything began with the Creator. Today, everything is sustained by the Creator, and tomorrow, everything ends with the Creator. Other values, such as generosity, kinship with all living beings, kindness, gentleness, tolerance, patience, endurance, love, and friendliness, derive naturally from the worldview characterized by the omnipresence of the Creator. For example, generosity is a characteristic of the Creator and is therefore to be practiced by his creation. It is a teaching, a law—one which early explorers to the Americas experienced first hand when they were fed by the First Peoples they encountered, as seen in the words of Simon Fraser concerning the Nlaka'pamux (Thompson) of the Fraser Canyon:

We had every reason to be thankful for our reception at this place; the Indians shewed us every possible attention and supplied our wants as much as they could. We had salmon, berries, oil and roots in abundance. . . . (19 June 1808)[19]

VALUES AS REFLECTED IN TRADITIONAL LIFESTYLES AND ATTITUDES TOWARD THE ENVIRONMENT

A different (as in holistic, interactive, reciprocal, sacred, spiritual) view of the Earth and resources

Since all sustenance and life forms that people need to survive are regarded as gifts of the Creator, to be respected and valued, they are approached differently by traditional Aboriginal people. Rather than cut down trees without ceremony or without thought for the life of the tree as is always done by modern forest companies, Roy Haiyupis, a Nuu-Chah-Nulth, describes a typical traditional activity when a tree is to be cut down: "Talk to it like a person. Explain to the tree the purpose, why you want to use it—for the people at home and so on. It may seem like you're praying to the tree, but you're praying to the Creator."[20]

> All gathering practices have a prayer and story to acknowledge the greatness and spirit of the plant as well as remind us of our need for humility. . . .[21]

Many specific examples of interactions of people with the resources they need, such as the words spoken to a salmonberry bush before its bark is taken for medicine, are provided in *The Religion of the Kwakiutl Indians* by Franz Boas:

> Don't be startled, Supernatural One, by my coming and sitting down to make a request of you, Supernatural One . . . . This is the reason why I come to you . . . to pray you, please, to [let me] take some of your blanket, Sore-Healer, that it may heal the burn of my child, that, please, may heal up his burn, Supernatural One. . . . (Kwagiulh)[22]

The differences between traditional and modern views of the Earth and its resources are likely best described by the differences between the physical and metaphysical. Traditional views exemplified by Black Elk, Recalma-Clutesi, Haiyupis, and Sewid-Smith focus upon the metaphysical, the spirits of the other life forms such as plants and animals, while the modern views may focus more upon the physical or scientific characteristics of the same life forms. The traditional approach to the environment is also personal, interactive, and reciprocal while the modern approach is impersonal. A cedar tree is a living personal being deserving respect because it sprang from "Mother Earth" and was given life by the Creator just as the human sprang from the Earth and was given life by the Creator. Thus, all of creation are kinfolk.

> See, Brothers: Spring is here.
> The Earth has taken the embrace of the Sun,
> and soon we shall see the children of that love.
> All seeds are awake, and all animals.
> From this great power we too have our lives.
> And therefore we concede to our fellow creatures,
> even our animal fellows, the same rights as
> ourselves, to live on this earth.
> —Sitting Bull, 1877[23]

Although natural resources, such as trees and animals, are to be respected they are still "requirements" for human survival. The resources are accessed by a protocol guided by the value of respect.

The following myth account illustrates the need for a protocol, not from the human perspective, as the Western world understands "human," but from the perspective of a salmon who is also, in spirit and in flesh, like a human. For want of an adequate English description, because there is none, the being who speaks in this myth may be called a "wise old salmon person."

> We had better tell *ynathloo7a* what we want his people to do for us, and what we should like them to put on the water for us to get. Now, the first thing we always liked to get from them is eagle's down; and mussel shells, the large ones; and the *hap'achim'thl*—these three things we always like to have. We also do not want them to use blunt-pointed spears on us, for it hurts; and whenever they make salmon traps to catch us with, let them shave the sticks well and put a good sharp point on them [at the funnel entrances]. Also, whenever they cook salmon in any way, and whenever they finish eating it, let them pick up all the bones

and pieces of skin and throw them into the salt water. Then we can come home again. If they do not do that, we can not come to life again.[24]

Other, similar protocols were followed in relationships with game and other food resources. For example, among the Sliammon Coast Salish, "Deer bones from deer tracked by dogs were never given to the dogs to chew; instead, they were thrown into the water and asked to come back again as real deer."[25]

In this way the process of life is acknowledged to be cyclical and reciprocal. The Creator is One and gives to all, and everything in creation gives, each to another. The Creator sends rain to water the earth which then blooms to provide food for Nature which in turn provides food for the human, who eventually dies and returns to the earth, which will bloom again to provide food for Nature, which in turn provides food for the human, again and again, in endless cycles. Cycles, in this belief system can be broken. If salmon, or deer, are not accorded the proper respect they eventually disappear; if forests are continuously clear-cut they, too, eventually disappear.

Integration of sacred religious thought with all activities

In a work published in 1986 entitled "The Spiritual Legacy of the American Indian," Joseph Epes Brown echoes what many observers have said before, that for traditional aboriginal people, religion "pervades all of life and life's activities."[26] In terms of attitudes and practices toward resources then, the following quote may make some sense in the context of the sacred.

If you respect things and look at them . . . as having a spirit or being, then you're at a place where you're . . . at a balance . . . you look at the world that way and respect it and you see that it's providing you with a way of life, and your kids. . . . (Gabriel George, Angoon, Alaska)[27]

Strategies to access resources might differ from place to place but the principles remain the same. Fasting, cleansing, purification, prayers, and supplications in isolation were the principles often practiced. This is seen in the following passage relating to Sliammon mountain goat hunting:

Only a very few men were mountain goat hunters. The hunting of mountain goats was a highly specialized skill, engaged in only by those who had trained and received a guardian spirit power enabling them to do so.[28]

Relationships to place

> Sacred areas are pivotal to the Nuu-Chah-Nulth culture. They are important to the well-being, survival, and sustenance of the Nuu-Chah Nulth. . . . (R. Atleo, Nuu-Chah-Nulth)[29]

In order to access resources properly, traditional peoples required special places in which to perform the necessary rituals, prayers, supplications, fastings, and purification; only in private isolation would they receive visions, instructions, and power so that, through them, the well-being of the community might be served. Sacred areas might be pools, caves, remote areas of a river or mountain, private wooded areas, or offshore islets and isolated coves. Each of these places would have a traditional name.

Although a specific place is not mentioned in the following account (sacred places were also secret places), the principle and purpose of rituals and places relating to the well-being of a community is well illustrated. In this narrative, a young Sliammon man had been judged lazy by his father. He was embarrassed and humiliated by his people. He left home and went out and trained for a full year.

> The young man had trained very hard and received a special guardian spirit power. He asked the people what type of fish or meat they wanted. One man who wanted porpoise went out hunting with the young man near Marina Island. So many porpoises came to the young man that it appeared as if he was calling to them. The young man filled their canoe with porpoise. The next day, the young man went hunting and the same thing happened. Before they returned home their canoe was filled with seals. The following day, he filled the canoe with fish. When the young man went hunting for deer, they ran towards him to be killed. He was able to get any type of fish or game that he desired. . . .[30]

Although sacred areas are important, it sometimes happens that a person may acquire spirit power in a secular, mundane setting, as happened to Andrew Ahenakew, an Anglican priest who became a reluctant medicine man. Having been thoroughly indoctrinated by Anglican theology, Ahenakew was skeptical that a great white spirit bear who appeared to him one night in a motel room and spoke to him could be in the employ of the Almighty. As usual, the Almighty prevailed and Andrew Ahenakew eventually followed the great white spirit bear's instructions to make medicine to cure cancer. Subsequently, between 1960 until his death in 1976, Ahenakew treated many cancer patients successfully, as well as other ailments that were apparently incurable.[31]

Cultural institutions reflecting values

Perhaps the best known traditional cultural institution along the Northwest Coast of the Americas is what was called "potlatch" by the Europeans. The term is derived from the Nuu-Chah-Nulth verb *pachitle*, meaning "to give" and the noun *pachuck*, which means "article to be given." The potlatch incorporated social, economic, political, and spiritual aspects of life. From a resource perspective its function was to redistribute wealth to promote the well-being of the community without doing damage to the environment, without violating the principles of balanced stewardship over the land, and in such a way as to render respect and honor to chiefs, nobility, people, plants, animals, spirit powers, and through all these, to the Creator. George Clutesi, a Nuu-Chah-Nulth of the Tse-sha-aht Nation, attended a potlatch, otherwise known as Tloo-quah-nah, during the first half of this century. The following is an excerpt of an opening welcome oration give by the official speaker.

> Hear again the stories that are old;
> Traditions that our ancestors told.
> The laws they made are still with us.
> They are here and have not changed.
> Our lands, our streams, our seas remain
> To provide for wants, that are yours and mine.
>
> See again my dance of joy and gladness.
> Cast your woes to the winds from the north.

Stand with me and share my happiness;
Take my hand, with me stand forth.
Do the dance your forebears and also mine
Did leave for us to perform as one.

Thanks, many thanks are due you for your own.
The presence of your House here in mine
Reassures that friend is nigh.
Arise, renew the friendship of all time
Show the goodwill to all mankind
Share with me the abundance of our seas.[32]

Ancient stories, teachings, laws, songs, dances, names, and lineages are emphasized during the potlatch to validate sovereignty over territories. This is an occasion of joyful sharing of resources and the renewing of friendships and goodwill, all in the attitude of respect and honor. Also reflected in the potlatch is the institute of *HaHuulhi*, a Nuu-Chah-Nulth term for a hereditary chief's rights and stewardship over his territories and resources, and for the responsibilities he incurs to the environment, to the resources, and to his people to sustain all of them wisely and fairly.

Many other rituals and ceremonies are relevant in reflecting aboriginal attitudes and values toward the environment and resources. Their importance and context in contemporary life is summarized:

Our well being (mental, physical and spiritual) is absolutely dependent on the intricate rituals and use of plants as well as our ceremonial or ritual acknowledgment of those precious gifts. It is extremely important to remind ourselves that while plant use is important it is only one part of a whole system that even at this time has been translated into a modern context using the old value systems. The use of modern tools has not significantly changed the gathering practices, but the restricted land and sea use has.[33]

Sustainability strategies

Sustainability is a modern economic concept often discussed in isolation from other societal concepts such as politics and religion. Aboriginal peoples focused upon the quality of their relationship to other life forms which were part of traditional economy. Traditional reality is moral reality. Callicott, for example, makes the following observations:

> The American Indian posture toward Nature was, I suggest, neither ecological nor conservative in the modern scientific sense so much as it was moral or ethical. Animals, plants, and minerals were treated as persons, and conceived to be coequal members of a natural social order. . . .

> To point to examples of wastage—buffaloes rotting on the plains under the high cliffs or beaver all-but-trapped-out during the fur trade—which are supposed to deliver the coup de grace to all romantic illusions of the American Indian's reverence for Nature is very much like pointing to examples of murder and war in European history and concluding therefrom that Europeans were altogether without humanistic ethic of any sort.[34]

Over and over, traditional people speak of taking only what is needed: Just take enough salmon for your winter needs, just take enough cedar to build your homes, make your canoes, objects of ritual, utensils, clothing, and leave the rest. What ever you take, be respectful towards it.

CONTRASTING WORLDVIEWS ABOUT THE ENVIRONMENT

Prevailing modern approaches to the environment and its resources have been profit oriented. The best of traditional approaches to the environment and its resources have been spiritually oriented. A spiritual orientation tends to holism, tends toward unification, because of the pervasive nature of a Creator who is in, and through, all things. A profit orientation, in contrast, is highly focused and tends to fragment reality. The strength of what may be termed holistic reality is a tendency toward balance, toward harmony. This becomes necessary when traditional people, through their spiritual experiences, become aware of forces and powers within the universe that are much greater than themselves. It becomes ultimately necessary when it is realized that the Creator of all things is omnipotent, omniscient, and omnipresent. Thus, the spirit of the Tloo-quah-nah of the Nuu-Chah-Nulth might be best expressed in the phrase, "Walk carefully upon the earth for it is filled with the unseen powers of the Almighty."

Left to themselves, traditional people, including everyone and everything else, might now be extinct. A good example is in accounts of the Great Flood. Without warning, and without instructions about how to survive, all humans may have been lost in the Great Flood. Here is one traditional account of the Kwagiulh people:

> And my ancestor *ts'eqamey'* was told that this flood was coming, and he was told how to prepare for it. And he was told to go to look for a large cedar tree, and to hollow it out. . . . And so that's what he did. He prepared the tree and he put all the food and all the things he would need in the tree, and then he sealed himself and his family in this tree. . . . When he entered the cedar tree, his name was *Hawilkwalalh*, which means "cedar tree," but when he came out, he was told you will no longer be *Hawilkwalalh*; your name will be *ts'eqamey'*, which means that you will be the first person to ever perform the cedarbark ceremony.[35]

This ceremony is still an important part of Kwagiulh life. In contrast, the predominant trend is to separate humans from their religious traditions. There is a profit orientation toward the environment which, with the aid of technological advances, has enabled people to create great wealth. The weakness in this approach is the tendency toward imbalance, toward disharmony: while great wealth is generated, great poverty is also created. This contrast was noted from the very outset of culture contact between the Europeans and the First Peoples. Sagard, a French missionary Recollet, observed:

> [Those] of their Nation . . . offer reciprocal Hospitality, and help each other so much that they provide for the needs of all so that there is no beggar at all in their towns, bourgs and villages . . . so that they found it very bad hearing that there were in France a great number of needy and beggars, and thought that it was due to a lack of charity, and blamed us greatly saying that if we had some intelligence we would set some order in the matter, the remedies being simple.[36]

The modern approach to the environment has helped to produce the infrastructure and technology of Western civilization and there is much in this production that is beneficial to society. It incorporates the social, political, and economic activities of society. However, because of the assumption that reality is fragmented, the worldview upon which the modern approach is based tends to create an imbalance within society. On the other hand, the best of the traditional approach to the environment is focused more upon a holistic worldview which tends toward balance and harmony.

TOWARD A RESOLUTION OF TENSIONS BETWEEN TRADITIONAL AND MODERN APPROACHES TO THE ENVIRONMENT

There appears to be an insurmountable gulf between the orientations of the two approaches to the environment and its resources. The rift is so wide and deep that it has created polarity within Canadian society, and indeed, within the world community, so much so that violence threatens to tear the very fabric of law and order. How then can society move toward a resolution of tensions between traditional and modern approaches to the environment without resorting to violence?

Traditional approaches to the environment have much to contribute to modern approaches. Perhaps the greatest contribution of traditional people might be in the area of attitude toward resources. Treat resources with respect. Resources are living beings that give their lives so that people might live. It is not necessary for modern, profit-oriented corporations to adopt this belief system, but it would be necessary for them to respect such beliefs. In a sense, profit-oriented corporations who extract resources may not change their belief system much, if at all, but the practices of resource extraction can change through public pressure, official institutional policy, and government legislation. A prime example is the work of the Scientific Panel which managed to integrate scientific and traditional ecological knowledge into its recommendations for forest practices in Clayoquot Sound.

The Panel's vision stresses ecological relationships before development objectives, while recognizing that environmental protection and economic development are mutually dependent. Although scientific in its approach to forest ecosystems, it treats people and their aspirations within those ecosystems as a critical component. The vision has six tenets:

- the key to sustainable forest practices lies in maintaining functional ecosystems;

- hierarchical planning is required to maintain ecosystem integrity from the subregional down to site-specific levels, and to ensure that the intent of higher level plans is reflected in lower level plans;

- planning must focus on those ecosystem elements and processes to be retained rather than on resources to be extracted;

- cultural values and desires of inhabitants and visitors must be addressed;

- scientific and traditional ecological knowledge of Clayoquot Sound must continue to be encouraged through research, experience, and monitoring activities; and

- both management and regulation must be adaptive, incorporating new information and experience as they develop.[37]

Recommendations that flow from this vision statement emphasize the shift away from a focus upon volume-based resource extraction, away from a focus upon trees removed, to a focus upon trees retained. From a scientific perspective such recommendations represent a paradigmatic shift away from the fragmented approach of the profit orientation to the more integrated, interrelated, interconnected holistic approach characteristic of the traditional orientation. There is an attempt in these recommendations to strike a balance, to create a harmony, between and among all life on a part of planet Earth known as Clayoquot Sound. The striving for balance and harmony between and among all life is, again, characteristic of the best of traditional thinking and practices.

Noteworthy of the Scientific Panel's work is that it is an integrated effort between traditional people and members of the scientific community from the dominant society. Its recommendations embody First Nations' perspectives, blended with progressive scientific views on sustainable use of the Clayoquot ecosystems. Fortuitously, the provincial government of British Columbia has endorsed all of the Panel's recommendations. Members of the forest industry, too, have indicated their support. With this new type of collaboration, in which the tensions between traditional and modern approaches are recognized but ameliorated through mutual respect and efforts at understanding, some balance and harmony might begin to prevail.

CONCLUSIONS

The tensions between traditional and modern approaches to the environment are so different from the perspectives of worldview and values that common terminology does not necessarily apply. Callicott's observation is a case in point. "Conservation," "ecological," and "sustainability" are all necessary ideas for products of modern approaches to the environment. Maximum exploitation of resources for maximum profit is part of the modern approach to the environment, which from its inception created the wealthiest nations upon the face of the Earth. So long as the negative environmental effects of this modern approach remained relatively unknown, and so long as the resources appeared to be unlimited, the accumulation of vast wealth was seen to be acceptable because it also created large numbers of highly paid, relatively unskilled jobs, particularly in the extractive industries such as forestry. From this perspective, these types of jobs are completely predicated upon the untenable modern precept of maximum exploitation of resources for maximum profit. These types of jobs create lifestyles and expectations that cannot be maintained. The philosophy is flawed. It is a type of corporate scam of gigantic proportions where local citizens always lose, and the scapegoats are usually the poor and powerless.

In reductionist terms, the tensions between traditional and modern approaches to the environment may be expressed in the differing philosophies of "need" versus "greed." Who can deny the obvious preoccupation of the modern world with greed, the private accumulation of wealth, government and institutionally sponsored lottos? It is, however, a point of focus rather than an either/or situation.

It is important to note that a preoccupation of society is a focus of that society. It does not mean that other values are absent. In both traditional and modern approaches to the environment one can discern both of the philosophies of need and greed at work. One can discern respect and a lack of respect in both approaches, but one can also discern prevailing tendencies, prevailing values, and prevailing practices, which ultimately are the deciding influences. The prevailing economic practice of maximum exploitation of resources for maximum profit has created an environmental crisis. The philosophy that underlies this practice must be either modified or restrained. Otherwise, survival of the human species may be questionable.

One modification possible is an adaptation of the traditional philosophy of "need," which might be translated into economic policies the outcome of which would mimic the balance and harmony found between traditional peoples and the environment. Again, this philosophy is not peculiar to traditional approaches to the environment; it is also found, for example, in modern approaches to personal health, marriage relationships, gender issues in the workplace, and human rights issues in general. Whether modern approaches to the environment can or will be modified is uncertain. If they are not, what is certain is that the decision will be taken out of human hands.

NOTES

1. First Peoples, First Nations, Aboriginal Peoples, Indigenous Peoples, Indian, and Native may be used interchangeably.

2. For example: J. Baird Callicott, "Traditional American Indian and Western European Attitudes Toward Nature: An Overview," *In Defense of the Land Ethic. Essays in Environmental Philosophy* (Albany: State University of New York Press, 1989), pp. 177–219; Joseph E. Brown, "Modes of Contemplation through Action: North American Indians," *Main Currents in Modern Thought* 30 (1973–74): 58–63; Sam D. Gill, *Native American Religions. An Introduction* (Belmont, California: Wadsworth Publishing Company, The Religious Life of Man Series, 1982).

3. Joseph E. Brown, "Modes of Contemplation through Action: North American Indians," p. 60.

4. Daisy Sewid-Smith, personal communication to NT, October 1994; see also Daisy Sewid-Smith, Chief Adam Dick, and Nancy J. Turner, "The Sacred Cedar Tree of the Kwakwaka'wakw People." *Alocoa Foundation Hall of Native Americans*, Museum Exhibit Background Book (Pittsburgh: The Carnegie Museum of Natural History, in press, 1995).

5. Scientific Panel for Sustainable Forest Practices in Clayoquot Sound,

First Nations' Perspectives on Forest Practices in Clayoquot Sound (Victoria, British Columbia, 1995a), p. 1.

6. From: Scientific Panel for Sustainabile Forest Practices in Clayoquot Sound, *First Nations' Perspectives on Forest Practices in Clayoquot Sound*, p. 15.

7. Janet Hodgson and Jayant S. Kothare, *Vision Quest: Native Spirituality & the Church in Canada* (Toronto: Anglican Book Centre, 1990), p. 23.

8. Joseph Epes Brown, ed., *The Sacred Pipe* (Norman, Oklahoma: University of Oklahoma Press, 1953), pp. xx.

9. Maisie Shenandoah, Oneida Nation (Iroquois), quoted in: Steve Wall, *Wisdom's Daughters. Conversations with Women Elders of Native America* (New York: Harper Collins, 1993), p. 135.

10. Vickie Downey, Tewa, Tesuque Pueblo, quoted in: Steve Wall, *Wisdom's Daughters. Conversations with Women Elders of Native America* (New York: Harper Collins Publishers, 1993), p. 6.

11. Joseph Epes Brown, ed., *The Sacred Pipe*, p. 59.

12. Kim Recalma-Clutesi, Kwagiulh, personal communication to NT, December 1992.

13. John D. Loftin, *Religion and Hopi Life in the Twentieth Century*, p. xv.

14. John D. Loftin, *Religion and Hopi Life in the Twentieth Century*, p. xviii.

15. Cecilia Mitchell, Mohawk, Akwesasne, quoted in: Steve Wall, *Wisdom's Daughters. Conversations with Women Elders of Native America*, p. 232.

16. Scientific Panel for Sustainable Forest Practices in Clayoquot Sound, *First Nations' Perspectives on Forest Practices in Clayoquot Sound*, pp. 6–7.

17. Dorothy Kennedy and Randy Bouchard, *Sliammon Life, Sliammon Lands*, (Vancouver, British Columbia: Talonbooks, 1983), p. 39.

18. Pablo Piacentini, ed., "We Have Been Pushed to the Edge of a Cliff," *Story Earth: Native Voices on the Environment* (San Francisco: Mercury House, 1993), p. 14.

19. W. Kaye Lamb, ed., *Simon Fraser. Letters & Journals, 1806–1808* (Toronto: The Macmillan Company of Canada Limited, 1960), p. 87.

20. Personal communication to NT, 2 February 1995.

21. Kim Recalma-Clutesi, personal communication to NT, December 1992.

22. Franz Boas, *The Religion of the Kwakiutl Indians*, Columbia University Contributions to Anthropology, Volume 10, Part 1, Texts [in the Kwakwala language]; Part 2, Translations. (New York: Columbia University Press, 1930), p. 218. Daisy Sewid-Smith notes that the original identification of Boas's passages as "prayers" in English is incorrect. "Words of praise, acknowledgment, and thanks" would be a more accurate characterization. The Kwagiulh term corresponding to "prayer" would be used only in addressing the Creator. Sewid-Smith notes, "We do not worship plants and animals; we worship the Creator, who made them."

23. Estell Fuchs and Robert J. Havighurst, *To Live on This Earth: American Indian Education* (Garden City, New York: Anchor Books, 1973), p. xix.

24. Franz Boas, 1916, pp. 929–30, cited by E.Y. Arima, *The West Coast People: The Nootka of Vancouver Island and Cape Flattery* (Victoria: British Columbia Provincial Museum, 1983), p. 59; the importance of recycling salmon bones is emphasized in many other stories and narratives; cf. Dorothy Kennedy and Randy Bouchard, *Sliammon Life, Sliammon Lands*, p. 26.

25. Dorothy Kennedy and Randy Bouchard, *Sliammon Life, Sliammon Lands*, p. 38.

26. Joseph Epes Brown, *The Spiritual Legacy of the American Indian* (New York: Crossroad Publishing Company, 1986), p. 123.

27. Thomas R. Berger, *Village Journey: The Report of the Alaska Native Review Commission* (New York: Hill and Wang, 1985), p. 59.

28. Dorothy Kennedy and Randy Bouchard, *Sliammon Life, Sliammon Lands*, p. 38.

29. Scientific Panel for Sustainable Forest Practices in Clayoquot Sound, *First Nations' Perspectives on Forest Practices in Clayoquot Sound*, p. 21.

30. Dorothy Kennedy and Randy Bouchard, *Sliammon Life, Sliammon Lands*, p. 51.

31. Janet Hodgson and Jayant S. Kothare, *Vision Quest: Native Spirituality & the Church in Canada*, p. 23.

32. George Clutesi, *Potlatch* (Sidney, British Columbia: Gray's Publishing Ltd., 1969), p. 35.

33. Kim Recalma-Clutesi, personal communication to NT, December 1992.

34. J. Baird Callicott, "Traditional American Indian and Western European Attitudes Toward Nature: An Overview," pp. 194–95.

35. Daisy Sewid-Smith, personal communication to NT, October 1994.

36. C. J. Jaenen, "Amerindian views of French culture in the seventeenth century," *Out of the Background: Readings on Canadian Native History* (Toronto: Copp Clarke Pitman Ltd., 1988), p. 121.

37. Scientific Panel for Sustainable Forest Practices in Clayoquot Sound, *A Vision and Its Context*, Report 4 (Victoria, British Columbia, 1995a), p. vii.

JAN WALLS and MASAO KUNIHIRO

7. Mountains, Water, Wood, and Fish: Chinese and Japanese Perspectives on Nature and Ecology

On the west coast of Canada today, most of us who think of Chinese people almost immediately think of two things: real estate and *feng-shui*. We think of real estate because we have heard that property is the first thing most Chinese think about acquiring when they come here. We think of *feng-shui* because we know that Chinese people are sensitive to the manifold connections and relationships that exist between human artifice, the lay of the land, mountains, waters, and trees.

When we think of Japan we think, among other things, of the exquisite gardens that attempt to embody the natural world of mountains, waters, trees, and plants in a balanced but dynamic backyard microcosm. Scholars have told us that the Japanese islands "are endowed with an abundance and diversity of natural beauty to which the Japanese have ever been susceptible" (Saunders 1961, 411), and that "in a country in which natural calamities such as typhoons, earthquakes, and floods are a frequent occurrence, the Japanese view of Nature has always been a singularly benign one, stressing the qualities of tranquillity and beauty, rather than those of turbulence or menace" (1961, 412).

Harmony with Nature has been taken as a fundamental aspiration in the world of traditional Japan:

> This all-important harmony with Nature, fundamental in the Japanese outlook, led to an animistic view of the world. The things

125

of Nature, like human beings, were considered animated by, or imbued with, a vital spirit; they had a kind of personal vitality. This vitality in things which depart from the ordinary through shape or color, or in any other way, was felt to be "superior." It was hence characterized by the word *kami*, the fundamental meaning of which is "above," "upper part," "superior." Anything with unusual power or beauty or form was an object for reverence, or more precisely, was entitled *kami*, and the list of *kami* is infinite: an awe-inspiring mountain, an oddly shaped rock, a torrential mountain stream, a secular tree. . . . (Saunders 1961, 412)

We also know that Buddhist thought and practice, which has had widespread influence throughout East Asia, emphasizes respect for all forms of life, which are intertwined in unfathomable chains of cause-effect relationships (Brown 1993). Taoist philosophy, which originated in China but has influenced thinking throughout East Asia, goes so far as to equate the Natural Way (Tao) with the source of Truth (Tao) (Chan 1963, 136).

On the surface, therefore, East Asia would seem to provide a most hospitable cultural context for environmental sensitivity as a way of life. Yet we notice today that more harm has been done to the biosphere in China than we would ever allow to occur in North America (Smil 1984, 1993), and Japanese industry is one of the world leaders in deforestation overseas (Ofreneo 1993, 204–205). Recent evidence indicates that urban air pollution in Asia has reached critical levels—five of the seven most polluted cities in the world are in Asia (Caswell 69). Toxic wastes dumped into rivers have contaminated coastal fishing areas of China, 30 percent of whose land area has been degraded (Caswell 69).

> Taiwan, one of the "tiger" economies, now has the dubious reputation of being the dirtiest place in Asia. The lower reaches of the island's rivers are nearing biological death—the result of unregulated dumping of industrial and human waste. A third of its rice crop is contaminated with heavy metals and even by Taiwan's lenient standards, air quality is officially harmful for 17 percent of the year. (Caswell 69)

It appears that in the race to industrialize China, demands for fuel and building materials are creating an economy that is environmentally unsus-

tainable. Official policy requires productivity without increasing environmental degradation, but at enterprise levels the practice has been that
whenever there is a conflict between the promise of increased production
and increased environmental degradation, production usually wins. Japanese industry has had an embarrassing history of environmental degradation, and most environmental protection progress enjoyed to date has
been the result of grassroots public movements that have literally forced
industry to withdraw from past harmful practices (Griffith 1990, 90).

There is in the great traditions of East Asia ample philosophical and
cultural grounding in the virtue of the unspoiled natural state of the universe (see chapter 3). This, complemented with the notion of "doing without overdoing, with nothing left undone," would seem to provide a
cultural shield against environmental degradation. Yet, as we have noted,
five of the seven most polluted cities in the world are in Asia, and environmental degradation seems to have been accepted as the price one must
pay for economic development. In many cases, the "dragons" have spoiled
their own nests.

Yet there is also evidence that the great "naturophile" traditions of
East Asia can also spawn solutions to modern problems of environmental
degradation. The following Japanese case study offers one impressive
example.

CASE STUDY: WOODS, WATERS, AND FISH IN JAPAN

> The woods are here, the seas there.
> This I call but secretly, Heaven's dispensation.
> The woods love the sea, the sea the woods.
> And they have weaved love from time immemorial.
> —Mrs. Ryuko Kumagai,
> Miyagi Prefecture

The Japanese are known worldwide as huge consumers of seafoods, their
intake of marine life running well over 45 percent of their total consumption of animal protein. Their fishing fleets of various sizes and for various
purposes, to the consternation of much of the rest of the world, both
developed and developing, have earned themselves the inglorious nick-
name of "indiscriminate and predatory hunters" of the catch of the sea.

More recently, they have been purchasing all kinds of fish and marine products from the farthest corners of the world, thereby jacking up their world prices much to the dismay of less fortunate people of the Third World. Of course, it must be recognized that they have made enormous strides in fish farming, perhaps leading the world, thus contributing to the propagation of fish farming technology among Third World countries.

Also, we may take solace in the fact that some of the fish and marine products purchased by Japanese offshore are the kinds that were mostly left untouched by the indigenous people as something weird if not totally inedible. Now they can discover wealth in resources previously discarded.

Nevertheless, the world's dependence on marine life as sources of low fat animal protein is on a rapid rise, and the world's population is expected to increase by well over 90 million per year. On the other hand, production of feed grains, for various reasons, is expected to be in an unstable supply/demand situation. Therefore, a country of Japan's economic power and technological capability should refrain from buying up the available seafood by flexing its economic muscle, but rather should lead the world by discovering new avenues for sea catch, other than the already well-known regular technology of fish farming.

We should make it clear at this point that our purpose here is not to advance an economic or political argument about the problems of fish in the context of world hunger, or of resource warfare among nations. Rather, we would like to discuss the Japanese concept of "wood-sea reciprocity," which might also be rendered as "reciprocity in the existence of woods and seas." The poem by Ryuko Kumagai quoted above, although a non-literary rendition of the Japanese original, may help clarify the point by dwelling on the importance of a holistic approach to the question of resource development by focusing on the "live-and-let-live" kind of symbiosis that exists between the woods and the sea. The woods, the darling of the sea, is not mere poetic imagery: it is in fact a straightforward statement of a very important aspect of ecological life with philosophical implications.

The desertification of the sea, particularly in Hokkaido and the coastline facing the Sea of Japan, has become conspicuous since around 1965. The depletion of marine resources has become a great source of fear at the same time. The catch of herring that used to be on the order of one million tons annually, is now practically nil since the Taisho Period in the 1910s and 1920s.

Since at least the Tokugawa Period (seventeenth to mid-nineteenth centuries), Japanese fishermen have known empirically that there is a close link between woods, river, and sea. There were many *sakana-zuki hayashi*, literally "fish-bonded woods," all over the country, and because of their reciprocity with marine life they were closely guarded by the authorities, who needed the catch from the rivers and seas. For instance, there was a phrase "One tree, one neck," implying that if a tree in the fish-bonded woods were violated, the price would be one's neck in the form of decapitation. In the Murakami fief (now in Niigata Prefecture) there was an edict ordering preservation of all of the trees around the Sammo River (where schools of salmon came). However, the term itself has become practically dead, and fish-bonded woods represent a mere 0.1 percent of the total wooded acreage under state control.

Recently, however, there has arisen a new ecological awareness of the link between woods, river, and sea in the face of growing depletion of various kinds of marine resources. This is a major departure from 1934 when a survey conducted by the then Ministry of Agriculture left very vague the supposed interrelationship between woods and fish in the fish-bonded woods and sea.

Today, it is a well-documented empirical finding that by reforestation on land, the nurturing of seaweed was made possible, which in turn helped fish to return to the coasts that had been left barren. The reforestation project at Erimo National Forest in Hokkaido, after forty years of strenuous effort, has proven this interconnection beyond any shadow of doubt. A writer from Hokkaido, Mr. Tatsuno Aragami, in his *Fish That Came from the Woods* (subtitled *Green Returns to Erimo Point*), provides testimony to this successful experiment in which the resuscitated woods helped fish to come back and kelp to grow abundantly. In fact, on 29 April 1989, to celebrate the miraculous comeback of fish, the townfolk of the fishing town of Erimo convened an arboring ceremony under the general themes of "Rooted Green Nurtures the Sea" and "Woods are Home to Fish." Again in 1992, they held a festival in honor of Forest and Fish, although ironically, that year marked a record poor catch of salmon, which indicates that the planting of trees and cleaning of the sea alone cannot be expected to lead to an enhanced catch; Nature is far more complex than is assumed by simplistic laws of causation.

Mr. Hatakeyama, an oyster farmer, has long held the belief that a river's stable flow is guaranteed by the water contained deep in the woods of broad-leafed trees, fertilizing it with bacteria and plant plankton, feeding the river life. His belief is now regarded as a scientifically viable proposition, and very much encouraged.

Hatakeyama and his seventy fellow oyster fishermen set out to plant trees, and they named the planting area "Oyster Woods." The Oyster Woods Appreciation Society was founded in 1989, and has since expanded the scope of its activities, with all sorts of people, notably youngsters, now planting seedlings along the Okawa River. Their activities are attracting a great deal of public attention throughout Japan, thanks to the ecologically and commercially aroused media as well as the education community.

Mr. Hatakeyama was fortunate in that his project based on his native instincts as a veteran oyster farmer was lent scientific credence by a noted marine chemist, Professor Katsuhiko Matsunaga of Hokkaido University. In explaining the woods-sea reciprocity Professor Matsunaga argues in a number of articles, including his best-selling scientific treatise entitled "When the Woods Vanish, So Does the Sea," that iron is an indispensable material for the growth of seaweed and plant plankton, and that the woods are importantly connected to the propagation of marine life. According to Professor Matsunaga, plants cannot absorb nitrogen without first taking in iron, and when iron combines with the acid produced as leaves of broad-leaved trees decay, the resulting mush can be directly absorbed by plants.

Be that as it may, there is a steadily growing realization that equates the preservation of the woods on land with the preservation of the sea, and efforts at "forestation" as a revival of fishing have become popular in such diverse places as Hokkaido, Miyagi, and Kumamoto prefectures. What is remarkable about these efforts is that fishermen, foresters, and the general public are banding together for various events. It must be added however that plant life in the sea itself, such as various kinds of seaweed, provides spawning and growing grounds for fish, and must therefore be encouraged. Similarly, water systems that connect the woods to the sea—rivers, lakes, and marshes, as well as underground water channels—should not be deterred from their proper functioning. To this end, embankments of rivers with concrete should be limited, and preservation of rice paddy fields should be promoted. In any case, if you compare the sea to the Mother, the mountain is to be likened to the Father. When the mountain is covered with an abundance of trees, important supplies of water and dropped insects are ensured and plant plankton is provided.

In this connection, consider the work of Mr. Shigeatsu Hatakeyama, whose Mizuyama Aquafarm facing Kesennuma Bay in Miyagi Prefecture supplies 10 percent of the *hors d'oeuvre* oysters served in Japanese restaurants. Mr. Hatakeyama coined the phrase "woods, the darling of the sea" which inspired Mrs. Ryuko Kumagai's poem quoted at the beginning of this chapter. The poet was inspired by Mr. Hatakeyama's enthusiasm for his tree planting project that began in 1989. He decided to plant trees on Mount Murone, a village near the source of the Okuma River, which flows into Kesennuma Bay and beautifies the Mount Murone area.

CONCLUSION

The final point touches on religious and philosophical dimensions: in the non-Aristotelian traditions of East Asia, it is possible that something *is and is not* at the same time. Japanese peoples do not feel compelled to make a rigid distinction, for instance, between woods and sea or between fish and fowl (to borrow the familiar English idiom). They feel rather ill at ease when called upon, if not compelled, to resort to binary opposition or mutual exclusivity. Most East Asian peoples feel more at home in a "both-and" situation than in an "either-or" situation. Perceptually, it is not too terribly hard for them to deal with fish and fowl on the same plane.

At the same time, mention should be made of the symbiosis in the perception as exemplified in Lord Shakamuni's statement in the Nirvana Sutra, "Grasses and trees, grounds and soils, all are capable of attaining Buddhahood." This statement was often quoted in the Heian Period (794–857 A.D.), and is held to be one of the salient features of Heian Buddhism. It is also widely quoted throughout the Buddhist communities of East Asia. Symbiosis was the name of the game, and the East Asian proclivity toward ambiguity and holistic approaches may have one of its roots in this philosophical/religious orientation.

Fuzziness may well be a virtue among Japanese, as proponents of Fuzzy Algebra and earlier of General Semantics have put forward in the West. Of course, we should remind ourselves that it could be the very absence of binary opposition in Japanese thinking, such as between singleminded pursuit of economic growth in quantitative terms on the one hand, and preserving the natural environment on the other, that has contributed to the enormous environmental degradation that the gung-ho period of economic growth and industrial expansion of the 1960s and 70s left in its wake.

There is a Chinese and Japanese proverbial phrase that says "to seek a fish by climbing a tree," alluding to the incompatibility of one's method and one's goal. This expression, often used with a sense of disdain, appears to have hit the mark in these days of ecological thinking: fish may be found by planting trees.

REFERENCES

Brown, Brian. 1993. "Toward a Buddhist Ecological Cosmology." *Bucknell Review* 37, 2: pp. 124-137.

Caswell, Tricia. 1995. "Australia and Asia—the environmental challenge," in Gred Sheridan, ed., *Living with Dragons: Austrailia Confronts its Asian Destiny*. St. Leonards, New South Wales: Allen & Unwin Pty Ltd., pp. 66-81.

Chan, Wing-tsit. 1963. *A Source Book in Chinese Philosophy*. Princeton: Princeton University Press.

Chan, Wing-tsit. 1967. "The Story of Chinese Philosophy." In Charles A. Moore, ed., *The Chinese Mind: Essentials of Chinese Philosophy and Culture*. Honolulu: University of Hawaii Press, pp. 31–76.

Fung, Yu-lan. 1966. *A Short History of Chinese Philosophy*. Edited by Derk Bodde. New York: The Free Press.

Giles, Herbert A. 1965. *Gems of Chinese Literature*. New York: Dover Publications.

Griffith, Jim. 1990. "The Environmental Movement in Japan." In *Whole Earth Review* No. 69 (Winter, 1990): 90–96.

Itoh,Teiji. 1982. *The Gardens of Japan*. New York: Kodansha International.

Liu, Wu-chi. 1966. *Introduction to Chinese Literature*. Bloomington: Indiana University Press.

Morris, Edwin T. 1983. *The Gardens of China: History, Art, and Meanings*. New York: Charles Scribner's Sons.

Ofreneo, Rene E. 1993. "Japan and the Environmental Degradation of the Philippines." In Michael C. Howard, ed., *Asia's Environmental Crisis*. Boulder: Westview Press, pp. 201–20

Reischauer, Edwin, and John K. Fairbank. 1960. *East Asia: The Great Tradition*. Boston: Haughton Mifflin Company.

Saunders, E. Dale, 1961. "Japanese Mythology." In Samuel Noah Kramer, ed., *Mythologies of the Ancient World*. Garden City, N.Y.: Anchor Books, pp. 409–42.

Smil, Vaclav. 1993. *China's Environmental Crisis: an inquiry into the limits of national development.* Armonk, N.Y.: M. E. Sharpe.

Smil, Vaclav. 1984. *The Bad Earth: environmental degradation in China.* Armonk, N.Y.: M. E. Sharpe.

Walls, Jan, and Yvonne L. Walls, trans. 1982. *100 Allegorical Tales from Traditional China.* Hong Kong: Joint Publishing Company.

FAZAL RIZVI

8. Immigration, Environment, and Public Policy in Australia

Of all the nations in the Pacific, Australia, New Zealand, the United States, and Canada stand out. Each regards itself as a "new nation" that has been established by mass migration. Each has drawn the great majority of its settlers from Europe over the past two centuries. Each is now predominantly an English-speaking society. Significantly, however, each has been created as a result of the displacement of its indigenous peoples, who have been reduced to small and disadvantaged minorities. This displacement has not only consisted in the reduction, often by brutal means, in the total number of indigenous peoples now living in Australia, New Zealand, the United States, and Canada, but also in the trivialization of the physical and spiritual values that form the basis of their lives. From the point of view of indigenous peoples, each wave of immigration has damaged their environment irreparably. In Australia, the tension between traditional and modern approaches to the environment is manifested strongly in immigration policy.

That immigration has environmental consequences is a fact that has always been recognized by indigenous peoples. However, it is a realization that has not, until recently, been widely discussed within the settler communities in the immigrant nations of the Pacific. For most of this century, immigration has been viewed in these nations as an engine of economic growth. What the new environmental movements have succeeding in doing in recent years, however, is to show how unchecked economic

135

growth and immigration have environmental costs. They have demonstrated that population growth is not only a problem for the Third World countries but also for the First World nations such as Australia and the United States. Large-scale immigration, they have suggested, puts considerable pressure on the nonrenewable resources of nations. Unplanned population growth, they have argued, creates a heavy burden on the native flora and fauna and on the wilderness areas.

These are of course legitimate concerns that should clearly be the subject of public debate. However, in this chapter I want to suggest that such debates always run the risk of sliding into a populist anti-immigrant rhetoric. This has clearly been the case in the anti-Mexican sentiments in California,[1] in the discourse of "monster houses" in British Columbia[2] and in calls for a halt to immigration from Asia in Australia[3] and New Zealand.[4] Great caution is therefore needed in exploring the complex relationship between immigration and the environment. In what follows, I explore the nature of this relationship not only as it is articulated by the environmental movements but also as it can be used to promote a racialized politics around legitimate environmental concerns.

I argue that in order to prevent environmental issues from becoming an instrument of anti-immigrant propaganda, we need to consider the relationship between environment and immigration *historically,* and develop a more *democratic understanding* of the environment utilizing the knowledges of not only the various settler communities but also the indigenous peoples. If new and creative solutions to our environmental problems are needed then we should regard the plurality of knowledges available in multicultural societies as a valuable asset rather than a hindrance. My discussion here is based largely on Australia, though I believe that much of it has relevance too for other immigrant nations in the Pacific.

I

When Europeans first came to Australia, they saw a largely uninhabited land whose abundant natural resources were ready to be exploited and developed. They dismissed the Aboriginal approaches to the management of the environment as primitive. The indigenous people were thought to lack the scientific knowledge and the intellectual capacity to fully utilize the environment. They were believed unable to practice agriculture in any systematic fashion—in the way the Europeans had done. Through the course of the nineteenth century, these beliefs became an ideology of development that continues to define the manner in which many Australians approach their relationship to the environment. In more recent years, however, the meaning ascribed to the idea of development has become highly contested. Most contemporary environmental debates are now centered around such issues as what kind of development there should be; who should control the processes of development; toward what purposes should development be directed; and what should be the relationship between the needs of the present inhabitants and those of future generations.

Historically, the indigenous and settler Australians have had radically different views on these matters. For more than 40,000 years, Aborigines had moved seasonally through their land to manage it and obtain only those foods and materials upon which their livelihood had depended. Their views of the environment were derived from the experience of their ancestors in obtaining a livelihood and in adapting their knowledge systems to that experience. On the other hand, as Coombs has pointed out, "Europeans had, since the industrial revolution, become units in a complex system, based on a different division of labour, producing commodities for sale through a widely-spread market."[5] Thus, Europeans did not only produce what they needed to consume but also what they could sell. This has been the basis of the European ideology of development. Development has required the ready availability of finance capital and natural resources, the use of complex technology, large-scale operations and extensive systems of marketing and transport—as well as human resources necessary for producing commodities and for creating new consumer markets.

This view of development stands in a sharp contrast with the Aboriginal experience, which carries the authority of religion and ancestral law. Indigenous peoples of Australia speak of their environment as essentially immutable. For centuries, Aborigines had known how to manage cyclical fluctuations of droughts and rainfall and the composition of the wildlife and vegetation, particularly through the use of fire. But the European ideology of development has imposed upon them an unprecedented amount of change, both materially and culturally. According to Coombs, "destructive and sudden changes, especially those which contravene the ethics of environmental management prescribed by ancestors are deeply resented"[6] by Aborigines (see also chapter 6). Environmental damage is seen as "wounding" and is responded to emotionally. It is viewed as a breach of property rights, especially when its purpose is unknown and permission has not been sought. It is considered a great dereliction of duty if there is a failure to prevent damage; and retribution by spiritual forces is feared.

This sense of anxiety needs to be understood in terms of the religious and emotional relationship Australian Aborigines have to the environment and its creatures. Environmental damage has always been acknowledged by Aborigines, and compensation paid to the spirits. The reasons Aborigines give for acting upon their environment in particular ways are thus linked to their cosmology, which informs their sense of duty. What hurts many Aboriginal people about the European developers is their failure to take responsibility for their actions—and to consult the traditional owners. While many traditional owners deeply resent the degradation of rivers, mountains, and forests, which are held to be sacred, they recognize that traditions are not static. Far from being hostile to change most Aborigines are pragmatic and flexible—many attach positive value to change. They realize that many of their traditions have now become refracted through European social and religious knowledge systems which have been imported to Australia. Non-Aboriginal technology has been accommodated within the traditional modes of living.[7] But Aboriginal people do care deeply about wanting to be consulted and having some power over their own destiny—and not having change simply imposed upon them, and becoming displaced, within their own land, by the successive waves of immigration.

In Australia, as in Canada, New Zealand, and the United States, immigration has been an essential ingredient of the European ideology of development. Immigration has provided labor and the technical, organizational, and managerial skills necessary for the exploitation of natural resources such as land and mineral deposits; and for sustaining national infrastructures. It has thus been essential for the accumulation of capital. Americans readily acknowledge that their history is based on immigration, and that it is immigration that is responsible for their great economic wealth. In contrast, as Higham points out, Australia has no comparable myth of immigration as a great nation-making experience.[8] Instead, Australia has been able to create a sense of itself as having been formed and developed by a largely British people. Within this fiction, people of

British background do not regard themselves as "immigrants," a label that seems reserved for other ethnic groups. Historically, this has made the colonization of indigenous peoples in Australia appear natural; and the issues concerning their prior ownership of land have been easily evaded. It is the colonizers who have made the rules about who can or cannot immigrate to Australia. Aborigines have never been in a position to have a say in these matters, though they have been keenly aware of what immigration, articulated to an ideology of development, represents: the destruction of the only cultures that have proved able to thrive in these environments.

This lack of consultation has resulted in Aborigines becoming quite distrustful of each generation of immigrants.[9] They are also, understandably, quite suspicious of the principle of equality to which immigrant groups aspire. Since this principle treats all social groups as equal, they believe that it undermines their distinctive claims to a range of historically specific rights, and in particular land rights, which are central to their political struggle. For most indigenous Australians, the relevant conceptual and political distinction is between the indigenous and the non-indigenous, and not among the different groups that have migrated to Australia over the past two hundred years. To them, the dominant Anglo-Australian group occupies the same historical status as do all other ethnic groups. But this approach fails to recognize the reality of ethnic politics in Australia which is fundamental to an understanding of social and political inequality in Australia.

II

The development of migration policies by any government requires a series of compromises. Migration policies are based on judgments concerning the financial and political costs of migration and the benefits particular types of migrants might bring. Through their policies, governments regulate the movement of people across societies with varying degrees of rigidity, often making harsh assessments about the appropriateness of particular kinds of people for particular needs. Governments often set quotas on the number of people allowed to immigrate either to fill particular jobs or to reunite with families. These quotas respond to a whole variety of factors and competing interests. And while some of these factors are macroeconomic and structural, others have their origin in the political and cultural myths and demands of a society, and sometimes even in the mass influence that certain individuals or groups are able to exercise over policy processes. As Offe has pointed out, a public policy is a combination of "social demands" and "state requirements": the often conflicting interests and needs of various groups in a community and the imperatives of capital. According to Offe, a policy is determined by the need to "react consistently to the two poles of the 'needs' of labour and capital" while maintaining "the compatibility and practicability of the existing institutions of social policy."

So it has been with Australia's immigration policies for most of this century. These policies have responded to popular xenophobic myths about those constituted as the Others on the one hand and the requirements of the capital on the other. In the early part of this century, so strong were the popular xenophobic sentiments that one of the first acts passed in Australia's federal parliament in 1901 was the Immigration Restriction Act.[10] This Act was designed to keep Asians out of Australia and to repatriate Pacific island laborers, who had been brought to Australia a generation earlier. The parliamentary debates on these Acts were extensive, and revealed much about the manner in which Asians were seen as a major threat to Australian social life.

The movement to keep Asians out was fueled also by a scientific racism prevalent at that time, as well as the growing tide of nationalist sentiment which aspired to a homogenous Australian culture. Constant references were made in the parliamentary debates to the way Asians were supposedly either incapable of surviving in the harsh Australian climate or else were not able to look after its fragile environment. Misinformed ideas about how the Chinese had only served to damage the gold field communities of Victoria and New South Wales were invoked. In defending the Immigration Restriction Act, Australia's first Attorney General suggested that the fragile beauty of Australia required that immigration to Australia be restricted only to those people who desired that "we should be one people, and remain one people, without the admixture of other races." [11]

Between the two world wars, these popular sentiments became institutionalized in Australian law. As Miles points out, "The demand to keep out 'coloured inferior races' was dialectically linked with an emerging sense of an imagined community of Australians, a collectivity that signified 'whiteness' as a sign of superiority and of inclusion."[12] The primary theme of Australia's immigration policy was that racial unity was essential for national unity; and that social cohesion required that all Australians adhere to a common and uniform set of values. It was argued that it was natural for people of supposedly different "races" to live apart. The goal of a common identity grounded in a particular combination of cultural and biological homogeneity implied certain practices of racialized exclusion, which were justified by the same normative cultural logic which had also marginalized Aborigines within their own country. As a nation, Australia was hostile to all forms of difference.

III

Since World War II, however, the cultural landscape of Australia has changed dramatically. So much so that while in 1947 only nine percent of the Australian population was not from the British Isles, this figure has now risen to more than twenty-five percent. The changes that have occurred in Australia as a result of immigration have appropriately been referred to as constituting a "demographic revolution."[13] A whole range of considerations led Australia to encourage and accept a higher number of immigrants following the World War II. The war had shown Australia— a very small nation by the standards of its neighbors—to be particularly vulnerable to external aggression, especially by Asian countries whose cultures Anglo-Australians had viewed with considerable suspicion. A response to this perceived threat was encapsulated in the phrase "populate or perish."[14] Australia also needed more people in order to stimulate its postwar reconstruction. A larger population thus seemed necessary for both security and economic growth. It was recognized moreover that the nation's population could not increase naturally and a massive immigration program appeared the only other alternative.

After the war, Australian industries, assisted by international capital, expanded rapidly. This in turn created a further need for an extended labor force, especially at the lower end of the occupational structure. Using the rhetoric of development, major private employers, therefore, pressed the state relentlessly for immigrant labor, and successive Australian governments responded with programs of active recruitment.[15] Viewed in this way, the state actively assisted the development of monopoly capital in Australia. But the demand for a more extensive migration program did not only come from private employers. The state instrumentalities, such as electricity and transport authorities, also sought workers to build up the infrastructure required to support private enterprise. The enormous Snowy Mountains Hydroelectric project in New South Wales and the Yallourn Power stations in Victoria could not have been completed without immigrant labor.[16]

For much of the postwar period, the Australian economy has depended on agriculture and mining. Large tracts of land have been cleared for pasturing of cattle and sheep, leading to widespread land degradation. Land degradation is now recognized as Australia's most serious environmental problem. The introduction to Australia of animals such as cattle, horses, sheep, and donkeys has led to the problem of soil erosion as Australian land has a very thin layer of soil which cannot easily support animals with hard-hoofed feet. The land management practices around questions of tenure, property size, and allocation of responsibility for rehabilitation of degraded land have largely been *ad hoc*, growing primarily out of the desire to achieve maximum profit. Old-wood forests have been cleared to sustain a woodchip industry that has at best a very ambivalent attitude toward the environment. Land formations have also been changed with major irrigation projects, often constructed with migrant labor, to produce crops that are mostly shipped abroad. The introduction of predators has led to the destruction of the local wildlife. Intense aerial spraying of chemicals and the slow leaching of pesticides and herbicides from the soil into the streams have resulted in the degradation of rivers and lakes. Large-scale mining has been justified in Australia on the grounds that the exploitation of minerals is necessary for the accumulation of capital; and that it involves simply the conversion of "idle" natural resources into more flexible and productive ones. This development thinking has often been disdainful of environmental arguments for greater government regulation of the mining and agricultural industries.

As in most other Western countries, there is now widespread public recognition of these environmental problems in Australia. However, this recognition has come at precisely the time when Australia is witnessing a major downturn in its previously buoyant economy. The deregulation of trade, investment, and other financial activities has meant that Australia is now integrated into the global economy. And as a result, it has become increasingly vulnerable to the fluctuations in world commodity prices.[17]

The world recessions of 1974–75 and 1981–82 and the stock market crash of 1987 have had severe consequences for the small Australian economy, triggering domestic recession and increased unemployment. Despite various policy initiatives, the unemployment rate in Australia has remained between eight to ten percent for most of the past two decades.

Australia's open market economic policies have also induced a new open approach to Asia. Global and regional pressures have forced Australia to change its explicit hostility towards Asians, as it has increasingly recognized that its economic future lies in its own geographical region, and that it can no longer rely upon its traditional allies—Britain and the United States. The White Australia policy was thus finally abandoned in the late 1960s, and the past two decades have witnessed an increasing number of Asians immigrating to Australia. The proportion of Asians of the Australian population has now reached nearly five percent.[18] Nearly nine per cent of Sydney's population is now of various Asian backgrounds.

This demographic shift has led also to a change in Australia's ethnic affairs policy—away from assimilation to multiculturalism. Unlike the United States, where multiculturalism is a term that denotes an oppositional social movement, in Australia, it is a policy developed by the state to "manage" ethnic diversity. Australian multiculturalism emerged in the 1970s as a compromise formation designed to pacify increasingly volatile ethnic communities on the one hand and allay the fears of the dominant Anglo community alarmed by a changing Australian demography on the other. It turned out partly to be a strategy for managing inter-group relations and for accommodating the interests of the ethnic middle class.[19] At the same time, however, multiculturalism provided symbolic resources around which it became possible for ethnic communities to organize themselves politically and secure a range of concessions from the state.

Even more significant have been the changes in Australia's attitude toward its indigenous peoples. There is now a general acceptance within the Australian community that their nation came into existence as a result of the conquest and dispossession of indigenous peoples, and that Australia has a moral responsibility to right the historical wrongs. In 1992, the High Court of Australia finally overturned the view that Australia was *terra nullius* before white settlement.[20] The Federal Parliament subsequently passed a Native Titles Legislation which enshrines the principle of Aboriginal land rights into Australian common law. The Government has also institutionalized the idea of reconciliation with indigenous peoples as one of its highest policy priorities.

However, despite the rhetorics of multiculturalism and reconciliation, many Australians continue to view these policy principles with a great deal of suspicion. Leaving aside those who hold extreme Anglo supremacist views, the response of many Anglo-Australians to these principles is deeply contradictory. Nowhere is this more evident than in their views about Australia's relationship with Asia. While much has been said and written about the importance of Australia negotiating a new role for itself in the Asia-Pacific region, most Australians remain suspicious of this rhetoric, unable to determine the ways in which they must change to accommodate "the new realities" of which the governments speak. They have been told that Australia's economic future is now inextricably tied to Asia and that they should see themselves as part of Asia. Yet they remain unclear of the extent to which this involves a rejection of the dominant European values and traditions. Australians have been asked to make a decisive ideological shift in their thinking, away from the colonialist frame that has traditionally informed their perceptions of Asia to a post-colonial outlook which challenges the racist assumptions of cultural dominance and superiority. Yet most of their attempts to revise their thinking have been at best clumsy, with the new practices of representation failing to make a decisive break from the residual racist expressions that had rendered Asians as a homogenized mass, socially inept and culturally inferior.

IV

It is in terms of this historical context that the complex relationship between the environment and immigration may be understood. For there is a sizable body of opinion in Australia that suggests that it is "the inappropriate and excessive levels" of immigration that are largely responsible for the environmental problems that Australia is currently experiencing. In Australia, the term "inappropriate and excessive levels of immigration" has become a coded phrase to refer to Asian immigration in particular. In recent years, anti-Asian activities have increased, as Asian immigrants are blamed for a whole range of social and economic problems. In a sense, the coded anti-Asian discourses are continuous with the earlier discourses of the White Australia policy—no longer as explicit but nonetheless based on an ambivalence that simultaneously fantasizes and fears Asia.[21]

This much was clearly evident in a recent public debate over the environmental problems confronting the city of Sydney. During this debate many Asians were left with a distinct feeling that "they are not wanted here," and that they have only reluctantly been permitted to reside in Australia—that diversity is something to be tolerated but not encouraged. The debate[22] originated with a statement issued in May 1995 by the Premier of New South Wales, Bob Carr. He described Sydney as a city "bursting at the seams," and ordered a major inquiry into its development. The terms of reference for the inquiry were broadly based and included Sydney's transport, environmental protection, housing, and other urban infrastructure concerns. Carr pointed out that Sydney will, for example, need an extra 520,000 homes within the next twenty-five years to accommodate the forecast rise in the city's population, which is projected to grow from 3.7 million to more than 4.5 million by 2020. He believed that Sydney needed "a more holistic and strategic approach to its problems of environmental degradation, neighbourhood amenities, and transport and employment."[23]

Bob Carr acknowledged that issues of immigration were clearly relevant to the scope of this inquiry into the development of Sydney. He insisted however that: "I do not think that we can solve the problems of Sydney simply by dealing with the problem of immigration. This is one factor but only one factor. I want to consider all those factors that governments can influence, and which affect things like air quality, water quality, neighbourhood, amenities, etc."[24] Despite Carr's clear warning that the debate about Sydney's development was much more than simply a debate about immigration, predictably, the popular media chose to focus most of its attention on immigration. Ethnic affairs were put in the spotlight in highly racialized terms, with more than a hint of a suggestion that it was the recent immigrants, particularly those from Asia, who were largely responsible for Sydney's environmental problems.[25] The juxtaposition of environmental problems and what were considered to be inappropriate immigration policies seemed deliberate, and served to highlight the difficulties one encounters in Australia in discussing urban environmental problems in a (de)racialized manner.

The debate shows that a high level of anxiety exists in the Australian community about its changing demography. This anxiety is evident in the way Bob Carr's policy intervention concerning the development of Sydney has been used as an opportunity by many Australians to express an anti-immigration sentiment that remains barely hidden in popular media. In this debate, the letters to the editors of major newspapers suggest that most writers believe that immigration, and in particular Asian immigration, is largely responsible for the problems of air, water, and soil pollution, as well as for other social problems that have lowered the quality of life in Sydney. It is suggested that the influx of immigrants has put severe pressure on the city's infrastructure, and that their different lifestyles "have made the city unrecognizable."

V

Those intent on blaming immigration simply dismiss as irrelevant the point made by the Bureau of Immigration, Multicultural and Population Research that Sydney's rate of population growth had actually fallen below the national average, and that Queensland has in fact become the preferred state for migrant settlement. According to the *Australian* newspaper (24 May 1995), "the fact that Sydney's problems are continuing to mount shows they are more complex than can be explained simply in terms of immigration numbers." However, such is the highly ideological nature of the debate surrounding immigration that evidence appears to be one of its first casualties.

Over the past decade, governments throughout Australia have instituted a number of reports on the impact of immigration on environment. The overwhelming interest governments appear to have in this issue is linked directly to the repeated calls by environmental lobby groups such as the Australian Conservation Foundation (ACF) for the nation to develop a coherent population policy. ACF and a number of smaller conservation groups have argued that at eighteen million Australia may have already reached the level of population it can sustain.[26] However, this argument is often presented as a technical fact; which it clearly is not. It is based on a set of normative assumptions about people's lifestyles and the pattern of their use of natural resources. It masks a range of ethnocentric beliefs that are seldom made explicit. It also appears to presuppose that it is immigration that has contributed soil degradation, land and water degradation, and air and sound pollution. But as Jock Collins[27] has suggested, the basic proposition here is at best simplistic. The view that little or no immigration will create a more congenial environment simply cannot be sustained.

Most of the critics of Australia's immigration program on environmental grounds insist that race is not an issue—that their concern is simply with economic and environmental issues. However, when these issues are so clearly juxtaposed, it is hard to take such a disclaimer seriously. According to Collins (1991, 34), the environmental case for turning off the immigration program is weak at best and shabby at worst. This is so because most of the environmental degradation had already occurred in the way new subdivisions for housing had been developed—well before the arrival of Asian immigrants in the early 1970s.[28] Many of the large industrial plants and refineries situated close to the center of Sydney and Melbourne were in fact established in the 1960s—well before people became environmentally conscious. It is the unattractive combination of residential and industrial areas that have contributed to the environmental problems that Sydney is currently experiencing. So to use immigrants as a scapegoat for the lack of proper urban planning is not only incorrect but also disingenuous.

That this whole debate has become racialized can also be shown by looking at the public statements of those prominent Australians who are known for their opposition to Asian immigration to Australia. In Australia, one of the leading opponents of Asian immigration is the historian Geoffery Blainey. While addressing a convention of the Australia Water and Wasteland Association in Perth in 1990, Blainey argued that maps of Australia were too attractive to its neighbors, who looked enviously at its space and resources and demanded to share it. The present maps seemed to indicate that Australia was a country with a lot of fertile land that could be used for settlement by eager foreigners, he said. Blainey suggested that our maps should be redrawn so that they did not appear so attractive.[29] This piece of chauvinism clearly demonstrates the persistence of the ethnocentric views which most Australians held both before and immediately after the World War II about the Asian "design" on Australia, encapsulated in the phrase, "the danger from the yellow peril."

Blainey seems to have jumped on the environmental bandwagon as it supports his wider political agenda. His argument also shows the simple conceptual slide that is often made from an expression of concern for the environment to views that are intolerant of cultural differences and seek to reinstate a regime of Anglo-hegemony. Indeed, the extraordinary success of a lobby group called Australians Against Further Immigration (AAFI), established in 1990, indicates the extent to which popular opinion in Australia has conflated the issues of environment and immigration.[30] The Group's electoral success hit a high point in 1989 when it secured 17 percent of the vote in an Adelaide by-election. AAFI, a coalition of a number of smaller right wing bodies, has used almost any research analysis it can find to suggest that high immigration intake is the root cause of environmental problems. However, what is more significant about the group's claims is its populist interpretation of the term "environmental" to refer not only to the physical environment but also the nation's cultural and moral environment which it claims is being spoiled by entry into Australia of people from "foreign" cultures.[31] For AAFI, then, a commitment to environmentalism simply represents a convenient pretext against which to pursue a racist agenda.

This agenda feeds on discontent, anger, insecurity, and resentment and flourishes on backlash politics. The discourse of the "threat posed by immigration to our way of life" further marginalizes the most recent immigrants to Australia, many of whom are refugees from Southeast Asia. Such a discourse operates on a set of taken-for-granted generalizations about particular minorities and in the discursive constructions of the Other. It is in the media that these constructions are most evident. As the Moss Report notes, the reporting of Asian-Australian activities, and the use of unnecessary ethnic identifiers in media is a continuing problem for Australian Human Rights and Equal Opportunity Commission.[32] The manner in which Asian-Australians are depicted in the media simply confirms their status as "outsiders"—those who are "not-Australian."

Somewhat romantically, the views AAFI promotes hark back to the days when Australia was allegedly a socially cohesive nation, free of the kind of economic, social, and political problems it currently confronts. The reference to the dangers to "our" lifestyle, which is under threat through environmental damage allegedly caused by high levels of immigration, suggests a belief that the recognition of the problems implies changes to immigration policy rather than changes in lifestyles that the available resources can support. On the contrary, in my view, public policies that need to be revised include current land use policy, from soil depletion to forest destruction, and policies concerning the use of limited resources. As a report of the Australian Bureau of Immigration Research[33] points out, just to abide by current pollution prevention commitments,

Australians would have to halve their current per capita use of petrol and coal. The Report notes that environmentally there is much that Australia can and should do to improve present conditions and inhibit further deterioration in the future.

VI

Australia certainly faces severe environmental problems, as it has experienced considerable land damage and resource depletion in its pursuit of development. Water has always been a precious commodity in Australia, and many scientists believe that the greenhouse effect will lead to even drier conditions within the next fifty years.[34] There is also widespread evidence of continuing land degradation, soil erosion, salinity, and excessive use of chemicals leading to a reduction in land that might be considered arable. These are significant environmental problems, but to isolate immigration, and in particular Asian immigration, and expect that such problems can be solved by curtailment of immigration programs is to overlook the complexity of the issues. Such calls fail to recognize that environmental degradation and resource depletion have more to do with the inappropriate use and poor management of the land, the structure of the Australian economy, and poor urban planning than with the actual number of people living in Australia. They also ignore the historical fact that much of the environmental damage in Australia can largely be attributed to the unplanned and uncontrolled expansion of mining and agricultural industries immediately after World War II.

The environmental problems confronting Australian cities are due moreover to the urban sprawl that feeds one of Australia's most cherished myths of "every family needing a quarter of an acre block to live."[35] This coupled with poor planning processes and the lack of adequate consultation has led Australian cities to approach a critical point about which environmental groups are quite understandably concerned. One of the main sources of environmental problems in Australia is its tradition of highly centralized planning procedures, which result in a very few "technical experts" being given enormous powers. These experts work within a very narrow technical framework, and make judgments that often bear little resemblance to the complexities of social and cultural life.

The issue of consultation is crucial to proper environmental planning, especially in a multicultural society where there needs to coexist a whole variety of often conflicting cultural values. Since such planning does refer not only to the protection of natural resources but also to the manner in which people relate to and utilize the environment, it is essential that they be widely consulted. In a multicultural society, different groups are likely to have different ways of interpreting the environment. If this is so, then some way of negotiating "difference" needs to be established. Moreover, if there is a close relationship between their ecological knowledge and their cultural values then differing environmental values cannot be negotiated outside their moral and cultural frames. In my view, negotiation of such values requires a *democratic* understanding of the environment; that is, an ethical engagement that defines the way decision making takes place in light of both the technical "scientific" knowledge as well as the cultural knowledge that various groups possess.

Such a democratic understanding is particularly important in a political climate in which considerable anxiety exists in some sections of the Australian community. The sources of this anxiety are not only the recent demographic changes but also economic decline, social fragmentation, and environmental degradation. In the past, the understanding that Australians had of their environment had been framed by narrowly defined economic criteria. However, as old certainties concerning development at any price fast disappear, it becomes patently obvious that sustainable development requires a more complex view of the environment, a more holistic view that seeks to bring together our cultural and moral concerns with our need to be economically productive.

In a multicultural society like Australia there are already present a whole range of traditions of thinking about the environment that are consistent with this aspiration. The knowledges about environmental care and protection that already exist within Australia's multicultural communities should clearly be utilized. And indeed, Australia need not go much further than to consult its own indigenous peoples about how to manage its delicate environment. As Baines and Williams have pointed out, the value of traditional ecological knowledge has been grossly undervalued not only by economists but also by Western "scientific" managers.[36] Traditional ecological knowledge is not necessarily "behind" what we call "modern," but simply a different way of representing alternative forms of ecological knowledge. Indigenous peoples' classification of natural phenomena and their perceptions of environmental causes and effects can contribute directly to either challenge or support the Western scientific perceptions. Traditional ecological knowledge can thus provide a basis for comparison, and also teach Western environmental scientists how their knowledge is not as value neutral as it is sometimes supposed. This clearly requires a commitment to dialogue grounded in both moral and practical reasoning about the coexistence of indigenous and settler cultures in an environment that is more fragile than many of us imagine.

NOTES

1. F. D. Bean and M. Fox, "The Significance of Recent Immigration Policy Reforms in the United States," in G. Freeman and J. Jupp, eds, *Nations of Immigrants* (Melbourne: Oxford University Press, 1992), pp. 41–55.

2. J. Gillard and M. Whyte, "The House that Ate the Neighbourhood," *Metropolis* 12 (July–August) pp. 16-17.

3. J. Collins, *Migrant Hands in a Distant Land* (Sydney: Pluto Press, 1988).

4. New Zealand Planning Council, *On the Move: Migration and Population—Trends and Policies* (Wellington: New Zealand Planning Council, 1991).

5. H. C. Coombs, H. McCann, H. Ross, and N. Williams, *Land of Promises* (Canberra: Centre for Resource and Environmental Studies, Australian National University, 1989), p. 2.

6. *Ibid.*, p. 8.

7. For example, Aborigines have accepted the presence of the use of firearms for hunting and motor vehicles for traveling to social and religious sites.

8. J. Higham, "The Movement of People 1788-1789," in G. Withers, *Commonality and Difference* (Sydney: Allen and Unwin, 1991), p. 1.

9. A. Barlow, "The relationship between Aboriginal Education and Multicultural Education," in D. J. Phillips and J. Houston, eds., *Australian Multicultural Society: Identity, Communication and Decision-Making* (Melbourne: Drummond, 1984).

10. J. Jupp, *Immigration* (Sydney: Sydney University Press, 1991), p. 46.

11. Cited in M. Willard, *History of the White Australia Policy to 1920* (Melbourne: Melbourne University Press, 1967) p. 119.

12. R. Miles, *Racism* (London: Routledge, 1989) p. 93.

13. R. Appleyard, *Immigration: Policy and Progress* (Canberra: Australian Institute of Political Science Monograph, No. 7, 1972).

14. *Ibid.*, p. 12.

15. J. Martin, *The Migrant Presence* (Sydney: George Allen & Unwin, 1978).

16. Jupp, *Immigration*, chapter 6.

17. S. Castles, "The New Migration and Australian Immigration Policy," in C. Inglis, S. Gunasekaran, G. Sullivan, and Chung-Tong Wu, eds., *Asian in Australia: The Dynamics of Migration and Settlement* (Singapore: Institute of Southeast Asian Studies, 1992), chapter 3.

18. I. Moss, *State of the nation: A report on the people of non-English speaking background* (Canberra: Australian Government Publishing Service, 1993).

19. F. Rizvi, *Multiculturalism as an Educational Policy* (Geelong: Deakin University Press, 1985).

20. T. Rowse, *After Mabo: Interpreting Indigenous Traditions* (Melbourne: Melbourne University Press, 1993)

21. A. Broinowski, *The Yellow Lady: Australian Impressions of Asia* (Melbourne: Oxford University Press, 1992).

22. The statement was made on 22 May 1995 and reported widely in the national newspapers.

23. Reported in *Sydney Morning Herald*, 23 May 1995, p. 1.

24. *Ibid.*

25. Letters to the editors of major Australian newspapers carried comment for more than a month after Carr's statement.

26. T. Flannery, "Australia: Overpopulated or Last Frontier?" paper presented at the Second National Outlook Conference, Bureau of Immigration Research, November 1992.

27. J. Collins, "Immigration and the Environment," in *Nuovo Paese*, (July 1990), pp. 6–7.

28. J. Collins, "Turning off the Tap," *Australian Left Review* 134 (1991): p. 34.

29. Speech reported under the title, "Blainey Redraws Our Map," in the Department of Immigration, Local Government and Ethnic Affairs Staff News Bulletin, Number 533, 22 March 1991, p. 1.

30. Australian Against Further Immigration, *Look Beyond Your Own Issue*, (Melbourne: Australian Against Further Immigration, 1990).

31. *Ibid.*, p. 3.

32. I. Moss, *State of the nation: A report on the people of non-English speaking background* (1993), p. 163.

33. Bureau of Immigration Research, *BIR Bulletin*, Number 5 (December 1995).

34. H. R. Clarke, "Immigration, Population Growth and the Environment: Australian Studies," in H. Clarke, A. Chisholm, G. Edwards, and J. Kennedy, eds., *Immigration, Population Growth and the Environment* (Canberra: Australian Government Printing Service, 1990).

35. M. Kalantzis, "Human Movement: A Democratic Right," in *Australian Author*, Volume 22, Number 3 (Spring 1990), p. 19.

36. G. Baines and N. Williams, "Partnerships in Tradition and Science," in N. Williams and G. Baines, eds., *Traditional Ecological Knowledge: Wisdom for Sustainable Development* (Canberra: Centre for Resource and Environmental Studies, Australian National University, 1993), p. 1.

PART III

RECONCILING TRADITIONAL AND
MODERN APPROACHES

STEPHEN OWEN and DAVID GREER

9. Forest Management in British Columbia: The Transition to Sustainability

Worldwide concern about the impact of human activity on the natural environment has led in recent years to growing recognition of the need to emphasize sustainability—the capacity to be maintained indefinitely—in the management of natural resources. Moreover, governments committed to achieving sustainability are coming to appreciate the importance of balancing a range of interests—economic, environmental, and social—that may appear to conflict but in fact are interdependent. In many ways the search for sustainability requires the reduction of tension between traditional and modern approaches to the environment.

For almost a century, the economy of Canada's westernmost province, British Columbia, has been largely dependent on the forest industry, operating primarily on the public lands that occupy more than 90 percent of the province. In the late 1980s and early 1990s, two factors impressed upon the provincial government, the forest industry, and interest groups advocating a variety of values the need to act in a concerted and decisive manner to develop a comprehensive strategy for the management of the province's land and resources. First, a declining ratio of jobs per unit of timber cut since the mid-1960s, resulting from sophisticated timber-harvesting technology and reflected in significant unemployment in resource-based communities, focused attention on the continuing depletion of available timber supplies. Second, concern about the impacts of clearcutting among a wide range of groups—including environmental associa-

tions, outdoor recreation clubs, the tourism and fishing industries, associations of water users, and aboriginal First Nations—was reflected in bitter conflicts in several areas where timber operations were underway or
planned.

The friction surrounding these issues revealed a changing public
awareness of the importance of forests to a diversity of interests, a recognition that the myth of natural abundance that had been central to British
Columbia's identity for more than a century was no longer credible, and
an inability of governmental and economic institutions to adapt to circumstances far removed from those that prevailed during the province's
early decades. The conflict and unemployment of the 1980s and 1990s
served as a catalyst for vigorous government action to develop and implement a strategy for achieving sustainability. The current transition to the
sustainable management of British Columbia's forests is a small yet
important example of a fundamental and enlightening change in attitudes,
resulting in a gradual shift from an exploitive ethic to one that emphasizes
a balancing of economic, environmental, and social values.

DIMINISHING SPLENDOR:
FOREST MANAGEMENT, 1871–1992

Early European settlers regarded British Columbia's forests as little more
than an obstacle to agriculture and an ever-present reminder of the
remoteness of British Columbia from civilization. By contrast, aboriginal
peoples valued the forest as a vital provider of material, cultural, and spiritual needs. Coastal societies, for example, transformed cedar wood and
bark into a remarkable variety of goods including house planks, posts and
beams, roofing, canoes, bentwood boxes, implements, carved monuments,
ceremonial ornaments, rope, baskets, mats, skirts, towels, and diapers.[1]
Several thousand years' dependence for day-to-day living needs on the
natural wealth that surrounded their communities was reflected in aboriginal value systems characterized by respect for all living things that sustained existence.

With the imposition of a European form of government in the nineteenth century, traditional aboriginal lands were claimed in the name of
the Queen, generally without treaty, and aboriginal peoples were confined
to small "reservations" that bore little resemblance to the territories that

had traditionally sustained their way of life. The forests that covered Crown land—which then, as now, included well over 90 percent of the land base of the province— became hugely valuable as British Columbia entered the twentieth century. Substantial markets for its timber were created by railway construction, settlement of the Canadian prairies, and housing construction in Pacific countries including Chile, Australia, and China. Between 1890 and 1910, timber production in the province increased fourfold, to six billion board feet. With a seemingly endless supply of fine timber and markets opening up around the world for British Columbia's "green gold," the forest industry quickly boomed and became the central economic activity.

Forest depletion

The British Columbia motto, *Splendor Sine Occasu* ("splendor without diminishment"), adopted in 1906, reflected pride in the seemingly limitless natural abundance and scenic majesty of the young province. Nevertheless, there was already concern about the rapidity with which the most accessible forests were being cut. The 1910 Royal Commission on Forestry noted that "British Columbia occupies a position of great advantage among the forest companies of the world, for she can undertake the care of her timber resources before—instead of after—fire and waste have squandered the bulk of them."[2]

During subsequent decades, the question of how best to sustain the province's forest capital was addressed by a series of royal commissions, with inconclusive results. In the absence of comprehensive timber inventories, and with limited understanding of the conditions needed to restore a west-coast forest once it had been cut, it was difficult to prescribe and enforce meaningful standards for sustainable forest management. In 1945, the head of one such commission, Chief Justice Gordon Sloan, noted the growing urgency of the problem:

> Our basic, fundamental and vital forest problem, in this province, is to see to it that our forests are perpetuated for the use, profit and pleasure of future generations. If we fail in this objective, then the economic future of British Columbia will, indeed, present a very dark and dismal picture. Fortunately, it is not too late to plan now for the future, but the sands are running

out and the time is now upon us when the present policy of unmanaged liquidation of our forest wealth must give way to the imperative concept of a planned forest policy designed to maintain our forests upon the principle of sustained-yield production.[3]

Following Sloan's recommendations, a new form of tenure, the tree farm license, was introduced to encourage careful management and replanting of forests by providing companies with long-term renewable tenures on vast areas of forest land. However, the effectiveness of the policy was hampered by postwar trends that saw corporate modernization accelerate the momentum of timber harvesting. Technological advances and the transformation of the industry into a few massive, vertically integrated companies made possible not only the use of timber that had previously been considered unmerchantable, but also the harvesting and processing of higher volumes. In the two decades between 1956 and 1976, the annual cut in B.C. increased by 400 percent.

Conflicting values

Prior to the late 1960s, in the general enthusiasm for economic development, there was limited public awareness of or concern for the impact of several decades of intensive logging on the province's forests. However, the affluence created by the boom in British Columbia's resource-based economy created several conditions that contributed to a broadening of public interest in forest management. Highway construction opened up large areas of the province that had previously been inaccessible to the general public. The rapidly growing tourism industry owed its success in large part to the province's spectacular mountain landscapes and ocean shorelines, and interest in outdoor recreation pursuits mushroomed with increased public mobility. Fish and wildlife protection had become a significant public concern, as had the quality of water needed for domestic and agricultural uses. But above all, interest in environmental protection in B.C. reflected growing concerns worldwide about the environmental impacts, many of them still little understood, of urban and industrial development.

Acknowledgment of the increased importance of planning for a variety of non-timber values received statutory recognition in 1979, with the passage of a new Ministry of Forests Act. Section 4(c) described the ministry's responsibility to

> plan the use of the forest and range resources of the Crown so that the production of timber and forage, the harvesting of timber, the grazing of livestock and the realization of fisheries, wildlife, water, outdoor recreation and other natural resource values are coordinated and integrated, in consultation and coordination with other ministries and agencies of the Crown and with the private sector.[4]

As the agency responsible for the management of all forest lands, the Ministry of Forests faced the formidable task of setting the conditions for a prosperous forest industry while attempting to accommodate a range of other values that often appeared to conflict directly with the interests of the forest industry. Increasingly vocal advocates of non-timber values frequently charged the ministry with demonstrating a timber bias and merely paying lip service to the protection of other interests. By the early 1980s, bitter conflicts over timber harvesting plans had surfaced in several communities. Citizens' groups that opposed clearcutting frequently complained that they had too little say in decisions made by a ministry that regarded forest companies as its clients; and First Nations became increasingly organized in their demands for recognition of aboriginal rights, including rights to land, on their traditional territories.

Meanwhile, in communities whose economies depended almost wholly on the forest industry, workers began expressing growing frustration at protests that had the potential to affect their livelihoods. Forest workers and resource-dependent communities were justifiably fearful for their economic well-being. As a result of automation, the annual amount of timber cut in the province more than doubled from 43,413 to 90,591 cubic meters between 1965 and 1987, while the number of forest industry jobs decreased by 2,000 during the same period.

A new level of conflict began in 1987 with the publication of *Our Common Future* by the United Nations World Commission on Environment and Development (commonly known as "the Brundtland report"). The report's emphasis on sustainable development in all nations provided a sharpened focus for interest groups advocating non-timber values. Existing land use conflicts intensified and new ones came to prominence. The list of contentious areas began to seem endless: Clayoquot, Walbran, Carmanah, Nahmint, Khutzeymateen, Kitlope, and many others.

DEVELOPING A SUSTAINABILITY STRATEGY

The Canadian government responded to the Brundtland report by setting up a task force that recommended the creation of federal and provincial strategies for achieving sustainable development. The federal strategy included the establishment of a National Round Table on the Environment and the Economy, Canada's Green Plan, and subsequent initiatives such as a new Canadian Environmental Protection Act, an Environmental Assessment Act, and the signing of an international convention on biodiversity, ozone depletion, and climate change. At the provincial level, governments across the country began to review their land and resource planning systems, and most provinces undertook initiatives to increase the protection of representative ecosystems.

In British Columbia, conflicts over land use and resource management were becoming increasingly destructive and costly, both economically and socially. The need to address these conflicts and the sustainability issues popularized by the Brundtland report led several private and government initiatives, including a Forest Resources Commission and a Round Table on the Environment and the Economy, to identify the need for a comprehensive land use planning system to reduce conflicts, increase the credibility of decision-making processes and promote sustainable land and resource uses.

In 1992, the provincial government announced a commitment to develop a wide-ranging and long-term strategy for resource and environmental management, under the auspices of an independent, statutory body, the Commission on Resources and Environment. The *Commissioner on Resources and Environment Act*, enacted in July 1992, empowered the commission to develop and oversee the implementation of the strategy.

The commission identified five components to be essential to the development of a sustainability strategy:

1. A clear government vision of sustainability, expressed through principles set out in a Land Use Charter, and through a legislative and policy framework;

2. Meaningful public participation, emphasizing consensus-seeking processes in the development of land use and resource management plans, to encourage stable and sustainable land uses that balance a range of values;
3. Careful coordination among all government agencies involved in resource and environmental management;
4. A comprehensive, consistent and accessible system for the resolution of disputes and of appeals against decisions; and
5. Independent oversight of the progress of the strategy towards achieving sustainability.[5]

Development of the sustainability strategy is well advanced, as reflected in a broad range of government initiatives and full or partial completion of strategic land use plans over more than half the area of the province. The initiatives include a Forest Practices Code that sets high standards for forest management; a Forest Renewal Plan to rehabilitate damaged forest lands, restore their ability to grow commercially productive forests, and encourage diversification in the forest industry; designation of about 15 million hectares of public lands as a forest land reserve, providing certainty for the forest industry; designation of 2.7 million hectares of new parkland, in partial fulfillment of the government's commitment to double from six to twelve percent the area of the province contained in protected areas; growth strategies legislation to manage urban growth; comprehensive environmental assessment legislation; land use plans, created through consensus-seeking public negotiation, fully or partially completed over more than half the area of the province, that delineate zones for intensive industrial use, complete protection, or human uses (industrial, recreational, settlement) that protect natural values such as wildlife travel corridors and significant ecosystems; and negotiation of treaties with First Nations (aboriginal peoples) to address their claims regarding their traditional lands from which they were displaced by European settlement during the nineteenth century.

The combined effect of these initiatives has been to help defuse land use conflict by addressing the root concerns of the disputants, and to begin to reverse the debilitating trends that have characterized forest management during the past several decades. A threatened forest industry is being stimulated by certainty of operating areas. Diversification in the industry, through an increase in value-added jobs and through forest rehabilitation, has the potential to improve the ratio of jobs per unit of timber cut, revive failing resource-dependent communities, encourage reforestation, and reduce the demand for timber supplies. And the creation of protected areas and sensitive management zones will help satisfy the need for wilderness and habitat conservation and for recreational opportunities.

It would be premature to pronounce the strategy a success after three years of development. It appears to enjoy broad public support, although this is to some extent masked by a "paradox of noise"—the dissatisfaction expressed by interest groups who maintain that the strategy has disturbed the status quo too much or too little. The long-term effectiveness of the strategy will depend on several factors: an ability to develop and employ a broad range of sustainability indicators to measure progress toward sustainability; preparedness to evolve to meet changing information and social needs; and continuing public and government commitment. The best hope for this is growing public recognition of the need to act decisively on issues that are increasingly accepted as being related: the effect of industrial development and urban growth on water and air quality, and on the sustainability of vital industries such as fisheries, forestry, and tourism; and dependence of healthy communities and quality of life generally on a sound economy and an undamaged environment.

GOVERNANCE ISSUES

Ensuring the continuing success of the sustainability strategy will require learning, practice, and commitment. Most especially, it will require a fuller understanding of the need for and avenues of cooperation among divergent interests and integration of different values, from local to global levels.

Dysfunction in public policy decision making

Due to the extraordinary demands on government and the increasing complexity of society over the last several decades, we have delegated more and more authority to our elected and appointed representatives. On the spectrum between representative and participatory democracy, our form of government has swung far to the representative side. While there are many practical reasons for this, the public is demanding a correction toward greater participation.

The sense of public alienation from public decision making is increased by the apparent inability of our decision-making structures to address individual needs. Our political system appears increasingly unrepresentative to many as parliamentary authority is subordinated to executive control supported by a government party that often represents significantly less than a majority of the population. Our judicial system has become irrelevant to many citizens through the excessive cost and delay of participation and through its inability to deal with dynamic, multi-party, public policy dispute, which simply cannot be adjudicated on a right versus wrong basis. And our administrative agencies are often seen as hierarchical structures that are insensitive to the individual needs of citizens and focus the attention of public servants upward toward the source of authority and accountability, rather than toward the individuals directly affected by the discretionary and sometimes arbitrary decisions of the bureaucracy in carrying out statutory mandates.

The dysfunction arising from this increasing alienation must be addressed through processes that provide the opportunity for meaningful participation in government decisions by those most directly affected by them. For some categories of decisions that affect a broad spectrum of interests, a fair hearing is no longer sufficient to achieve a lasting and equitable result. Direct participation in the decision-making process is necessary.

Procedural dysfunction in forest management has been demonstrated by the rejection of the results of planning processes and has been manifested in the bitter public conflicts that plagued British Columbia in the 1980s and early 1990s. Parties from across the spectrum of interests in land use would regularly attempt to do "end runs" around decisions reached by processes from which they felt excluded. If the chief forester reduced the annual allowable cut for a corporate timber licensee, the company would seek judicial review; a permit issued for a logging road into a pristine watershed would incite an environmental group to resort to civil disobedience and set up a blockade; cabinet ministers would be lobbied by various interest groups against administrative land use decisions; and media campaigns, often spiced with exaggerated claims, were launched at home and abroad. A common tendency is for government to react to such pressures with ad hoc decisions outside of formal planning processes. This creates inconsistency and enhances public distrust and alienation.

Confrontation has played an important part in the development of Western civilization through the dialectical challenge of ideas and philosophies; the search for truth through an adversarial justice system; the redistribution of wealth through labor-management tension; and the development of political ideologies through the parliamentary opposition dynamic. However, we have perhaps reached a point in our history where the demand on resources, increasing social pluralism, and challenge of global competition make us unable to afford the debilitating cost in goodwill and resources of confrontation. This suggests that the determinants of successful societies in the future will be those that can temper the confrontational dynamics in the fundamental political, social, and economic institutions of society with substantive results that are based on a broad consensus. These decisions will be better informed, more balanced and more stable.

In a forestry context, substantive dysfunction has existed in British Columbia, notwithstanding an apparent abundance in natural resources and environmental splendor. This dysfunction has been reflected in significant debt, unemployment, and conflict, and in an ongoing loss of environmental options, resource jobs, community stability, and business certainty. It is becoming widely understood that such continuing losses can only be halted through the application of land use principles of broad sustainability. It is clear that social stability will only be achieved through economic strength, which can only be maintained through environmental integrity. Achieving balanced land use decisions that respect this interdependence can only realistically be achieved through the development of a broad consensus.

The role of public participation in achieving sustainability

Partisan politics and representative government are not alone capable of dealing with the dysfunction in governance. Diluted ideology often renders the "business plan" of the right largely indistinguishable from the "manifesto" of the left. Yet as the public then seeks political definition in the credibility and competence of its representatives, rather than in their distinctive ideas, simplistic, personalized, and negative politicking can ravage reputations and divide us further. And as the media accelerates and amplifies the relationship between public opinion and government reaction, issues can get trivialized and solutions become even more elusive. Such "hyperdemocracy" bears little resemblance to Edmund Burke's slow and thoughtful horseback ride from Bristol to London.

Disillusionment with the effectiveness and integrity of government is a major contributing factor to the public demand for a more direct role in governance. This raw democratic energy can be a powerful and positive force for the development and implementation of more relevant and stable public policy that meets the needs of the broad spectrum of society and represents a true populism. However, there is also a danger of political manipulation of public anger into coalitions of otherwise unaligned negatives which have only destructive power, exercised through both the advocacy of powerful interest groups and the easy surrender by politicians to the direction of referendums. Yet both the public negotiation of issues by sectoral interests and direct democracy can be constructive supplements to representative government, which seems so often unable to deal with the complex issues that confront us.

The major risk of interest group advocacy is that it mobilizes and concentrates political and economic power in the hands of those with selective rather than broad public interest. When such special interests dominate the public policy agenda they distort it against the general public good, making the dysfunction and conflict in governance even worse as weaker interests are left out of the solution.

Distortion can also occur where political leadership simply defers to the majority will in referendums, in which individuals vote their preferences without personal accountability. A hallmark of our parliamentary system is that our representatives must publicly present and defend their ideas. The public interest is usually more than the sum of the individual interests in society, and clearly more than a bare majority of anonymous likes or dislikes, whether motivated by altruism, ignorance, self-interest, or indifference. There are, of course, issues well suited to referendums where a clear choice must be made between irreconcilable yet broadly acceptable options. Referendums may not be suitable, however, to decide complex relationships between legitimate, competing, yet interdependent interests such as arise in environmental, resource use, and native rights cases.

However, representative government can be supplemented effectively with greater public participation by drawing on the best of both direct democracy and sectoral interest negotiation. The key is that such participation is open, so as to be responsible; balanced, so as to be fair; and advisory, so as to leave decision making with accountable, elected officials. An effective example is the "shared decision-making" processes being pioneered in B.C. to negotiate long-term, sustainable uses of public forests and other natural resources.

Shared decision making means that on a certain set of issues for a defined period of time, those with authority to make a decision and those affected by that decision are empowered jointly to seek an outcome that accommodates rather than compromises the interests of all concerned. Parties distinguish their interests from their demands or positions that fail to take into account the needs of others. Because different groups will value things differently, clear self-analysis, communication, and understanding of each others' interests can lead to a package solution which can provide better outcomes to each party than if they were simply competing on their own. (See also chapter 10 for use of a similar process.)

An example in the B.C. experience is the issue of timber harvesting. Broadly stated, the interests of environmentalists are to protect biodiversity and to ensure that other non-timber values such as visual quality, recreational use, and aesthetics are sustained. Labor interests want secure employment, rural communities want economic diversification and stability, and corporate interests want certainty of return on investment. Shared decision making can lead to an all-gain solution where more sensitive harvesting techniques encourage greater employment through forest restoration projects and smaller-scale operations, a more diversified rural economy through protection of fish stocks and tourism values, and corporate certainty through settled zoning and sustainable fiber flows.

Consensus is one measure of success in a shared decision-making process. Full agreement represents the ideal outcome. However, the process should not be seen as unsuccessful just because it does not achieve the ideal result. Where full agreement cannot be reached, the efforts of the participants can still narrow the scope of the conflict and richly inform the decision-making process. Whether or not the parties come to terms, the building of working relationships and mutual understanding among the participants will have far-reaching consequences. The value of this process should not be underestimated. Small, interim victories may pave the way for future agreement.

A second measure of success in a shared decision-making process is the quality of the decision ultimately reached, whether or not by consensus. If the decision is seen as reflecting a better outcome than would have been the case without this form of public participation, it should be seen as invaluable to the policy development process. While longer-term and more subjective, criteria such as balance, effectiveness, and durability are all useful means of evaluating the "better outcome," and they are most likely to be met by directly involving those who are most knowledgeable, interested in, and affected by the decisions.

Achieving sustainability through the implementation of integrated social, economic, and environmental policy is an ongoing, dynamic process of public involvement in decision making and oversight at the local level; impact monitoring through the development and measurement of sustainability indicators; monitoring and enforcement of standards; public review and reporting; and amendment of policies and plans to respond to ongoing experience.

Incentives offered by government to motivate adoption of sustainability plans have proven to be not only helpful but also essential in regional land use planning negotiation processes. British Columbia's Forest Renewal Plan, drawing on large financial resources made available through increases in the public rent on public land timber harvesting, is providing for forest rehabilitation, increased and diversified employment, value-added manufacturing, intensive forest management, and research and development, all of which provide the motivation for a wide range of interests to support transition to sustainability. Enlightened self-interest is not necessarily inconsistent with good public policy.

Aboriginal participation

In 1991, the British Columbia government reversed a century-old policy by acknowledging the right of aboriginal peoples to use their traditional territories and by making a commitment to enter into negotiations regarding their land claims. Some negotiations are currently underway. For the most part, First Nations have been reluctant to participate actively in land use and resource management planning processes, in order to ensure that their rights are not prejudiced during treaty negotiations. This absence is having a major impact on the effective management of the public forest resource.

Historically, government treatment of First Nations was characterized by exclusion, through the creation of Indian reservations, and by attempts to assimilate aboriginal populations by eroding their languages and cultures. The commitment to treaty negotiation is the most significant indication of a new relationship based on respect rather than contempt and integration rather than exclusion. However, there is a major risk of backlash and militancy fueling each other in an explosive circle. This issue need not and must not be approached as "us against them"—it is "our" problem, and we must address it together with common understanding and expectations.

The most basic right of native people is the same as that of everyone else in Canada: the opportunity to be healthy, proud, and contributing members of society. The tragic experience of the past 150 years is that they have not enjoyed this right. In all the dialogue on this issue—and the accompanying law suits, protests, political threats and promises, inquiries, hand wringing, and cross-claims of racism—we risk losing sight of the central issue: we are not solving one of Canada's greatest tragedies.

Whatever the intentions—good, evil, or thoughtless—dominant society's simplistic attempt to assimilate native people into the mainstream has been a failure. By any indicator of despair—poverty, suicide, illness, abuse, addiction, incarceration—native people are the most desperate. As a society, we must take responsibility to end this tragedy—and to do so, we cannot ignore the distinctiveness of native history and culture. Forced residential schooling, outlawed cultural ceremonies, banned traditional languages, and smothering federal laws and bureaucracy have been a disaster for the self-esteem and self-sufficiency of native society. And the subsequently declared equal right to participate in general society has not secured the opportunity to do so.

The situation of native people must be understood and respected as being distinct from those with immigrant roots. The rest of us share a tradition of having made a choice, rather than having had one violated. Perhaps our cultural expectations prepare us collectively to change and integrate into a general pattern, in a way that seems inconsistent with the aspirations of native people. The situation of native people must also be distinguished from the past injustices to minority immigrant groups such as the internment of Japanese and the Chinese head tax. Perhaps, again because of expectations, these people have been able to adapt and prosper within the mainstream. Native people generally have not.

How then are we to address this tragic situation? The first steps have been for the federal and provincial governments to accept the principles of self-government and native rights. Such rights have been recognized, though not fully defined, by the courts and in the Constitution. Extended negotiations will have to take place over the next decade to settle and implement new arrangements which draw on the historical and cultural distinctions of native people. This is particularly true in British Columbia where, for the most part, treaties were never settled.

Negotiations over self-government and native rights must be moderate and realistic. Political and community leaders in native and general society must help tone down both the expectations and the fears of their constituents. Discussions must be as open as possible if they are to avoid descending into mistrust and anger. Hatred is often close to the surface and all of us have a responsibility to ensure that it is not promoted for political or economic ends. Ironically, we must all work together to recognize the distinctiveness that is necessary both to allow the successful realization by native people of the benefits of general society, and to allow us all to draw on the strengths of a revitalized native culture which are so relevant to some of the most pressing challenges of modern life.

In this context, self-government means the responsibility to have a direct say in those aspects of native community life that are closest to their culture—education, health, justice, child welfare, and forest management—within the general security of Canadian constitutional laws and institutions. Native self-government parallels the aspirations of all communities to gain more control over decisions that affect them most directly and of which they are most knowledgeable. A range of native self-government mechanisms already exist, including joint stewardship agreements to manage resources, municipal government-like powers, public utility, policing, and taxation responsibilities on reserve land, native law enforcement officers, and child placement and sentencing panels of elders to supplement court processes.

Native rights are the essential link to economic self-sufficiency. They do not mean displacing existing private ownership, but rather will be recognized through a combination of non-exclusive traditional use rights on public land, sharing of public resource rents, resource use tenures, training and employment opportunities, and land and cash settlements. Far from reducing current economic activity, settlement of these rights will reduce dependency and stimulate opportunity and development through land use certainty and increased investment.

Negotiations to settle self-government and native rights issues will take many years. In the meantime, public resources are being depleted and settlement options are being foreclosed, for the most part without the participation or benefit of native people and at times contrary to their legal rights. It is in everyone's best interest that resource use not be halted by court injunctions during negotiations, but that it continue in the interim on a clearly sustainable basis. It is also essential that native communities begin immediately to gain experience in forest management and benefit economically from resource use. Native participation in public land use planning processes and interim measures agreements are required to deal openly and lawfully with sustainability, co-management, and economic opportunity until treaties are signed.

Resolving outstanding issues of self-government and native rights will increase the self-esteem necessary for a full and healthy revival of native culture. It is remarkable that the spark and promise have survived such long and intensive injustice, and still exist for the benefit of all Canadians. Without over-romanticizing the past, we can look positively to traditional wisdom for guidance in moving from confrontation to consensus in decision making, to more sustainable forest use, to greater respect for the young, old, and weak in society, and to greater personal responsibility for wrongs against the community.

We must not fool ourselves into thinking we can simply vote this issue away in a referendum, or hide it under the false reasoning of an equality of convenience. A century of neglect and oppressive law has brought us only shame without resolution. The pressure for just settlement will continue to mount, ever increasing the cost in goodwill and resources. Expectations and fears, both political and economic, must be realistically and openly discussed by all sides. Every Canadian will benefit from addressing historical injustice, reversing the tragedy of despair, rekindling traditional wisdom, and ending conflict.

The sustainability strategy is justifiably heralded as a great step forward in the way we manage our resources and environment, and the contrast with the practice of the past century is indeed significant. It is useful to remember, however, that the fundamental premises of the strategy—sustaining a balance of values and striving for consensus in decision making—have been practiced by aboriginal cultures in British Columbia for many hundreds of years. As British Columbia progresses toward sustainability, it is imperative not only to redress past injustices to aboriginal peoples but also to benefit from their traditional knowledge. (See chapters 6 and 10.)

The irrelevance of borders

As we become more conscious of the common interests of the global community, political borders are becoming increasingly irrelevant. World War II made evident the illusory nature of military security and led to the founding of the United Nations. While the effectiveness of the U.N. has often been held up to examination, the global commitment to the institution has steadily increased to the point where more than 99.9 percent of the world's people are now represented in the U.N., compared to 70 percent in 1945.[6]

The role of the U.N. has changed considerably over the years, reflecting a growing recognition that global security in the modern world must be defined as much in economic, social, and environmental as in military terms, and that the way lands and resources are managed in any political jurisdiction may have significant implications not only for local ecosystems but for the global ecosystem. Increasingly, reliance is being placed on broad, participatory consensus-building processes for the resolution of international conflict. Examples include the labor and environmental side deals to the North American Free Trade Agreement and increasing involvement of non-governmental organizations in helping to shape the underlining policy for international conventions such as that developed at Rio de Janeiro.

Today, forest management frequently has international implications, as concerns increase about the relationship between destructive forestry practices and diminishing biodiversity, ozone depletion, and global warming. When a chainsaw rips into an old-growth fir in a British Columbia clearcut, the sound of its falling is heard in Germany, and the parent transnational based in New Zealand may bear the consequences of the resulting boycott. The consequences may be felt, too, at a local round table advising government on forest management decisions in a small British Columbia community, where representation of a multinational company at the negotiation table may become a matter of discussion, and issues raised at the table may range from local to international.

As a part of the global economy, resource industries must take a strong role in developing extraction, manufacturing, employment, and marketing strategies that will ensure that they are responsible and competitive and that demonstrate a commitment to remaining so in decades to come by supporting the goals of sustainability. The forest industry has a responsibility to shareholders and citizens alike to ensure responsible resource use. Rather than viewing the national and international attention being given to certifiably sound resource extraction practices as a competitive threat, resource-based industries can use this government and public interest in certified products as a competitive advantage through marketing. Appropriate environmental regulation can both ensure environmental integrity and enhance corporate competitiveness; in addition, the technologies developed to meet higher environmental standards can themselves be marketed to other jurisdictions, as they move themselves to sustainable resource management.

Responsibility to the world community

The predominant image of British Columbia elsewhere in the world is one of natural abundance and magnificent scenery. In recent years, this image has been somewhat tarnished by the furious debate, carried on both locally and internationally, about the province's forest practices. As the attention of the world turns increasingly to sustainable development issues in the wake of Brundtland and Rio, British Columbia has a responsibility to demonstrate to other jurisdictions its commitment to sustainability. In large part, this responsibility derives from the fact that British Columbia, unlike many jurisdictions, possesses the attributes most needed to make sustainability achievable—an abundance of natural resources, a large land base with considerable ecological diversity, a strong economy, and political stability.

On a small scale, the need for sustainable management in British Columbia forests is a metaphor for the need for a commitment to global security. Economic, environmental, and social principles, inextricably linked at the local level, are similarly linked at the global level. Nations have regularly practiced concepts of peace, development, democracy and the environment as both domestic and independent concerns. This has contributed to violence, poverty, oppression, and pollution which together seriously threaten global security. If we are to survive and advance as a global community, we must recognize that these concepts can only be sustained to the extent that they are practiced as both universal and interdependent principles.

British Columbia's responsibility to act in accordance with these principles is increased by its identity for over a century as a province of Canada. Canada is perhaps uniquely qualified to demonstrate international leadership through a bold approach to foreign policy which builds on our considerable experience in peacekeeping, development aid, human rights and democracy, and, more recently, environmental management. Unless we can understand that our individual and state security is dependent on some reasonable level of universal well-being, we will be unlikely to defend against the consequences of inequity. Canada's multicultural society demonstrates the potential both to import violence from other countries and to harmonize relationships among a wide range of human experiences and needs. In addition, our effective role as honest broker and peacekeeper equips us to provide leadership in international understanding and cooperation. Canada is well placed through its experience in international trade and development programs, its wealth and opportunity, and its mixed economy to understand the challenge and provide innovative leadership in encouraging parity in economic development.

Canada can be justly proud of its contribution to international peace, development, democracy, and resource management. Faced with international threats of recession, injustice, civil strife, and environmental degradation, we often seem to doubt our ability to promote comprehensive global security. Yet we have the ability and the responsibility to develop a bold and integrated foreign policy. It is not so much a banker or a policeman that will ensure global security, but a leader. Canada should self-confidently demonstrate this leadership.

CONCLUSION

In recent years, approaches to forest management in British Columbia have been transformed by a growing emphasis on the importance of managing for a broad range of values in addition to the economic value of timber, and by increased understanding both of what is required to sustain the timber resource and of the interdependence of economic, environmental, and social values. Intense "valley-by-valley" conflict in the 1980s, combined with significantly decreased employment in the forest industry, served as a catalyst for concerted government action to develop a comprehensive strategy for sustainability of forestry and other resource and environmental values. The continuing success of the strategy will depend on its ability to adapt to changing conditions and on careful development and monitoring of indicators that enable progress towards sustainability to be measured reliably.

The effectiveness of the strategy depends as well on its continuing ability to address dysfunction in governance by achieving solutions through cooperation rather than conflict and by maintaining an appropriate balance between representative and participatory democracy in making decisions that affect the public interest. This cooperative approach requires a broad focus, with a recognition that issues such as forest management not only affect a range of interests but have implications ranging from local to international. Global security requires a united approach to pressing and related issues that transcend national boundaries, including poverty, human rights, militarism and terrorism, and environmental degradation. Nor can forest management be separated from such unresolved land use issues as First Nations claims to their traditional territories taken from them in the nineteenth century and appropriated for Crown forest land.

In the last decade, forest management in British Columbia has shifted from a pattern of conflict, separate treatment of economic and environmental interests, and resource depletion to a model based on consensus, respect for and accommodation of a broad range of values, and sustainability. This departure from the practices that accompanied economic growth in the modern era is essential to the achievement of long-term economic, environmental, and social well-being; it also suggests an emulation of principles that were common to many aboriginal societies before they were displaced by European cultures. In that sense, we have come full circle, and should keep in mind that, in preparing for the future, we have much to learn from traditional approaches.

NOTES

1. Wayne Suttles, ed., *Handbook of North American Indians:* vol. 7, *Northwest Coast* (Washington: Smithsonian Institution, 1990), p. 24.

2. *Final Report of the Royal Commission of Inquiry on Timber and Forestry, 1909–1910* (Victoria, 1910), D66.

3. *Report of the Commissioner Relating to the Forest Resources of British Columbia* (Victoria, 1945), pp. 9-10.

4. *Ministry of Forests Act*, RSBC Chap. 272.

5. Commission on Resources and Environment, *British Columbia's Strategy for Sustainability* (Victoria, July 1995).

6. Commission on Global Governance, *Our Global Neighborhood* (Oxford and New York: Oxford University Press. 1995), p. 8.

DAVID H. GETCHES

10. Water in the Columbia River Basin: From a Source of Permanence to an Instrument for Economic Growth

The history of water use in the Columbia River Basin reveals a clash in values between traditional and modern societies. Traditionally, indigenous people of the Northwest coastal region respected and interacted with natural processes of the river. Because salmon (and other fish) were essential to their sustenance, community organization and structure, and commerce, tribal societies reflected the transcendent importance of protecting the waters that brought the fish to them. They placed the highest priority on preserving water in its natural state, believing that it was necessary to maintain the health of the rivers to ensure the return of the salmon, thus ensuring the stability and permanence of their society.

Modern people came to the region encouraging development and expansion of economies. They used water as the essential ingredient in building flourishing economies. In the process, they radically altered natural systems, effects that rippled far into the future and throughout the Pacific region. They valued the river as an instrument of growth. Thus, modern water laws and policies—from the arrival of white people in the mid-nineteenth century—were built on the idea that water was a resource to be exploited for the immediate satisfaction of human demands.

Water is—and has always been—the key economic factor for societies in the region. It offers bounties of food, eases transportation, fuels power supplies, turns and cools the wheels of industry, and nourishes crops. As in the past, people of the Pacific draw much of their regional identity from the waters that touch their shores and thread through their lands. The reality of the water linkage is shown by the heroic journey of the salmon, a valued resource shared by communities throughout the Pacific. These magnificent fish are Nature's emissaries, reminding us of the common bonds that make the Pacific a region tied together by water, and of the permanence of Nature's ways. Fish born in a mountain stream in Idaho pass a thousand miles downstream through the Snake and Columbia rivers and more thousands of miles out to sea, south to California or up to Alaska and perhaps Siberia or Japan. They range across the national frontiers and the wide distances that separate Pacific peoples.

In the last twenty years a new consciousness of the ecological interrelationships of water use with other matters of value to modern inhabitants has arisen. Attempts to reverse destruction of the Columbia's ecosystem have followed, and water policy and laws in the region are responding to this new conception of the values served by water and the river. The current shift in approach to water use suggests a resurgence in respect for natural processes and a return to the ideal of permanence held by Native peoples of the region.

NORTHWEST INDIANS, WATER, AND SALMON

For 11,000 years, salmon has been the central focus of Northwest Indian society. When the Lewis and Clark expedition explored the Columbia River in 1805, protein-rich salmon—coho, sockeye, chinook, chum, and humpback—sustained a well-fed population of more than 50,000 Indians.[1] The salmon so venerated by Northwest Indians are anadromous fish. After hatching from eggs laid in headwaters streams, they navigate through fresh water that takes them downstream to range about the Pacific Ocean to feed and grow. Years later they make a reverse trip, eventually reentering fresh water and struggling back up the Columbia to spawn in their natal stream. To end this epic journey, they lay their eggs in the gravel of the same headwaters streambeds where they hatched and, after spawning, expire at the spot where their spectacular odyssey began, completing a perpetual cycle.

Northwest Indian mythology reflects the centrality of salmon to aboriginal value systems and spiritual life. Petroglyphs found along the banks of the Columbia reveal a society whose core beliefs centered on the salmon.[2] Legends tell of salmon people who lived under the sea in a huge house. Donning salmon skin and converting into fish when the time came for their annual journey up the Columbia, the salmon people struggled upriver to perpetuate the species, and sustained the Indians' every need. The Indians saw the salmon run as a voluntary sacrifice by the salmon people for their benefit.[3]

At the time of contact with non-Indian settlers, all of Indian society was organized around the migrating and spawning habits of the salmon. Salmon was important to Indian society not only as the mainstay of the Northwest Indians' diet. The roles of men, women, and children were defined according to the migration, harvest, preparation, and use of salmon. Villages and family units followed the fall and spring salmon runs.[4] They had summer and winter homes—places they customarily used and land resources on which they seasonally depended. But, according to custom, the only vested property interests of the Northwest Indians were their fishing sites.[5] Economic activity was centered on the salmon and controlled by the seasonal runs; salmon was their chief unit of barter. The Indians traded with tribes in the region and over the mountains to the east, using salmon as the medium of exchange for other foods and commodities.

Celilo Falls provides perhaps the most dramatic image of the importance of salmon to aboriginal Northwestern Indians. Each spring, thousands would gather as the salmon made their way to this sacred place, 200 miles upstream from the mouth of the Columbia. As salmon jumped and struggled to overcome the falls, Indian fishers reached their long-handled dip nets down from suspended platforms extending out precipitously over the falls and scooped up the salmon.[6] Harvests were dried and stored to sustain tribes throughout the year; excess catch was used for barter.

The tribal people honored the natural forces, especially the river that brought salmon to them. When the first salmon arrived each season, it was a cause for ceremonial thanksgiving. In the first salmon ceremony each spring, following a ritual partaking by each member of the village, the bones of the fish were returned to the river, where they were said to reassemble and come back to life.[7] By this ritual, the Indians paid homage to the salmon people, who represented eternal cycles of life, and sought to ensure their return. They also had practices and rituals that treated the water as a sacred resource to be kept pure and pristine. For instance, there was a taboo against menstruating women passing over the river.[8]

The Indians of the Northwest were relatively wealthy. They had plenty of food and built comfortable wood houses. Wealth for them, however, meant the ability to make gifts, not simply to accumulate belongings. They did not assert dominion over expanses of land, "owning" only the right to fish at particular places, and they used only the resources they needed for community well-being. At the time of contact, the Columbia produced more salmon than any other river system in the world.[9]

NON-INDIAN EXPANSION AND
A CONFLICT OF VALUES

Growth of the Columbia River fishing industry

Almost from the moment of contact, the non-Indian settlers came into conflict with Indian values. The newcomers were relentless in their efforts to take possession of land and resources. They procured the tribes' agreement to let them occupy virtually all the land. Leaving groups of Indians with typically small (or no) land reservations, often with little access to rivers, the treaties secured the one thing the tribes valued most: the continuing right to fish "at all usual and accustomed grounds and stations . . . in common with all citizens of the Territory."[10] Thus, tribes were dispossessed of most of their lands, with only vestiges for homes and the promise of being able to fish as a kind of easement on the lands owned by the non-Indians.

The treaty fishing right proved to be a hollow promise as non-Indians took up homesteads along the river and began to monopolize the fishery.[11] When the tribes could muster the resources to press their treaty-guaranteed fishing rights, however, they usually prevailed against the non-Indians. In the 1880s, treaty Indians complained of a fence obstructing access to their Tum Water fishery. In the lawsuit that followed, the appeals court forced the landowner to honor the Indians' easement under the 1855 treaty.[12] But conflicts continued, and in 1890, Audubon and Linneus Winans began to deny the Yakima Indians access to The Dalles area and erected fish wheels that harvested huge quantities of fish. Deprived of use of their traditional fishing sites, the Yakimas called on the United States to sue on their behalf. The case went to the United States Supreme Court where the tribe's continuing right to fish was vindicated. In an opinion at once eloquent, perceptive, and beneficent for the times, Justice McKenna captured the essence of the Indians' relationship to the Columbia River and the salmon, saying that rights of access to the river to fish "were not much less necessary to the Indians' existence . . . than the atmosphere they breathed."[13]

But the right of access to the rivers was not enough. The economic value of fish stimulated markets that tested the limits of the fishery. Until the treaties and for a time afterwards the settlers were content to allow the Indians to harvest fish to be sold locally. With the perfection of canning in the late 1860s, however, came the prospect of huge distant markets for Columbia River fish. This led to non-Indian domination of the fishery, and the decimation of the salmon population began in earnest. It took only twenty years until commercial canners were packing about forty million pounds of salmon annually. Indians were crowded out of their usual and accustomed fishing places and by the late 1880s serious depredations in the spring and summer chinook runs were apparent and fishers turned to other stocks.[14] Commercial harvests proceeded virtually unchecked until the 1930s.[15]

Diversion of water for irrigation

As the tribes were confined to reservations, non-Indian populations grew and spread their settlements across the land.[16] In the late nineteenth century a host of federal land acts awarded now public (formerly Indian) lands to the settlers descending on the Columbia River Basin and plateau. Non-Indians were drawn to the Yakima, Willamette, and other sprawling Northwest valleys by a mild climate and fertile soils. The aridity of this area required irrigation, however, for successful farms.[17]

The homesteaders were encouraged to divert water from streams and bring it to their lands, with the promise that they would gain a legally protected right to the water used. The territories, later states, throughout the West accepted the "prior appropriation doctrine." The rule was simply that the first person to divert water from the stream and put it to a "beneficial use" would be assured the right to continue using it and have a better right than those who came later. Priority in time gave the better right.

Historically, "beneficial use" was interpreted broadly enough to include just about any use that might possibly be construed as beneficial to society. The uses considered most beneficial, however, were those that generated economic activity and growth. Thus, prior appropriation was ideally suited to the early development of the West. Irrigated agriculture required out-of-stream uses of water; the law of prior appropriation provided the certainty, convenience, and order necessary for its success. Early mining methods from sluicing to hydromining also required that water be taken out of the stream. Later, urban development demanded similar policies and laws because they allowed water to be transported away from its source.

Initially, small diversions of water had little impact on the flows of neighboring streams and certainly were of little consequence to the mighty Columbia. But the settlers soon recognized that their individual diversions could not remove, store, and transport to their thirsty lands enough water to realize the full potential for crop production and to cushion the vicissitudes of climate. They needed federal investment and planning to build dams, canals, and irrigation systems.

The federal Reclamation Act of 1902 financed ever-larger irrigation projects until irrigated agriculture became the largest diverter of water from the Columbia, withdrawing more than 30 million acre-feet a year and returning less than half of that water to the river.[18] But irrigation development came at the expense of the salmon habitat; fish died in unscreened diversion canals; silt destroyed the gravel salmon needed for spawning.[19] Agricultural irrigation combined with other resource development undertaken by the settlers to cause grave damage to the river. For instance, clear-cut logging promoted erosion that poured huge amounts of silt into the streams and accelerated runoff, alternately clogging and washing away gravel spawning beds.[20] (See also chapter 7 on the relation between forests and fish.)

Harnessing the river for hydropower

Attempts to recover from the Depression spurred construction of public works projects and the Columbia's impressive flows attracted interest as a source of power development. In 1932, Presidential candidate Franklin D. Roosevelt declared in a stump speech to the residents of Portland:

> We have, as all of you in this section of the country know, the vast possibilities of power development on the Columbia River. . . . This vast water power can be of incalculable value to this whole

section of the country. It means cheap manufacturing production, economy and comfort on the farm and in the household. . . . There will exist forever a national yardstick to prevent extortion against the public and to encourage the wider use of that servant of the American people—electric power.[21]

The Columbia also was seen as having potential for navigation, with visions of oceangoing vessels being able to penetrate far up the river. The first federal project on the Columbia mainstem, Bonneville Dam, was begun in 1933. The dam provided hydroelectric power and eventually created a safe channel for ships to reach several inland ports, as well as the means to control floodwaters.[22]

The commitment of federal spending power to develop the water resources of the Northwest furthered the Reclamation policy begun a few decades before. There followed a frenzy of dam building to produce hydropower as well as water for irrigation. The Columbia River quickly became the most developed river in the world. The capstone of the multitude of federal projects was Grand Coulee Dam, called "the biggest thing on earth," by Oregon Senator Richard Neuberger.[23] By 1985 there were 19 mainstem dams and 128 hydropower and multipurpose projects in the basin, with a total storage capacity of more than 67 million acre-feet of water. The projects made the river navigable for 500 miles by tug and barge from the mouth up to central Idaho on the Snake River.[24]

The Columbia River system suffered enormous damage—becoming a series of slack water ponds and reservoirs—as a result of the water development policies set in motion by decisions and laws made by states and the federal government. The same institutions that enabled economic expansion and westward movement of population thus destroyed the salmon fishery and undermined the Indian societies whose permanence was tied to the permanence of the rivers and the salmon. One of the most tragic episodes in the creation of the Columbia-Snake hydroelectric complex involved the inundation of Celilo Falls in 1956. Seventy-five feet of water drowned more than a hundred centuries of cultural and historical traditions when the Army Corps of Engineers closed the gates at the Dalles Dam. The Indian tribes received cash settlements, but few believed that their loss could be measured in dollars. Hydropower—and raw political power—won out over traditional and treaty-promised fishing rights.

Dams impede access to much of the salmon's original spawning habitat. An estimated one-third to one-half of the habitat is now completely inaccessible to migrating fish. But the adult fish struggling upstream may have it easier than the smolts heading for the sea. Until fish screens were installed, many of the young fish perished in hydroelectric turbines. Still, the highly regulated flows in the Columbia River fail to flush those young fish at anywhere near the speed of the unharnessed river. It now takes young chinook salmon an additional forty to fifty days to reach the ocean during low-flow years, increasing their susceptibility to predation and impeding their ability to convert from a freshwater to a saltwater environment.[25]

Anadromous fish runs in the Columbia system before non-Indians arrived are estimated to have been 10–16 million. Today's numbers are around 2.5 million (three-quarters of which are from hatcheries).[26] Entire stocks have been wiped out, and others are nearly gone. In the spring of 1991 the American Fisheries Society published a comprehensive report on the status of Pacific salmon. It concluded that, in addition to one hundred now extinct stocks, seventy-six native salmon and steelhead stocks in the Columbia River basin are in danger of extinction or otherwise deserve "special concern." Some of the remaining stocks, it acknowledged, may already be extinct; many others are in danger of losing their genetic identity through interbreeding with hatchery stocks. The report attributed the declines to a variety of factors: loss of and damage to habitat; inadequate passage and flows caused by hydropower, agriculture, logging, and other developments; overfishing; and negative interactions with other fishes, including non-native hatchery salmon and steelhead. Among these, historical overfishing and hydroelectric dam operations are likely the most important.[27]

The effects of the hydropower system on salmon are felt by fishermen throughout the Pacific region, and legal questions have been raised by states upstream from the dams. When the National Marine Fisheries Service issued a biological opinion in 1993, incredibly concluding that the Columbia River power system could operate without jeopardizing the Snake River salmon in violation of the Endangered Species Act, Idaho challenged the ruling. This resulted in the federal court throwing out the federal agency decision. The court found that the federal agency had used data and modeling methods selectively in order to minimize the perceived likelihood of extinction of the salmon.[28]

Our expansionist commitment to growth has led to the virtual destruction of a resource that was once at the center of the tribal societies. Irrigation and the Bureau of Reclamation in some places, hydropower and the Army Corps of Engineers in others, have combined to submerge traditional Indian values. The hydropower system on the Columbia is vastly, and tragically, overbuilt in anticipation—and encouragement—of ever-growing power demands. While the *price* of power was low, the *costs* were high. Planners did not consider the value of ecosystems, of free-flowing rivers, of gene pools lost and ignored, of the salmon, and of the tribal societies that depended on them.

While Indians continued to fish with dip nets, spears, and weirs, fishers from the east shoveled up salmon by the ton with fish wheels and huge traps. When Indian society was oriented to the river and the migratory cycle of the fish, settlers hungered for commerce, profit, land, and the extension of Jeffersonian ideals all the way to the Pacific. Where Indians valued fishing sites, settlers valued real estate. Where Indians were tied to the river and the salmon by centuries of tradition, ceremony, and barter, settlers spread out to cultivate the arid Columbia plateau, diverting water from the river for irrigation.

The conflict between Indians and non-Indians was, indeed, fundamental. It became a legal conflict when Indian fishing was effectively outlawed by the states and eighty years of long and bitter litigation ensued. The dispute became violent as state and local officials tried to force Indians not to fish with traditional gear or at times non-Indian authorities decided to close the river.[29] Eventually, the United States pressed the Indians' cause, but by the time the courts conclusively acknowledged the tribes' right to fish, the river had been so altered that the fishery was nearly destroyed.

ECOLOGICAL REALITY AND BROADENING VALUES

Western water law and policy is largely to blame for permitting and even encouraging what has happened to the once mighty Columbia and the Pacific salmon. With a fuller understanding of the wide-ranging and unfortunate consequences of focusing water policy on the single-minded goal of development, the question now is: what water policy reforms are needed to satisfy the broader range of values that are affected? The answers inform the issue of water policy reform throughout the American West.

Basic concepts of western water law, such as the beneficial use doctrine, are being expanded and applied to reflect a new water ethic that expresses a broader range of societal values than economic growth and production. "Beneficial use" has always operated to limit and define the private right in water by constraining waste. Uses required for mining and agriculture were generally considered beneficial, while extravagantly wasteful uses were deemed not to be beneficial. Only recently has the anti-waste principle been viewed in a broader social context. The uses for which western water is valued today—from swimming pools to hydropower, to river rafting, to aesthetics, to salmon habitat, to biodiversity—are far more complex and numerous than those of the nineteenth century. As a consequence, courts and legislatures have begun to modify the definition of "beneficial use" to provide for today's more extensive water values.

Nearly every western state constitution has always required that water be used in the "public interest" or to promote the "public welfare." The vesting of private water rights by putting water to a "beneficial use" effectively transfers water from a public to a private resource. It follows that courts and public agencies charged with determining whether a private use is "beneficial"—with determining whether the transfer to a private use is justified—must measure that use against the interests of the whole public.

Federal environmental laws—outlawing water pollution, protecting wetlands, conserving wildlife, requiring ecological considerations in licensing hydropower projects, and demanding assessments of the impacts of federal decisions—have become a force in water law and policy that is at least as great as state water allocation law. The Endangered Species Act in particular has awakened all the Northwest to the distress of the Pacific salmon. Its mandates are as strict as any environmental law in the world, going well beyond the curtailment of commercial harvesting of endangered fish. More fundamentally, a salmon recovery plan focused on fish passage and habitat improvement will require annual public and private expenditures and foregone economic benefits in the hundreds of millions of dollars. More than one billion dollars already have been spent building fish ladders, screening turbines, building hatcheries, increasing flows, controlling predators, and building juvenile fish bypasses.[30]

A further remedy for the ailing salmon fishery lies within the vast network of irrigation and hydroelectric water projects that itself has subverted and submerged natural systems. As with the concept of beneficial use, the built environment along the Columbia—the vast system of canals and reservoirs and dams—has the potential to be transformed into a vehicle to satisfy changing western water values. While constructed to address the demands for irrigation, hydropower, and urban development, the system also can be operated to manage the river and the ecosystem and to achieve publicly beneficial purposes never imagined originally. Dams are being re-operated to give higher priority to fish and lower priority to irrigation and power generation, and they are being retrofitted with facilities that allow better conditions for fish survival. There is actually talk of removing some dams.

The Yakima Project in the state of Washington enabled a 400 percent increase in irrigated acreage and greater crop yields per acre. But salmon populations in the river have declined an estimated 99 per cent since the turn of the century.[31] Several years ago the Yakama Indian Nation received an award of more than $2 million for the destruction of their treaty-secured fishing rights by the Yakima Project.[32] More recently, the state courts have ruled that the Yakama Nation has certain minimum streamflow rights.[33] The Yakima Project was required to operate to ensure the instream flows necessary for the tribe's fishery. The Cle Elum Dam, for example, has been operated since 1933 to hold back water until irrigators need it, and then to release it. The result was devastating to the spawning salmon, either keeping water away from their beds when it was most needed, or inundating them to the point of annihilation. However, the irrigators and the Bureau of Reclamation have devised a "flip-flop" method whereby the Cle Elum Dam is operated in conjunction with another Yakima system dam, achieving flows that correspond much more closely to Nature, while also satisfying irrigation demands.[34] Further, Congress passed legislation that provides for altering the use of the Yakima Reclamation facilities in ways that are compatible with survival of the fish and the tribal fisheries.[35]

Also on the Columbia system, the upper Snake River in Idaho was historically the richest habitat for salmon in the basin. Today few fish can migrate that far up the river. By operating the seven major reservoirs on that part of the system to release water down the river in sequence with the needs of salmon the effects of the dams can be mitigated and migration can be enhanced. The solution is complicated legally, however. There are contracts for delivery of the water to irrigators and for hydroelectric power generation so that the Bureau has to *pay* for water it uses to maintain streamflows for fish.

There are other problems. The *amount* of water needed for the river and its fishery may be delivered through operational changes, but salmon only respond to a particular *temperature* of water which signals them when and where to go. Water stored at the bottom of a reservoir is, of course, colder than the water at the top, so that dams with high outlet works release warmer water that does not meet needs for fish. Modifying the dams is an expensive proposition. For instance, redesigning the release system at Shasta Dam on the Sacramento River to meet salmon needs will cost $80 million, but it is being done.[36]

Changes in operations and structural reconfigurations may not be enough to restore habitat. Plans are afoot to remove a number of dams in the Pacific Northwest that have destroyed ecosystems. For instance, the Elwha River in Washington once produced copious salmon runs. However, since early in the century a hydroelectric dam has obstructed the river and ended salmon migration. It is now generally conceded that the best solution is to remove the dam, sacrificing a modest power source for the benefit of a rich ecological resource. Similar decisions, unheard of a few years ago, are becoming more common.

The *way* decisions are made, apart from the strict legal principles that define rights in water, is significant. Water policy today is understood more broadly to include all the environmental laws and policies that express society's shared values concerning natural resources. Therefore, broadening the concerns represented in water decisions usually requires increasing the number of participants in the process. Interests of the public, as distinguished from well-represented "special interests," can be represented in formal and informal processes that inform or actually resolve questions such as which permits are granted and determine what actions shall be taken to improve resource use. Several remarkable efforts by groups of citizens and public officials, usually within identifiable watersheds or sub-watersheds, have been initiated in the Northwest. (See chapter 9 for similar efforts in Canada.)

Managing water resources by watershed rather than according to political boundaries or narrow, single-mission government agencies can lead to more sensible ecological decisions and more equitable results. In the past, the institutions that managed our water have had little relation to the people most affected by the decisions. Upstream users have had little respect for the impacts of their water development on those downstream users. Groundwater users have paid little attention to others depending on the same hydrologically related resource. Managing the Columbia and its salmon presents particularly intriguing challenges because of the utter lack of regard the salmon, in their migratory habits, have for political boundaries.

Some states are providing frameworks and incentives for watershed-based efforts in which problems are solved locally rather than leaving them to state or federal agencies. Oregon in 1993 passed legislation encouraging the creation of watershed councils and establishing a Watershed Health Program.[37] One example of the Oregon program is on the Illinois River, a tributary to the Rogue. An initial effort to work together in dealing with problems of water quality and deteriorating fish habitat causing a decline of anadromous fish was hampered by the polarization of commodity interests and environmental interests. After the Watershed Health Act was passed the local Natural Resources District convened people and applied for the available state funding that comes from lottery proceeds. The Illinois Valley Watershed Council now includes not only district board members, but representatives of the fishing industry, educators, miners, environmentalists, and the city of Cave Junction.[38]

A distinct advantage of the watershed is that it is, in fact, an amalgam of countless, nested tributary drainage basins that can be grouped together or separated to define just the geographic area necessary to deal with a problem. Clearly, some issues in the Columbia Basin have a scope that demands consideration of a much larger area than a sub-watershed. Salmon survival depends on seeing the entire river as an integrated natural system and on managing the built environment in a coordinated fashion to protect the natural system. In 1980, Congress recognized the need for a concerted effort to protect the salmon after government agencies and power interests had made disastrous, single-minded decisions that resulted in a financial crisis for the power generating complex on the Columbia. The Northwest Power Planning Act created the Northwest Power Planning Council and required that management of the hydropower system throughout the Columbia River Basin address the interests of fish and wildlife, in addition to the interests of power supply and conservation, irrigation, Indian treaty fishing, and urban growth.[39] The Act said that future energy planning for the Columbia system must be a process that includes the public and considers the full economic and ecological effects of alternative sources of energy. And it mandated that there be a program to reverse the effects of the string of giant dams on the waning fishery.

The Northwest Power Planning Council has been somewhat successful, although recently the Ninth Circuit Court of Appeals rejected the Council's initial Salmon Strategy and chastised it for failing to take leadership, thereby "sacrificing the Act's fish and wildlife goals."[40] The Council then began to take greater leadership and has promulgated a plan to replace the one the court found to be deficient. The new plan, estimated to cost power users $171 million per year, provides not only for endangered salmon recovery but ensures that there will be more water left in the river for protection of other species and values.

The changes in water policy that are being made in the Columbia River basin cannot all be justified by economics. They are animated by a broader range of values. In essence, people and institutions are responding to information about the consequences of past actions that implicate concerns beyond the "modern" veneration of economic growth and production. Ecological imperatives, aesthetics, and demands for equity have given rise to a greater consciousness of the ethical implications of water use, one that has elements of the Indian cosmology that places the river at the center of life and values.

A RETURN TO THE IDEAL OF PERMANENCE?

People increasingly demand that water be used with greater care, fairness, and ecological respect. For most of this century, fulfilling utilitarian goals was paramount, but increased understanding of ecological science and hydrology has awakened a sense that water is being used in ways that seem "wrong"—destroying fisheries, polluting streams, depriving Indians of treaty rights. Thus, a fuller understanding of the consequences of water uses has created pressures for reforming water policy and for moving away from the single-minded goals of greater production and growth.

It has been suggested that water policy ought to be founded on ethical principles that eschew waste, favor equitable distribution, and comport with ecological interrelationships and needs.[41] Several water policy reforms emerging in the western United States are consistent with these principles. To the extent that policy is pursuing such a water ethic, it is beginning to emulate the Indians' traditional approach, an approach apparently based on the ideal that the salmon, the river, and other resources are to be here and coexist with the people permanently.[42]

Our greater ecological awareness, then, may be moving us away from the utilitarian, instrumentalist approach that dominated "modern" water policy for more than 150 years and toward water policies and institutions closer to the traditional ones they supplanted. These changes hold out hope for the Pacific salmon because it is clear that the only hope of restoring the Columbia River system to any semblance of long-term sustainability lies in a realignment of laws and behaviors relating to Nature.

NOTES

1. Charles F. Wilkinson and Daniel K. Conner, "The Law of the Pacific Salmon Fishery: Conservation and Allocation of a Transboundary Common Property Resource," *Kansas Law Review* 32 (1983): p. 27.

2. Beth and Ray Hill, *Indian Petroglyphs of the Pacific Northwest* (Seattle: University of Washington Press, 1974), pp. 30–31.

3. Philip Drucker, *Cultures of the North Pacific Coast* (San Francisco: Chandler Publishing Co., 1965), p. 84.

4. Barbara Lane, *Political and Economic Aspects of Indian-White Culture Contact in Western Washington in the Mid-19th Century* (unpublished, 1973); *United States v. Washington*, 384 F. Supp. 312, 350 (W. D. Wash. 1974); Eugene S. Hunn, *Nch'i-Wána: The Big River* (Seattle: University of Washington Press, 1990), pp. 148–49, 151.

5. Erna Gunther, "The Indian Background of Washington History," *Pacific Northwest Quarterly* 41.3 (July 1950): pp. 192, 194–95.

6. Anthony Netboy, *The Columbia River Salmon and Steelhead Trout: Their Fight for Survival* (Seattle: University of Washington Press, 1980), p. 15.

7. Franz Boas, "Second General Report on the Indians of British Columbia," *British Association for the Advancement of Science, Report on the Northwestern Tribes of Canada* 1, p. 569, summarized in Beth and Ray Hill, *Petroglyphs*, p. 35.

8. Barbara Lane, *Political and Economic Aspects of Indian-White Culture Contact*, p. 9.

9. R. J. Childerhose and M. J. Trim, *Pacific Salmon and Steelhead Trout* (Seattle: University of Washington Press, 1979), p. 9.

10. *United States v. Winans*, 198 U.S. 371 (1905).

11. Robert H. Ruby and John A. Brown, *Indians of the Pacific Northwest: A History* (Norman: University of Oklahoma Press, 1981), p. 259.

12. *United States v. Taylor*, 3 Wash. Terr. 88, 13 P. 333 (1887).

13. Robert H. Ruby and John A. Brown, *Indians of the Pacific Northwest*, p. 259; *United States v. Winans* at 381.

14. Charles F. Wilkinson and Daniel K. Conner, "The Law of the Pacific Salmon Fishery": pp. 31–33.

15. Sarah F. Bates, David H. Getches, Lawrence J. MacDonnell, and Charles F. Wilkinson, *Searching Out the Headwaters: Change and Rediscovery in Western Water Policy* (Washington D.C.: Island Press, 1993), p. 96.

16. Robert H. Ruby and John A. Brown, *Indians of the Pacific Northwest*, pp. 259–68.

17. Sarah F. Bates et al., *Searching out the Headwaters*, pp. 29–36.

18. *Ibid.*, p. 96.

19. Anthony Netboy, *The Columbia River Salmon*, pp. 55–71.

20. Jim Stiak, "Why Logging and Salmon Don't Mix," *High Country News* 23.7 (22 Apr. 1991): p. 18.

21. Anthony Netboy, *The Columbia River Salmon*, p. 72.

22. Sarah F. Bates et al., *Searching Out the Headwaters*, pp. 96–97.

23. Donald Worster, *Rivers of Empire* (New York: Pantheon Books, 1985), p. 270.

24. Sarah F. Bates et al., *Searching Out the Headwaters*, p. 97.

25. *Ibid.*, p. 98.

26. Northwest Power Planning Council, *Columbia River Basin Fish and Wildlife Program—Strategy for Salmon* (1992), p. 5.

27. Willa Nehlsen, Jack E. Williams, James A. Lichatowich, "Pacific Salmon at the Crossroads: Stocks at Risk from California, Oregon, Idaho, and Washington," *Fisheries* 16.2 (Mar.–Apr. 1991).

28. *Idaho Dep't of Fish and Game v. Nat'l Marine Fisheries Serv.*, 850 F. Supp. 886 (D. Or. 1994), *vacated as moot*, 56 F. 3d 1071 (9th Cir. 1995).

29. American Friends Service Committee, *Uncommon Controversy: Fishing Rights of the Muckleshoot, Puyallup, and Nisqually Indians* (Seattle: University of Washington Press, 1970), pp. 60, 125–37.

30. Pat Ford, "How the Basin's Salmon-Killing System Works," *High Country News* 23.7 (22 Apr. 1991), p. 15.

31. Natural Resources Law Center, *Report on Environmental Enhancement of Bureau of Reclamation Facilities*, 1 (pending 1995), p. 12.

32. *Yakima Tribe of Indians v. United States*, 20 Indian Claims Comm'n Dec. 76, 84 (1968).

33. *State Dep't of Ecology v. Yakima Reservation Irrigation Dist.*, 850 P. 2d 1306 (Wash. 1993).

34. Natural Resources Law Center, *Report on Environmental Enhancement of Bureau of Reclamation Facilities*, 1 (pending 1995), pp. 28–29.

35. Northwest Power Act, 16 U.S.C. § 839 (1980).

36. Paul McHugh, "Plumbing the Depths," *San Francisco Chronicle* 1Z1 (4 June 1995).

37. Or. Rev. Stat. § 536.600 (1993).

38. Natural Resources Law Center, *The Watershed Sourcebook: Citizen Initiated Solutions to Natural Resource Problems* 2 (pending 1995), p.76.

39. Northwest Power Act, 16 U.S.C. § 839 (1980).

40. *Northwest Resource Info. Ctr., Inc. v. Northwest Power Planning Council*, 35 F. 3d 1371, 1395 (9th Cir. 1994).

41. Sarah F. Bates et al., *Searching Out the Headwaters*, pp. 178–98.

42. See the study by Nancy J. Turner and E. Richard Atleo entitled "Pacific North American First Peoples and the Environment" in this volume discussing the influence of traditional values in resource decisions and drawing on the specific example of a scientific panel's integration of traditional values in its recommendations regarding forestry practices in Clayoquot Sound. See also Arthur Hanson's chapter in this volume entitled "The Pacific after Rio," which considers how traditional values can be reasserted as societies enter their postmodern or postindustrial phase.

VASSILY I. SOKOLOV

11. Changed Land, Changed Lives: Energy and Aborigines in the Russian Pacific

In all, about 58 percent of Russian territory is inhabited by approximately twenty-nine Aboriginal peoples. Their total number is still a subject of scientific and administrative debates, but it is estimated at almost 185,000 (1989 census),[1] most of whom live in the Russian Far East (Pacific) and North. At present, the population of Russia's arctic zone alone—extending from the European part to the Far East—is about two million. Of these, nearly 70,000 are ethnic minorities of the North. The current situation of Aborigines in Russia provokes large public concern about their future. The destruction of the Aboriginal natural habitat and the loss of traditional skills and adaptive abilities to survive in extreme conditions are to a large extent the result of the imposition of new "modern" values by modern society on the Aboriginal community. The history and consequences of this process in relation to energy supply and use are a clear example of the tension and clash between traditional and modern approaches to the environment.

THE ABORIGINES OF THE RUSSIAN PACIFIC

The Aboriginal peoples of the Pacific region do not form a single ethnic community, as they are different in origin, in cultural and religious aspira-

195

tions, and in economic traditions. Among them are Chukhi (15,100 in 1989), Evenks (17,200), Nanai (12,000), Koryaks (9,200), Nivkhi (4,700), Ul'chi (3,200), Itel'men (2,500), Eskimos (1,700), Yukagirs (1,100), Orochi, Aleuts, Neguidals, and Oroki (each less than 1000).

However, three major ethnic regions within the Russian Far East can be distinguished on its vast territory.[2]

1. The Northern regions within the Russian Arctic (Chukotsk and Koryak National Autonomous Regions, Magadan, and Kamchatka Regions): Every ethnic group in this region can be divided in two major subgroups on the basis of the orientation of their economic activities: the coastal subgroup, which obtains its food supply mainly from sea hunting and fishing, and the nomad subgroup, involved mainly in such activities as wild reindeer hunting and domestic reindeer stock management;

2. The Okotsk Sea coastal zone inhabited mainly by Evenks and covering the South of Magadan Region and the North of Khabarovsk krai (region);

3. The Southern part of the Russian Far East (Amur River Basin, Primorsky Krai, and Sakhalin Island) is inhabited by different ethnic groups (Nanai, Nivkhi, Udegue, Ul'chi, Neguidal, Oroki) who also speak paleo-asian languages but who have more diversified economic activities compared to the other two ethnic regions. Recently the Republic of Yakutia (Sakha) started to be considered as a part of the Russian Far East. On its vast territory (more than 3.1 million km^2) the Evenks (9,100) and Yukagirs (500) represent the Aboriginal population. The Yakuts themselves (about 300,000) were migrants by origin, but over many centuries they have adopted most of the traditional practices and approaches to the natural environment.

Great diversity can be found even within each ethnic group, because of the large size of their territory, which sometimes comprises thousands of km^2 (e.g., Yukagirs and Evens). This has resulted in different dialects, in some cases close to different languages.

THE RICHES AND POVERTY OF
THE ABORIGINAL POPULATION

The territories inhabited by Aborigines in Russia contain from 70 to 90 percent of all oil and natural gas deposits, gold and other precious metals, nickel, lead, tin, and other crucial natural resources discovered in the country. The Far North of Russia with only 7.4 percent of the population provides 20 percent of GNP. These territories provide 91 percent of the annual production of natural gas, 75 percent of oil, 15 percent of all coal, and 17 percent of hydroenergy. The Far North of the Russian Federation provides 60 percent of export earnings.[3]

All the territories of the Russian Far East with Aboriginal populations have certain commonalities. Among those should be mentioned: vast, remote territories which are hard to administer; a high rate of immigrant populations; raw material production as a major economic activity. However, the major commonality unifying all Aboriginal families is the religious attitude toward the natural environment: "in the heathen religions of practically all Aborigines the major attention is given to the issues of conservation and strict economic use of natural resources."[4]

Externally imposed development has threatened the indigenous cultures and the ecology of large territories of the Russian Far East. In particular, environmental changes introduced by development projects may well threaten future opportunities and scope for indigenous developments. The extent to which the minorities are deprived of their rights has very few analogies in the rest of the world. This is especially evident in their relationship with governmental agencies, such as the Ministries of Industry, that supervise the exploration and extraction of mineral deposits and energy resources. Industrial expansion to the remote Far Eastern regions was carried out by governmental and industrial agencies without significant attention being paid to the environmental and social impacts on local Aborigines. In many cases it has led to the irreversible destruction of natural resources and living conditions. Additionally, the State's strategic interests in the Pacific have resulted in a heavy military buildup in the Far Eastern region.

This expansion was primarily responsible for the contamination of Northern ecosystems and directly threatened the health of indigenous peoples, dependent as it is on natural ecosystems as far as food supply is concerned. As a result of these processes the territories and resource bases used by Aborigines for traditional activities have been reduced to such an extent that the pressures of physical survival have forced the Aborigines to adopt—in a very short historical time—the values and priorities of "modern society." This adaptation has resulted, in particular, in a critical health situation which has now been detected in the Aboriginal community of Russia. Aborigines have the highest mortality rate in the country: life expectancy is ten to twelve years less than the Russian average; the rate of mental disease exceeds the Russian average by 3.7 times; that of alcoholism by 4 times; that of drug abuse by 7 times; etc.[5]

Environmental protection as an issue of Aboriginal survival is a relatively new issue in a country like Russia.[6] The relevant debates started in the former Soviet society around two decades ago, but reached most public attention only after the USSR's disintegration, when ethnic rights and sovereignty emerged on the national agenda as a focus point for reforming the former Soviet society.

RUSSIAN ABORIGINES: HISTORY OF
STATE REGULATION

The first legal statute for Aboriginal people was developed and adopted by the Russian Imperial government in 1822. Before this date, in the seventeenth to nineteenth centuries, the administration of Aboriginal activities was carried out by a traditional system of tribal chiefs, incorporated into the local administration system of the time. The 1822 Statute allocated special rights to Aboriginal people based on their traditional lifestyle and provided them with an exemption from Russian common law regarding, in particular, taxation, land trade and transfer to other users, restrictions on the trade of alcohol, etc. However, the absence of a law enforcement mechanism, the expansion of the traditional Russian bureaucratic system, and a Realpolitik aimed at the "russification" of local peoples raised serious problems for the implementation of the concept of self-administration for Aboriginal peoples as designed by the 1822 Statute and by subsequent legislation.

A radical change in the overall concept of Aboriginal administration took place in Russia after the 1917 Revolution when the Soviet social system emerged. A system was conceived of "equal rights and equal consumption", which assumed that equal opportunities for peoples with different cultural, economic, and other backgrounds could be reached through direct state control of all activities. This resulted, in particular, in uniform education, collective economic activities, and industrialization of all regions, including the peripheral ones. This policy had important effects for Aborigines because of their heavy involvement in common social processes and the virtual destruction of the traditional management system.

On the other hand, the Soviet Constitution provided special provisions for ethnic groups' development, and the Soviet Union itself was formed as a multi-ethnic state with clearly defined ethnic territories. In 1924, the Soviet Union created the State Committee on Northern Affairs (Goskomsevera), which had as its major brief the administration of the Northern territories, including the administration of Aboriginal communities. From the very beginning of the Soviet political regime, the debate on the future of Aboriginal management followed two major directions. The proponents of Aboriginal management in the form of "reservations" appealed to the model of American Indians' status and emphasized the need for central government control and for restrictions within reservations on settlement and modern economic activities, etc. However, their opponents, the so-called progressivists, had clearly more success in Soviet Society and gained special support from governmental and business structures. Their view was in line with the ideological imperatives of the Soviet system and was based on the involvement of Aboriginal peoples in regular activities, thereby creating "equal opportunities" for the whole population, regardless of cultural, social, or other differences.[7]

From the very beginning of the 1930s, the Soviet system of public administration (local, rural, regional committees exercising powers within strict control from central government) was implemented in the Far East regions. The judicial system there was introduced only in 1933–34. The conservation of cultural specificities of Aboriginal peoples and a certain level of self-administration were realized through the concept of national (ethnic) counties and districts—special administrative entities for Aboriginal people living in compact ways on defined territories. This process started with the creation of three ethnic counties in the Russian Far East in 1930 (Chakotsk, Koryaksk, and Okhotsk [Evenks]) and several Aboriginal districts (such as Zeisko-Tursky and Djeltulakski districts for Evenks, or Norym district for the Aleuts of Kamchatka).[8]

This administrative approach aimed at preserving Aboriginal rights could not protect the local population from assimilation and cultural "intervention." For example, in Chukotsk national county the Chukchi constituted 96.2 percent of the population in 1931; by 1989 the proportion of Aborigines in Chukotsk national county had been reduced to 37 percent.[9] This reduction has had a clear impact on the traditional lifestyle, notably in the reduced use of the native language. In 1959, 87.5 percent of the Chukchi population spoke the native language; by 1989 the rate had been reduced to 70.4 percent. The corresponding figures for the Koryaks are 87 percent and 52.4 percent; for Udegue 67.6 percent and 24.3 percent; for Orochi 50.5 percent and 17.8 percent, etc.[10]

The economic expansion into the Russian Far East has had a clear impact on the Aboriginal population in several ways. Land nationalization within the Soviet Union accelerated the alienation of Aboriginal lands—a process that actually goes back to long before the 1917 Revolution—and led to the destruction of traditional land ownership. Having been nationalized, the lands had no clearly defined owner, and open access to the lands, especially on the part of industrial ministries, was practiced for decades in these remote locations. Under such conditions Aboriginal lands can easily be transferred for other uses under the pretext of "national interests." In fact, the lands and resources were ministries-owned rather than state-owned. The monopolistic position of the industrial ministries and agencies was strengthened from the mid-1950s onward when many development projects focused on the natural resources of the Russian Far East were put on the national agenda. The departmental (*vedomstvennyi*) interests were extended far beyond specific development projects and covered trade, transportation, services, and social development. Among the most monopolistic agencies acting in the Russian Far East were the Dal'stroi (Far East Construction Agency), the *Glavsevmorput'* (Northern Transportation Agency), the Ministry of Geology, and diverse energy development ministries such as the Ministry for Oil and Gas, the Ministry for the Coal Industry, and others.

A governmental migration policy (giving extra payments and tax reductions for resettlers) and especially the collectivization process imposed by the Soviet state since the 1930s also contributed to the decline of Aboriginal activities—sometimes indirectly. For example, the food supply system for resettlers was mainly based on the creation of collective farms (*sovkhozes* and *kolkhozes*) with high levels of specialization (livestock management, fishing, etc.) and large-scale production. Thus, six fishing farms organized within Chukchi county increased the catch there from 10,000 tons in 1930 to 70,000 tons in 1981.[11] By the mid-1940s almost 90 percent of reindeer in the Russian North were owned by collective farms; in that way, however, the traditional system of livestock management was almost destroyed. Another important result of collectivization and production intensification was overgrazing; there were also other, similar, environmental effects, e.g., the average permissible density of thirty to ninety reindeer per km^2 of grazing land supported by traditional Chukchi practice was exceeded in many locations. A real threat to the basic natural resources used in the traditional economies had emerged.

Urbanization too led to new environmental challenges. Large cities built in the Soviet era—such as Norilsk, Bilibino, Mirnyi—in the Far North and urban expansion in the southern part of the Russian Far East led to unprecedented pollution; e.g., the cumulative emissions of sulfur dioxide by the Norilsk industrial complex were estimated at 2,000,000 tons in 1994. In search of job opportunities and basic needs, local people moved to the cities, putting traditional housing around cities and thus contributing to the urban spread. "Population concentration" for the purpose of facilitating basic supplies was a governmental policy that also had negative effects on the cultural and economic traditions of Aborigines in the Russian Far East and Siberia from the mid-1950s. One result of this process was a noticeable reduction of traditional activities; e.g., during the 1970–87 period alone the reindeer livestock population in Magadan Region was reduced by 15 percent, by 30–40 percent in Krasnoyarski krai, and on Sakhalin Island it virtually disappeared.[12]

The loss of traditional skills and activities was accelerated by specific education policies introduced by the Soviet State. In particular, mandatory free education for all children, introduced since the mid-1960s, had visible effects on intergenerational relations and on traditional life and practices. All children were taken to often remote schools, sometimes for the whole academic year, isolating them from day-to-day family life and destroying intergenerational links, thereby bringing new priorities into Aboriginal life. In recent years this situation seems to be changing: now 240 dormitories provide residence and teaching for about 10,000 Aboriginal children; 35,000 other children have a chance to study in 270 ethnic schools where most of the teaching is based on native language and on the inclusion of traditional activities.[13] (See chapter 6 for parallel Canadian examples.)

All the side effects of modern life's intervention in Aboriginal life were so obvious that from time to time the central government was forced to elaborate certain regulations and decrees aimed at preserving traditional activities. Thus, in 1957 the ruling Communist Party and the USSR Council of Ministers in a joint decree, "On the Further Development of Economies and Cultures of Aborigines in the North," tried to implement a state assistance program for traditional hunting, fishing, reindeer stock management, etc. In the 1960s every local or regional Soviet committee in the Russian Far East was already supposed to have a special department of Aboriginal affairs.

However, every single time, state policy on Aborigines has been contradictory and inconsistent. The new Russian Federation Law on Autonomous Counties of 1980 radically changed the status of ethnic entities—by changing the designation of "national" to "autonomous"—providing equal electoral rights to the whole population of a specific county. Since in most cases they are a minority within a county, the Aborigines in fact lost their representation in local administrative bodies. Besides that, the "pyramidal" structure of public administration set up in the former Soviet Union left no space for Aboriginal people to defend and promote their vital interests. In the central budget all Union subsidies were allocated among "pyramid" components, often not reaching the ethnic minorities to satisfy their basic needs and cultural development. Throughout the whole Soviet era the governmental agency *Goskomsevera* was in charge of governmental regulations and of the coordination of other activities affecting Aboriginal peoples. Despite its relatively broad mandate, the Committee failed to provide appropriate policies in support of traditional activities.

ABORIGINAL POPULATIONS AND THE
DEVELOPMENT OF ENERGY SYSTEMS

Energy clearly became the bloodstream of modern economic life, bringing tremendous opportunities for human survival, for meeting basic needs of individuals, for the gradual or radical improvement of well-being. From the very beginning of humanity, the possession of energy sources symbolized the power to endure in a hostile environment, to overcome natural threats to human life. This is still relevant to Aboriginal life, which is heavily concentrated around the supply of energy.

Motorized life and heated homes

The new values imposed on Aborigines by modern society are partly based on policies of cheap energy provision and high energy consumption— policies, incidentally, posed as crucial national and ideological goals by the creators of the Soviet Union. The implementation of these goals had both positive and negative effects on the Aboriginal community. The changes brought about by high energy consumption can easily be traced in traditional hunting and fishing practices and tools: motor-driven boats replaced the traditional boats; aviation, particularly in the form of helicopters, became generally used by hunters as means of transportation; etc.

Other side effects of modernization are clearly visible in all aspects of Aboriginal life. Because of the poor modern infrastructure in the remote regions of the Russian Far East, caterpillars and tracked vehicles are heavily used as means of transportation, leaving the tundra soils damaged and unrecoverable for many decades. Experts of the Academy of Sciences consider motorized transportation as a major environmental problem for the remote areas of the Far East and North.[14] That is why, for instance, the government of Yakutia has been enforcing limits on motorized transportation since 1978.

Another bothersome result of the use of liquid fuels are the thousands and thousands of metal fuel barrels that were used for the transport of the fuel and then discarded anywhere throughout large areas of the Far North and East, polluting land and water and changing the landscape. The disposal of these barrels was never subject to state regulation.

In the residential sector too, energy systems have changed, in many cases dramatically. In many regions of the Far North and East, Aboriginal housing could not escape the policy of population concentration, uniform building construction, and the expanded use of central heating systems. These changes were considered an integral part of social reforms in the former Soviet Union, and they led to new demands for energy and to losses of traditional skills in human adaptation to the extreme weather conditions through traditional housing (*yurta*), adaptations in dress, biomass and coastal wood debris use for fuel, etc. Fortunately these losses are not absolute and many Russian Aborigines have managed to preserve their traditional housekeeping practices. This latter was especially important because during these last few years of economic chaos many regions of the Far East and North have faced severe shortages of external energy supplies.

Property rights over energy resource-rich lands

As stated earlier, the dominance of industrial interests on aboriginal lands has affected the population in many, often contradictory, ways. Because of shortages in central government budgets, many industrial agencies acting in the Far Eastern regions were obliged to provide financing for the social and economic infrastructure, including schools, hospitals, transportation facilities used by the local population and primarily by Aborigines (a practice regulated through government resolutions and legislative acts adopted during the Soviet era).

Energy supplied via long-distance transportation became a normal practice for the majority of the Far East regions. Most other basic needs were satisfied and survival was guaranteed. Basic prices for traditional products were fixed and guaranteed by the state. In exchange for such charity Aboriginal land rights were in fact transferred to the exploration and mining enterprises without "formalities."

These kinds of relations between the ministries and the Aborigines had created a heavy dependence of Aboriginal life on industrial activities for the provision of basic needs, including cheap energy, heating equipment, and even sometimes modern housing for locals, thereby diverting natives from traditional activities. In some cases this led to the loss of experience gained over generations.

In the last twenty-five years special emphasis has been placed in remote regions of Russia on oil and natural gas exploration. In many cases such activities have led to the polarization of interests regarding land use and benefits sharing patterns. The crucial point in the emerging conflicts is related to financial compensation to Aborigines for the lands alienated for energy or mineral production. The Russian Federation Law on Subsurface Resources (1992) and the Law on the Protection of the Natural Environment (1991) make special provisions in this respect: the use of natural resources should be chargeable to the industrial entities. However, whatever money transfers there are, in the existing bureaucratic environment they are not reaching the intended addressees: royalties and fines for environmental damage are paid to the local administration, often located hundreds of miles from the affected Aboriginal community, and the funds in question are often allocated to other users.

The most controversial case in this respect concerns natural gas exploration and production on Yamal Peninsula in West Siberia. The

richest deposits of fuels in West Siberia (Surgut and Samotlor) were discovered in the 1960s on the lands of local Aboriginals—the Khanty—and
gave enormous economic gains to the former Soviet Union: oil export
revenues alone were estimated at 440 billion dollars over two decades of
exploration. They are still the major export revenues nowadays in the
Russian Federation. Further investment in the oil and gas sector has led
to the discovery of very rich deposits of gas condensate on the land of
other local Aborigines, the Nenets. Major constraints on the development of new sites (Bovanenskoye and Kharasaveyskoye) are linked to
environmental and Aboriginal factors.[15] The essential threats to local
Aborigines come from large industrial construction on grazing fields,
from railway construction, and especially from the technological accidents that are increasing in scope and impact on the territory of the former Soviet Union.[16]

In the Yamal case, attempts on the part of local government made
since 1985 and even the decrees of the Federal government in 1989 to put
limits on oil and gas development on the Yamal Peninsula have been
unsuccessful—the deposits are now being developed, largely under the
pretext of "national interests": the urgent need for export commodities.
The fate of local Aborigines is hard to predict due to the absence of any
legislative and enforcement mechanism regulating industrial-Aboriginal
relations.

An almost identical situation can be traced in the case of oil and gas
development on Sakhalin Island. The fields discovered on the Sakhalin
offshore shelf in 1991 have a total potential deposit of 230 million tons
of oil and condensate and about 600 billion cubic meters of natural gas
(the biggest natural gas site, Lun'skoye, contains around 400 billion
cubic meters). Large international companies (Exxon, Mobil, Royal
Dutch/Shell, Amoco, and others) as well as companies from Japan and the
Republic of Korea have started a competition game around these new
energy deposits, stimulated by certain Russian industrial agencies' policies
designed to attract foreign capital to the Russian Far East. None of the
negotiations and bidding processes that have taken place over the last several years have focused on the interests of Aboriginal communities living
on Sakhalin Island. Even the local administration that opposed the central
government's plans to attract selected foreign investors for the development of natural gas sites never mentioned the land rights of local Aboriginal people.[17]

Modern energy systems and the creation of dangerous environments

Some energy development projects can be seen as directly threatening to the traditional way of life. The problem under consideration here is primarily about the interrupted plans to introduce atomic energy systems in the Russian Far East. The plans include both small- and large-scale nuclear facilities to provide energy for the industrial and residential sectors. In particular, mobile atomic stations are proposed by several industrial groups (NPO "Raduga," NPO "Yuzhnoe," "VetroEn") for use in remote regions. The prototypes for such stations have been developed in the country since the 1960s–1970s and are supposed to be installed on the Arctic coast to reduce the vast amounts of oil now transported by ship in the summertime.[18]

At the same time, the Federal Government is involved in the construction of large-scale nuclear power stations across the country, despite all the environmental and social impacts of the Chernobyl accident. Bilibino nuclear power station in the Arctic sector of the Far East is expected to have three power reactors by the year 2010 in addition to the three existing ones. One nuclear station is designed for Prmiorski krai, another—the Far East Atomic Power Station (with a capacity of 600 Mwt)—is scheduled to be put into production by the year 2004 in the region of Evoron Lake (Khabarovsky krai). The Second Congress of Aboriginal Peoples of Russia, which took place in November 1993, made a special appeal to the President and Government to stop any nuclear developments in Amur and Khabarovsk Regions in order to avoid the threat to the local population, including Aborigines.[19] However, there is no indication of considerable changes in state policy regarding further nuclear developments.

A similar appeal on the part of Russian Aborigines has been made in relation to nuclear arms testing and highly radioactive wastes disposal in the area of Novaya Zemlya (Arctic region). In fact, during the several decades that these large islands were used for such purposes, they lost their Aboriginals (they have been relocated to other regions in the Soviet Union since 1957). More than 130 nuclear arms tests have take place on the territory of Novaya Zemlya, leading to dangerous contamination of the natural environment.[20]

Dozens of military submarines, most of them with nuclear engines, are stored on the Pacific, hiding the potential risk of nuclear materials leakage. Low-level radioactive wastes are still being buried in the sea waters, both in the North and East of the country. The plutonium production facilities are the largest source of radioactive contamination of Krasnoyarsky krai, where a lot of Siberian Aboriginals live. Thousands of miles away from these facilities, in the wildest areas, it is still easy to find traces of contamination. So far no early warning systems have been put in place for the local population.

Energy development projects: Ethno-environmental impacts

One of the most controversial cases demonstrating the deepening tensions between traditional life and modern approaches to carrying out economic activity relates to the construction of hydrostations. Several huge projects planned by the former USSR government generated intense debate on the feasibility of large constructions in the territories occupied by Aborigines. The most debated case was the construction of Turukhanskaya Hydrodam in the middle of Krasnoyarsky krai. The realization of such a project could lead to the inundation of three million cubic meters of forests and to the displacement of many hundreds of Evenks living in these territories. The environmental impacts of such energy development projects were so obvious that the government was forced to stop the project despite important investments already made.

The difficult lessons learned from Turukhanskaya Hydrodam could not stop similar projects on other Aboriginal territories. Recently, in the middle of Ussuri taiga in Primorski krai, the Russian Ministry for Fuels and Energy started to plan a series of hydrostations to increase the energy supply for selected Far Eastern regions. The reservoir is supposed to cover 400 square kilometres of virgin forests that are now being used by the local Aboriginal people—Iman Udugue—who practice hunting and the collection of honey and wild grasses. All the major locations of this people's traditional activities will be destroyed or considerably changed. The dams on the local rivers will destroy the fishing habitat used intensively by Aborigines. Independent experts have shown that the implementation of such projects would not change the energy situation in the region, but would create new environmental problems, especially regarding traditional activities. Among the seventy species of local wild animals, twenty have important value for Aboriginals in terms of food supply and trade.[21] (See chapter 10 for a U.S. parallel.)

Deforestation has been the result of the development projects and minerals prospecting that have taken place in the Russian Pacific region at an unprecedented rate: by the beginning of the 1990s, 30 percent of all Far Eastern forests had disappeared; 34 percent in Primorsky krai; 42 percent in the Amur region; 39 percent on Sakhalin Island; etc.[22] Such conditions create additional ethnic tensions and conflicts regarding land use patterns.

All these conflicts and failures in the adoption of modern approaches to development were derived—as members of the Russian Parliament E. Gaer and V. Khasnulin indicate—from our "mistaken perception of the cultural backwardness of Aborigines when compared to a technocentric type of civilization. This is an attempt to transform to a European style of life the life of peoples who had chosen a type of civilization based on spiritual relations with the environment and ecological balance."[23]

RECENT DEVELOPMENTS

Three major approaches are now being considered by Russian scientists in relation to the tensions between traditional life and modern approaches: non-interference, or the "laissez-faire" approach; the adoption of reservation status for Aboriginal lands; and the stimulation of "cultural assimilation." However, most of the scientists (Bogoslovskaya L., Kalakin V., Krupnik, I., Vakhtin N., and others) support the idea of reservations,[24] where the Aborigines would be able to manage the natural resources in the traditional way. They also emphasize the lack of any ethnological impact assessment during the industrial and other development projects.[25]

The legislative steps undertaken during the last few years seem to take into account these scientific views. The political reforms in the former Soviet Union and especially the decentralization have created a new basis for local actions, including those aimed at the protection of Aboriginal life.

The radical changes in the former Soviet society since the middle of the 1980s had opened the door to Aboriginal peoples for political activities. Numerous ethnic and political associations were formed, such as the Chukotka Peoples Association; the Regional Eskimo Society; the Yukagir Congress; and others. The First Congress of the Northern Aborigines took place in March 1990. It resulted in a unification of Aboriginal efforts in defending their interests; now the Association of Northern Aboriginals of Russia is in charge of representing Aboriginal interests in the legislative and executive branches. The first NGOs have started to promote environmental goals, such as "Yamal—for the next generation" which united Nenets community leaders.

Some positive changes have been introduced in the administrative structure for Aboriginal regions. For example, after the adoption of the Law on Local Self-Administration (1991), now under revision, the administrative powers for such regions are based in two branches: local administration, and a senior citizens council consisting of tribal chiefs or Elders. The most important changes brought about by the Russian Federation Constitution concerns property rights: natural resources have been declared the property of the people living in a particular territory. This constitutional provision offers large opportunities for Aboriginal peoples. However, no enforcement mechanisms are in place and real application is nonexistent; most of the attempts to come to a fair agreement between Aboriginal communities and industrial companies or ministries have failed or, if agreements were signed, they were not met.

In 1992, the President of the Russian Federation signed a special decree, "On Urgent Matters to Protect the Living Conditions and Traditional Activities of Northern Aborigines," designed to identify the territories supporting traditional nature management and to prevent other uses of these lands. This important step taken by Russian leaders could have had noticeable results for preserving the traditional activities of Russian Aborigines if the national economic situation had not been in such a deep crisis. Just two months later the President signed another decree, "On Urgent Measures to Develop Large Natural Gas Deposits on the Yamal Peninsula, the Barents Sea, and the Sakhalin Island Shelf," which put in doubt the implementation of the previous decree, because most of these natural gas deposits are located on Aboriginal lands.

The International Convention on Aborigines adopted by the UN International Labor Organization in 1989 has not been ratified by the Russian Government and this step is high on the Russian Aboriginal agenda. The other important issue with international dimensions and debated by the Aboriginal community in Russia is the concrete realization of the idea of circumpolar cooperation in the protection of Aboriginal rights and traditions.[26]

The most urgent need on the national political agenda is for the development and adoption of comprehensive legislation on the Aboriginal situation in the Russian Federation. Three major bills are under consideration by Russian federal legislative bodies: "On Aboriginal Status and Ethnic Territorial Entities"; "On Ethnic-Cultural Associations"; "On Territories for Traditional Nature Management."

It is important to state that the Aboriginal peoples of Russia have no special legal status: conditions for them were always subject to the federal government's one-sided interpretation of its responsibility under certain governmental decrees. The major achievement that could be gained from adopting the bill on Aboriginal Status now being debated in Parliament is the definition of "territory of traditional nature management." Such territories should be defined for every Aboriginal people according to their traditional activities needs, and any alienation of these lands should be forbidden. The regime of land use within allocated territories, state regulations, and financial assistance for traditional activities are to be developed and adopted by special legislative acts.[27]

The bill of ethnic-cultural associations provides the legal framework for groups of common cultural origin or aspirations to realize their rights. The bill extends Aboriginal rights to self-administration, political activities, cultural and traditional practices, and increases Aboriginal representation in elected bodies.[28] Special attention is paid to framing the legal rights of Aborigines and other minorities within ethnic territorial entities.[29]

Great expectations are attached in the Russian Aboriginal community to the federal law on traditional nature management drafted by the Russian Parliament. The major goal of such a bill is to identify and protect the areas of traditional Aboriginal activities and to create legal and institutional conditions for Aboriginal self-governance within selected territories. Certain regional governments in Russia have already adopted similar legislation providing a favorable regime for Aboriginal community development in the traditional way, among them the Republic of Yakutia (Sakha) and Khanty-Mancy Autonomous Regions.[30] Since the early 1990s the Yakutia government has allocated 250 billion rubles for Aborigines and other local people in exclusive support of traditional forms of economic activity.[31]

All these legislative and other steps recently undertaken show the urgent need for society to take measures regarding conditions for Aborigines who are under pressures of modern development and severe economic crises that could result in the loss of their ethnic and cultural identity and could threaten their long-term survival. This is especially important for the transitional period of radical change in the economic system. Aborigines now have the highest unemployment rate: 30–35 percent in the Amur region; 90 percent among the Ul'chi, Nanai, and Udegue who live in remote areas of this region; even in the most productive oil and gas regions of West Siberia unemployment among Aborigines has risen by 2.5 times in the last few years.[32] The shutdown of many industrial enterprises has led to large migrations from the Far East and North: in Magadan region alone the population has been reduced from 450,000 to 270,000; the total expected migration from the North and Siberia is estimated at about 3,000,000.[33] All this forces the Aboriginal population to look for the recovery of their traditional lifestyle, but extensive assistance is required. The Director of the Institute of Ethnology and Anthropology of the Russian Academy of Sciences emphasizes that "economic reform should comprise the set of special measures and programs to protect specific interests and rights of Aborigines of the North and Siberia living in a fragile environment and keeping traditional activities. The Aborigines should be provided with special protection on the part of the state, and the principles and conditions of the market economy should not be applied to them in full."[34] The recognition by society of the fairness and rationality of traditional nature management practices is a slow but irrevocable process.

CHRONOLOGIES OF MAJOR EVENTS FOR ABORIGINAL COMMUNITIES IN RUSSIA

1822	First Legal Status is adopted for Aborigines in the Russian Empire.
1918	The First Soviet Constitution incorporates equal rights provisions for ethnic entities.
1924	Institutional and Legal initiatives relating to Aborigines are introduced by the Soviet government. The State Committee on Northern Affairs is formed.
1930	Territorial self-administration is applied to Aborigines.
1930s	Collectivization process in the Soviet Union: Aborigines are gradually involved.

1950s	Economic expansion takes place in the remote areas of the Soviet Union, including the Pacific. Population concentration policy.
1957	First governmental resolution on the revitalization of and state support for traditional Aboriginal activities.
1960s	Mandatory education policy.
Late 1980s	Perestroika and the emergence of Aborigines on the Soviet political scene.
1990	First Congress of Russian Aboriginal peoples. The Russian Aborigines' Association is formed.
1991	USSR disintegration. National debate on sovereignty—Aborigines are involved.
1992	Russian Federation Presidential resolution "On Urgent Measures to Protect the Northern Aborigines Living and Economic Activities Territories."
1993	The new Russian Federation Constitution defines property rights over natural resources as rights of the people living in the relevant territory.
1994–1995	New legislative bills on Aboriginal status, territorial self-administration, and on areas of traditional activities are introduced in the Parliament of the Russian Federation.

NOTES

1. The present estimate of the Aboriginal population at about 200,000 is an underestimation, due particularly to the fact that during the population census and in practical ways some Aborigines prefer to be declared as Russians in order to benefit from all the extra payments offered to resettlers to Nordic and remote regions. Some estimate the Russian Aboriginal population at twice the official figure (see, e.g., *Rossiiskie vesti*), 3 March 1995, p. 12).

2. *Narody Dal'nego Vostoka SSSR v XVII-XX vekakh* (Moscow: 1985), 240 p.

3. Federal Assembly of the Russian Federation, Hearings on the "ILO Convention 169 Ratification" and "On Aboriginal and Nomadic Peoples," 22 November 1994.

4. *Severnye prostory*, 1994, N 4, p. 20.

5. *Meditsinskaya gazeta*, 30 August 1995, p. 22.

6. Regarding the destruction of the Aboriginal living environment it should be noted that many effects and trends have not been documented until recently. In many cases ecological impacts cannot be predicted or discovered until they occur. The other important factor is connected to the restrictions imposed by the former Soviet leadership on environmental and health information flows.

7. It is interesting to note that in 1924 the Far East Soviet Republic—which had the status of a sovereign state until it was abolished and incorporated into the Russian Federation within the Soviet Union in the mid-1920s—had adopted a "Provisional Statute on the Management of Aboriginal Tribes of the Far East." Despite certain opportunities for self-administration left to Aborigines, the document reflected in its major provisions the dominant ideological goals: the assimilation of Aboriginal peoples into modern (Soviet) society.

8. Among the Far Eastern people only the Yakut, who had a relatively high population, were allocated the higher status of self-administration—Autonomous Republic within the Russian Federation.

9. Vachtin, N., *Indigenous People of the Russian Far North: Land Rights and the Environment* (St. Petersburg: 1994), p. 5.

10. *Narody Sovetskogo Severa (1960–1980 gody)* (Moscow: 1991), p. 264.

11. *Traditsii i sovremennost' v kul'ture narodov Dal'nego Vostoka* (Vladivostok: 1983), p. 45.

12. Krupnik, I., *Arkticheskaya etnoekologia* (Moscow: 1989), 225 p.; Vakhtin, N., *Korennoe naselenie Krainego Severa Rossiskoi Federatsii*, (St. Petersburg: 1993), 129 pp.

13. *Severnye prostory*, 1993, N 5–6, p. 11.

14. *Problemy ratsional'nogo prirodopol'zovania i kontrolia kachestva prirodnoi sredy Sibiri* (Yakutsk: Akademia nauk SSSR; 1979), pp. 10–11.

15. Buks, I., Prokhorov, B., "Mestorozhdenia Yamala: komplexnaya otsenka ekologicheskogo riska osvooeniya," *Energiya: economika, technika, ekologia*, 1994, N 5, pp. 2–4.

16. Pipeline explosions and leakages are best known: according to official estimates around 15 percent a year of all oil transported is being lost due to leakages. Recent events in Komi Republic show the tremendous environmental impacts from pipeline accidents; non-governmental groups estimates show that around 200,000 tons of crude oil have contaminated the northern ecosystems.

17. *Novoye vremya*, 1992, N 7, pp. 21–23.

18. *Severnye prostory*, 1993, N 7–8, p. 93.

19. *Severnye prostory*, 1994, N 4, p. 5.

20. *Severnye prostory*, 1993, N 7–8, pp. 22–23. Besides that, during the period 1961–1990 these islands and sea waters were heavily used for the disposal of highly

radioactive wastes: thousands of containers, dozens of nuclear engines, and even nuclear ship reactors. Disclosure of the relevant information during "perestroika" led to strong public protests, and as a result to the prohibition of old practices. The cleanup of abandoned wastes posed a cascade of technical, social, and economic problems that will be hard to solve in the foreseeable future. At the same time the Novaya Zemlya situation is considerably aggravated by the recent decision of the Russian government to create a permanent disposal site for radioactive wastes: the total amount of radioactive waste per year is estimated at 7 billion tons and just 28 percent of this amount is reused (*Izvestia*, 15 June 1995, p. 1).

21. *ECOS Magazine*, 1991, N 2, pp. 40–46.

22. Vakhtin, N., *Op. cit.*, 1993, p. 9.

23. *Rossiishe vesti*, 13 March 1995, pp. 12–13.

24. It is important to note that large areas of the Arctic zone in Russia have very few natural reserves, unlike other parts of the country where the natural reserve system is rather well developed.

25. For more details see Krupnik, I., *Op. cit.*, 1989.

26. See, for example, Romanov, G., "Daleko ne rai. Desyatiletie korennykh narodov mire i tsirkumpolyarnaya tsivilizatsia," *Polyarnaya zvezda*, N 2, pp. 100–102.

27. Federal Law of the Russian Federation. Draft. "On the Main Principles of Local Territorial Self-Administration in Aboriginal and Minorities' Areas," Moscow, 1994.

28. Federal Law of the Russian Federation. Draft. "On Ethnic-Cultural Citizens' Associations," Moscow, 1994.

29. Federal Law of the Russian Federation. Draft. "On National Minorities' Rights Protection," Moscow, 1995.

30. *Status malochislennykh narodov Rossii. Pravovye akty i dokamenty* (Moscow: 1994), pp. 257–321.

31. *Severnye prostory*, 1994, N 1, p. 23.

32. *Severnye prostory*, 1994, N 6, p. 14; RIA *Novosti. Goryachaya linia*, 25 April 1995.

33. *Sovetskaya Rossia*, 26 September 1995, p. 2.

34. *Natsional'naya politika v Rossiiskoi Federatsii. Materialy mezhdunarodnoi nauchno-prakticheskoi konferentsii, Lipki, sentyabr'* (Moscow: Nauka, 1993), p. 31.

GRAHAM E. JOHNSON and
YUEN-FONG WOON

12. Social Values and Development Patterns in South China: The Case of the Pearl River Delta Region in the 1990s*

Economic development in the post-Mao era can have a significant impact upon the environment. Such development is marked by two major policy initiatives: the Open Door policy and the decentralization of economic decision-making power to the *zhen*, each of which is a rural community made up of an average population of 60,000 to 100,000 or thirty natural villages. This decentralization policy has made it meaningful for us to study the economic strategies of the *zhen*, the *guanliqu* (brigade), the natural villages, and the individual households in the Pearl River Delta region.

Historically, the Pearl River Delta region was the point of origin of a majority of the Overseas Chinese in Hong Kong and North America. Being the earliest recipient of the new economic policies of the post-Mao era, this region has become one of the fastest developing economies in the world. In this chapter we are focusing on the impact of industrialization,

* This research project has been made possible by the generous support of the Research Grants Division of the Social Sciences and Humanities Research Council of Canada to which we are deeply grateful. Our heartfelt thanks also go to the Chinese Consul General in Vancouver, the Guangdong Overseas Chinese Affairs Office, and to all the local hosts, cadres, and villagers in our field sites. We would also like to thank Dr. George Lin for the use of the map designed by him. We take full responsibility for the interpretation and errors in this chapter.

215

commercialization, and globalization on four *zhen* in this region in the 1990s—viz. Fuching Zhen of Dongguan County, Leliu Zhen of Shunde County, Lougang Zhen of Guangzhou Municipality, and Duanfen Zhen of Taishan County. Our study, which concentrates on questions of agricultural and non-agricultural land use in each locality, does have significant environmental implications for South China.

Our findings suggest that from a macro perspective, all four *zhen* in the 1980s and 1990s are following a development path similar to that of parts of East and Southeast Asia of the 1970s. However, from a micro viewpoint, the unique blending of Confucian, Maoist, and Post-Mao values and approaches has resulted in *each zhen*'s creating its own unique pattern of development and response to the environment.

THEORETICAL ISSUES

In the 1960s, social scientists subscribing to the modernization theory believed that industrialization and commercialization necessarily result in rapid urbanization. Development in Third World countries would mirror the processes observed in Western Europe and North America. These changes were interpreted as signs of progress.[1] In the 1970s, dependency theory in turn became the dominant paradigm in the literature of development.[2] It emphasizes the detrimental effects of globalization on the peasantry. It also asserts that as a result of industrialization and the subsequent urbanization of the population, peasant communities suffer from disintegration and peasants lose their cushion for survival.[3]

In the 1980s, McGee's study of rural development in Asia seems to provide an alternative paradigm.[4] He notes that in some parts of East and Southeast Asia, those characterized by high population densities and formerly dominated by wet rice agriculture, "desakota zones" have emerged in the wake of the region's development.[5] These zones, stretching along linear corridors between large city cores, are characterized by an intensive mixture of agricultural and non agricultural activities. Inside these zones, peasants work in rural industry, petty commodity production, small service concerns, and other non-agricultural employment while still staying in their home communities. As a result, the already crowded cities have not become more crowded, the peasants have not suffered from dislocation, and the environment has not been seriously degraded.

Neither modernization theory nor its major theoretical challenge, dependency theory, is able to account for the "desakota process." Both conventional approaches, despite their differences, agree upon a rural/ urban dichotomy. McGee and his associates argue that the rural/urban dichotomy imposes an analytical rigidity and is too closely based upon the experience of Europe and North America, presuming a commonality on development processes which is unfounded.[6]

Using the Pearl River Delta region as a case study, this chapter will first describe the "desakota process" in South China in the 1980s and 1990s. We will divide the whole delta region into four differing areas: the eastern delta, the central delta, Guangzhou and its immediate hinterland, and the western delta, and examine the distinct pattern of rural transformation in each of the sites. This will be followed by an analysis of the political, economic, and social factors that account for these places' unique characteristics. The purpose is to illustrate that peasant communities are *not* necessarily victims of industrialization, commercialization, and globalization. Instead of turning into members of a mass society, peasants and local leaders may work out distinct community strategies to make full use of opportunities in the wake of economic reform and the open door policy in the period after 1979.

THE PEARL RIVER DELTA REGION

Guangdong Province, located strategically along China's south coast, is a large province of substantial geographic, economic, and cultural diversity. Its economic core is the Pearl River Delta, with Guangzhou as its regional center. The delta also contains Hong Kong, Macao, and two of the three Special Economic Zones that were located in Guangdong after the promulgation of the new open door policy in 1979 (see map, p. 218) .

A mere twenty years ago, the Pearl River Delta region was a well-defined rural area, dominated by double cropping rice. Its development through the late 1970s was the result of a national strategy to give the province's development an agricultural focus. This had been in place for almost thirty years, since the incorporation of Guangdong Province into the People's Republic of China. Its potential for light industrial development was compromised and there was hostility to the long-established commercial skills within the province.[7] Nevertheless, the Pearl River

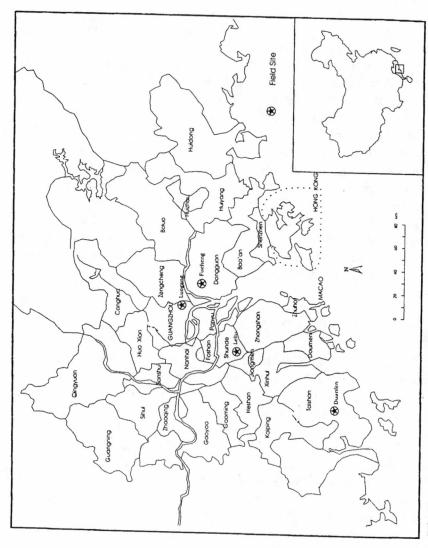

The Pearl River Delta Open Economic Region

Delta region was still the major provincial producer of cash crops such as fish, sugar cane, silk cocoons, fruit, and vegetables.

For the production of grain or cash crops, the Central State insisted on a collective approach. Like other parts of China, natural villages, lineages, and marketing communities became production teams, brigades, and communes.[8] A large state-organized planning apparatus intervened in the Chinese peasant economy.

The Pearl River Delta region has long been an area of outmigration. From the mid-nineteenth century large numbers of emigres from south and southeast China did unskilled labor in the Americas, southern Africa, and Southeast Asia. Between 1949 and 1979, national policies toward Overseas Chinese dependents were marked by misunderstandings and hostility. This, naturally, caused estrangement among Overseas Chinese and produced difficulties and privations for their dependents in the Pearl River Delta region.[9]

Under different circumstances, many delta residents left for Hong Kong in the late 1940s and early 1950s, and contributed to Hong Kong's post-1950 economic transformation. Just across the border, the Pearl River Delta region was insulated from the global economy through national policy, which discouraged international trade and investment. Out of touch with Hong Kong and the global economy, the region in the intervening decades suffered results that contrasted sharply with Hong Kong's boom.[10]

ECONOMIC REFORM AND THE OPEN DOOR

Starting from late 1978, the reforms associated with the leadership of Deng Xiaoping have brought about a shift from an insulated, state-dominated economic system to one that is more open to market forces and the global economy.[11] This has been accompanied by the drastic decentralization of economic decision-making power. Since 1985, the Pearl River Delta region has been designated as an "Open Economic Region." Both rural and urban areas can exercise considerable autonomy in order to seek foreign investment and they are allowed to retain a large percentage of the foreign exchange earnings.

Coming at the end of a ten-year period of xenophobia that characterized the Cultural Revolution, China's "open door" policy was, in fact, not wide open to Western investment in the early 1980s. Rather, it was the entrepreneurial skills and capital of Chinese in Hong Kong and in North America that were actively sought. Kinship connections and local loyalties became a central part of development initiatives.

The Pearl River Delta region is home for the large majority of Hong Kong and North American Chinese. To take advantage of this fact, decentralization of economic decision-making power in this region has been extended to the level of the counties and municipalities (shi), and in many cases to the level of the zhen (formerly people's commune) and the guanliqu (formerly production brigade). Local cadres and inhabitants of rural communities have therefore become part of a collective strategy responding to new opportunities implicit in the region's incorporation into the world system.

In December 1991, the national government passed an organic Law, extending the decentralization policy even further. This law called for the establishment of democratically constituted Villagers' Committees and Community Shareholding Cooperatives to manage collective rural enterprises and redistribute net profits to members of indigenous households.[12]

However, the passing on of economic decision-making power to rural communities does not mean the Central Sate has no control over the reform process, particularly when it comes to protecting major city interests and state enterprises' economic integrity. For example, the Guangdong Government and the Guangzhou Municipal Government both allow a certain amount of labor mobility. They try, however, to confine this mobility to small and medium size towns as much as possible, instead of allowing peasants to settle permanently in the already-crowded metropolis of Guangzhou.

In addition, the Central State retains significant influence over generalized land use. In the 1990s, in response to the mass transformation of land from agricultural to non-agricultural uses, the Beijing Government decided to tighten land regulations. In March 1994, Agricultural Land Protection legislation came into effect. Thereafter, local areas could shift land out of "an agricultural reserve" only under the most stringent conditions, thus protecting the rural environment against industrial erosion.

FOUR FIELD SITES IN THE PEARL RIVER DELTA REGION

For more than a decade, we have observed the process of rural transformation in the Pearl River Delta region in the wake of economic reform and the open door policy. We have come to the conclusion that such a transformation confirms McGee's description of the "desakota process" that is occurring in other parts of East and Southeast Asia. We also find, however, diversities within the Pearl River Delta region.

We have identified four patterns of development, broadly corresponding to the different locations within the region: the eastern delta as represented by Dongguan Shi, the central delta as represented by Shunde Shi, the Guangzhou hinterland as represented by Luogang Zhen, and the western delta as represented by Taishan Shi. The purpose here is to describe the "desakota process" for each area, focusing particularly on the development of one *zhen* (formerly people's commune) and within each zhen, the development of one *guanliqu* (formerly production brigade).

DONGGUAN SHI IN THE EASTERN DELTA: FULLY OPEN TO THE WORLD

Dongguan Shi lies along the Hong Kong-Shenzhen-Guangzhou corridor. It is representative of the eastern delta "desakota process." Here, we have selected Fucheng Zhen, a former commune, and Wantong Guanliqu, a former production brigade, as our focus.

Dongguan Shi has taken full opportunity of new policy options after 1979, utilizing investment resources and skills of Hong Kong capitalists for economic development. In the thirteen years after 1979, US $1,375 billion was invested by outside interests. At the end of 1992, 8,000 enterprises were established with capital from external sources.

The dramatic transformation of Dongguan began with a massive local strategy of infrastructural development, which put in place an effective telephone system (including a cellular network), an augmented electricity generating capacity, a top of the line water supply system, and an elaborate highway system.

Four major highways and a network of ten subsidiary highways have led to a major transformation of the landscape. Hills are being leveled while paddy land and other formerly marginal areas (forested or low productivity land) have disappeared from view. These have been replaced by roads or factory buildings and, since 1991, enormous commercial-residential complexes.

Fucheng Zhen is a former commune adjacent to Dongguan City. The gradual shift from agricultural to industrial land use has accelerated since

1985. Up until 1994, this has been the major policy goal. At present, Fucheng has more than 500 enterprises, employing over 30,000 workers.

The links of Fucheng as a whole to the global economy are direct. Many of the village-run enterprises, producing such things as garments and plastics, are subsidiaries of Hong Kong-based manufacturers. The products are destined for Hong Kong and for re-export to Europe and North America. All the *guanliqu* in Fucheng have established industrial estates with new plants and dormitory immigrant work force, at a cost far below the present average in Hong Kong.

Wantong Guanliqu, like the rest of Fucheng Zhen, has responded quickly to the changed circumstances after 1979. The *guanliqu* thrived under collectivization —a star performer in land reclamation projects during the Great Leap Forward resulting in high grain yields and relatively high per capita income even before 1979.

Reform policies resulted in Wantong's rapid industrialization. Currently, only 34 percent of the indigenous labor force is engaged strictly in household-managed agricultural production. The rest work in enterprises, mostly collective entities run by the village.

Not all village-run enterprises in Wantong have been industrial. Starting in the mid 1980s, vegetables were cultivated year-round for Hong Kong markets by a collective enterprise working jointly with a Hong Kong-based entrepreneur. It employs wage workers, mostly villagers.

Wantong is also making major inroads into tourism. It has gone into partnership with another Hong Kong capitalist to create a "holiday village," complete with villas, a handsome restaurant, and a variety of leisure activities. This business venture was set up with the leisure needs of the increasingly affluent Hong Kong residents clearly in mind.

In general, the development of Dongguan Shi has significantly improved villagers' earnings in the 1990s. The Villagers' Committees and the Shareholding Cooperatives owning the land have accumulated an enormous amount of net profit from collective agricultural and non-agricultural enterprises. This has resulted in substantial dividends redistributed to indigenous households.

Openness to the global economy through Hong Kong has definitely raised the standard of living in Dongguan. This, however, has had its costs, including industrial pollution and loss of productive agricultural land. Dongguan saw its arable land diminish by 25 percent in the 1980s.

The process continues, accelerated, in the 1990s. Since 1993, five of the nineteen *guanliqu* in Fucheng Zhen are completely lacking in agricultural land. In 1979, Fucheng boasted self-sufficiency of all its food needs in addition to a substantial export of foodstuffs. Since 1994, pork and grain have had to be imported from outside.

To prevent further deterioration of this situation, Dongguan has yielded to Central State directives and installed stringent land control legislation as of March 1994. Wantong, for example, has become one of four *guanliqu* in Fucheng Zhen designated as an "agricultural reserve area."

This national policy prevents Dongguan Shi from becoming completely urbanized. Its rural areas are centers for mixed agricultural and non-agricultural activities and development. The "desakota" nature of the landscape described by McGee for other parts of Asia remains a feature of the Dongguan development.

SHUNDE SHI IN THE CENTRAL DELTA: SUSTAINABLE DEVELOPMENT

Shunde Shi lies along the central corridor from Guangzhou south to the Zhuhai Special Economic Zone bordering on Macao. It is our central delta representative for the "desakota process." Here, we have selected Leliu Zhen and within it, Nanshui Guanliqu as our focus of study.

Shunde Shi, even during the pre-reform period, was a center for commercialized agriculture. Fish, silk cocoons, and sugar cane were the core of this vibrant agriculture that was rice deficient, even during the 1970s' Maoist "grain first" policy.

In the wake of rural reforms, Shunde's agricultural sector has flourished. Cocoons, sugar cane, and peanut crops have been victims of pollution and low market demand. The production of fish, fruits, vegetables, flowers, and high quality livestock, however, has expanded dramatically. The products are destined for domestic markets, Hong Kong/Macao, and beyond. The fish ponds, in particular, remain the central element in the delicate ecology of Shunde. They symbolize local pride and identity, but also form an extremely lucrative industry.

As Shunde Shi has a centralized location, it has attracted substantial Hong Kong investment. Hong Kong's role in Shunde's industrialization is, however, muted because the prosperous commercialized agriculture of

Shunde provides much investment funding. As a result, the pressure to convert land from agricultural to commercial and industrial uses is not as intense as in Dongguan. Nevertheless, such conversions are occurring.

Since the late 1970s, Shunde Shi has moved rapidly along the road of rural industrialization. In 1992, its industrial output was among the highest of any comparable units in Guangdong, including Dongguan Shi. Much like Dongguan, the private sector in Shunde is small in comparison to the collective sector. The market towns have become centers of industrial growth, dominated by factory complexes, banks, restaurants, and other service facilities. They are important for local employment.

Because it is less reliant on Hong Kong capital, Shunde's industrial product mix differs significantly from that of Dongguan. It is less involved with textiles, toys, and plastics destined for re-export through Hong Kong. Shunde is known throughout China for its high quality domestic appliances, such as fans, refrigerators, rice cookers, sterilizers, washing machines, and air conditioners. China's domestic market is in fact more significant than the world market in Shunde's industrial development.

Leliu Zhen, our research unit in Shunde, possessed no rice paddies even during the Maoist era. As in the rest of Shunde, commercialized and export-oriented agricultural production, particularly fish, allowed its peasant cultivators to enjoy relative prosperity.

Leliu's economic activity is no longer dependent on the complex of rivers. It is oriented toward an elaborate modern road system. Non-agricultural development is dispersed throughout the *zhen*, and industrial value is equally distributed between the *zhen* and the *guanliqu* levels.

Nanshui Guanliqu in Leliu Zhen has changed less than other places in Shunde since reform. At present, its industrial development is still modest, and about 70 percent of the village labor force remains in agricultural production. During the Maoist era, Nanshui was regarded as a model unit for learning from Dazhai. Despite the reform policies in the post-Mao era, this *guanliqu* chooses to remain aloof from rapid rural transformation. There is intense village solidarity: its agricultural economy is efficient and its commitment to collectively managed village economy is strong.

The organization of production in Nanshui Guanliqu does not differ dramatically from the 1960s and 1970s. Fish ponds are usually contracted by older men in cooperation with men from other households. In 1994, management was resumed by the *guanliqu* itself. The fish ponds were put up for short-term competitive bidding because production value had increased dramatically since the last round of contracts in 1983–84.

In general, our study indicates that in Shunde, there is continuity even in the middle of dramatic changes. Like Dongguan, Shunde has changed, but unlike Dongguan, these changes have not been beyond recognition.

At present, Shunde people have the highest per capita rural income in Guangdong Province. They also receive substantial dividends redistributed by Villagers' Committees and Shareholding Cooperatives, which were established around 1992. Such dividends are derived mostly from rural industrial enterprises, among the most productive in the whole of China. A minor portion of dividends have also come from collectively owned fish ponds which are traditionally organized around cooperative principles.

Lucrative dividends from collective assets are often cited by our interviewees as their major reason for not wanting to move to the cities. We have also found very little resentment or reluctance from our subjects regarding the "agricultural reserves" policy put into place in Shunde in March 1994. This is because this policy dovetails nicely with their own desire to preserve their community's ecology, in spite of the major transformation taking place.

The rural area of Shunde is still the site of both agricultural and non-agricultural activities, which indicates that the "desakota zones" are still alive and well. In contrast to Dongguan, Shunde's "desakota zones" are maintained by choice rather than legislation from the Central State.

LUOGANG ZHEN IN THE GUANGZHOU HINTERLAND: TIES THAT BIND

Baiyun District is officially an "urban" district directly under the control of the Guangzhou Municipal Government. The population of its thirteen *zhen* is, however, predominantly rural. For our study of the Guangzhou hinterland, we have chosen Luogang Zhen of Baiyun District and its component village of Jianjiang Guanliqu as our focus.

Luegang Zhen, like Shunde Shi, has a strong commercialized agricultural base. Its comparative advantage is a long history of growing fruits such as oranges, lychees, and pineapples. However, in complete contrast to Shunde, there has been very little growth in industry in the last decade.

Luogang's fruit production is geared toward the local market particularly the urban core of Guangzhou. It is true that some of its fruits, particular lychees, are exported to Hong Kong. However, this does not result in prosperity for the producers. Luogang is part of the Guangzhou Metropolitan Region, so that all its exports have to go through the buying agents of the Provincial Foreign Trade Corporation which may not offer high purchasing prices.

In the early 1980s, Luogang Zhen prospered because the terms for domestic sales had improved dramatically. Household income in Luogang was substantially increased in the early reform period partly because the government offered a higher purchase price for all farm products. As well, much of the red tape was reduced for domestic sales: Luogang no longer had to sell all its fruits to the highly bureaucratic state agencies stationed in Guangzhou. It could now engage actively in domestic private marketing, which had become lucrative in this period. The increased economic activities that had arisen in the wake of the reforms led to a dramatic increase in disposable household income throughout the Pearl Delta region, and Luogang's fruits sold well in the open market.

However, domestic market forces soon shifted to Luogang's disadvantage. In the early stages of reform, fruit specialists from Luogang were extensively recruited to assist other localities' diversification of agriculture. These other locations in the delta became Luogang's competitors. At the end of the 1980s, when newly established citrus groves came into production throughout the delta, fruit prices tumbled, and Luogang suffered. It is lucky that Luogang is close to centers of labor demand (especially in construction work), which has permitted villagers to seek employment outside agriculture. Many now commute to work in downtown Guangzhou while still maintaining residence in Luogang Zhen.

All in all, Luogang has not undergone any fundamental change in the last decade. It remains firmly embedded in the agricultural sector. The town center has a population of only 3,000, and has remained virtually unchanged since the 1970s. The local cadre we interviewed indicated that the *zhen* town would soon expand and an area of about 1,000 mu has been prepared for its commercial development, but even this is a joint venture with Baiyun District.

Jianjiang Guanliqu, our field site, has similarly undergone little change in the past decade. In 1993, more than 100 mu of village land was repossessed by provincial authorities for road improvements, after a compensation of RMB 50,000 per mu was paid. Some of the monies were distributed to peasant households, while others were used for collective welfare. The remaining money was not used for setting up collective industrial enterprises; it was deposited in the bank to earn interest instead.

In general, Luogang Zhen did not undergo the kind of rural transformation that similar units in Dongguan Shi or Shunde Shi experienced. This is largely because it has been firmly linked to the state agencies in a fashion that is atypical of units outside the Guangzhou urban core. Any of Luogang's future plans for industrial or commercial development must be "studied" by a Guangzhou Government which obviously has numerous other priorities in mind. As of March 1994, long term development prospects for Luogang are further constrained by the aforementioned Central State legislation's freezing much of its land as "agricultural reserves."

There are two reasons why rural inhabitants of mountainous Luogang Zhen have not left to join downtown Guangzhou's mass society. The first reason is that the net profits from collective enterprises are being redistributed by the Villagers' Committees and Shareholding Cooperatives as dividends to the indigenous households. The second reason, perhaps the more important one, is that the Guangzhou Government has not allowed Luogang natives working in the urban core to formally apply for permanent settlement there.

Thus, it is largely the migration and land protection legislation upheld by the Central State which prevents Luogang and its rural population from being absorbed by Guangzhou's urban sprawl. Currently, Luogang Zhen can adequately be described as a "desakota zone." It does have several collective industrial enterprises such as a pharmaceutical plant, a furniture-making workshop, and a garment factory, the products of which are geared toward the export market. Its rural inhabitants, however, are engaged more in agricultural activities than non-agricultural ones.

TAISHAN SHI IN THE WESTERN DELTA:
OVERSEAS CHINESE LINKS

Taishan Shi is on the western fringes of the Pearl River Delta region. It does not have proximity to Hong Kong, Macao, the Special Economic Zones of Shenzhen and Zhuhai, or Guangzhou Shi. In our examination of the "desakota process" in this area, our focus is Duanfen Zhen and a component part, Jianglian Guanliqu.

Taishan Shi lacks economic transformation because of its inadequate communications system and relatively remote geographical location. Even in the 1990s, it is still a bucolic rural landscape firmly based on grain production. Industrial activities are modest and enterprises are rarely found at the village level. Unlike our three other case studies, the opportunity for Taishan Shi to attract outside investments in commercialized agricultural enterprises or industrial enterprises is limited.

The private economy, however, is thriving. The service and commercial sectors, as well as petty commodity production centered around the household are well developed. This is because of the consumer market created by the dramatic increase in overseas remittances and the presence of an increasing number of high-income Overseas Chinese visitors in the community.

Taishan's history has indeed been dramatically shaped by Overseas Chinese connections. Relying largely on overseas remittances for funds, it reached a golden era in the 1920s and 1930s. These same remittances and overseas connections unfortunately became the basis for discrimination once Taishan became incorporated into the People's Republic, especially during the Cultural Revolution. After 1979, as a result of the new Overseas Chinese policy, many of the harsh political judgments were reversed. Since then, the overseas emigres have been renewing links with their ancestral communities.

At present, the funds that flow into Taishan from the North American and Hong Kong/Macao Chinese, substantial as they are, are put primarily into the private economy or public projects such as schools, roads, bridges, homes to respect the aged, and hospitals, in much the same way as during the pre-1949 period.

Duanfen Zhen, our research site in Taishan Shi, is a typical Overseas Chinese homeland. Its collective economy is very weak in comparison to the private sector. This is because much overseas remittance is directed toward supporting relatives in the home villages rather than investing in collective enterprises. While some Overseas Chinese dependents use this money for small businesses, many are not so enterprising. They await their chance to join relatives abroad instead of taking an interest in local economic endeavor. Out-migration, as opposed to entrepreneurship, is the dream of rural households of Duanfen Zhen, the so-called "Overseas

Chinese mentality," obsessed with the possibility of a life abroad. There is still the belief that "Golden Mountain" exists to improve the life chances of these people and their descendants.

Jianglian Guanliqu in Duanfen Zhen is deeply affected by this "Overseas Chinese mentality." Since 1979, many have left in response to family reunification initiatives in such countries as Canada and the United States. Forty percent of the houses are left empty and many plots of land abandoned as a result. To deal with the problem, Jianglian Guanliqu subcontracts the land on a short-term basis to outsiders, mostly from Guangxi Province.

In general, the emergence of "desakota zones" in Taishan Shi is even slower than that of Luogang Zhen because of the lack of rural industrialization. Villagers are engaged more in agricultural than non-agricultural activities. Collective enterprises are not prosperous enough for the Villagers' Committees or Shareholding Cooperatives to distribute any dividends to indigenous households.

The agricultural nature of Taishan Shi will remain for an indefinite period of time, because the Central State decided in 1994 to freeze a large majority of its land as "agricultural reserves." Industrialization and commercial development will be confined to Taishan City and a small number of *zhen* in its immediate hinterland.

Our study shows that while Taishan Shi has substantial links abroad, such global connections have not resulted in dramatic rural transformation similar to that of Dongguan. Overseas ties have only caused massive emigration, development of the private sector, and impressive public welfare and social infrastructural developments.

DISCUSSION: SOCIAL VALUES AND PATTERNS OF DEVELOPMENT

As can be seen from the above, the concept of "desakota" adequately sums up the process of economic transformation in the Pearl River Delta region in the last fifteen years. There is, however, no single pattern of development. In this paper, we have outlined four different development paths. This diversity is the result of the interaction between state policies, market forces, and an array of local social values.

State policies promulgated by Beijing have the most immediate impact on the patterns of development of the Pearl River Delta region. It is the decentralization of economic decision-making power that has given more leeway to the *zhen* and the *guanliqu* in Shunde, Dongguan, and Taishan to develop in their own unique ways. In contrast, Luogang's economic development and labor mobility are hampered because it lies within the Guangzhou Government's orbit and any initiative must be channeled through municipal bureaucracy.

The policy of setting up agricultural reserves, which was applied across the board in March 1994, has had a differential impact on various localities within the Pearl River Delta region. It retards rural industrialization in Luogang and Taishan but, at the same time, prevents Dongguan from becoming urbanized and industrialized to the point of no return.

Market forces constitute another variable with an immediate impact on development patterns within the Pearl River Delta region. The degree of proximity to the large urban markets of Guangzhou, Hong Kong, Macao, and the Special Economic Zones affects our research sites in a profound way. For example, the highly commercialized agriculture in Shunde Shi and Luogang Zhen, already prominent during the Maoist period, has become more so with the rise of private marketing and the increased household incomes in these large urban centers. Such market forces have favored Shunde's fish production but worked to the disadvantage of Luogang's fruit orchards.

Likewise, the rise of land and labor costs in Hong Kong has caused massive amounts of Hong Kong capital to flow across the border. This led directly to a more thorough industrial transformation in Dongguan than in any other of our research sites. By the same token, Dongguan's rapid incorporation into the global economy through Hong Kong has changed it into a dependent economy. By contrast, Taishan Shi, the most remote of these sites, has been the least transformed.

While it is clear that economic and political factors have played direct roles in shaping different development patterns and impacts upon the environment in the Pearl River Delta region, we believe that the role of *social values* cannot be ignored. As the Pearl River Delta is an "Open Economic Region" set up to involve the Chinese abroad, we must additionally examine roles played by the values system of both Overseas Chinese and locals in economic development.

The social values of Overseas Chinese in the 1990s are derived from their Neo-Confucian philosophy. The Chinese emigres, whether in Hong

Kong, Macao, North America, or elsewhere, have remained loyal to ancestral points of origin, in spite of decades abroad and unjust and hostile treatment by the People's Republic. Once political persecution of their dependents ceased and confiscated houses and property were returned, the Chinese abroad again became involved with their home communities.

To be admired and remembered as "benefactors" of their ancestral village, the Chinese in Hong Kong and North America have been enthusiastic in donating to public projects. By contrast, to avoid being regarded as "exploiters," they have shown reluctance to invest in productive enterprises at home. This attitude has had the most profound effect on Taishan's development. As a region that is remote geographically, making investment less profitable, there are far more donors than investors among its emigres abroad.

The social values of the local inhabitants and the local cadres is another factor shaping the patterns of development in the Pearl River Delta region. By tradition, South China's rural inhabitants possess an intense local loyalty—loyalty to their lineage and their marketing community. It is a loyalty furthered during the period of intensive agricultural collectivism in the 1960s and 1970s directed by three layers of bureaucracies created by Mao—the commune, the brigade, and the production team.[13]

Economic reforms in the post-Mao era have not caused major changes in property rights structure or institutional arrangements in the rural area.[14] The rural industrialization process has largely operated within pre-reform administrative structures, notably the people's commune.

The modus operandi of the recently established Villagers' Committees and Shareholding Cooperatives is a unique example of continuities with the past. Net profits from collective assets are redistributed only to the indigenous households, which for centuries have held topsoil rights by virtue of descent or marriage. This practice is reminiscent of the policy of distributing basic grains during the commune period or of the lineage pork distribution in the pre-1949 period.

In Dongguan, Shunde, and Luogang, the redistribution of dividends has been cited as a major reason why many rural inhabitants do not forgo their native village membership. This factor, however, is not significant in Taishan, because its collective economy is too weak to yield any dividends. Its inhabitants are more deeply affected by another set of social values—the "Overseas Chinese mentality" which makes them desire to leave for Overseas reunification.[15]

As can be predicted, intense local pride has played a significant role in shaping development patterns in the Pearl River Delta region. The most obvious example is Shunde's community. Rather than offering subsidiaries of Hong Kong-based manufacturers producing labor-intensive items for the world markets, Shunde uses its own capital to produce high quality appliances for China's domestic markets. It also insists on retaining its distinctive landscape created by commercial aquaculture over a lengthy period of time. In villages such as Nanshui Guanliqu, the rural landscape has hardly been changed in the last decade, because the local cadres and inhabitants have chosen to remain aloof from rapid industrialization.

The above analysis shows that peasants and their local leaders are still very much in control of economic transformation in the Pearl River Delta region. Far from showing "dependency" to the forces of industrialization, commercialization, and globalization, Pearl River Delta communities have preserved their unique character and relationship with Nature and are protected against uncontrollable elements.

Looking into the future, we believe that the "desakota zones" of the Pearl River Delta region will continue to exist. Rural communities there will not disintegrate, nor will urban sprawl take over agricultural land use, making rural inhabitants into members of the mass society and destroying the environment.

As the results of our investigation made clear, the *zhen* of the post-Mao era is not an artificial unit. It is an administrative, social, and economic unit superimposed upon the commune which has gone through thirty years of Maoist intensive collective socialism and local self-reliance. The commune, in turn, was built upon a marketing community with a deep history (some say over 1000 years) and a well-entrenched peasant subculture with topsoil rights. The decentralization of decision-making power in the post-Mao era has enabled each of these communities to take advantage of economic reforms and the open door policies to carve out its own development paths in the 1980s and 1990s. It is inconceivable that the local inhabitants or the local officials will easily give up their entrenched rights.

Helping these internal forces of community cohesion is a confluence of three external forces that help to prevent urban sprawl from eating up agricultural land in the "desakota zones." The first one is the presence of a strong Central State which insists on preserving farmland. The second is the presence of a large number of urbanites in Hong Kong and other major cities in the Pearl River Delta region whose food culture creates an incessant demand for fresh fish, livestock, vegetables, and fruits—a demand that can only be satisfied by commercialized agriculture in their immediate rural hinterland. Last, though certainly not the least important, is the nostalgia of the Overseas Chinese and their Neo-Confucian concerns to preserve Nature and to beautify their home villages. One can therefore conclude that the development of "desakota zones," while following the general East Asian pattern described by McGee, can also be seen as a manifestation of development with "Chinese characteristics," which values the natural environment.

NOTES

1. Wilbert E. Moore, *The Impact of Industry* (Englewood Cliffs, N.J.: Prentice Hall, 1965); Walt Whitman Rostow, *The Stages of Economic Growth: A Non-Communist Manifesto* (Cambridge: Cambridge University Press, 1960); Neil Joseph Smelser, "Mechanism of Change and Adjustment to Change," in B. F. Hoselitz and W. E. Moore, *Industrialization and Society* (The Hague: UNESCO and Mouton, 1963), pp. 32–54.

2. Samir Amin, *Unequal Development* (New York: Monthly Review Press, 1976); Gavin N. Kitching, *Development and Underdevelopment in Historical Perspective* (London and New York: Methuen Press, 1982). See also Alvin Y. So, *Social Change and Development; Modernization, Dependency and World System Theories* (Newbury Park: Sage Publications, 1990).

3. Peter Worsley, *The Three Worlds: Culture and World Development* (London: Weidenfeld and Nicholson, 1984).

4. Terry G. McGee, "Urbanisasi or Kotadesasi? Evolving Patterns of Urbanization in Asia," L. Ma, A. Noble, and A. Dutt, eds., *Urbanization in Asia* (Honolulu: University of Hawaii Press, 1989), pp. 93–108; Terry G. McGee, "The Emergence of the Desakota Regions in Asia: Expanding a Hypothesis," in Norris Ginsburg; Bruce Koppel, and Terry G. McGee. eds., *The Extended Metropolis: Settlement Transition in Asia* (Honolulu: University of Hawaii Press, 1991), pp. 3–26.

5. "Desakota" is a Malay term meaning market-town community. It is neither completely urban nor completely rural. Within the community, many villagers are doing "city-type jobs" but are not members of the mass society. While

"desakota zones" began to develop in the freer economies of East Asia in the 1970s, the centralized economies of the socialist bloc, including that of the PRC, had to wait until economic reforms were initiated by the governments in the 1980s and 1990s.

6. See, for example, Bruce Koppel, "The Rural-Urban Dichotomy Examined: Beyond the Ersatz Debate?", in N. Ginsburg, T. McGee, and B. Koppell, eds., *The Extended Metropolis: Settlement Transition in Asia*, pp. 47–90.

7. Helen F. Siu, *Agents and Victims in South China: Accomplices in Rural Revolution* (New Haven: Yale University Press, 1989).

8. George William Skinner, "Peasant Marketing in China," (in three parts), *Journal of Asian Studies* 24, 1–3 (1964): 3–43, 195–228, 363–99; H. F. Schulman, *Ideology and Organization in Communist China* (Berkeley and Los Angeles: University of California Press, 1968); William Parish, "China—Team, Brigade, or Commune?" *Problems of Communism* 25, 2 (Mar-Apr 1976): 51–76.

9. Glen D. Peterson, "Socialist China and the Huaqiao: The Transition to Socialism in the Overseas Chinese Areas of Rural Guangdong, 1949–1956," *Modern China* 14, 3 (July 1988): 309–35.

10. Ezra F. Vogel, *One Step Ahead in China: Guangdong Under Reform* (Cambridge: Harvard University Press, 1989).

11. Dali Yang, "China Adjusts to the World Economy: The Political Economy of China's Coastal Development Strategy," *Pacific Affairs* 65, 1 (Spring 1991): 42–64.

12. Kevin J. O'Brien, "Villagers' Committees: Implementing Political Reform in China's Villages," *Australian Journal of Chinese Affairs* 32 (July 1994): 33–60; Ricky Tung, "The Development of Rural Shareholding Cooperatives Enterprises in Mainland China," *Issues and Studies* 30, 5 (May 1994): 1–30; Tyrene White, "Reforming the Countryside," *Current History* 9, 556 (September 1992): 273–77.

13. William Parish and Martin Whyte, *Village and Family in Contemporary China* (Chicago: University of Chicago Press, 1978).

14. Victor Nee, "Institutional Change and Regional Growth: An Introduction," in Thomas B. Lyons and Victor Nee, eds., *The Economic Transformation of South China: Reform and Development in the Post-Mao Era* (Ithaca: Cornell East Asia Program, 1994); Philip A. Huang, *The Peasant Family and Rural Development in the Yanazi Delta 1350-1988* (Stanford: Stanford University Press, 1990); Sulamith H. Potter and Jack M. Potter, *China's Peasants: The Anthropology of a Revolution* (Cambridge: Cambridge University Press, 1990).

15. See Yuen-fong Woon, "International Links and the Socioeconomic Development of Rural China: An Emigrant Community in Guangdong," *Modern China* 16, 4 (1990): 139–72; Graham E. Johnson and Yuen-Fong Woon, "The Response to Rural Reform in an Overseas Chinese Area: Examples from Two Localities in the Western Pearl River Delta Region, South China," *Modern Asian Studies* (in press).

HAROLD COWARD

Conclusion

In the chapters of this book we have ranged across the Pacific sampling today's tensions between traditional and modern approaches to the environment. Through the voyages of Captains Cook and Vancouver, Europeans came to know of the Pacific as a place of enchanting beauty and bountiful sustenance. Today that beauty can still be found but now in stiff competition with the forces of rapid industrial development. The tension between Nature's bountiful beauty and its ability to sustain modern development is especially acute in the Pacific—as our chapters have shown. The ancient Chinese wisdom of Lao Tzu counsels us to take no activity that is contrary to Nature—to practice *wu-wei*. As humans we are to follow Nature and in doing so our wishes are not eliminated but rather fulfilled.[1] Neither Taoism nor any other traditional wisdom of the Pacific teaches human inactivity, but instead counsels action in harmony with Nature—of which we as humans are but a part. Gro Harlem Brundtland states a similar wisdom in more modern terms: "the 'environment' is where we all live; and 'development' is what we all do in attempting to improve our lot within that abode. The two are inseparable."[2] Too often, as our case study chapters show, we have engaged in development without limiting our activity so as to stay within the bounds of what Nature can provide on a sustainable basis.

In many areas of the Pacific—the forests of British Columbia, the salmon of the Columbia River, the oil, gas, and hydroelectric energy of

Siberia, the fish catch off Japan, and the industrial development of the
Pearl River Delta in China—the tension between development and sustainability has approached the breaking point. But in all of these areas, one
can find attention to traditional values that is guiding human interaction
with Nature into new directions that offer hope for the future. In Part I,
both Head and Hanson identified new trends. Observing that the original
captains of industry, people such as Josiah Wedgwood or Matthew Boulton, showed both a social conscience and a sensitivity to Nature, Head
goes on to point out that at the 1995 Copenhagen World Summit development activity was reconnected with the social and environmental values
of the local people. Thus, the World Bank's use of per capita GNP as a
standard measure of development (a destructive and misleading comparison of progress across societies) is being replaced by the concept of Net
Human Benefit (NHB), which attempts a holistic evaluation. Any criteria
put forward to measure development success must reflect the traditional
values of the Pacific society being considered and not simply impose the
economic values of Europe or America, which credit development in
terms of aggregate economic growth disconnected from social or environmental costs. Hanson notes the post-Rio emergence of the non-governmental organizations (NGOs) as powerful voices in this debate.
Indeed, it is suggested by many that world power now operates on three
levels: (1) the market economy; (2) governments; and (3) NGOs. And it
is the NGOs that have especially taken up the cause of social and environmental damage that modern development often visits on poor and
indigenous peoples.

This was very evident at the 1994 Cairo UN Conference on Population and Development. There, the views of women and the religions had
a strong influence on the drafting of preliminary documents, the Conference discussions, and the resulting "Programme of Action."[3] Unlike earlier summit conferences where the discussion was between governments,
the Cairo meetings opened the doors to input from NGOs, including
many women's and religious groups from the Pacific Basin. This was the
case at the three preparatory meetings at which agenda, themes, and drafts
for the Cairo Conference were prepared. It was also true at Cairo itself
and the subsequent UN meetings in Copenhagen and Beijing. While the
Cairo Conference was focused on the population problem and the development (especially in the education, social status, and employment of
women) needed to deal with it, the analysis quickly made clear that the

issue of environmental degradation could not be left out. As Ruether points out forcefully in chapter 5, wherever women have been exploited for development purposes so has the environment. Her call for a "double transformation of both women and men in their relation to each other and to Nature"[4] has become a clarion call adopted by many NGOs. Ruether offers militarism as the strongest example of the double rape of both women and the earth, and concludes that the change of consciousness needed "is one that recognizes that real 'security' lies, not in dominating power and the impossible quest for total invulnerability, but rather in the acceptance of vulnerability, limits, and interdependency with others, with other humans and the earth."[5] Perhaps the best Pacific illustration of the truth of Ruether's contention is Sokolov's analysis of the destructiveness of militarism on indigenous people and the environment in Eastern Russia (chapter 11).

NGOs as a new third level of organization have begun the "change of consciousness" called for by Ruether. They represent a force and mechanism for global regional democratization and the engagement of traditional values with development processes. Although not yet well developed in many Asian Pacific countries, NGOs are exerting increasing influence in the area. As Hanson makes clear in chapter 2, today international agencies such as the World Bank and the Asian Development Bank are far less likely to support projects destructive of local values and ecology. Also, NGO information channels between developed and developing countries are exerting influence on transnational companies. Corporations working in the Pacific, but headquartered in Europe or North America, are being pressured in those countries to apply the same ecological standards abroad as they do at home. Plants of American corporations in Taiwan are monitored by American NGOs for the same stringent standards the corporation requires of its U.S. plants. However, for companies originating in Japan, Taiwan, Korea, Hong Kong, or Thailand, where strong NGOs have yet to develop, there are far fewer domestic pressures to ensure that the corporation employs the same standards in plants elsewhere as are employed at home. While the NGOs have flourished in the liberal democratic societies of Europe and North America, it remains to be seen how successful they will be in the more hierarchical Asian cultures. As Walls suggests in chapter 3, E-mail and the Internet may help in the development of Asian NGOs. But perhaps there are other approaches based on traditional values and family patterns (e.g., those described in chapter 12's analysis of the Pearl River Delta) that will be employed to limit industrial development. In the pluralistic context of the Pacific Basin a variety of approaches will likely be used.

If NGOs do succeed in Asian countries, it will be because they embody local values regarding human interaction with the environment. And here there are differences! While the notion of undeveloped wilderness ("wildness" as Thoreau called it) is well established in the modern West (witness the national parks of North America) and indeed is a basic principle of the "Deep Ecology" movement, there is disagreement as to its acceptability in Asian cultures. According to Walls in chapter 3, the Chinese widely follow an allegorical tale of Zhuang Zi which teaches the dangers of imposing too much civilization on primal Nature—wilderness is to be preserved and respected in its natural state. It is good to have undeveloped spaces between the developed spaces of civilization. Thus national parks and Buddhist gardens. However, another Third World writer does not agree. Guha argues that not only is the wilderness approach antithetical to traditional Asian values, but when introduced to Asia the emphasis on wilderness is harmful. In North America it may make sense to save pristine real estate from greedy developers by designating it a National Park. But this approach does further emphasize the view that people are separate from Nature, and that some unspoiled piece of Nature should be kept pure for viewing, much as endangered animals may be seen in a zoo. Guha, however, offers an analysis that is radically different. In long-settled and densely populated countries the agrarian populations have developed a finely balanced relationship with Nature—as the Pearl River Delta analysis of chapter 12 demonstrates. The creation of a park or wilderness area would not only dislocate large numbers of peasants from their ancestral lands but would also put at risk the ecological care of those lands that the peasants' traditional values foster—to say nothing of the loss in food production that would also result. In such a context, the Chinese government's move to freeze the lands in the Pearl River Delta as Agriculture Preserves may well be ecologically superior to the creation of parks.

Guha offers an example (Project Tiger in India) of how North American values, exported to Asia by powerful NGOs, may end up damaging both the environment and the traditional values of the local populations.

Project Tiger, a network of parks hailed by the international conservation community as an outstanding success, sharply posits the interests of the tiger against those of poor peasants living in and around the reserve. The designation of tiger reserves was made possible only by the physical displacement of existing villages and their inhabitants; their management requires the continuing exclusion of peasants and livestock. The initial impetus for setting up parks for the tiger and other large mammals such as the rhinoceros and elephant came from two social groups: first, a class of ax-hunters turned conservationists belonging mostly to the declining Indian feudal elite, and second, representatives of international agencies, such as the World Wildlife Fund (WWF) and the International Union for the Conservation of Nature and Natural Resources (IUCN), seeking to transplant the American system of national parks onto Indian soil.[6]

Guha notes that nowhere in the process were the needs of the local peasant population taken into account, the result being a direct transfer of resources from the poor to the rich. Also, by giving such projects high profile, funds and attention are diverted from environmental problems that impinge more directly on the lives of the poor (e.g., water shortages, soil erosion, and air and water pollution). In this example the action of powerful Western NGOs has perhaps served to heighten rather than reduce ecological tensions. The Deep Ecology approach (consistent with the above example) of separating people and Nature to preserve Nature runs counter to the traditional teaching of India, China, Japan, and the indigenous peoples of the Pacific that people are an interdependent part of Nature and not separate from it. Thus, rather than giving money to NGOs like the WWF to use to buy land from which people would be removed to create wilderness parks, the practice of Chinese immigrants to North America of sending money back to maintain their ancestral home or village in its traditional ecological agricultural practice may well be a better approach. We see here that the NGOs as the third force alongside governments and corporations have the capacity to create as well as reduce tensions between traditional and modern approaches to the environment. Homegrown NGOs (e.g., those of Japan, Korea, China, etc.) stand the best chance of intervening in ways that will bring the most positive result—both because they will likely embody local ecological values and because they can politically bring pressure to bear on corporations that behave well at home but poorly abroad.

A major problem that comes up in many chapters and is not solved by either the National Parks approach to preserving Nature or the Pearl River Delta ownership model is the so-called "tragedy of the commons." How will we care for the air, earth, and water, which no one owns but are common to all? This issue is especially crucial for the Pacific Basin dominated as it is by the vast international waters and wealth of the Pacific Ocean. Is it all simply up for grabs—with greed rather than need dominating? In their study of the problem, Wilman and Burch (chapter 4) found that the influence of religion was crucial in fostering behavior directed to the larger good. In traditional and aboriginal societies the goal was to help the individual restrain pursuit of self-interest for the good of the community. This, however, excluded concern for those outside of the community. What is needed now is the expansion of "community" to include all people and the global commons. For this to happen, traditional religious values need support from governments and NGOs worldwide. Traditional communities need the help of modern science so as to be able to integrate traditional and modern approaches to resource management.

The dominant religious value of traditional and aboriginal societies, namely, that everything is interconnected and sacred, does offer a basis to approach the problem of the commons. In such societies the attitude toward Nature is not conservative in the modern scientific sense, rather it is deeply ethical. Together, humans, animals, plants, and minerals are treated as persons who are all part of the same family. Also, in traditional societies, the ethical agent is not the autonomous choosing individual of the modern West, but the larger collective of family, tribe, nation, or, at its broadest moral extension, the cosmos itself. From that perspective, there is no difficulty in valuing the commons, for it (air, earth, and water) is experienced as a part of oneself—or perhaps better, oneself as part of it. One overfishes the ocean, pollutes earth, air and water, and leaves one's neighbor cold and hungry if they are seen as outside one's self-identity and self-interest. The teachings of Chinese and Aboriginal religions that we are part of the larger interconnected and interdependent self of Nature helps us to realize that in protecting the commons our own self-interest is not eliminated but fulfilled. Or as Gro Harlem Brundtland put it, the environment is where we all live and work to improve our lot. It is all one abode. Adopting a larger sense of self-identity gives us the basis for an ethical concern that extends outward from our body and possessions to include other persons living now, the generations to come, the animals, plants, earth, air, and water. To conserve it all is in my own self-interest for it is all "me." As some aboriginal elders teach, we are to make our decisions by including the needs of seven generations into the future. Adopting such an ethical approach would not only protect the fish in international waters, but would lead Japan to stop protecting its own ecology by polluting and exploiting in an unsustainable way the ecology of its Pacific neighbors. It would also cause Europe and North America to stop exporting pollution and unsustainable practices to developing countries in order to meet stringent environmental guidelines at home. As the atmosphere and the oceans are rapidly teaching us, pollution does not recognize political boundaries. If one person, city, or country "fouls their nest" all of us end up experiencing it. The Aboriginal Elders were right, we are all sharing "the same nest"—the global commons of Nature.

Seeing the interconnectedness of everything is not just an abstract ethical value, it has important practical considerations—as the four case study chapters make clear. Getches's analysis of how the Columbia River went from the world's richest salmon stream to one in which the salmon barely survive is a case in point. Rather than being sensitive to the ecological values of the river and its salmon—as the Native Peoples had been for centuries—white settlers and their governments used the river as an instrument for growth. Dams were built for agricultural irrigation without due regard for the impact on the ecology of the river, its fish, and the native communities and culture that depended upon the salmon. Getches notes that in 1956 when the Army Corps of Engineers closed the gates at the Dalles Dam, Celilo Falls were inundated and seventy-five feet of water drowned more than one hundred centuries of cultural and historical traditions—not to mention the impact on the salmon. While the Native society was oriented to the river and the salmon's migratory cycles, the settlers sought land, commerce, and profit. The result is that spawning streams are flooded, returning fish face dams blocking their way, and the slack flows of the Columbia fail to flush the young fish out into the ocean efficiently so that many die en route. The once-mighty fish runs of 10–16 million salmon are now down to 2.5 million, three-quarters of which are from hatcheries. But Getches indicates that lessons are being learned and water policy changed. Dams, reservoirs, and canals are being re-operated to give higher priority to fish and lower priority to irrigation and power generation. Large sums of money are being spent on fish ladders, turbine screens, and increasing river flows. Some dams may even be removed. A key to further progress is to find political processes that engage all of the stakeholders (including those who will speak for the fish) and solutions in which everyone, farmers, fishers, and fish, are winners. Thus, the value of interconnectedness can be put into practice. The Yakima Project in Washington and the Illinois Valley Watershed Council in Oregon are positive examples. While such actions are local, the effects are felt far out into the Pacific Ocean.

The principle of interconnectedness has also been successfully applied to forests in British Columbia, Canada. As the Owen and Greer case study shows, the transition to sustainability in British Columbia forest management has been achieved by a consensus approach of shared decision making including forest companies, native people, NGOs, scientists, and governments. The resulting Forest Practices Code and Forest Renewal Plan to rehabilitate damaged forest lands allows for commercial development but protects natural values such as wildlife travel corridors, fish spawning streams, and significant ecosystems. Aboriginal approaches to forestry have been given recognition and approval, and treaties are being concluded allowing Native Peoples to address their claims to traditional lands and forests from which they were displaced by Europeans during the nineteenth century. The hopefulness of this process is exemplified in the chapter by Turner and Atleo in which they report on activities that are part of the same overall British Columbia process described by Owen and Greer. Turner (a scientist) and Atleo (a Native Elder) report on the work of "The Scientific Panel for Sustainable Forest Practices in Clayoquot Sound" on which they served. The panel, made up of scientists, native elders, and government representatives, wrestled over the development desires of modern society and traditional values and approaches of the Native peoples. Although polarized at the start the panel did succeed in learning from each other's approaches so that in the end all agreed that the key to sustainable forest practices lies in maintaining functional ecosystems. This is a clear shift away from the profit orientation that dominated previously (remove the trees) to a focus on retaining the trees. With retained trees come resources and work for future generations, recognition of the value of native traditions and maintenance of the fish spawning beds in the upper reaches of the streams. The work and recommendations of the Panel have been endorsed by the British Columbia government and are now being implemented as policy. The interconnectedness principle operating here evokes the stories Walls and Kunihiro told of the connection proved between forests and fish in Japan. Just as the unsustainable cutting of the forests on Hokkaido led to the desertification of the adjacent Sea of Japan, and subsequent loss of fish stocks, so also after forty years of reforestation, the fish have returned to the previously barren sea coasts. Thus the Japanese saying, "find a fish by planting a tree."

In Australia, the interconnectedness principle has indeed taken a strange twist. In chapter 8, Rizvi demonstrates that in Australia immigration has functioned as an engine of economic growth but at a cost to both the environment and the traditional Aboriginal culture. As in Canada, the United States, Russia, and New Zealand, European immigrants brought an attitude to Nature and an approach to development that quickly displaced the Aboriginals from their lands, trivializing the physical and spiritual values that formed the basis of their lives. Immigration has damaged their environment irreparably. (See also Sokolov's analysis of the fate of Indigenous peoples in Eastern Russia.) Today, however, it is the white Australians who feel threatened by the increasing pressure from immigration, especially from Asia. A time-honored way to oppose such immigration in Australia is, as Rizvi demonstrates, to link immigration to the environment and claim that Asians should be kept out because they would not look after Australia's fragile environment. Such an argument was used in defending Australia's Immigration Restriction Act by the first Attorney-General of the country. A resonance of the same idea is heard today in the current debate over problems caused by the city of Sydney's rapid growth. Recent immigrants, particularly those from Asia, are held largely responsible for Sydney's environmental problems. The recognition of the interconnectedness between people and the environment in which they live can be used for negative purposes, as the Australian example shows. In the main, however, the recognition of our interconnectedness with each other and Nature has helped to overcome tensions between traditional and modem approaches to the environment.

The economist Herman Daly recently argued that "human economy has passed from an era in which human-made capital was the limiting factor in economic development to an era in which remaining natural capital has become the limiting factor."[7] What is natural capital? It is the source that yields the flow of natural resources upon which our developed industrial and technological world depends—the forest that yields the flow of cut timber and newsprint; the petroleum deposits that yield the flow of crude oil and natural gas; the fish populations of the sea that yield the flow of caught fish. The interdependent nature of natural and human-made capital, says Daly, "is made obvious by asking what good a sawmill is without a forest; a refinery without petroleum deposits; a fishing boat without populations of fish."[8] No longer is the limiting factor in economic development the lack of human-made capital. In the fisheries, for example, our technology has produced fishing boats and techniques that are rapidly exhausting fish stocks on the Pacific Coast of North America.[9] Now the limiting factor in the catch of fish is not our human-made capacity to catch them but rather the reproductive capacity of the fish themselves. Rather than humans taming and wresting a living from limitless but cruel Nature, now it is the limited capacity of Nature itself that is leading us to come to grips with our insatiable desire for more. On the human-made capital side, if we run out of one component, another can be substituted. In building a house, for example, if we run out of carpenters we can substitute more power saws or if we run out of power saws we can substitute more carpenters and still build the house. But can we equally easily substitute one natural resource for another on the natural capital side? While technology can and does allow us to use a natural resource more efficiently, and therefore make it last longer, there is still a limit. Once the oil (a non-renewable resource) is gone, it is gone forever. Fish (although renewable) if fished too hard, or blocked from reproduction by dams, can also disappear. Warnings from environmental scientists around the globe suggest that in our rapidly increasing use and pollution of Nature due to population pressure and technological consumption, we are at the limit of what Nature can provide to support the demands of its human part. Thus the tension we have examined in this book as it is found throughout the Pacific. The wisdom of traditional cultures studied offers values and practices that are helping us to begin to live within the limits of Nature. Yet at the same time, the push of economic development in the Pacific is constantly expanding. It seems clear, as Daly and others warn, that we are at a historic turning point. Our challenge is to learn to limit our reproduction and consumption so that we do not go beyond the limits of what nature can support. For as the Chinese sage Lao Tzu said,

> To hold and fill to overflowing
> Is not as good as to stop in time.[10]

NOTES

1. Wing-tsit Chan, *A Source Book in Chinese Philosophy* (Princeton: Princeton University Press, 1963), p. 137.

2. Gro Harlem Brundtland, *Our Common Future*, "Preface" (Oxford: Oxford University Press, 1987).

3. A. L. Grist and L. L. Greenfield, "Population and Development: Conflict and Consensus at Cairo," *Second Opinion* 20/4: 41–51.

4. Rosemary Radford Ruether, *Gaia and God: An Ecofeminist Theory of Earth Healing* (San Francisco: Harper, 1992), p. 265.

5. *Ibid.*, p. 268.

6. Ramachandra Guha, "Radical Environmentalism: A Third-World Critique," in *Key Concepts in Critical Ecology*, ed. by Carolyn Merchant (New Jersey: Humanities Press, 1994), p. 284.

7. Herman E. Daly, "From empty-world economics to full-world economics," in *Environmentally Sustainable Economic Development: Building on Brundtland*, ed. by R. Goodland, H. Daly, S. Serafy, and B. von Droste (Paris: UNESCO, 1991), p. 29.

8. *Ibid.*, p. 31

9. See Terry Glavin, *Dead Reckoning: Confronting the Crisis in Pacific Fisheries* (Vancouver: Greystone Books, 1996).

10. In Wing-tsit Chan, *A Source Book in Chinese Philosophy*, p. 143.

ABOUT THE AUTHORS

RICHARD ATLEO is a researcher who received an Ed.D. in Educational Administration from the University of British Columbia in 1990, and has taught at both Simon Fraser University and at the University of British Columbia. Currently he is an Arts One First Nations instructor at Malaspina University-College. He has not only engaged in diverse research activities ranging from Education in British Columbia to Residential School Experiences, to Cervical Cancer among First Nations Women, but also served as Co-chair on the Scientific Panel for Sustainable Forest Practices in Clayoquot Sound. Dr. Atleo is Chief Umeek of the Ahousaht First Nation of the Nuu-Chah-Nulth.

R. DOUGLAS BURCH is a research associate with the Arctic Institute of North America at the University of Calgary. He received a Master of Economics Degree from the University of Calgary in 1988. His current interests focus on community development and environmental planning in small First Nation communities in Northern Canada.

HAROLD COWARD is the Director of the Centre for Studies in Religion and Society and Professor of History at the University of Victoria. His main fields are comparative religion; psychology of religion; and environmental ethics. He serves as an Executive Member of the Board, Canadian Global Change Program. His wide variety of publications include

249

Jung and Eastern Thought (State University of New York Press 1985), *Population, Consumption, and the Environment: Religious and Secular Responses* (State University of New York Press 1995).

DAVID H. GETCHES is the Raphael J. Moses Professor of Natural Resources Law at the University Of Colorado School of Law. He was formerly the Executive Director of the Colorado Department of Natural Resources (1983–87) and the founding Executive Director of the Native American Rights Fund (1969–78). While at the Native Rights Fund he litigated the case of *United States v. Washington* which recognized the treaty fishing rights of several tribes. Prof. Getches is author of numerous articles and books on water law, Indian law, and natural resources policy. Recent books include: *Water Law in a Nutshell; Federal Indian Law* (with Wilkinson and Williams); *Water Resource Management* (with Tarlock and Corbridge); and *Searching Out the Headwaters: Change and Rediscovery in Western Water Policy* (with Bates, MacDonnell, and Wilkinson).

DAVID GREER is an Associate with the Commission on Resources and Environment.

ARTHUR HANSON is President and CEO of the International Institute for Sustainable Development (IISD) located in Winnipeg (Canada). Over the past twenty-five years, he has initiated a number of major programs in environment and development, especially in Southeast Asia and North America. He has held management and advisory positions with research councils, universities, foundations, international development agencies and banks, and non-government organizations, and currently serves on Canada's Round Table on the Environment and the Economy (NRTEE).

From 1978 to 1991 he was Professor of Environmental Studies at Dalhousie University and was Director of the School of Resource and Environmental Studies for a decade. Prior to that he worked for five years with the Ford Foundation in Indonesia.

IVAN HEAD is Professor of Law, and Chair of South-North Studies, at the University of British Columbia. He has been a foreign service officer, a Professor of Law at the University of Alberta, special assistant to the Prime Minister of Canada, and President of the International Development Research Centre, and has written extensively on issues of international law and international relations. His most recent book, co-authored with Pierre Trudeau, is entitled *The Canadian Way: Shaping Canada's Foreign Policy 1968–1984* (Toronto: McClelland and Stewart, 1995).

GRAHAM E. JOHNSON is Associate Professor of the Department of Anthropology and Sociology at University of British Columbia. He received his Ph.D. from Cornell University in 1971. He works primarily in rural development and urbanization in South China and Hong Kong, and secondarily on Chinese-Canadian communities. He is the co-author of *Walking on Two Legs: Rural Development in South China* (1976) and *From China to Canada: A History of Chinese Communities in Canada* (1982). Dr. Johnson also published numerous articles on development in the Pearl River Delta region in the 1980s and 1990s.

MASAO KUNIHIRO is Distinguished Visiting Professor at the Institute for Advanced Studies in the Humanities, University of Edinburgh; Overseas Advisor for the Institute on Global Conflict and Cooperation, University of California, San Diego. He was Professor of Cultural Anthropology at Tokyo International University and also at Sophia University for over twenty years. He was a Member of the House of Councilors (Senate) of the National Diet (Parliament) of Japan for six years until mid-1995. He is the author-translator of more than 65 titles, the author of numerous articles in Japanese and some in English, and Foreign Affairs Special Advisor to Prime Minister Takeo Miki.

STEPHEN OWEN, Q.C., served the province of British Columbia as Deputy Attorney General, Ombudsman, and the sole commissioner for the Commission on Resources and the Environment. He recently joined the University of Victoria as the David Lam Professor of Law and Public Policy.

FAZAL RIZVI is Professor of Educational Policy at Monash University in Australia. He received his Ph.D. from Kings College at the University of London in 1984. He has written extensively on educational and cultural policy, racism, multiculturalism, social justice, and democracy. His books include *Dilemmas of Reform* (1987) and *Culture, Difference and the Arts* (1993). He edits the journal *Discourse: Studies in the Cultural Politics of Education*, published by Carfax Press, Oxford. He has served on numerous government bodies concerned with educational and cultural policy, including the Australia Council for the Arts and the Australia Foundation for Culture and the Humanities.

ROSEMARY RADFORD RUETHER is the Georgia Harkness Professor of Applied Theology at the Garrett Theological Seminary and member of the Graduate Faculty of Northwestern University in Evanston, Illinois. She is a columnist for the *National Catholic Reporter* in the United States and is a frequent contributor to books and magazines on issues of religion and women, peace and justice, and ecology. Her most recent book is *Gaia and God: An Ecofeminist Theology of Earthhealing* (San Francisco: Harper, 1992).

VASSILY I. SOKOLOV is Academic Coordinator and Core Faculty member for the International LEAD (Leadership for Environment and Development) program being carried out in Russia by the Development and Environment Foundation. He also holds the position of Senior Research Fellow at the Russian Academy of Sciences and has more than a hundred publications in books and articles on environmental policy, management, and institutional arrangements at national and international levels, on environmental economics and international comparative studies. His advisory activities to federal and regional governments in Russia are related to the implementation of environmentally sound practices, particularly in Far North regions, Siberia, and the Russian Pacific.

NANCY TURNER is an ethnobotanist and Professor in the Environmental Studies Program, University of Victoria. Since 1993 she has been a member of the Faculty Program Committee for the Centre for Studies in Religion and Society and served on the Scientific Panel for Sustainable Forest Practices in Clayoquot Sound. She received her Ph.D. in Botany in 1974 from the University of British Columbia. She has authored and co-authored many books and papers on topics relating to traditional plant knowledge, mostly from northwestern North America.

JAN WALLS is Director of the David Lam Centre for International Communication at Simon Fraser University's Harbour Centre campus in downtown Vancouver. He has taught Chinese language and culture courses and contributed to Asia-focused program development at the

University of British Columbia (1970–78), the University of Victoria (1978–85), and Simon Fraser University (1987–present). From 1981 to 1983, he served as First Secretary for Cultural and Scientific Affairs in the Canadian Embassy in Beijing, and from 1985 to 1987 he was Senior Vice President of the newly established Asia Pacific Foundation of Canada, where he developed their first programs in cultural and educational affairs.

ELIZABETH A. WILMAN is a Professor in the Department of Economics at the University of Calgary. She received her Ph.D. from the University of Michigan in 1974. Her teaching and research are in the area of environmental economics. She is the author of *External Costs of Coastal Beach Pollution* (1984) and a number of articles on nonmarket valuation, property rights regimes, wildlife economics, and economic instruments for pollution control.

YUEN-FONG WOON, is Associate Professor in the Department of Pacific and Asian Studies at the University of Victoria. She received her Ph.D. from University of British Columbia in 1975. She works primarily on lineage history, family strategies, and economic development in the Pearl River Delta Region, and secondarily on Asian Canadian communities. She is the author of *Social Organization in South China 1911–1949: The Case of the Kuan Lineage of Kaiping County* (1984) and numerous articles on socioeconomic development in South China and the Sino-Vietnamese community in British Columbia.

INDEX

ISRAEL

PROFILES • NATIONS OF THE CONTEMPORARY MIDDLE EAST
Bernard Reich and David E. Long, Series Editors

Israel: Land of Tradition and Conflict, Bernard Reich

The Republic of Lebanon: Nation in Jeopardy, David C. Gordon

Jordan: Crossroads of Middle Eastern Events, Peter Gubser

South Yemen: A Marxist Republic in Arabia, Robert W. Stookey

Syria: Modern State in an Ancient Land, John F. Devlin

Turkey: Coping with Crisis, George S. Harris

The Sudan: Unity and Diversity in a Multicultural State,
John Obert Voll and Sarah Potts Voll

Libya: Qadhafi and the Green Revolution, Lillian Harris

The United Arab Emirates, Malcolm C. Peck

North Yemen, Manfred W. Wenner

Iran, John W. Limbert

Algeria, John P. Entelis

Afghanistan, Ralph H. Magnus

Also of Interest

*The New Arab Social Order: A Study of the Social Impact of
Oil Wealth*, Saad Eddin Ibrahim

OPEC: Twenty Years and Beyond, edited by Ragaei W. El Mallakh

Economic Growth and Development in Jordan, Michael P. Mazur

The United Arab Emirates: Unity in Fragmentation,
Ali Mohammed Khalifa

Libya: The Experience of Oil, J. A. Allan

Food, Development, and Politics in the Middle East,
Marvin G. Weinbaum

Israel's Nuclear Arsenal, Peter Pry

ISRAEL
Land of Tradition and Conflict

Bernard Reich

Westview Press • Boulder, Colorado

Croom Helm • London and Sydney

The photographs are courtesy of the Embassy of Israel, Washington, D.C., and the World Zionist Organization Press Service. Paperback cover photos: The Western (Wailing) Wall (*upper left*); demographic mosaic in Jerusalem (*upper right*); Shrine of the Book and the Knesset (*center*).

Published in 1985 in the United States of America by Westview Press, Inc., Frederick A. Praeger, Publisher; 5500 Central Avenue, Boulder, Colorado 80301

Published in 1985 in Great Britain by Croom Helm Ltd., Provident House, Burrell Row, Beckenham, Kent, BR3 1AT

Library of Congress Cataloging in Publication Data
Reich, Bernard.
  Israel, land of tradition and conflict.
  (Profiles. Nations of the contemporary Middle East)
  Bibliography: p.
  Includes index.
  1. Israel. I. Title. II. Series.
DS102.95.R45 1985   956.94   85-5327
ISBN 0-8133-0211-0
ISBN 0-8133-0215-3 (pbk.)

British Library Cataloguing in Publication Data
Reich, Bernard
  Israel: land of tradition and conflict—(Profiles:
  nations of the contemporary Middle East)
  1. Israel
  I. Title II. Series
956.94'054   DS126.5
ISBN 0-7099-4215-X

Printed and bound in the United States of America

10   9   8   7   6   5   4   3   2   1

For my children

Barry, Norman, Michael, and Jennifer

Contents

Tables and Illustrations

Acknowledgments

Any book results from a substantial effort over an extended period during which a large number of people make valuable contributions. This volume has benefited from my numerous visits to Israel, including a year as a visiting research associate at Tel Aviv University's Shiloah Center, where personal observation and discussions with academics, journalists, government officials, and others added to the understanding of Israel gained from more traditional and formal research. The work has also been enhanced by the probing and observations of my students in Political Science 179 at the George Washington University over the past decade and of others with whom I have discussed these topics in universities, public forums, and government offices in the Middle East and elsewhere.

A number of friends and colleagues, expert in the subject matter of the manuscript, have reviewed all or part of it and offered suggestions that have improved its accuracy and contributed to its interpretations. I owe a debt to Cheryl Cutler, Robert Goldfarb, Marvin Gordon, Aryeh Idan, Gershon Kieval, Maurice Roumani, Marsha Rozenblit, Ken Stammerman, Don Stein, Renee Taft, and Max Ticktin. My coeditor for the series, Dr. David Long, has made his usual sage contribution, and Libby Barstow has been extremely helpful in ensuring the quality of the final product through expert editing. Others who have been particularly helpful cannot be mentioned. As usual, my wife, Suzie, proved to be indispensable in the preparation of this book. Though many have provided assistance to improve this work, the responsibility for its contents remains mine alone.

Bernard Reich

Introduction

Israel is a state imbued with tradition and beset by conflict. It was born of Jewish tradition with thousands of years of history but has been beset by conflict deriving from the Arab-Israeli dispute and from internal tensions arising from the division between Arabs and Jews and between Jews of differing traditions and backgrounds.

The modern State of Israel is a product of centuries of Jewish heritage and history that affect all aspects of its national life. Yet, at the same time, it is the result of a unique confluence of forces and events that have characterized the nineteenth and twentieth centuries, including two world wars and the Holocaust. Other states have achieved independence in this same period and have been influenced by similar forces, but Israel remains unique because of its Jewish and Zionist heritage.

Israel's special role as the world's only Jewish state, and its consequent linkage to Jews everywhere, has had a manifold and multifaceted effect on its activities and has generated interests and policies, and created situations, unparalleled elsewhere. It sees itself as a spiritual center for world Jewry and as a haven for its persecuted numbers: Israel has been the focal point for worldwide Jewish concern and cultural, philanthropic, and political activity.

Although small in size and population, Israel elicits substantial international interest as a consequence of its unique situation. Its rapid development and impressive accomplishments in the social and scientific arenas have been widely

1

admired, and it has been the region's most politically and socially innovative state. Notwithstanding its estrangement from much of the Third World with which it shares numerous characteristics, it has become increasingly important as a central actor in the Middle East, and the Arab-Israeli conflict has been the focal point of attention of much of the international community.

Although Israel is a modern country—independent for less than four decades—the historical forces that formed it, led to its independence, and shaped its society and culture, its political culture and ideology, and its politics and policy are a product of thousands of years of Jewish history. Born of tradition, Israel seeks to maintain and enhance its past while struggling to deal with present domestic and foreign challenges. Israel has built a democratic system unlike that of any other state in the Middle East and has melded immigrants from more than seventy countries into a uniquely Israeli population. In a country almost devoid of natural resources, it has developed a thriving, if atypical, economy, and its people have achieved a high standard of living. All of this has been accomplished while it remains at war with the Arab world, except Egypt.

The story of modern Israel, independent since the withdrawal of the British mandatory government in 1948, is often recounted in terms of the wars it has fought with its Arab neighbors who have challenged its right to exist since the days prior to independence. These wars have been important turning points in Israel's domestic development and foreign policy and have marked watersheds in its history. During its first three and one-half decades of independence it has fought six major wars and engaged in countless skirmishes with its Arab neighbors in an effort to achieve the peace and stability essential for its domestic development.

Israel's ability to capture world attention has focused on such actions as wars and military achievements, but other events are equally noteworthy. Such dramatic actions as the rescue of hostages at Entebbe and Operation Moses (the dramatic effort to rescue thousands of Ethiopian Jews—Falashas—from refugee camps in the Sudan and bring them to Israel) have generated the admiration of many. This fits in with Israel's self-perception as guardian of world Jewry and its determination to serve as a safe haven for persecuted Jews, no matter what their origin.

The Israel that gained independence in 1948 was significantly different from the state that continues to celebrate its independence each spring. Israel is a dynamic country and is constantly undergoing change in all sectors. Israeli society is characterized by extensive debate over virtually all aspects of state activity—from the nature of the governmental process to political leadership, to the substance of foreign and security policy, to the role that religion might play, to the questions of demographic change and their implications. These alterations in society and national life affect all aspects of contemporary activity and characterize the Jewish state. They are examined in the following chapters.

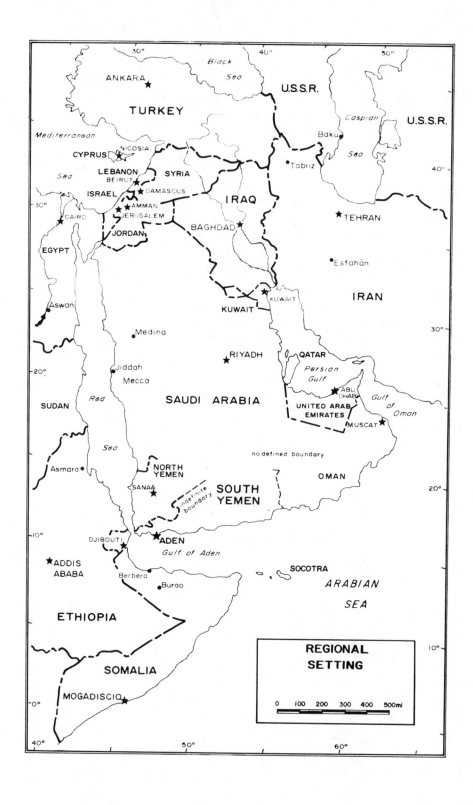

1

The Land and Its People

THE LAND OF ISRAEL

Israel lies at the southwestern tip of Asia, on the eastern shore of the Mediterranean Sea. The modern State of Israel corresponds geographically to an area that has been known historically by various names, including—most recently—Palestine. It is a small country whose land borders (except with Egypt) are not permanent and recognized and, hence, whose size has not yet been fully determined. Within its current frontiers it is bounded on the north by Lebanon, on the northeast by Syria, on the east by Jordan and the Dead Sea, on the south by the Gulf of Aqaba (Gulf of Eilat), on the southwest by the Sinai Peninsula of Egypt, and on the west by the Mediterranean Sea.

The new Jewish State of Israel envisaged by the United Nations Palestine partition plan in November 1947 would have had some 5,600 square miles (14,500 square kilometers). In reality, various changes resulting from wars and from subsequent agreements have enlarged the area within the 1949 armistice lines to about 8,000 square miles (20,700 square kilometers).

Within Israel's pre–1967 Six Day War frontiers, the variations of topography are considerable, and it has substantially dissimilar geographic regions. The hilly to mountainous area of Upper and Lower Galilee stretches from Haifa on the Mediterranean to the borders of Syria and Lebanon. It is one of the country's major agricultural areas, along with the Hula Valley and the Plain of Sharon. The region between

5

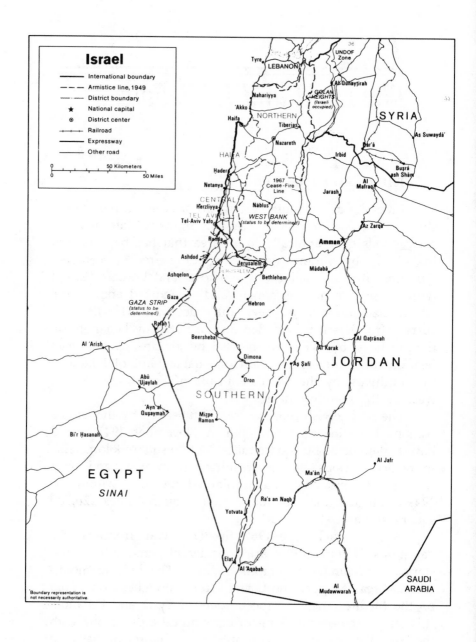

Israel

- —— International boundary
- - - - Armistice line, 1949
- —·—· District boundary
- ★ National capital
- ⊙ District center
- +—+ Railroad
- —— Expressway
- —— Other road

0 — 50 Kilometers
0 — 50 Miles

Tyre
LEBANON
UNDOF Zone
Al Qunaytirah
GOLAN HEIGHTS (Israeli occupied)
SYRIA
Nahariyya
'Akko
Haifa
NORTHERN
Tiberias
As Suwaydā'
HAIFA
Nazareth
Irbid
Dar'ā
Buṣrá ash Shām
Ḩadera
1967 Cease-Fire Line
Al Mafraq
Netanya
Jarash
CENTRAL
Herzliyya
Nāblus
TEL AVIV
WEST BANK (status to be determined)
Az Zarqā'
Tel-Aviv Yafo
Amman
Ramla
Ashdod
Jerusalem
JERUSALEM
Mādabā
Ashqelon
Bethlehem
Gaza
GAZA STRIP (status to be determined)
'Hebron
Rafaḩ
Al 'Arīsh
Beersheba
Al Qaṭrānah
Al Karak
Dimona
Aṣ Şāfī
JORDAN
Abū 'Ujaylah
Oron
'Ayn al Quṣaymah
SOUTHERN
Bi'r Ḩasanah
Mizpe Ramon
Al Jafr
EGYPT
SINAI
Ma'ān
Ra's an Naqb
Yotvata
Elat
Al 'Aqabah
SAUDI ARABIA
Al Mudawwarah

Galilee and the central sector, from the Jordan depression to the Mediterranean, includes the fertile Jordan Valley (Israel's most prosperous wheat and vegetable area), the Bet She'an Valley, and the Jezreel Valley. The western coastal plain extends roughly from Mount Carmel south past Tel Aviv to the flat plain in the region beyond Rehovot, Ramle, and Lod. The coastal plain is devoted to the cultivation of citrus and to other types of agriculture, such as vineyards. The location of a considerable amount of small industry around Tel Aviv and the other sizable towns and cities of the plain, however, has converted some of the cultivable land to urban uses. The hills of the Samaria area contain a number of fertile valleys, whereas the Hills of Judea that stretch south from Jerusalem are mainly barren. The Negev desert stretches south from Beersheba and the Dead Sea to Eilat on the Gulf of Aqaba; geographically it is an extension of the Sinai desert. It is almost entirely arid and accounts for more than half of the country's land area. About one-third of the country is cultivable.

Israel is situated between subtropical wet and subtropical arid zones of climate. As a result rainfall is light in the south and heavy in the north. The country is generally sunny because of its subtropical location and extensive desert areas. Rainfall usually takes place between November and May—with about three-quarters in December, January, and February.

Israel has a number of permanent rivers, but none is substantial by international standards. The Jordan, the largest river, originates in the Dan, the Banyas, and the Hasbani rivers and flows from the north to its terminus in the Dead Sea—the lowest point on earth at more than 1,300 feet (about 400 meters) below sea level. Israel's water-based resources include Lake Tiberias (also known as the Sea of Galilee or Lake Kinneret), a source of fresh water and fish. Israel's water needs and the scarcity of resources lead it to utilize most of its water potential to the fullest, primarily for agriculture. Water resources have been tapped at substantial cost and effort; water is derived primarily from the upper Jordan, Lake Tiberias, and the Yarkon River and from groundwater on the coastal plain. The National Water Carrier, put into operation in 1964, brings water from Lake Tiberias through a series of pipes, aqueducts, open canals, reservoirs, tunnels, dams, and pumping stations to various parts of the country, including the northern Negev.

Israel is relatively poor in natural resources, although it has copper and phosphates, glass sand, and building stone. The Dead Sea, shared by Jordan and Israel, is a major source of minerals (including potash, bromine, and magnesium). Much of the mineral resource is exported and is an important source of foreign exchange. Energy resources (coal, gas, and oil) provide only a small portion of the country's needs, making oil imports a heavy burden for the economy.

The majority of Israel's population is located in the narrow coastal plain along the Mediterranean. Haifa, the country's third-largest city and a major port, is the site of much heavy industry. Tel Aviv, the second-largest city, is the center of a large metropolitan area and serves as the economic, business, and banking center; the headquarters of the trade unions and the political parties; and the location of the Defense Ministry and General Staff. It is also a center of newspaper publishing, art, theater, and music. The largest city, Jerusalem, is the capital (although virtually all foreign embassies remain in Tel Aviv) and the country's spiritual center.

Agriculture and agricultural settlements have played an important role in the Zionist efforts to create a Jewish state and in Israel's efforts to develop a flourishing society. Jewish settlement in Palestine from the beginning of the Zionist movement until the end of the British mandate stressed agriculture as a means of reclaiming land and as a way of demonstrating the pioneering spirit central to Zionism. This focus has remained important, and the governments of Israel have encouraged immigrants (and others) to work the land and have considered agricultural training in border areas (in the Nahal program) the equivalent of military service.

In the early days of the new state, the development of agriculture was a major concern in order to provide food for a rapidly growing population and to conserve scarce hard currency through self-sufficiency in food. In more recent years, after meeting its own needs, Israel has become more oriented toward agricultural exports. Citrus has been the most important crop and substantial exports, primarily to Western Europe, have helped to earn important foreign exchange. Over time, the focus on agriculture has diminished as advances in agricultural techniques have made it possible to generate greater yields with fewer participants, and Israelis have become more oriented toward industry and urban life.

Israel's population is overwhelmingly urban, with heavy concentrations in the three largest cities. Despite this, Israel is associated in the minds of many with agriculture and with its unique experiment—the legendary kibbutz, one of the unusual forms of habitation developed for Israel's population to realize the goals of the state. The others are the *moshav* and the development town.

The kibbutz (a word meaning *collective settlement* that comes from the Hebrew for *group*) is a socialist experiment— a voluntary grouping of individuals who hold property in common and have their needs satisfied by the commune. Every kibbutz member participates in the work. All the needs of the members—from education to recreation, medical care to vacations—are provided by the kibbutz. The earliest kibbutzim (plural of *kibbutz*) were founded by pioneer immigrants from eastern Europe who sought to join socialism and Zionism and thus build a new kind of society. They have been maintained by a second and third generation as well as by new members. Initially, the kibbutzim focused on the ideal of working the land and became known for their crops, poultry, orchards, and dairy farming. As modern techniques, especially automation, were introduced and as land and water became less available, many of the kibbutzim shifted their activities or branched out into new areas, such as industry and tourism, to supplement the agricultural pursuits. Kibbutz factories now manufacture electronic products, furniture, plastics, household appliances, farm machinery, and irrigation-system components.

The popular and romantic image of the kibbutz conveys the impression of a movement of major proportions, but actually it is relatively small. The first kibbutz—Degania—

was founded in 1909; today there are some 250 kibbutzim with a membership of some 120,000, or about 3.5 percent of Israel's population. Despite their small proportion of the country's population, the kibbutzim have substantial influence in Israel's political and official life. Kibbutz members are found in the Knesset (parliament) and the cabinet and in the senior ranks of the Histadrut (the General Federation of Labor) and other agencies and organs of official and semiofficial Israel. Kibbutz members are disproportionately overrepresented in the Israel Defense Forces' (IDF or Zahal—the Hebrew acronym for Tzvah Hagana Le Yisrael) officer ranks and elite units (such as the air force, paratroop, and commando units).

The kibbutzim are divided, with some exceptions, into several federations reflecting various political and ideological perspectives. Ihud Hakevutzot Vehakibbutzim was affiliated with Mapai elements of the Israel Labor party. Hakibbutz Haartzi is affiliated with Mapam, which advocates a stricter Marxist ideology; Hakibbutz Hameuchad was identified with the Ahdut Haavoda wing of the Israel Labor party. Hakibbutz Hadati combines communal life and a socialist ideology with Orthodox Judaism and is affiliated with the National Religious party, although some kibbutzim identify with Poalei Agudat Yisrael. The Ihud and Hameuchad federations have merged into what is known as the United Kibbutz Movement (Hatnuah Hakibbutzit Hameuhedet).

A *moshav* is a village composed of a number of families— the average is about sixty—each of which maintains its own household, farms its own land, and earns its income from what it produces. The *moshav* leases its land from the Israel Lands Authority or the Jewish National Fund (Keren Kayemet Le Israel) and, in turn, distributes land to each of its members. Each family belongs to the cooperative that owns the heavy machinery and deals collectively with marketing and supplies and provides services such as education and medical care. Some now engage in industry under similar conditions. The first *moshav*, Nahalal, was founded in 1921 in the Jezreel Valley. Private homes, rather than communal living, are the rule, as are private plots of land and individual budgets. *Moshavim* (plural of *moshav*) have become more numerous than kibbutzim, and by 1980 they numbered about four hundred with more than 135,000 participants. Many of the postindependence immigrants to Israel were attracted to the concept of cooperative activity based on the family unit rather than the kibbutz's socialist communal-living approach.

Peculiar to Israel is the third type of settlement, the development towns. They were established in the 1950s and became focal points for new immigrants, predominantly those from Asia and Africa who arrived with few personal resources. The towns were created as part of a conscious government policy to serve as urban centers for new immigrants, to spread Israel's population throughout the country, and to provide a nucleus for the development of specific areas of the country. They have become integrated into Israeli life, and some have made significant contributions to the country.

ISRAEL'S JEWISH POPULATION

Israel has a small population, numbering some 4 million in 1984. On independence in May 1948, Israel's population was approximately 806,000—650,000 Jews (about 81 percent) and 156,000 non-Jews (mostly Arabs). By the end of 1984 Israel's population was 4,235,000—3.5 million Jews (about 83 percent) and 735,000 non-Jews. The increase in the non-Jewish population was a result of high birthrates; the increase in the Jewish component was due primarily to immigration. An estimated 53 percent of Israel's Jewish population were sabras (native born). Table 1.1 presents data on Israel's population.

Israel is by self-identification a Jewish state, and more than 80 percent of its population is Jewish. Israel's Jews are of a single religious faith and share a spiritual heritage and elements of historical experience. Ethnically and culturally, however, they are heterogeneous. The connection of the Jewish people with the land of Israel has continued throughout history. Jewish presence in the area was maintained even after the creation of the Diaspora, although the numbers and the status of Jews declined as that of other populations increased. The Jewish community in Palestine prior to the

TABLE 1.1
Population of Israel (in thousands), by Religion, Origin, and Birthplace
(1948, 1961, 1972, 1982)

	1948[a]	1961[b]	1972[b]	1982[a]
Total	881.7	2,179.4	3,147.7	4,063.6
Jewish population	716.7	1,932.3	2,686.7	3,373.2
European-American origin	591.4	1,007.1	1,187.3	1,343.6
Born in Europe or America	393.0	672.1	749.7	785.3
Second generation, born in Israel	198.4	335.0	437.6	558.3
African or Asian origin (Oriental)	105.0	818.3	1,273.6	1,496.7
Born in Africa or Asia	70.0	529.8	665.0	628.1
Second generation, born in Israel	35.0	288.5	608.6	868.6
European-American and Afro-Asian third generation, born in Israel	20.3	106.9	225.8	532.9
Non-Jewish population	165.0	247.1	461.0	690.4
Moslem Arabs	—	170.8	352.0	530.8
Christian Arabs	—	50.5	72.1	94.0
Druze and others	—	25.8	36.9	65.6

[a]As of year end
[b]As of mid-year

Note: First-generation Jews are those born outside Israel; second generation are those born in Israel of foreign-born parents; third generation are those born in Israel of Israeli-born parents.

Source: Dov Friedlander and Calvin Goldscheider, "Israel's Population: The Challenge of Pluralism," *Population Bulletin* 39, no. 2 (Washington, D. C.: Population Reference Bureau, 1984), p. 9; and Israel, Central Bureau of Statistics, *Statistical Abstract of Israel 1983*, no. 34 (Jerusalem, 1983), p. 60.

waves of Zionist immigration was concentrated in a number of important cities, notably Jerusalem, and focused on religious interests and activities. Between World War I and 1948, the size of the Jewish community increased substantially, and following Israel's independence and the ensuing Arab-Israeli war, a Jewish majority existed within the postwar frontiers.

The Jewish population is composed of immigrants from numerous countries and reflects a variety of ethnic and linguistic groups, religious preferences, and cultural, historical, and political backgrounds. The dispersion of the Jews had led to the creation of numerous communities located throughout the Diaspora, each of which was influenced by local customs that it integrated into its rituals and the practice of its faith. Each community developed diverse institutions, customs, languages, physical traits, and traditions. These were transferred to Israel with the communities. No single ethnic group constitutes even 20 percent of the total Jewish population (the largest group originated in Morocco).

The two main groupings are the Ashkenazi Jews and the Sephardim. Ashkenazi Jews, primarily from eastern and central Europe, were the main components of the first waves of Zionist immigration to Palestine, where they encountered a small Jewish community that was primarily Sephardi in nature. The Ashkenazi had fled from the Jewish ghettos of Europe (including Russia) and sought to build a new society, primarily secular and socialist in nature. The more religious brought with them their East European customs, fashions, and language (Yiddish, a German-based language written in Hebrew letters, was their language of everyday communication). Today the Ashkenazi community includes sizable groups from Western Europe, North America, and the British Commonwealth. The more religiously orthodox include in their number very small, but active and vocal, sects (such as the violently anti-Zionist Neturei Karta of Jerusalem and its colleagues in the United States) that refuse to accept the legitimacy of the state and of the everyday use of Hebrew (the language of the Bible and thus for them holy).

Israel's non-Ashkenazi Jews are a majority of the country's population. These people, of Afro-Asian origin, are referred to as Edot Hamizrach (eastern, or Oriental, communities), Sephardim, or Orientals. The term *Sephardim* is often used to refer to all Jews whose origin is in Muslim lands, although it properly refers to the Jews of Spain and the communities they established in areas to which they migrated after their expulsion from the Iberian peninsula during the Inquisition. Although technically incorrect, *Sephardim* has increasingly come to include both those whose origins were in the Iberian peninsula and those who had been located throughout the Arab world and the more broadly defined Middle East (including Turkey, Greece, Iran, and Afghanistan) for centuries following the exile from the historical Jewish state. The Iberian Jews generally spoke Ladino, a Judeo-Spanish language originally written in medieval Hebrew letters and later in Latin letters (much as the Ashkenazi Jews spoke Yiddish), whereas those of the Middle Eastern communities did not. Most of the Oriental immigration came after Israel's independence from the eastern Arab states (such as Iraq) and from Iran, where the Jews had resided for more than two thousand years and often had substantial centers of learning. The community is diverse and pluralistic, although a collective "Oriental" identity appears to be emerging.

Immigration

Israel's role as the world's only Jewish state has led to its national commitment to a policy of virtually unrestricted immigration—an outward expression of a bond of faith between Israel and world Jewry that results from Israel's view of its mission as the emissary of the exiled and scattered Jewish people (see Table 1.2). This approach serves the needs of world Jewry by removing Jews from areas of distress and serves the needs of Israel by providing the people necessary for its security and development. Israel's 1950 Law of Return assures all Jews who wish to immigrate that they are free to do so; Israel is also concerned about the well-being of Jews everywhere.

In Jewish tradition, immigration to Israel is *aliyah* ("going up"), resulting from a deep-rooted view that "in the end of days" Jews would return to Zion—to the Holy Land. Zionism made this ancient concept a contemporary reality. Immigration to Israel has been rooted in Jewish religious ideology and in secular nationalistic ideology. Religious concerns prompted individuals to migrate to Palestine, and Zionist ideology later impelled larger groups to follow a similar course, although until World War I relatively few Jews settled in Palestine. Subsequently, the Zionist leadership in Palestine and else-

TABLE 1.2
Immigration to Israel

Period	Total	Last Continent of Residence				
		Asia	Africa	Europe	America & Oceania	Not Known
1919–1948[a]	482,857[b]	40,895	4,041	377,381	7,754	22,235
1948–1951[c]	686,739	237,352	93,951	326,786	5,140	23,510
1952–1954	54,065	13,238	27,897	9,748	2,971	211
1955–1957	164,936	8,801	103,846	48,616	3,632	41
1958–1960	75,487	13,247	13,921	44,595	3,625	99
1961–1964	228,046	19,525	115,876	77,537	14,841	267
1965–1968	81,337	15,018	25,394	31,638	9,274	13
1969–1971	116,484	19,700	12,065	50,558	33,891	270
1972–1974	142,755	6,347	6,821	102,763	26,775	49
1975–1979	124,827	11,793	6,029	77,167	29,293	545
1980–1982	46,750	5,368	3,732	23,869	13,596	185

[a]Up to May 14, 1948

[b]Includes about 11,000 illegal immigrants and about 19,500 tourists who remained in Israel

[c]From May 15, 1948

Source: Israel, Central Bureau of Statistics, *Statistical Abstract of Israel 1983*, no. 34 (Jerusalem, 1983), pp. 137–138.

where, in the spirit of Zionism, adopted policies to increase immigration in order to assure the growth of the Jewish population both in absolute size and relative to the Arab population of Palestine.

Modern Israel's history may be dated from the establishment of the farming communities in Palestine in 1882 by the first wave of Jewish immigrants. The First Aliyah (1882–1903) consisted mainly of individuals and small groups from the Hibbat Zion and Bilu movements. Combined with the existing local community and its institutions, the immigrants of the First Aliyah established the initial political and social structure of the Jewish community in Palestine. Some twenty-five thousand immigrants, primarily from eastern Europe, arrived in Palestine during this period.

The Second Aliyah (1904–1914) was the most significant in terms of Israel's future political system. Some 40,000 immigrants of Russian and eastern European origin laid the foundations of the labor movement and established the first Jewish labor parties and kibbutzim. They were secularists who sought to modernize and secularize Jewish life in the Diaspora, and they brought their political ideas, especially socialist ideology, to Israel. The Third Aliyah (1919–1923) reinforced these principles. Composed of some 35,000 immigrants, primarily young pioneers of Russian and eastern European origin, it helped to establish the Histadrut and additional communal agricultural settlements. The Fourth Aliyah (1924–1928) included some 67,000 immigrants, mostly of Polish middle-class origin, who tended to settle in the major cities of Palestine and to establish small factories and shops there. The Fifth Aliyah (1929–1939) consisted of some 250,000 individuals, primarily from Central Europe (especially Nazi Germany), who brought with them large amounts of capital and substantial skills and experience.

Aliyah continued during and after World War II. In these, sometimes referred to as the Sixth Aliyah and the Seventh Aliyah, about 100,000 immigrants reached Palestine.

From the outset, immigration has been a major tenet of Zionism, which saw it not only as a means of increasing the size of the Yishuv (the Jewish community in Palestine) but also as a logical activity of a movement that believed that the future of Jews could be assured only in a Jewish state. Between World War I and 1948 immigration into Palestine was controlled by the British mandatory authorities then in control of the territory, and relatively large numbers of immigrants were initially permitted to enter Palestine. Immigration soon became a major source of tension between the Jewish and Arab communities in Palestine and of controversy between the Zionists and the British government. The Arabs sought limitations on Jewish immigration to Palestine; the British, in a 1939 White Paper, restricted both immigration and land purchases, an action that contributed to increased Zionist militancy and opposition to British authority in Palestine. The 1939 White Paper came at a particularly unfortunate time because of growing European anti-Semitism leading to the Holocaust and because of the need for the development of the Jewish community in Palestine. Despite the restrictions, some "illegal" or unofficial immigrants, known as Aliyah Bet, reached Palestine through various clandestine procedures.

With the end of World War II hundreds of thousands of European Jewish refugees sought to locate new homes and begin new lives by entering Palestine, and immigration became a major concern. Israel's first prime minister, David Ben-Gurion, was committed to rapid increases in Jewish numbers for both ideological and security reasons. The nation's commitment to unfettered immigration, for the same reasons, was enshrined in the guiding principles of the new state. The Declaration of Independence provided that "the State of Israel will be open for Jewish immigration and for the Ingathering of the Exiles." As its first act, Israel's provisional Council of State abolished all immigration restrictions.

The Law of Return, adopted by the Knesset on July 5, 1950, assures virtually unlimited and unfettered Jewish immigration to Israel by providing that every Jew has the right to immigrate to Israel to settle there unless the applicant is engaged in an activity "directed against the Jewish people" or one that may "endanger public health or the security of the state." An amendment in 1954 also restricted those likely to endanger public welfare. The 1950 law has provided the formal basis for the substantial immigration that has taken place since independence. The concept of unlimited immigration, which has been reinforced by the programs and actions of successive governments and has had overwhelming support in parliament and from Israel's Jewish population, has resulted in hundreds of thousands of Jewish immigrants from more than seventy countries.

The open immigration policy has been implemented almost without regard to the economic costs and social dislocations caused by a rapid and massive influx of people. Israel has admitted whole communities, virtually without regard for their economic usefulness or for its own absorptive capacity. In the initial years after independence, the added burden was reflected in an economy affected by shortages, rationing, and austerity. Housing became a particular problem. Transit camps (ma'abarot) were established in 1950 to help provide facilities for the new immigrants, although later they were brought to housing in the development towns that became the focal point of new settlement.

It is not surprising, therefore, that numerous difficulties have beset Israel's efforts to absorb the masses of immigrants. Rapid economic, social, and cultural assimilation would have been a formidable undertaking for a small country even under the most favorable conditions. In Israel, the problem was compounded by limited resources, extensive defense needs, and the composition and character of the new immigration. Israel was obliged to prepare the immigrants for gainful employment and to provide housing, schooling, and medical facilities. Although the material problems have not yet been fully solved, they are well defined, and manifold activities are directed toward their solution. These include systematic establishment of new agricultural communities in which newcomers are settled soon after their arrival and are provided with training and work, medical treatment, and a well-developed system of national insurance and housing.

The waves of immigration have reflected changing conditions in Israel, in the countries of immigrant origin, and in the international community. About 90 percent of the immigrants during the mandate period came from Europe or other Western countries. The first postindependence immigrants from the British internment camps on Cyprus (where they had been sent after attempting illegal immigration to Palestine) were followed soon by displaced persons from camps in Germany, Austria, and Italy. Large segments of the Jewish communities of Bulgaria, Libya, Poland, and Romania followed. During the nascent years of Israel's independence, European Holocaust survivors were joined by Jewish communities from the Middle East and North Africa. The Jews of Yemen (about 45,000) migrated in 1949 in Operation Magic Carpet, as did virtually all of Iraq's ancient Jewish community (about 123,000) in the 1950 Operation Ali Baba. Subsequent immigration waves came from Morocco and Tunisia, Poland and Hungary, and—in the aftermath of the Sinai War of 1956—from Egypt.

By the time the waves of mass immigration had been completed in the early 1950s, they had significantly altered Israel's population profile. Whereas at independence the Yishuv was overwhelmingly Ashkenazi in number, organization, and institutions as well as in political, economic, and social lifestyle, after mass immigration the proportion of the Jewish population of Oriental origin increased from 15 to 33 percent. The Jewish population had more than doubled, and the Jewish proportion of the total population had increased to 90 percent.

Mass immigration was a special case that resulted from the substantial reservoir of Jews anxious to immigrate to Israel and from the unusual efforts made by Israeli and Zionist authorities to bring the largest possible number of Jewish immigrants to Israel in the shortest amount of time. In the early 1960s, Eastern Europe and North Africa were the major sources. After the Six Day War of 1967, immigration from the West—primarily Western Europe, the Americas, and the Commonwealth—began in earnest. Soviet immigration also became a factor—although the numbers have varied from year to year with the caprice of the Soviet authorities and the varying choices of the immigrants, once out of the Soviet Union, to go to Israel or elsewhere. After the Yom Kippur

War of 1973, immigration declined, and there was increased emigration, especially to Western Europe and the United States.

Jewish immigration has been declining dramatically since the early 1970s and in recent years has exceeded emigration only slightly. Declining immigration is a result of a number of factors, particularly a waning of Zionist ideology. Israel's attraction for immigrants has decreased, given the problems posed by political and security issues and the difficult economic conditions since the Yom Kippur War. Few large reservoirs of obvious sources of immigration are left, since the communities of Asia and Africa have virtually all been transferred to Israel or have migrated elsewhere. The Jewish communities in the West (especially North America and Western Europe) are under no significant pressures to change their location. The Soviet Union's large Jewish community remains unable to emigrate despite continuing evidence of a desire of many to do so. In addition, it seems likely that many of the Jews remaining in the Diaspora, including those in South Africa, South America, and the Soviet Union (if they were to have the option), would not opt to emigrate to Israel but would follow the patterns of recent years and emigrate to countries facing fewer problems.

In late 1984 and early 1985 a massive airlift brought thousands of Falashas (Jews of Ethiopia) to Israel from refugee camps in the Sudan. This complicated effort was known as Operation Moses.

Emigration

Yerida ("going down"), or emigration from Israel, has become a salient issue of public concern in recent years despite uncertainty as to its dimensions and the fact that it is not a new phenomenon in Zionist or Israeli history. During each of the major waves of *aliyah*, there also was emigration. The growing concern reflects the view that emigration is, to a certain extent, a barometer of Israel's national condition and that it affects national morale and the strength of Israel's national potential.

Yerida has a number of different aspects, and the problem is not fully delineated. A lack of agreed definition as to who is an emigrant makes it difficult to differentiate between the actual emigrant (*yored*) and the student or tourist who may go abroad and remain there for an extended period. There is also the matter of identifying the extent of *yerida*, since most Israelis who leave the country with the goal of emigrating are often not prepared to admit their intention. Thus, existing data are little more than estimates and vary considerably. In recent years, emigration has also taken on a different character. Previously most emigrants were members of immigration groups who departed the country after failing to be appropriately absorbed. Although some emigrants still come from this group, a large portion of the new emigration comes from individuals who were born and raised in Israel, fought in its wars, and participated in the shaping of its society. Their reasons for leaving the country are varied and include such contentions as "taking a break," seeking advanced study, or looking for better economic, social, and professional conditions.

The "why" of emigration elicits even less agreement than other aspects of the issue, although there appears to be accord on the explanation that the most important emigration cause is a weakened commitment to Jewish and Zionist identity rather than factors relating to personal well-being. Immigrants' intentions to stay in Israel appear to be related to the degree to which they feel themselves to be Israelis or to be "at home" in Israel rather than by how happy they are with their absorption into specific areas of life or activity. Thus, for example, the Jews from the USSR who generally settle and remain in Israel are those who came because of Jewish or Zionist conviction. The religiously observant Jews generally tend to remain rather more often than the secularized.

Yerida affects Israel in a number of respects. It questions the Zionist ideology that identified Israel as the center of the Jewish people, an ideology that attracts Jews to live in Israel and to contribute to the process of establishing and maintaining its independence. Constant emigration that includes many born in the country is in direct contradiction to the ideological and moral basis of Israel as a Jewish-Zionist state. Emigration also affects immigration, particularly the effort to attract new immigration from the West, which has always been difficult.

Emigration affects Israel's political image and the esteem in which it is held by the Jewish communities. *Yerida* is developing an image of a country weakened by the exodus of its citizens, and emigrants reinforce those views once abroad. Israeli national morale is also affected. Israel's citizens have numerous problems to face on a daily basis; emigration weakens their staying power, leading to further *yerida* that, in turn, reduces Israel's national potential.

The Oriental Question

At independence the majority of Israel's Jewish population was of Ashkenazi origin. The massive immigration to Israel of Jews from Oriental communities and their higher birthrate have changed the demographic nature of the state. Israel today has an Oriental majority.

Geographically and demographically Israel is an Oriental country; culturally, socially, and politically it is Western in nature and orientation. The early Zionists laid the foundations for an essentially European culture in Palestine, with the attendant concepts, ideals, and ideologies, and subsequent immigration accelerated the trend. The Western immigrants created and developed the Yishuv structure of land settlement, institutions, trade unions, and political parties, as well as an educational system—with its attendant assumptions and promises—all in preparation for a Western-oriented Jewish national state.

More recent immigrants have had to adapt to a society that had formed these institutions. Massive Oriental immigration has created a country in which a large portion of the population has societal and cultural traditions, customs, practices, and attitudes akin to the populations among whom they had lived for generations and different from those of their Western coreligionists. Among the Oriental population family loyalty is strong, and concepts of responsibility very often do not transcend the family. Suspicion of government is great; resistance to taxation, rationing, and other governmental controls is prevalent. In part because of a lack of education and experience, relatively few members of the

Oriental community have succeeded in attaining responsible senior government positions. For Orientals, living conditions are generally poorer than for members of the occidental community, and a relatively small proportion attend Israel's universities.

The migration of Oriental Jews to Palestine and, later, to Israel brought them into contact with a Zionist movement that had been founded by European Jews as a response to European anti-Semitism. The membership and leadership of the World Zionist Organization was overwhelmingly European; its programs and activities were almost entirely European oriented. As already noted, the majority of the early Jewish immigrants to Palestine (more than 85 percent) were European. The reasons for this are to be found in the fact that the Jewish communities in much of the Muslim world had reasonably favorable economic and social conditions and did not seek to emigrate; in addition, the Zionist movement's attention was riveted to Europe, where its organized efforts sought to recruit European Jews who were more immediately threatened.

After the Holocaust, this focus of attention shifted. When the creation of Israel and the resulting Arab-Israeli war generated impossible conditions for Jews in the countries of the Middle East and North Africa, the mass immigrations discussed earlier transported Jewish communities en masse to Israel from Iraq, Yemen, and Libya. Segments of Jewish communities were moved from Morocco, Algeria, Tunisia, Iran, Syria, and Egypt. Many of these non-European immigrants were also motivated by religious factors, in comparison to their European counterparts with their more secular and socialist approaches to Zionism.

Israel's communal problem is one of ethnic-cultural cleavages within the Jewish community. These differences have existed since the Oriental and occidental communities came into contact during the mandate period. At the outset, the communities had limited contact, in part because social groups with similar ethnic, cultural, and religious backgrounds tended to reside in specific neighborhoods with others of similar perspectives, separated or isolated from those with different backgrounds. The majority of the Oriental community held a larger portion of more menial jobs as the Ashkenazim moved out of those sectors of employment. The Oriental community was also undereducated compared to its Ashkenazi counterpart and included large numbers of uneducated and illiterate individuals. The communities were also separate in terms of their involvement in politics and public affairs, as the Oriental communities were not involved in public activity within the framework of Yishuv political life. The situation did not change dramatically or significantly once Israel gained independence, although both a Sephardim party and a Yemenite list were represented in the First Knesset (1949–1951) and the Second Knesset (1951–1955).

The major distinction between Israel's two major Jewish communities is in socioeconomic status. The "social gap" has been manifest in a number of inequalities. Israel's Oriental population has second-class economic and social status as a result not of government policy, but of unavoidable social conflicts and of the difficulty of making rapid progress toward equality in Israel's special circumstances. Progress has been slower than desirable, but tangible indicators of increasing improvement are now evident. Members of Israel's Oriental community have risen to high rank in the military, serve in respectable numbers in the Knesset (32 of 120 in the Eleventh Knesset are of Sephardi origin), and are ministers in the cabinet. One—Yitzhak Navon—became president. At the same time, there has been increasing social contact and intermarriage between the two communities, and improvements in housing and education have helped to reduce the gap between Israel's predominantly Ashkenazi upper class and its less-privileged Oriental ethnic majority.

The nonmaterial problems, which are essentially those of cultural and social integration, are more complex and will require time for solution. Although the religious tradition of the Jewish population is an asset, as it provides a common core of values and ideals, there are major differences in outlook, frames of reference, levels of aspiration, and various other social and cultural components. Army service, which emphasizes education and provides the experience of a common life-style while learning the Hebrew language, helps the

process of acculturation and encourages the evolution of a
unified, though multicultural, society. Despite these efforts,
the full integration of immigrants into Israel's society remains
a major social problem.

Elements of the problem have been manifest in various
ways. Often there is residential separation into distinct neighborhoods, a predominance of intragroup marriages, separate
and unequal schools, and a perspective that portrays the
Orientals as culturally deprived or backward. Together, these
elements helped to foster the inequality of Israel's Oriental
community in the 1950s and early 1960s. After the 1967 war,
the situation improved as economic expansion brought more
Orientals into white-collar occupations, and they began to
move into the political and social elite. Despite this movement,
Orientals still constitute the bulk of blue-collar workers in
Israel, and Ashkenazim still predominate in the government,
bureaucracy, and managerial, entrepreneurial, and professional
groups.

Israel's Oriental Jewish community has reacted in numerous ways to its unequal treatment in the Israeli system.
During much of the first three decades of Israel's independence,
the Oriental population was politically quiescent and its actions
low-key—mostly petitions, protests, demonstrations, and
strikes. Efforts to create interest groups and political movements to focus attention on the core issues were notably
weak: the Sephardim party and the Yemenite list in the first
Knesset elections and demonstrations in immigrant transit
camps for better food and jobs. Attempts to establish "communal" or ethnic political parties failed in the 1959, 1961,
and 1965 Knesset elections.

Although there had been riots in the Oriental neighborhood of Wadi Salib in 1959, no significant movement
developed in the Oriental community until the 1970s. Then
a militant group formed by some young Orientals of North
African background, who chose to call themselves Black
Panthers, took to the streets to oppose what they regarded
as discrimination against the Oriental Jewish community. They
helped to generate awareness and a plethora of public investigation or study commissions. Demands for more edu-

cational and social services were part of the effort to achieve
improvement in the Oriental community's socioeconomic status. These efforts achieved some amelioration of the situation
but did not effect substantial change.

Most significant was the slow emergence of the Oriental
population as a political force with increased support for the
Likud bloc led by Menachem Begin. The lack of political
organization in the Oriental population meant that its method
of expression was by casting votes for, or withholding them
from, the major established parties. This seemed to reach a
plateau in the 1981 Knesset elections, when the Oriental vote
for Likud led the Israeli press to speak of an "Oriental revolt,"
and the Jewish ethnic issue became more public during the
campaign. It seemed to suggest full-scale Oriental efforts to
be heard in the electoral process and to follow the pattern
foreshadowed in the 1977 election and replicated in the 1984
election, although the ethnic issue was all but eliminated
from the latter campaign.

Why the Oriental population has voted in support of
Likud remains unclear, but a number of factors seem to be
involved. There is appeal in Likud's nationalist and tradi-
tionalist approach to political and religious matters and in its
"hard-line" perspective in foreign and security policies. At
the same time, many in the Oriental community (as indeed
most Israelis) have had a significant increase in the standard
of living and in private consumption. The Likud is thus often
equated with prosperity, whereas the Labor governments are
associated with years of deprivation. These perceptions are
powerful generators of votes, and the Oriental Jewish community has become an increasingly significant political factor,
given its growing proportion of the population and its growing
political awareness and participation.

The Religious Issue and "Who Is a Jew"

The United Nations partition plan of November 1947
provided for the establishment of a Jewish state in Palestine,
and when that state became independent in May 1948 it
thought of itself as both Jewish and secular. Israel's Declaration

of Independence recalls the religious and spiritual connection of the Jewish people to the land of Israel, but also guarantees Israel's citizens "freedom of religion and conscience." The document does not address the meaning of a "Jewish state" or the roles that would be played by religious forces and movements (especially by their political parties) in the state.

Since independence, Israel has had to come to terms with the concept of its "Jewishness" and the definition of "who is a Jew," and thus it has had to address the meaning of a "Jewish state" and the roles to be played by religious forces and movements within the state. The conflict between secular and religious perspectives on these and related matters has been a continuing characteristic of Israel; indeed, it was foreshadowed in the drafting of the Declaration of Independence and was the cause of hot debate during consideration of the proposed constitution. One faction insisted on the primacy and enshrinement of Jewish religious values while the other sought to focus on more secular themes, thus limiting the role of religion in the state. Eventually a compromise, which precluded a written constitution, was reached, but Israel continues to face the issues.

"Who is a Jew" has been at the center of a religion-state controversy in Israel and has theological, political, and ideological overtones with specific practical dimensions. Secular and religious authorities and ordinary citizens have faced the question in connection with issues of immigration, marriage, divorce, inheritance, and conversion as well as in matters related to registration to secure identity cards and in the official collection of data and information. The question relates to the application of laws such as the Law of Return, the Nationality Law, and others passed by Parliament, as well as those relating to marriage and divorce and their interpretation by both secular and religious authorities.

Jews have special positions under the Law of Return (1950) and Nationality Law (1952), but the term was not defined in either piece of legislation. As a result, it became necessary to determine who was a Jew and to decide who would make such a determination. During the country's early years when there was a special effort to encourage immigration, then–Prime Minister David Ben-Gurion encouraged a broad and liberal interpretation, essentially permitting each individual to decide whether he or she was a Jew or not. The Orthodox leadership, on the other hand, sought to restrict Jewish identification and to ensure its conformity with Orthodox doctrine as determined by traditional Orthodox authorities. Thus the only person who could be Jewish, in this perspective, was one who met the requirements of Jewish law (halachah) that provided that an individual was a Jew only if born to a Jewish mother or converted to Judaism by an accepted Orthodox authority.

Over time a number of celebrated instances relating to the question of who is a Jew have arisen. In 1958 the issue became one of considerable significance and generated a major controversy, when the National Religious party withdrew from the coalition government because it opposed the Cabinet's definition of "Jew" in connection with the issuance of new identity cards for Israeli citizens. The Knesset debated the matter, but later it was postponed. Other prominent cases have included the Brother Daniel case (1962); the status of the Falashas of Ethiopia; the status of the Bene Israel of India; and the Shalit case (1970). These and others have focused on a particular aspect of the broader problem but have not resolved it. These matters threaten to strain relations not only between the various factions within Israel but also between Israel and some of its Jewish supporters abroad.

Israel's religious structure utilizes a modified millet system, the system used by the Turks when the Ottoman Empire controlled Palestine. Under this arrangement the various non-Muslim religious communities were allowed substantial autonomy to govern themselves through their own communal council, in accordance with their own canon law and under the jurisdiction and control of their ecclesiastical authorities. The system was retained, with alterations, during the mandate. At that time, the several non-Muslim religious communities organized their affairs under leadership of their chosen religious functionaries. Thus, the Jewish community remains organized today with two chief rabbis (one Sephardi and one Ashkenazi), rabbinical courts, and related institutions. Similarly, Jewish religious courts were granted jurisdiction over matters of personal status (for example, marriage, divorce, and alimony). Today these courts and other religious institutions of the state recognize only the Orthodox Jewish approach and interpretation. Conservative and Reform rabbis and organizations have been denied any real role in the religious system, although there are non-Orthodox congregations, institutions, and rabbis in Israel.

Israel utilizes a similar procedure in which the various religious communities (for example, Muslim, Christian, and Druze) and religious authorities exercise jurisdiction in litigation involving personal status and family law (for example, marriage, divorce, alimony, and inheritance) and apply religious codes and principles in their own judicial institutions. Various matters that are secular concerns in other states are within the purview of religious authorities; even though there is no established religion, all religious institutions have a special status and authority granted by the state and, to a substantial degree, are supported by state funds. The secular government takes into account the requisites of the segment of the population that observes religious tradition. Religious institutions receive governmental funding, and the public school system includes religious schools receiving state support. Laws pertaining to the Sabbath and to the Jewish dietary requirements are part of the state's legal system.

The Ministry of Religious Affairs has primary responsibility for meeting Jewish religious requirements, such as the supply of ritually killed and prepared (kosher) meat, for rabbinical courts, and for religious schools (*yeshivot*), as well as for the autonomous religious needs of the non-Jewish communities. These functions are noncontroversial; few dispute the duty to meet the religious requirements of the people. Nevertheless, a subject of sharp and recurrent dispute is the extent to which religious observance or restriction is directly or indirectly imposed on the entire population. The observant community, which faithfully follows all of the laws and rules of the Orthodox Jewish tradition, through its political movements and parties and through its membership in government coalitions has been able to achieve government agreement

for the establishment of separate school systems, exemption
of observant girls from army service upon application, curtailing of business and public activity on the Sabbath (although
subject to local exception), and limitations of the role of non-
Orthodox Judaism in Israel. Those who are less observant of
traditional Judaism often argue that they do not have full
religious freedom because of governmental acquiescence to
the demands of the observant Jewish groups. The religious
parties have been able to secure concessions because the need
for coalition governments has given them a larger voice in
politics than is dictated by their numerical strength.

Israel's religious structure stems partly from a compromise
to obviate clashes that took the form of a so-called status
quo agreement worked out by David Ben-Gurion on the eve
of Israel's independence. It retained the situation as it had
existed upon independence; individuals would be free to
pursue their religious practices in private as they saw fit while
public matters would be frozen with what prevailed before
statehood. This arrangement thus continued the millet system.
This allowed preservation of a large system of religious
(especially rabbinical) courts and other government-supported
religious institutions. The status quo has allowed the Orthodox
community to maintain and expand its efforts to assert control
over various activities, periodically engendering public conflict
and discussion. Although there is a split between the religious
and secular approaches to the problem of religion in the
Jewish state, there are also differences within the Orthodox
religious community that were manifested in part by the large
number of religiously based parties contesting the 1984 election
and the fact that a number of them were offshoots of existing
religious parties. Numerous factions, each with their own
leadership and agenda, compete with each other to secure
loyalty and votes and to secure program goals and political
patronage.

Israel's Jewishness is a basic element underlying its
political system, although citizens of Israel may be and are
of a variety of religious backgrounds, and the Jewish population is of differing backgrounds and traditions and diverse
in regard to observance of the faith. Despite the overwhelm-

ingly large proportion of Jews in Israel's population, this has not ensured agreement on the appropriate relationship between religion and the state, between the religious and secular authorities, or on the methods and techniques to be employed by the religious authorities. The approach to the role of religion has reflected a pragmatism born of compromise deemed essential by most Israelis.

The religious issue has its origins in the Zionist political goal of establishing a Jewish state. The Jewish return to the Holy Land was seen by Orthodox Jews as a divine pledge, but the ultra-Orthodox opposed the notion of a Jewish state established by man and wanted to await the messiah. At the same time, there were other anti-Zionists, including some Reform Jews who did not wish Judaism to be bound up with Jewish nationalism. Opposition to the creation of a Jewish state became academic after Israel's independence but continued to be expressed by small (but vocal) fringe groups at both ends of the spectrum. Reform opposition all but disappeared (with the exception of the American Council for Judaism and offshoots such as American Jewish Alternatives to Zionism), and the Reform movement, although concerned about the power and role of the Orthodox leadership in religious affairs within Israel, has been increasingly identified with the strongest Jewish supporters of Israel. Opposition within the ranks of the Orthodox dwindled, and the remaining group, consisting of some several hundred families, is the Neturei Karta (Guardians of the City) located in Jerusalem and in Brooklyn, New York. That group challenges the legitimacy of the state, expresses support for the Palestine Liberation Organization (PLO), and continues to refuse to recognize the authority of the state or to deal with it in any meaningful way.

The role of religion in Israel and the relationship between religious institutions and the state is an intensely emotional issue that deeply divides the population and affects many and diverse aspects of Israeli life. Although there are polarized extreme positions (including advocacy of total links and total separation between religion and the state), most Israeli Jews are prepared to accept some linkage between synagogue and state if only because of a perceived necessity to do so. The various views are strongly held, but all parties have accepted a working arrangement that prevents major clashes and reflects the reality of the situation as it developed in the period prior to independence. This has not resolved the issues, and a level of tension remains that periodically emerges in the form of political conflict.

The political reality of Israel has required coalition governments from the outset. That same reality has necessitated inclusion of the parties of the religious community in virtually all cabinets as coalition partners that have control of the Ministry of Religious Affairs and usually also of the Ministry of the Interior. This has given the religious parties substantial political power and thus an ability to enforce many of their demands and perspectives concerning the role of religion in the Jewish state.

For various reasons, the religious parties have tended to be "logical" coalition partners for Mapai/Labor and Likud since independence. Generally, the concessions sought by the religious parties from the main coalition party have been easier to grant than those sought by the parties with a more specific foreign policy or socioeconomic policy focus. Mapai/Labor was usually willing to maintain the status quo (or make concessions) on religious issues—concessions usually sought by the religious parties in exchange for their support on foreign policy or security matters of greater moment to Mapai/Labor. Coalitions were therefore relatively easily created, with Mapai giving ground on religious questions and the religious parties supporting Mapai's foreign policy and socioeconomic policy concepts. Whereas the demands of other parties were in the realm of foreign policy, security, or economics—all central to Mapai's thinking—the concerns of the religious parties were generally limited to matters impinging on religion and personal status, and generally these were of less concern.

As a result, state support of religious authority, including the maintenance of the Sabbath and dietary restrictions, became a feature of the state, as did numerous other factors of a more minor nature. For Mapai, these concessions seemed less onerous than those sought by Israel's other parties in exchange for their joining Mapai's coalition governments. As a result of cabinet participation and control of important ministries such as Religious Affairs, Interior, and Education, the religious minority has been able to exert significant influence on the nature, functioning, and decision making of the system. Despite religious party participation in the Cabinet, there continue to be government crises over religious questions.

Various religious-political issues have faced Israel's governments. The disagreement on incorporation of principles of religion in a constitution marked the Knesset debate on the preparation of that document. There has been discord over the religious education of children in immigration camps, compulsory military service for women, the question of uniform national education, and even on the criteria to be applied to determine if a given individual is to be considered a Jew according to Israel's laws. More recently the issues have involved the matter of conversion, the introduction of daylight saving time, and permissable activities on the Sabbath.

After Israel took control of East Jerusalem in 1967, a controversy developed with regard to the status of the Western (Wailing) Wall and the nearby areas where the Temple once stood. Although there was agreement that this was among the holiest of Jewish sites, there were differing perspectives concerning its treatment. In 1976 it was a religious issue—a no-confidence motion in the Knesset based on the charge that a government-organized ceremony precipitated violation of the Sabbath since those attending would be forced to travel on the Sabbath—that ultimately led to the resignation of the Rabin government, the call for new elections, and the coming to power of the Likud.

Although religious issues have always played a role in Israel's political and social life, they became particularly prominent following the accession to office of Begin and the Likud in 1977. At the same time, there has been an evolution in the religious parties and in their importance in the governmental structure. (These are dealt with in greater detail in Chapter 4 on politics.) Agudat Israel emerged after 1977 as a strong force that decided to join the coalition, for the first time since 1951, and to assert its views on religious issues, seeking to alter the status quo. It seemed to eclipse the National Religious party (NRP), which suffered from a number of internal difficulties (some of which were manifest in the decision of Aharon Abuhatzeira to bolt the party and establish Tami—his own North African–oriented religious party). Begin's accession to office fostered changes in the religious sphere as a reflection of his personal sympathy for many of the demands of the religious factions. The coalition agreements by which the 1977 and 1981 governments were established reflected the desire and ability of the religious parties to press for their particular interests in relation to the religious status quo. The religious parties, especially Agudat Israel and the National Religious party, insisted on substantial concessions from Begin and Likud prior to joining and supporting the coalition. The result was a lengthy coalition agreement that focused on important changes in the role of religion in Israel and on the question of who is a Jew.

THE NON-JEWISH POPULATION

Israel's non-Jewish citizenry is composed mainly of the Arabs who remained in what became Israel after the 1949 Armistice Agreements and their descendants. By 1984 that group had grown to nearly 700,000 as a result of a high birthrate (see Table 1.1). Another non-Jewish group, the approximately 1.3 million Arabs in the territories occupied by Israel in the Six Day War of 1967, is excluded from population totals. The Muslim population, which constitutes about three-fourths of the non-Jewish population, is predominantly Sunni. The Christians are about 14 percent of the non-Jewish population. Greek Catholics and Greek Orthodox constitute more than 70 percent of that number, but there are also Roman Catholics, Maronites, Armenians, Protestants, and Anglicans. The Druze are a self-governing religious community that broke from Islam, whose members live primarily in Syria and Lebanon. They number some 50,000 (about 9 percent of the non-Jewish population). The non-

Jewish communities have special positions, similar to those enjoyed under the Ottoman millet system.

After the 1949 Armistice Agreements, the activities of the Arab community were regarded primarily as concerns of Israel's security system, and most of the areas inhabited by the Arabs were placed under military control. Military government was established in those districts, and special defense and security zones were created. Israel's Arabs were granted citizenship with full legal equality but were forbidden to travel into or out of security areas without permission of the military. Military courts were established in which trials could be held in closed session. With the consent of the Minister of Defense, the military commanders could limit individual movements, impose restrictions on employment and business, issue deportation orders, search and seize, and detain a person if that were deemed necessary for security purposes. Those who argued in support of the military administration saw it as a means of controlling the Arab population and of preventing infiltration (from neighboring Arab states), sabotage, and espionage. It was argued that the very existence of the military administration was an important deterrent measure. However, as evidence developed that Israel's Arabs were not disloyal, and as Israel's security situation improved, pressure for relaxation (and then for total abolition) of military restrictions on Israel's Arabs grew in the Knesset and in public debate. The restrictions were gradually modified, and on December 1, 1966, military government was abolished. Functions that had been exercised by the military government were transferred to relevant civilian authorities.

The non-Jewish community has undergone other substantial changes since 1948. Education has become virtually universal. Local authority has grown, and through the various local authorities the Arabs have become involved in local decision making and provision of services. The traditional farm life of the Arab has been altered by new agricultural methods and by increased employment in other sectors of the economy—especially industry, construction, and services. Social and economic improvement have included more urbanization, modernization of villages, better infrastructure,

improved health care, and expansion of educational opportunities.

Arab-Jewish Separation

The Arab and Jewish communities in Israel have few
points of contact and those that exist are not intimate. The
Arabs tend to live in separate villages and in separate sections
of the major cities. The Jews and Arabs are separate societies
who generally continue to hold stereotypical images of each
other, often reinforced by the schools, the press, social distance,
and—most significantly—the tensions and problems created
by the larger Arab-Israeli conflict in its numerous dimensions.
There is mutual suspicion and antagonism, and there is still
a Jewish fear of Arabs—a result of wars and terrorism. The
Jewish educational system displays a lack of knowledge of
and information about Israeli Arabs, even while there is
considerable expertise about the Arabs of the surrounding
countries. The lack of knowledge and contact is reinforced
by the separateness of the two communities, and this is
apparently a result of a mutual desire to maintain the individual
cultures and societies.

Israel is not a melting pot, and neither the Arabs nor
the Jews apparently want it to be. There is opposition to
integrated schools and to mixed neighborhoods, and intermarriage remains a very complex and divisive issue. The two
groups seek to preserve their distinctiveness, although there
has been some cultural seepage across the line that divides
the two communities and their cultures and histories.

For the Arabs of Israel, both Muslim and Christian, there
is a major dilemma—they are torn between their country
(they are citizens of Israel) and their people (the Arabs). As
an Arab minority in a country threatened by the Arab world,
they are objects of suspicion, surveillance, and discrimination;
are denied certain jobs; and are subjected to extra scrutiny
because of the security factor. Yet, they possess virtually all
the rights and privileges of Israel's Jewish citizens. They have
a right to vote, secure seats in the Knesset, participate in
local government, serve in government offices, enjoy equality

before the law, receive economic and social-welfare benefits, have their own schools and courts, and prosper materially. The Arabs are not drafted for service in the army, although the Druze are, but they may volunteer, and some do so. There is discrimination built into the system in that those who serve in the military are entitled to more generous social welfare support; because the Arabs do not serve in the military, they are discriminated against in securing this support. There is also discrimination in the allocation of government funds to Arab towns as compared with Jewish villages, although the precise reasons for this remain obscure and appear to be a result of actions at both the national and local levels.

Overall, the socioeconomic status of the Arab population is lower than that of the Jewish population—Arabs have lower income than their Jewish peers, their larger families compound the financial burden, and their housing is generally of poorer quality. Centuries of foreign control left their impact on the political attitudes of the Arabs; that is, earlier despotic rule, violence, and extortion have engendered an attitude of suspicion and mistrust toward government.

Successive Israeli governments have sought to bring about a more complete integration of Arab citizens into the life of the country and to foster their economic, social, and cultural advancement. However, there are essentially no issue areas where the two groups are logical political allies. There is no political or other unit of society where Israeli Jews and Israeli Arabs meet to barter or bargain for the allocation of political, economic, or social resources. As a minority, the Arab community has no veto over policies affecting its future or affairs. There is no proportional distribution of appointments or positions within the system, nor has the Jewish community made concessions on political posts or on other matters to the Arab minority.

Arabs and the Political System

Israel is a democratic and open society whose citizens are equal before the law. Israel's Declaration of Independence sought to clarify the philosophical basis for Israel's future and noted that the state "will ensure complete equality of social and political rights to all its inhabitants irrespective of religion, race, or sex; it will guarantee freedom of religion, conscience, language, education and culture." The laws of Israel do not discriminate with regard to religion or nationality, with the exception of the special circumstances of the Law of Return (which facilitates *Jewish* immigration) and the Nationality Law of 1952 (which differentiates between Jews and non-Jews in naturalization in specific instances). There is universal adult suffrage, and Arabs can and do vote in large numbers and are periodically courted by many of the political parties for their vote.

Despite their ability to participate in the system, the Arabs of Israel have been relatively inactive politically. They have failed to form a significant independent Arab political party that could appeal to the Arab voter, represent the Arab minority in the quest for Arab rights, and express its opinions, perspectives, and positions. In part this is a result of the belief that the Arabs could achieve more by working within the Labor party and Labor Alignment than against it with their own parties. In addition, no significant independent Arab social, economic, cultural, or professional organization has come into being. Independent organs of opinion are similarly lacking. No Arab leaders of national stature have appeared on the scene, although some local leaders are relatively well-known nationally, partly because of the small size of the state. Additionally there have been few demonstrations or protests by Israeli Arabs to represent their perspective. Mass actions by the Arab population have been few in number and limited in effect.

Nevertheless, over time the Arab community has become increasingly politicized. Below the surface equanimity there is a discontent with the perceived second-class status resulting from various forms of unofficial discrimination. In the wake of the Yom Kippur War of 1973 and with the increased international standing of the Palestinians, most especially of the PLO, the Arabs of Israel seemed to become more restive and more politically aware. Increased support for the Communist party culminated in the election of a Communist mayor in Nazareth in 1975 and in increasing activity in student groups on university campuses among the more educated segments of the Arab society. In the spring of 1976, Israel's Arabs participated in their first general protest and staged the most violent demonstrations in Israel's history to that time.

The riots, whose extent and ferocity surprised both Israeli Arabs and Jews, grew out of a general strike, centered in Nazareth, that was called to protest land expropriations in Israel's northern section. The government had adopted a five-year plan to increase the number of Jewish settlers in the Galilee and had expropriated land, some of which was Arab-owned. Despite compensation, the Arabs protested that their land should not be expropriated to make it available for Jewish settlers. The expropriation served as a catalyst; the initial demonstrations escalated and eventually became broader and more general in their focus, incorporating various grievances and general complaints about the second-class status of Israel's Arabs. Although the immediate problems receded, the basic questions remain.

This growing political action reflects a number of factors. One is the erosion of traditional life-styles and patterns of activity and their replacement by modern and interactive life-styles more typical of Western societies. Another is an emergence of a sense of Arab identity—including links to Arabs beyond the borders of Israel, accelerated by the contacts made after the 1967 war. Between 1948 and 1967, Israel's Arabs were isolated from the rest of the Arab world. Because there were few direct contacts with other Arabs, Arabs in Israel were also cut off from contact with developments in the Arab states. The war and the Israeli occupation of substantial territories with hundreds of thousands of Palestinians gave Israeli Arabs a direct link to the Arab world—more specifically, to the Palestinians. In many instances they could reestablish connections with friends, neighbors, and relatives from whom they had been separated after 1948. Direct contacts with nearly a million additional Arabs in the West Bank and Gaza were possible. Travel between the occupied areas and Arab capitals allowed further contacts, albeit less direct, with the latest developments in the Arab states. This has helped to generate a new perspective among the Arabs of Israel.

Another factor in political development has been a growth of appropriate institutions for the expression of views and perspectives, as Israeli Arabs have become more exposed to the life-styles and activities of the Jewish population of Israel. Perhaps most important of these has been the increasing educational opportunities available. Education has become nearly universal at the lower levels, and tens of thousands of Israeli Arabs have graduated from high schools and universities. This has created a group of well-educated and articulate Arabs, which has helped to undermine the more traditional social structure of the Arab village and family.

To date, however, the Arabs have failed to organize on a mass communal basis to improve their position and status. Given the absence of important Arab political parties, the Communist party in its various incarnations has played an important role in the articulation of the Arab perspective and in promoting Arab positions. But it is not an "Arab" party, even though most of its voting support comes from the Arabs of Israel and much of its orientation has come from its Moscow connection.

The Arab issue has been of little prominence on the political scene; there has been little ethnic strife between the Arab minority and the Jewish majority. Issues concerning the Arab community of Israel have not attracted much sustained interest or attention within the Jewish community of Israel, whether in the media or political circles, or become a salient political issue over an extended period. The communal gaps between Jews and Arabs in various sectors have not become significant concerns of the system: The Knesset and the government rarely consider the matter. The issue was significant in the period prior to 1966, and the matter was discussed to some extent when Israel was considering the question of abolition of the military administration. This was perhaps the most prominent discussion of the issue of Israeli Arabs in Israel's political mainstream, although it has been raised periodically since that time.

It is surprising that the Arab community of Israel has not been more politically aware and active—there have been numerous factors and incentives to motivate that type of action and response. It would seem that strong irredentism on the part of Israel's neighbors, constant propaganda from the Arab world, and strong bonds of kinship and national identity between Israeli Arabs and Arabs (including refugees) across the border should have encouraged feelings of alienation in Israel's Arab minority, should have generated some action on its part, over and beyond the irritation of land expropriation and the socioeconomic gap.

Social and economic improvements do seem to have facilitated political organization and political action and have raised expectations and stimulated further political demands. The older and more traditional political style is declining relative to the newer approaches. Israel's Arabs are more nationally oriented and less parochial, and there is more sophistication regarding political goals and strategies along with an increasing ability to organize and mobilize on a national scale. Whether the political quiescence that has characterized Israel's Arabs will continue, in light of their growing political awareness, remains uncertain.

The sabra (cactus). Sabra is also the name for native-born Israelis (*left*). The Judean desert (*below*).

Housing in a typical neighborhood (*right*). Bringing water to the desert: Pipes for Israel's National Water Carrier (*below*).

Haifa, Israel's major port on the Mediterranean (*top*). Tel Aviv: Hotels and marina on the Mediterranean (*center*). Tel Aviv (*bottom*).

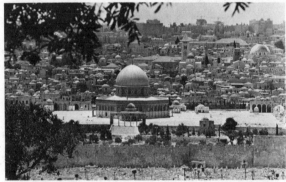

Jerusalem, capital and largest city in Israel (*top*). Dome of the Rock Mosque with the old city wall in the foreground and the old and new Jerusalem beyond (*center*). Ben-Yehuda Street in Jerusalem (*bottom*).

Tradition and conflict: (*top*) The Western (Wailing) Wall, a remnant of the Holy Temple compound, with the Dome of the Rock Mosque, a major shrine of Islam, above; (*bottom*) praying at the Western Wall.

Demographic mosaic: A street in Jerusalem (*top*). Café on a main street in Tel Aviv (*center*). Israel's bedouin meet at the market in Beersheba (*bottom*).

Operation Magic Carpet: Immigrants from Yemen come to Israel in 1949.

2

History

Israel is a young country, having achieved its modern independence in 1948, but it has an intimate connection to the ancient Jewish state and to Jewish history. The land of Israel was the ancient birthplace of the Jewish people, and it is in this area that the religious and national identity of that people was formed and developed. Later, the ancient Jewish state, the Holy Land, and Jerusalem became the spiritual focal points of the Jewish religion—a part of its hopes, rituals, and goals—in addition to providing the historical link for the Jews. Thus, the Jewish connection to Zion for centuries could be found at the heart of tradition, belief, and religion.

EARLY JEWISH HISTORY

The earliest connections between the Jewish people and the land of Israel are in the Biblical period when Abraham, the first of the patriarchs of Judaism, migrated from Ur of the Chaldeans to Haran and then to the Promised Land around the second millenium B.C. or B.C.E. The subsequent travails of the children of Israel in Egypt culminated in the Exodus (ca. thirteenth century B.C.) led by Moses, which was marked by various events of continuing significance in Jewish history and tradition. Notable Jewish holidays—Passover, (Pesach), Pentecost (Shavuot), and Tabernacles (Succot)—relate to the Exodus and the wanderings of the children of Israel through the desert from Egypt to the Promised Land.

Under Joshua and the Judges the Israelites conquered and settled much of the Promised Land (Canaan), and eventually a monarchy was established under King Saul (ca. 1020–1004 B.C.). He was succeeded by David (ca. 1004–965 B.C.), who unified the Jewish tribes, pacified the area, and made Israel into a major regional force. Jerusalem became his capital, and he established a dynasty that lasted some four hundred years. His son, Solomon (965–928 B.C.), inherited a strong, large, and peaceful kingdom, and Israel became a great trading nation. Solomon's wisdom was legendary, and he constructed the first Temple, which became the focal point of religious and secular life in the Jewish state. After Solomon's death the kingdom was divided. Ten northern tribes established the Kingdom of Israel that lasted from 928 to 722 B.C., when it was destroyed by an Assyrian monarch who exiled the tribes into obscurity. The Kingdom of Judah (Judea), in the south, maintained its capital at Jerusalem until 586 B.C., when the Babylonians destroyed the Temple, ended the kingdom, and took the leadership and much of the Jewish population in exile to Babylon. Under Cyrus of Persia the Jews were allowed to return to Jerusalem, and the rebuilding of the Temple began.

Subsequently (except for a period of independence under the Hasmoneans), Persian, Greek, or Syrian-Greek rulers controlled or sought control of the area. In 63 B.C. the Roman leader Pompey conquered Judea and Jerusalem, inaugurating a period of relative calm that ended with a revolt in A.D. 66. The revolt was put down, and Titus, commander of the Roman forces, conquered Jerusalem and destroyed the Temple in A.D. 70. After the revolt of Simon Bar Kochba (132–135), Jerusalem was destroyed, large numbers of Jews were killed or enslaved, and, most significantly, Jewish sovereignty over the area was terminated. Many Jews were dispersed throughout the world (a scattering known as the Diaspora), and the idea of an ultimate return to the Promised Land went with them. After a period of Christian control under the Byzantines, the region fell to the Arabs in the seventh century (they took Jerusalem in 638) and then to the Seljuk Turks. This period of Muslim control was interrupted when the Crusaders conquered Jerusalem in 1099 and established the Latin Kingdom, which lasted until 1291. They were succeeded by the Muslim Mamelukes (1291–1516). Ottoman rule was established in 1517 and lasted until the end of World War I.

Many Jews were in the Diaspora, but Jews remained in the area throughout the long period of outside domination, although their political, social, and economic status varied considerably as the ruling powers changed. Of those Jews living in Palestine, two-thirds were in Jerusalem; smaller communities resided in Safed, Tiberias, and Hebron. By the late nineteenth century, conditions were appropriate for the reestablishment of a growing Jewish link with the land of Israel. In the 1880s, Jewish refugees from the pogroms in Russia and from similarly adverse conditions elsewhere in Europe began to arrive in Palestine. There was also a group of Oriental Jews, mostly from Yemen. These and members of the Hibbat Zion movement (known as Hoveve Zion— Lovers of Zion) joined farm villages or established new ones (such as Rishon Le-Zion, Zichron Ya'akov, and Rosh Pina) in conformity with their view that immigration and settlement in Palestine would alleviate the problems of the communities in Europe. In 1878, a group of Jews from Jerusalem founded a new town, Petah Tikva.

The new immigrants, later known as the First Aliyah, faced many obstacles, some natural and some placed in their way by the Ottoman Turkish administration. But it was this immigration and the founding of agricultural settlements that revived modern Jewish life, along with the politically focused Jewish national liberation movement (political Zionism) and the founding of the World Zionist Organization.

ZIONISM

Theodor Herzl (1860–1904), the founder of modern political Zionism, was the driving force for the creation of the political ideology and worldwide movement that paralleled the actions taken by the first immigrants. He was an assimilated Jew who was born in Budapest but later moved to Vienna. As a journalist, he observed the Dreyfus trial and was affected by the false accusations leveled against the French Jewish army officer and by the episodes of anti-Semitism that accompanied the trial and the disgrace of Dreyfus. Herzl later wrote *Der Judenstaat* (The Jewish State), published in 1896, in which he assessed the situation and problems of the Jews and proposed a practical plan for resolution of the Jewish question. Subsequently, Herzl traveled widely to publicize and gain support for his ideas. He found backing among the masses of East European Jewry and opposition among the leadership and wealthier segments of the Western Jewish communities.

On August 23, 1897, in Basel, Switzerland, Herzl convened the first World Zionist Congress representing Jewish communities and organizations throughout the world. The congress established the World Zionist Organization (WZO) and founded an effective, modern, political, Jewish national movement with the goal, enunciated in the Basel Program, the original official program of the WZO, "Zionism seeks to establish a home for the Jewish people in Palestine secured under public law." Zionism rejected other solutions to the "Jewish Question" and was the response to centuries of discrimination, persecution, and oppression. It sought redemption through self-determination. Herzl argued in *Der Judenstaat*: "Let the sovereignty be granted us over a portion of the globe large enough to satisfy the rightful requirements of a nation; the rest we shall manage for ourselves."

Israel is a product of, and has adopted as its ideology, modern political Zionism, which had its origins in the historical-traditional pledges recorded in the Bible, linking the Jewish people to the land of Israel. Since biblical days the Jews of the Diaspora longed for the time that they would return to Zion, the Promised Land. Much of this hope was religious in nature and orientation and viewed a return to the Promised Land as an achievement that would result from some form of divine action. At the same time, Jewish writers developed spiritual, religious, cultural, social, and historical concepts linking Jews to the land of the historical Jewish state in Israel.

Zionism had a long history before its conversion at the end of the nineteenth century into its modern political form as the Jewish national movement that saw the establishment of a Jewish state as a logical consequence of its actions. This conversion was facilitated by the political currents and fertile conditions presented by nineteenth-century European nationalism and anti-Semitism. The movement built on centuries of Jewish history and tradition and identified a future goal— the creation of a Jewish state—that linked Jewish identity with a geographic area.

At the outset, Jewish nationalism was poorly developed. Jews were scattered throughout the world, although those in the Diaspora retained a strong spiritual, traditional, and emotional tie to the geographic area known as the land of Israel. Some intellectuals began to write about the Jews and the conditions in which they lived, thereby providing the underpinnings for an ideology. It was in the European atmosphere of numerous nationalist movements, blatant anti-Semitism, and Jewish nationalist literature by such authors as Moses Hess and Leo Pinsker that Herzl wrote the tract that provided the best-known operational basis for modern political Zionism.

The Zionist movement began its work after the Basel congress. Various organizations and units were created to carry on the work of the Zionist movement, including the Jewish National Fund, founded in 1901 at the Fifth Zionist Congress and charged with land purchase and development in Palestine. Like other nationalist movements, various internal divisions developed that reflected differing backgrounds and approaches, although the central goal of creating a Jewish state in Palestine was a strong cohesive force.

World War I provided an opportunity for the Zionist movement to make important gains. Among the more significant was the Balfour Declaration, issued by the British government on November 2, 1917. Substantial effort by the Zionist organization, with a special role played by Chaim Weizmann (a Russian-born Jew who was not only a British chemist who made significant contributions to the British war effort but also a prominent Zionist leader who later became the first president of Israel), preceded the government's decision, after lengthy discussion and some division. The declaration took the form of a letter from Arthur James Balfour, the foreign secretary, to Lord Rothschild, a prominent Zionist leader.

> His Majesty's Government view with favour the establish-
> ment in Palestine of a national home for the Jewish people,
> and will use their best endeavours to facilitate the achievement
> of this object, it being clearly understood that nothing shall
> be done which may prejudice the civil and religious rights
> of existing non-Jewish communities in Palestine, or the rights
> and political status enjoyed by Jews in any other country.

The declaration was vague and sought to assuage the fears of prominent Jews in England as well as those of the non-Jewish inhabitants of Palestine. Nevertheless, it engendered much controversy, then and since.

Among the problems was the Balfour Declaration's apparent conflict with arrangements made during World War I by the British with the French and the Arabs concerning the future of the Middle East after the termination of hostilities. Foremost among those was the Hussein-McMahon Correspondence, which the Arabs saw as a promise that an independent Arab kingdom would include all of Palestine, although the British later argued that they had excluded the territory west of the Jordan River from that pledge.

THE PALESTINE MANDATE

At the end of World War I, British control replaced Ottoman rule in much of the Middle East, including Palestine, and the fate of the Middle East was determined by the Allied powers. The future of the region was considered at length at the Paris Peace Conference and elsewhere, and eventually the British and French divided the area into spheres of influence and control. At the San Remo Conference (1920) the British and French agreed on the frontiers of the Palestine mandate and the disposition of the neighboring territories. Subsequently the British separated the territory east of the Jordan River from that to the west, created the Amirate of Transjordan, and accepted its control by Amir Abdullah, the son of Sherif

Hussein. The Palestine mandate to which the Balfour Declaration might apply was thus left with only the territory west of the Jordan River, although the various mandatory arrangements continued to apply to Transjordan.

The decision to separate the territory was a divisive factor within the Zionist movement, leading to the creation of Vladimir Zeev Jabotinsky's World Union of Zionist Revisionists (ultimately the New Zionist Organization) that has provided the ideological basis for Herut and Likud, under the leadership of Menachem Begin. Jabotinsky's goal was the establishment of a Jewish state, with a Jewish majority, on both sides of the Jordan River, and he opposed partition of Palestine into an Arab and a Jewish state. The revisionists also opposed efforts to place restrictions on Jewish immigration to Palestine and argued for the immediate establishment of a Jewish state in all of Palestine. The demand for Jewish control over the two banks of the Jordan was central to revisionism and separated it from other Zionist factions in mandatory Palestine. The Revisionist party, established by Jabotinsky in 1925, and his New Zionist Organization supported the principle of Shlemut Hamoledet, the right of the Jewish people to all of Eretz Israel, and rejected Arab claims for national and political sovereignty in Palestine.

Jabotinsky agreed that the Palestinian Arabs had a national identity and were conscious of their common past and future, but he opposed the creation of an Arab state in Palestine and sought to defeat Arab nationalist attempts to create such a state. Jabotinsky argued for increased militarism, self-reliance, and overt opposition to British authority. The Irgun Tzevai Leumi (the National Military Organization, or Etzel—known as the Irgun) was founded by the revisionists in 1937 as an armed Jewish underground movement after seceding from Hagana (Defense) because of the primarily defensive character of that organization, established earlier as the official defense force of the Jewish community. The Irgun was active against Arab attackers of the Yishuv and, following World War II, renewed its fight against the British presence in Palestine and retaliated against British actions taken against the Jewish guerrillas. Israel's new government under David Ben-Gurion finally forced the Irgun to dissolve as a demonstration of the regime's capacity to govern and to exert control over its territory and population.

The mandate for Palestine differed from the other mandates established after World War I in that, inter alia, it gave special recognition to Zionist claims and to the Zionist movement. The preamble to the mandate incorporated the Balfour Declaration, and throughout there was an emphasis on the rights and privileges of the Jewish community, including those of preparing for the establishment of the Jewish national home. The mandate formally acknowledged the Zionist organization as "an appropriate Jewish agency . . . for the purpose of advising and cooperating with the Administration of Palestine in such economic, social, and other matters as may affect the establishment of the Jewish National Home and the interests of the Jewish population in Palestine. . . ."

Between 1920 and 1948 Britain controlled Palestine and exercised its authority through a high commissioner and an executive council composed of senior British officials. The mandate established Britain's responsibility to help prepare Palestine for independence, and it contributed to the territory's development through the building of an infrastructure, the improvement of education and health conditions, and the fostering of agricultural and industrial productivity. Autonomous Arab and Jewish communal groups were established and were granted powers of self-government within the framework created by British Orders-in-Council and the regulations of the mandate system.

During the mandate period, the Yishuv established and developed institutions for self-government and procedures for implementing political decisions, thereby laying the foundations for the future state of Israel. All significant Jewish groups belonged to the organized Jewish community (with the exception of the ultra-Orthodox Agudat Israel, then anti-Zionist, which refused to participate) and chose, by secret ballot, the Assembly of the Elected (Asefat Hanivcharim) as its representative body. It met at least once a year, and between sessions its powers were exercised by the National Council (Vaad Leumi), which it elected.

The mandatory government entrusted the National Council with the responsibility for Jewish communal affairs and granted it considerable autonomy. The executive committee of the National Council—through a number of self-created departments concerned with education, culture, health, social welfare, and religious affairs—acted as the administering power for the Jewish community. The council also controlled the recruitment and clandestine military training of Jewish youth in the Hagana, which after independence formed the core of the IDF. The General Federation of Labor (Histadrut), founded in 1920, coordinated labor-related matters and engaged in social welfare and economic endeavors.

The National Council functioned concurrently with the internationally recognized executive of the Jewish Agency for Palestine. Article 4 of the Palestine Mandate had provided for the establishment of "an appropriate Jewish Agency . . . for the purpose of advising and cooperating with the administration of Palestine in such economic, social, and other matters as may affect the establishment of the Jewish National Home and the interests of the Jewish population in Palestine, and . . . to assist and take part in the development of the country." Chaim Weizmann, as president of the WZO, negotiated with leading representatives of Jewish organizations and communities throughout the world for their participation in the work of the Jewish Agency. In August 1929 these negotiations culminated in the establishment of a new body, the Jewish Agency for Palestine, popularly referred to as the Expanded Jewish Agency. It took over the activities—such as fundraising and maintaining liaison with foreign governments—designed to build a Jewish national home, a project in which concerned Jews everywhere could participate. It conducted negotiations with the mandatory authority (the United Kingdom) and the League of Nations and unsuccessfully sought accommodation with the Arabs.

Prototypical institutions, founded and developed by and for the Jewish community, laid the foundation for many of Israel's public bodies and political processes. The party system was initiated, and proportional representation was instituted. Procedures were established and tried, and the Yishuv gained experience in the functioning of the political process. Several of the semigovernmental organizations created, most notably the Histadrut and the Jewish Agency, continued to play important roles after Israel's independence. These have contributed to the growth of a highly developed system of Zionist political parties and the consequential prevalence of coalition executive bodies both in the Zionist movement and in the local organs of Palestinian Jewry. The political parties that were established contested the elections for the various political posts. The political elite filled roles in the organs of the Zionist movement, including the Jewish Agency, the Hagana, and the Histadrut, and in other political institutions and was concerned with relations with the British as the mandatory power and with the promotion of Jewish immigration to and settlement in Palestine.

During much of the mandate period the Jewish and Arab communities of Palestine were in conflict. The tensions were reflected in such events as riots by the Arabs in 1920 and 1921, the 1929 massacre by Arabs of Jewish inhabitants in Hebron, and the 1936–1939 Arab disturbances. Britain's responses to the clashes between the two communities took numerous forms; the most significant was limitation of Jewish immigration and land purchases. The Yishuv's response to the deteriorating security situation posed by Arab attacks was to create the Hagana.

In 1937 the Peel Royal Commission recommended partition of the Palestine mandate into an Arab state united with Transjordan and a Jewish state, while retaining a British enclave. The recommendation was later abandoned, but in 1939, in a new White Paper, the British dramatically restricted Jewish immigration to Palestine.

After World War I, when the British mandate replaced Ottoman rule in Palestine, the focus of Zionist political and diplomatic endeavor was Britain. However, during and after World War II, political necessity and reality resulted in a shift in focus to the United States. The Biltmore Program, adopted by the Extraordinary Zionist Conference in New York on May 11, 1942, in response to Britain's policy toward the Jewish national home (particularly the restrictions on land sales and immigration), became the basis for Zionist effort until Israel's independence and was a harbinger of change. The program rejected British efforts to restrict Jewish immigration to and settlement in Palestine and called for the fulfillment of the Balfour Declaration and the mandate, urging that "Palestine be established as a Jewish Commonwealth." The Biltmore Program reflected the urgency of the situation in which the Jewish leadership found itself as a consequence of the Holocaust and the need to provide for the displaced Jews of Europe.

Unable to satisfy the conflicting views of the Arab and Jewish communities of Palestine and to ensure public safety because of the conflicts between them and faced with the heavy burden entailed in retaining the mandate, which compounded the extensive costs of World War II, the British now conceded that the mandate was unworkable and turned the Palestine problem over to the United Nations in the spring of 1947. The United Nations Special Committee on Palestine (UNSCOP) examined the issues and recommended that the mandate bè terminated and that the independence of Palestine be achieved without delay. However, it was divided on the future of the territory. The majority proposed partition into a Jewish state and an Arab state linked in an economic union, with Jerusalem and its environs established as an international enclave. The minority suggested that Palestine become a single federal state, with Jerusalem as its capital and with Jews and Arabs enjoying autonomy in their respective areas.

On November 29, 1947, the United Nations General Assembly adopted the majority recommendation (the partition plan) over Arab opposition, by thirty-three votes to thirteen, with ten abstentions. The situation in Palestine deteriorated rapidly after the United Nations vote. Disorders initiated by the local Arab population, reminiscent of those of the 1920s and 1930s, broke out in all parts of the country, and as the end of the mandate approached, they degenerated into a virtual civil war.

ISRAEL'S INDEPENDENCE

The British decided to end the mandate on May 14, 1948, and David Ben-Gurion read the Declaration of Independence that established the State of Israel as the last British high commissioner departed. The temporary National Council of State unanimously passed an ordinance voiding the restrictions on Jewish immigration and land purchases contained in the 1939 British White Paper. The United States recognized the provisional government "as the *de facto* authority of the new State of Israel," and three days later the USSR granted *de jure* recognition.

First Arab-Israeli War

As Israel declared its independence, armies of the Arab states entered Palestine and engaged in open warfare with the defense forces of the new state, with the stated goals of preventing the establishment of a Jewish state and of assuring that all of Palestine would be in Arab hands. This first Arab-Israeli war (known in Israel as the War of Independence) involved troops from Egypt, Syria, Jordan, Iraq, and Lebanon, with assistance from other Arab quarters, against Israel. The war was long and costly: Israel lost some four thousand soldiers and two thousand civilians, about 1 percent of the Jewish population, and each side had successes and failures.

When the war ended in 1949 Israel was in control of about one-third more territory (some 2,500 square miles— 6,500 square kilometers) than it had been allocated by the partition plan. This area was acquired at the expense of the projected Arab state of Palestine, never formally established owing to the Arab refusal to accept anything less than all of Palestine. The remaining territory of the projected Palestinian Arab state was divided between Jordan and Egypt. The former incorporated what has become known as the West Bank (some 2,200 square miles—5,700 square kilometers) into its kingdom, while the latter established its military administration over the Gaza Strip (135 square miles—350 square kilometers). Jordan's decision to annex the territory was recognized only by Britain and Pakistan, was taken against the wishes of the other Arab states, and was condemned and not recognized by the Arab League. Jerusalem was divided between Israel and Jordan rather than becoming the international city envisioned by the partition plan.

The United Nations secured a truce, and the military situation was stabilized by a series of armistice agreements signed in the spring of 1949 between Israel and the neighboring Arab states. These agreements also delineated the frontiers (not recognized borders) between them and established a series of demilitarized zones between Israel and Egypt, Syria, and Jordan. Israel's frontiers at that point encompassed approximately 8,000 square miles (20,700 square kilometers). The United Nations Truce Supervision Organization (UNTSO) was established to oversee the armistice, but a general peace settlement was not achieved. Although it was agreed in the armistice accords that the goal was to achieve peace, the Arab states refused to negotiate for peace with Israel.

An armistice agreement between Egypt and Israel was signed on February 24, 1949. Israel retained the Negev extending to the Sinai border; the Gaza Strip remained under Eygptian military occupation. An agreement with Jordan established a 330-mile-long (530-kilometer-long), winding border that left the so-called West Bank under Jordanian occupation. The boundary ran through the streets of Jerusalem, dividing it between the Jordanian eastern sector and the Israeli western portion. The Jordanian Arab Legion replaced the Iraqi forces in the north-central "triangle" area of the country. An agreement with Lebanon established a demarcation line along the former international frontier between Lebanon and the Palestine mandate, and Israeli forces withdrew from the Lebanese villages they had occupied. Under the terms of the agreement with Syria, the latter withdrew from the areas occupied west of the former international frontier, and Israel agreed to their demilitarization and permitted the return of the Arabs who had fled during the fighting. Israel secured control over Lake Tiberias and the Hula Valley. Iraq did not conclude an armistice agreement.

A Palestine Conciliation Commission was established by the United Nations to settle the problem of those who had fled before and during the war from the territories that became part of Israel. It met in Lausanne on April 26, 1949. The Arab delegations insisted on the return of all Arab refugees as a precondition to negotiations, but Israel was prepared to discuss the problem only as an element of a comprehensive peace settlement. Israel later offered to admit 100,000 refugees as part of that settlement, but the Lausanne talks made no progress and were broken off in September. Subsequent efforts achieved no breakthrough on this matter.

Establishment of the State

The new state began to function even while the fighting continued. It was during this war that Israel's fledgling government was faced with a critical domestic challenge to its authority. Despite efforts at coordination and control of the various preindependence movements by the government, the Irgun Tzevai Leumi was still active. A ship, the *Altalena*, arrived from France with not only immigrants but also arms and ammunition for delivery to the Irgun. The government ordered that the ship and its cargo be placed at its disposal, but the Irgun refused. In the subsequent battle between the army and the Irgun the government prevailed, and the ship was sunk. Soon afterward the Irgun was disbanded, and its members were incorporated into the Israeli army. The incident, which added to the existing bitterness between the protagonists and pitted Menachem Begin and David Ben-Gurion against each other for decades to follow, made it clear that the government would not tolerate challenges to its authority or the existence of armed forces competing with the IDF.

A census taken on November 8, 1948, determined the population in Israeli-controlled areas to be 873,000—717,000 Jews and 156,000 Arabs. The majority of those eligible cast ballots on January 25, 1949, for members of the First Knesset. The largest party was the left-of-center Mapai, which won 46 seats out of 120. It was followed by the more leftward leaning Mapam with 19 seats and the United Religious Front, representing the Orthodox Jewish perspective, with 16. David Ben-Gurion became prime minister, and Chaim Weizmann took the oath as the first president of the State of Israel in February 1949.

Despite the failure to achieve peace with the Arab states, and the resultant continuation of the Arab-Israeli conflict with its potential for future wars, Israel began to consolidate its position at home and abroad in the late 1940s. Its international status improved rapidly; within a year after independence, Israel was recognized by fifty states, and on May 11, 1949, was admitted as a member of the United Nations. At home a major focus was immigration. The early years of statehood saw an ingathering of Jewish exiles, one of Israel's basic aspirations, under the terms of the 1950 Law of Return. In September 1952, after a bitter controversy within Israel, an agreement was signed with the Federal Republic of Germany for payment to the State of Israel, as the representative of the Jewish people, of DM3 billion (then worth US$715 million) as partial reparation for material losses suffered by the Jews under the Nazis. In November 1952 Weizmann died, and Itzhak Ben-Zvi, a Zionist Labor leader and prominent historian, was elected as president the following month.

Beginning in the late 1950s, Israel's relations with Asia and Africa grew significantly. Israel sought to develop friendly relations with Third World states that would help to counter growing Arab-sponsored anti-Israel pressure in various international forums. Israel embarked on an intensive and extensive program of economic aid and technical assistance to emerging black African states. Relations with Africa continued to expand steadily until the early 1970s, then declined rapidly during and after the Yom Kippur War of 1973.

Continued Hostilities

Although the armistice agreements had envisioned movement toward peace, the early 1950s were characterized by a heightening of tension in the area. In June 1950 the members of the Arab League concluded a joint defense treaty to improve their ability to respond to the perceived danger posed by the

Zionist state. Continuing to attack the "Zionist threat," they maintained the state of war with Israel. They demanded the implementation of United Nations resolutions that favored their cause and maintained their commitment to the destruction of the State of Israel and to the restoration of the rights of the Arabs in Palestine. The Arab League also maintained its boycott of Israel and sought to dissuade foreign concerns, through economic pressure, from trading with Israel or from investing in its economy. Egypt denied passage through the Suez Canal and the Strait of Tiran to ships or cargoes belonging to or traveling to or from Israel. Sabotage, shooting, and murders increased regional tensions. In the period from 1951 to 1956, over four hundred Israelis were killed and nine hundred injured in some three thousand armed clashes with Arab regulars or irregular forces inside Israeli territory; in addition, some six thousand acts of sabotage, theft, or attempted theft were committed by infiltrators coming primarily from Egyptian and Jordanian territory. Disputes arose between Syria and Israel over water rights and between Jordan and Israel over roadblocks by force as well as over demilitarized-zone violations.

Although secret contacts to achieve peace took place between King Abdullah of Jordan and representatives of Israel, starting prior to Israel's independence, hopes of a possible arrangement were dashed when he was assassinated by an Arab extremist in Jerusalem in July 1951. A vicious cycle of repeated Arab attacks, reprisals by Israel, and international condemnations of Israel occurred throughout 1954, and sporadic incidents in the Gaza Strip and on the Sinai border became more serious in that year. The situation continued to deteriorate.

By January 1956, it was clear that war was approaching. The arms race was continuing, and tension increased when the Czech-Egyptian arms deal, announced in September 1955, introduced the Soviet Union as a major arms supplier to the Arab-Israeli sector. Palestinian *fedayeen* (guerrilla/commando) attacks into Israel were on the increase. At the same time the British and the French opposed Eygpt's nationalization of the Suez Canal and its support of anti-French rebels in

North Africa. Britain and France agreed with Israel that action against the dangers posed by President Gamal Abdul Nasser of Egypt, who had emerged as the leader of postrevolution Egypt, and his policies was essential, and the three powers organized a coordinated operation. Israel moved into Sinai on October 29, 1956, and by the afternoon of the next day, Britain and France issued an ultimatum (as previously agreed) calling on both sides to stop fighting and to withdraw to positions 10 miles (16 kilometers) on either side of the Suez Canal. Israel accepted, but Egypt rejected the proposal, and the fighting continued. By November 5 Israel had occupied Sharm el-Sheikh, and the war was over. Britain and France managed to fight their way through only one-third of the canal before the United Nations called for a cease-fire.

The United States took a leading role in bringing about a cease-fire and the eventual withdrawal of Israeli, British, and French troops from Egyptian territory. U.S. pressure, as well as reassurances, eventually proved decisive in securing Israel's full withdrawal from the Sinai Peninsula and the Gaza Strip. As a consequence of the Suez crisis and the Sinai War, a United Nations Emergency Force (UNEF) was stationed in Sinai. In addition there were some tangible achievements for Israel that secured a considerable degree of quiet on its southwestern border and free access to Eilat, its outlet for trade with West Africa and Asia—gains that were preserved until the 1967 war.

For a decade after the 1956 Sinai campaign there was no large-scale outbreak of hostilities between Israel and the Arab states, although tensions remained high. Israel focused its attention on economic and social achievement at home and made considerable progress in transforming the country into a modern, urban, industrial society. Ben-Gurion's power and popularity reached their zenith in the late 1950s and early 1960s, only to decline later, and politics took on a new tenor with his replacement as prime minister by Levi Eshkol in 1963 and with continued alterations in the relationships among the various political parties. Foreign policy focused on improving international relationships, especially those with France and the United States. Israel continued to develop its

military capability to provide for defense in the face of Arab
hostility and potential conflict. The Arab-Israeli conflict receded
during much of the decade, but reasserted itself as the focus
of attention in the spring of 1967.

The Six Day War

In mid-May 1967, Egypt proclaimed a state of emergency,
mobilized its army, and moved troops across Sinai toward
the border with Israel. Nasser requested the removal of the
UNEF from the Egypt-Israel frontier, and United Nations
Secretary General U Thant complied. The UNEF positions
were then manned by contingents of the Egyptian armed
forces and of the PLO, which had been established in 1964
at the initiative, and with the assistance, of the Arab League.
Egypt and Israel faced each other with no buffer, and Nasser
announced that the Strait of Tiran would be closed to Israeli
shipping and to strategic cargoes bound for Israel's port of
Eilat. Israel regarded these actions as casus belli, illegal, and
aggressive. On May 30, Jordan entered into a defense pact
with Syria and Egypt, and Iraqi troops were stationed along
the Israel-Jordan front. The Israeli reaction to Egyptian mobilization and to the other actions appeared timid until it
became clear that the international system was not prepared
to take any action to support Israel beyond providing moral
support: Israel received no U.S. military assistance, and other
states preferred to avoid any involvement in the developing
conflict.

Israel than acted on its own. It created a "wall-to-wall"
political coalition (excluding the Communists) in a government
of national unity, and Moshe Dayan became the defense
minister. On June 5, 1967, Israel launched a preemptive strike
against Egyptian air forces and bases. The war was broadened
after Jordan and Syria joined in the conflict, initiating their
participation by respectively shelling Israeli positions in Jerusalem and from the Golan Heights. The Israelis decisively
defeated Egypt, Jordan, Syria, and their allies, and in six days
radically transformed the situation in the Middle East: They
were in control of territories stretching from the Golan Heights

in the north to Sharm el-Sheikh in the Sinai and from the Suez Canal to the Jordan River. The territories included the Sinai Peninsula, the Gaza Strip, the West Bank (referred to by Israel as Judea and Samaria), the Golan Heights, and East Jerusalem (annexed by Israel).

The Six Day War marked the inauguration of a new period in which the quest for an Arab-Israeli peace gained momentum. The war was neither launched nor waged with peace as the objective; Israel's goals were limited and tactical, primarily aimed at relieving the military threat posed by the actions of Egypt's President Nasser and his military forces. But once the magnitude of the Israeli accomplishment in the Six Day War became clear, there was hope that the military gains might be converted into political achievements. Peace suddenly loomed as an operational and practical objective of Israeli policy—a perspective stated by Prime Minister Eshkol and endorsed by the Knesset soon after the war in 1967. Withdrawal from the territories taken by Israel during the hostilities was linked to direct negotiations with the Arabs in order to achieve peace. Israel did not believe that peace was imminent or that it was achievable in the short term, but the changed circumstances (especially the occupation of territory the Arabs would seek to reclaim) shaped a hope that a negotiated peace, in which peace and security would be exchanged for territory, was possible.

In the Khartoum Arab Summit at the end of the summer of 1967, the Arab states agreed to unite their efforts "to eliminate the effects of the aggression" and to secure Israeli withdrawal from the occupied territories within the framework of "the main principles" to which they adhere: "no peace with Israel, no recognition of Israel, no negotiation with it, and adherence to the rights of the Palestinian people in their country." Later the United Nations Security Council, on November 22, 1967, adopted a British-sponsored resolution (United Nations Security Council Resolution 242) that emphasized "the inadmissibility of the acquisition of territory by war and the need to work for a just and lasting peace in which every state in the area can live in security." The resolution was deliberately vague but emphasized an exchange of territory for peace. The resolution affirmed that "a just and lasting peace" should

> include the application of both the following principles: (i) Withdrawal of Israeli armed forces from territories occupied in the recent conflict; (ii) Termination of all claims or states of belligerency and respect for and acknowledgement of the sovereignty, territorial integrity and political independence of every State in the area and their right to live in peace within secure and recognized boundaries free from threats or acts of force.

It also sought "freedom of navigation through international waterways" and "a just settlement of the refugee question." Gunnar Jarring, Sweden's ambassador to Moscow, was appointed by the secretary general to implement the resolution, but ultimately he failed to secure meaningful movement toward peace.

In the first decade after the 1967 war Israel retained control of the occupied territories, and despite various efforts, no significant progress was made in the achievement of peace. The Palestinians became more active—initially gaining publicity and attention through terrorist acts against Israel, some of which were spectacular in nature. However, the most serious threat to Israel came from Egypt, which embarked on the War of Attrition in the spring of 1969 in an effort, as Nasser put it, "to wear down the enemy." But the war soon took on a broader scope as the Egyptians faced mounting losses and minimal successes, and Nasser sought and received assistance from the Soviet Union. The Soviets soon were involved as advisers and combatants, and Israeli aircraft flying over the Canal Zone were challenged by Russian-flown Egyptian planes. The War of Attrition was ended by a U.S.-sponsored cease-fire in August 1970, and talks under Jarring's auspices were restarted, but no significant progress toward peace followed.

The Yom Kippur War

The relative calm on the Egyptian front lasted until October 6, 1973 (Yom Kippur), when Egypt and Syria launched a coordinated attack on Israeli positions on the Suez and Golan fronts. Taking Israel by surprise, the Arab armies crossed the Suez Canal, secured a beachhead in Sinai, and advanced into the Golan Heights while—during the first three days of combat—a skeletal Israeli force sought to withstand the invasion until additional troops could be mobilized. Ultimately Israel stopped the Arab forces and reversed the initial Arab successes; it retook the Golan and some additional territory, while Eygpt and Israel traded some territory along the Suez Canal following Israel's crossing of the canal and its advance toward Cairo.

The United Nations Security Council adopted Resolution 338, which called for an immediate cease-fire and the implementation of United Nations Security Council Resolution 242 and explicitly required negotiations "between the parties." Subsequently, U.S. Secretary of State Henry Kissinger negotiated the Egypt-Israel Disengagement of Forces Agreement of 1974 and the Sinai II accords of 1975 between Egypt and Israel, as well as the Israel-Syria Disengagement of Forces Agreement of 1974. These involved Israeli withdrawals from territory in the Suez Canal zone in the two agreements with Egypt and in the Golan Heights in the arrangement with Syria.

The Yom Kippur War resulted in an Israeli military victory, but that victory was accompanied by significant political and diplomatic disappointments and by domestic economic, psychological, and political stress. Israel underwent substantial turmoil during and after the hostilities. The war marked a watershed between a sanguine and euphoric Israel with its accompanying economic boom after the dramatic 1967 victory and a country stunned and troubled as a result of the "earthquake" associated with 1973. The failure of military intelligence, initial battlefield reverses, the "wars of the generals" concerning Israel's military capability, questions about war-associated political decisions, and deteriorating economic conditions all contributed to the uncertainty.

In purely tangible terms the 1973 war had perhaps the most far-reaching effects on Israel of any conflict to that time. Personnel losses and overall casualty rates were substantial. The mobilization of the largest part of the civilian reserve army of several hundred thousand caused dislocations in agriculture and industry. Tourism and diamond sales fell, and the sea passage to Eilat was blockaded at the Bab el-Mandeb. Numerous other aspects of the war added to the economic costs of the conflict, and austerity was the logical result.

At the same time Israel's international position deteriorated. Although it was not the initiator of the war, Israel was condemned, and numerous states (particularly in black Africa) broke diplomatic relations. The ruptures with Africa were a disappointment, but a shift in the attitudes and policies of the European states and Japan was perhaps more significant. The war also increased Israel's dependence on the United States. No other country could provide Israel, or was prepared to do so, with the vast quantities of modern and sophisticated arms required for war or the political and moral support necessary to negotiate peace.

The cease-fire of October 22, 1973, was followed by what Israelis often refer to as the "wars of the Jews"— internal political conflicts and disagreements. The initial domestic political effect of the war was to bring about the postponement to December 31 of the elections originally scheduled for October 30 and the suspension of political campaigning and electioneering for the duration of the conflict. The war not only interrupted the campaign for the Knesset elections, it also provided new issues for the opposition to raise, including the conduct of the war and the "mistakes" that preceded it. In November 1973 the government appointed a Commission of Inquiry, headed by Chief Justice Shimon Agranat of the Supreme Court, to investigate the events leading up to the hostilities (including information concerning the enemy's moves and intentions), the assessments and decisions of military and civilian bodies in regard to this information, and the Israel Defense Forces' deployments, preparedness for battle, and actions in the first phase of the fighting.

The war overwhelmed a population that believed that the Arabs would not attack, given the relative strength of the two sides. Israel's confident optimism was eroded by the war, and the subsequent reevaluation tended to breed a feeling of uncertainty. A mixture of anger and frustration was engendered by political and military factors associated with the conduct of the war. Despite significant military accomplishments, Israel was unable to achieve its desired goals, and the losses suffered in combat added to the sense of concern. Israel's prewar euphoria and self-assuredness were replaced by a more sober and realistic outlook that helped to foster political and social maturity. There was a greater turning inward but also a more heightened interest in politics. Israelis also were more cautious, questioned attitudes and policy more, and were more critical of both the system and the people who ran it. Deteriorating economic conditions contributed to the unsettling circumstances. The prewar economic boom was replaced by increasingly stringent conditions in the postwar period. Increased taxes and war-related levies were introduced, and a high rate of inflation began to have its effects.

Postwar Changes

The war accelerated the momentum for political change, though it did not create it. In a society in which political participation was widespread and in which views were intense and diversified, the war served to increase the concern for and participation in politics of the younger, better-educated, and generally native-born generation. The effects were only partially reflected in the 1973 elections for the Knesset. After the December elections Golda Meir received the mandate to form a new government, which she succeeded in doing. However, she soon resigned, and after considerable maneuvering within the Labor party, Yitzhak Rabin became Israel's prime minister in the spring of 1974, the first sabra to attain that position. He governed at the head of a tripartite leadership that included Yigal Allon as foreign minister and Shimon

Peres as defense minister. At the same time various protest groups and political movements were spawned by the war and its aftermath, and these affected future political developments. The Rabin government helped to restore Israel's confidence by its successful raid at Entebbe, Uganda, on July 4, 1976, that freed hostages held by Palestinian hijackers, but few other major achievements were recorded during its tenure.

In May 1977, after early elections for the Knesset, a new government was established. The Likud bloc, headed by Menachem Begin, was now the largest party in the Knesset; on June 20, 1977, Begin's coalition government gained the confidence of the parliament. This was the first time that the Likud had formed a government in Israel, and some regarded Begin's success as an aberration that could be explained by specific factors unique to the 1977 election, especially the rise of a new political party known as the Democratic Movement for Change (DMC), which helped to siphon votes from the Alignment. (The 1981 election suggested that this was inaccurate.)

The new government was committed to the attainment of a peace settlement with its Arab neighbors, but it was an initiative by Egyptian President Anwar Sadat that invigorated the slow-moving process. Sadat's announcement on November 9, 1977, that he was prepared to go to the Israeli Knesset to discuss the Arab-Israeli situation was a surprise to the international community but was not a precipitous action. Contacts between Egypt and Israel had taken place through a variety of channels, and there had been secret preparatory meetings in Morocco.

Sadat's historic visit to Jerusalem in November 1977 was followed by negotiations in which the United States—and President Jimmy Carter personally—played an active and often crucial role. In September 1978, President Carter, President Anwar Sadat of Egypt, Prime Minister Menachem Begin of Israel, and their senior aides held an extraordinary series of meetings at Camp David, Maryland, during which they discussed the Arab-Israeli conflict. On September 17, 1978, they announced, at the White House, the conclusion of two accords that provided the basis for continuing negotiations:

a "Framework for Peace in the Middle East" and a "Framework for the Conclusion of a Peace Treaty Between Egypt and Israel."

The Middle East framework set forth general principles and some specifics to govern a comprehensive peace settlement, focusing on the future of the West Bank and Gaza. It called for a transitional period of no more than five years during which Israel's military government would be withdrawn (although Israeli forces could remain in specified areas to ensure Israel's security) and a self-governing authority would be elected by the inhabitants of these areas. It also provided that "Egypt, Israel, Jordan and the representatives of the Palestinian people" should participate in negotiations to resolve the final status of the West Bank and Gaza, Israel's relations with Jordan based on United Nations Security Council Resolution 242, and Israel's right to live within secure and recognized borders. The Egypt-Israel framework called for Israel's withdrawal from the Sinai Peninsula and the establishment of normal, peaceful relations between the two states. In addition to the two frameworks there was a series of accompanying letters clarifying the parties' positions on certain issues.

A peace treaty signed in Washington, D.C., in March 1979 between the Arab Republic of Egypt and the State of Israel, under the auspices of the United States, ended the state of war between the two countries. Soon thereafter there began a withdrawal of Israeli forces from the Sinai Peninsula, the establishment of peace and diplomatic relations between Israel and Egypt, and the negotiation among representatives of Israel and Egypt, with the assistance of the United States, on the question of full autonomy for the Palestinian Arabs living in Judea and Samaria and the Gaza District. The treaty established the permanent boundary between Egypt and Israel as "the recognized international boundary between Egypt and the former mandated territory of Palestine."

The peace between Egypt and Israel marked a major turning point in the modern history of Israel, but it did not inaugurate a period of tranquility either at home or abroad. The 1981 Knesset elections, which returned a Likud government to power, suggested that 1977 was not a unique event. In these elections Labor and Likud emerged about equal in electoral strength and together held 95 of the 120 seats in the Knesset. The smaller parties became less significant (a trend that was not to be sustained in the 1984 elections).

Overall, Begin's tenure as prime minister (1977 to 1983) was a stormy one marked by significant accomplishments but also by major controversies. The major achievement, for which Begin shared the Nobel Peace Prize with President Anwar Sadat of Egypt, was the Egypt-Israel Peace Treaty of 1979. For Begin, and for Israel, it was a momentous but difficult accomplishment. It brought peace with Israel's most populous adversary and reduced significantly the military danger to Israel by neutralizing the largest Arab army, one with which it had fought five wars. But it was also traumatic, given the extensive tangible concessions required of Israel, especially the uprooting of Jewish settlements in Sinai. Israel withdrew fully from the Sinai Peninsula in April 1982, although there is a continuing dispute over a small area at Taba.

Other events generated controversy. The most significant included Israel's extension of its law and jurisdiction to the Golan Heights in December 1981 and the war in Lebanon. Operation Peace for Galilee—the war in Lebanon begun in June 1982—occasioned debate and demonstration within Israel, resulted in substantial casualties, and led to Israel's increased isolation. It also brought about major clashes with the United States. An agreement of May 17, 1983, between Israel and Lebanon providing for the withdrawal of Israeli forces from Lebanon noted that "they consider the existing international boundary between Israel and Lebanon inviolable." Although signed and ratified by both states, Lebanon abrogated the agreement in March 1984.

Another tragic aspect of the war was the massacre by Christian Phalangist forces at the Sabra and Shatila refugee camps in the Beirut area, with its resultant anguish within Israel and the decision to create a Commission of Inquiry, headed by Supreme Court Chief Justice Yitzhak Kahan. The commission's report led to the resignation of Ariel Sharon as minister of defense.

Within Israel, despite growing triple-digit inflation in the 1980s, Begin's tenure was marked by prosperity for the average citizen, although there were indicators that this might prove costly in the long term. The standard of living rose, as did the level of expectations. The religious parties increased their political power and secured important concessions to their demands from a coalition that recognized the increased role of the religious parties in maintaining the political balance. The major foreign relationship continued to be the one with the United States, although this underwent significant change as the ties were often tested amid tensions resulting from disagreements between the two states on various aspects of the regional situation and on the issues associated with resolution of the Arab-Israeli conflict. Nevertheless, U.S. economic and military assistance and political and diplomatic support rose to all-time high levels.

Menachem Begin's decision to resign as prime minister of Israel on September 16, 1983, paved the way for Yitzhak Shamir to establish a new government. He was soon forced to agree to early elections, which were held in July 1984. The results were inconclusive in determining Israel's direction, and the two major political forces—the Labor Alignment and Likud—initially were faced with a stalemate in their efforts to form a new government. Ultimately they agreed to form a government of national unity, in the fall of 1984, marking the beginning of a new phase in Israel's modern political history.

Masada, a stronghold perched on the hills of Judea, is the site of the Jews' last defense against the Romans, A.D. 72–73 (*top*). Yad Vashem: A memorial to six million Jews who died in the Holocaust (*bottom*).

David Ben-Gurion declaring Israel's independence, May 1948 (*top*).
President Chaim Weizmann taking the oath as Israel's president.
The picture on the wall depicts Theodor Herzl, who founded the
World Zionist Organization in 1897 (*bottom*).

3

The Economy

Israel's economy has undergone substantial change since independence, and the economic well-being of its people has improved significantly. Israel remains something of an economic "miracle" belying the preindependence prophecies that its troubled economy could not long endure. Instead, a country virtually bereft of natural resources and faced with substantial burdens imposed by massive immigration and by Arab hostility had achieved a relatively prosperous economic level by the 1980s. The standard of living in Israel and the productivity of its labor force are comparable to those in such West European countries as Italy and the United Kingdom, its life-expectancy levels are among the highest in the world, and it has maintained extensive social services for its population. These achievements are matched by similar statistics in other sectors.

FACTORS AFFECTING THE ECONOMY

Israel's small size and lack of mineral and water resources profoundly affect its economy. In particular, the lack of domestic energy resources makes its economy and economic policies particularly sensitive to international oil developments and external shocks. This dependence was exacerbated in the late 1970s when Israel returned the oil fields in Sinai and offshore in the Gulf of Suez (fields that it had mainly developed) to Egypt and had to resume purchasing large quantities of oil on the world market. Since 1979 Israel's oil imports have contributed significantly to its large balance-of-payments deficit, with oil imports costing more than US$1 billion a year.

Extensive irrigation and intensive farming methods have dramatically increased agricultural production for both domestic consumption and export. In part these increases have come from Israel's scientific innovations, especially in water conservation. The amount of irrigated land and of agricultural exports rose substantially between 1948 and the 1980s. Agricultural exports, though still substantial, have accounted for a declining percentage of total exports as Israel has developed its industrial base.

Population growth has also been substantial, with the Jewish population increasing about fivefold since 1948. In the first years after independence the growth rate was even more dramatic because of massive waves of immigration. This population growth has placed strains on Israel's economic and social systems; housing, capital growth, investment, and absorption have been costly. Although the immigrants are largely in their productive years, their transition from new immigrant to absorbed citizen is heavily dependent on government assistance. Nevertheless, as in the United States, immigration has been a major positive factor for the economy; the immigrants brought with them many and varied skills and a willingness to learn, making the work force one of the most diverse and technically advanced in the world.

In the early years this was not the case: The massive influx of immigrants generated numerous problems for Israel's economy. The initial immigrants faced high levels of unemployment, poverty, crowded living conditions, and inadequate housing and public services. In turn, many were unskilled (or prepared for activities unsuited to the new state), large numbers were elderly or ill, and they had numerous disabilities, including lack of knowledge of Hebrew and unfamiliarity with the types of government and conduct that characterized Israel. The sudden influx of large numbers of immigrants (Israel's population doubled during its first three years of independence) required the creation of an appropriate infrastructure, including roads, schools, hospitals, communications, housing, and special immigrant absorption and training facilities. In effect, the existing population became a minority seeking to integrate and absorb a population larger than itself. This early immigrant population utilized resources that might otherwise have been allocated for investment and industrialization.

Later immigration provided a pool of "human capital" and endowed Israel with skilled workers and professionals who have helped compensate for the lack of natural resources. Israel has developed its own highly regarded educational and scientific establishment that is in the forefront of accomplishment in such areas as energy technology and medical-scientific research, and its population is one of the most highly educated in the world. Illiteracy is virtually nonexistent. Israel's human-resource capability has allowed it to export, on a temporary basis, not only the products of its skilled workers but also the resource itself to assist other countries in development schemes. Thousands of Israeli experts have worked in diverse sectors of development in numerous developing and developed countries.

DEPENDENCE ON FOREIGN CAPITAL

Israel has lacked the physical and financial capital necessary to utilize its work force efficiently and therefore has had to import capital as well as raw materials. Since 1948, Israel has relied heavily on foreign capital inflows for the capital formation to finance the growing economy and current expenditures. Substantial capital inflows during the first three decades of independence permitted a large increase in the capital base, creating employment opportunities and leading to spectacular increases in domestic production. However, in recent years much of this imported capital has also been used to finance current consumption, a nonproductive use in the sense that it does not result in future income.

Some of Israel's achievements, particularly in the area of industrial development, can be traced to a significant investment program financed from outside sources, including U.S. government aid (both loans and grants), the sale of Israel bonds, investments, and German reparations and restitution payments. At the same time, donations from the world Jewish community in support of Israel-based philanthropies helped reduce the government's burdens in the social-welfare sector, thereby permitting the use of scarce funds for economic projects. This capital inflow has been complemented by an efficient economic machinery utilizing new industrial techniques and Israel's substantial and well-endowed human-resource base.

A large percentage of foreign capital has been provided by the U.S. government, through direct economic grants and loans and through military grants and loans that have released domestic resources that otherwise would have been utilized for the defense effort (see Table 3.1). From 1949 to 1983 U.S. aid totaled more than US$25 billion. This total included more than US$17.4 billion in military loans and grants; more than US$7.9 billion in economic loans and grants, including the Security Assistance Program (now called the Economic Support Fund); PL-480 Food for Peace; housing guarantees; Export-Import Bank loans; aid for resettling Soviet Jews; and other programs. Aid for Israel has evolved from a rather modest effort, oriented primarily toward economic assistance, to a substantial and multifaceted program. Between 1948 and 1971 the overwhelming portion of aid was economic, and most of that was loans, as was the military portion of U.S. assistance. The program shifted in the 1970s as the total amount of U.S. aid increased dramatically, and much of it then took the form of military assistance under the Foreign Military Sales (FMS) program, which is used primarily in the United States. In each year since 1974 authorized FMS credits have averaged over US$1 billion annually.

Since the Yom Kippur War of 1973 Israel's requirement for both economic and military assistance has grown considerably, in spite of the economic progress the country has made. Its increased needs result primarily from the growth of military expenditure, the rise in the price of oil and other essential imports, and the growing burden of external debt service, although domestic economic policies have also been a factor. Since 1974 almost half of the military assistance has been grant aid; since 1979 economic aid has taken the form of a cash transfer not linked to specific projects or commodity imports, although the funds cannot be used for military purposes. Since 1981 all U.S. economic assistance to Israel has been in grant form. U.S. aid to Israel in 1983 was approximately US$2.5 billion, and military assistance exceeded that provided to any other country. In the November-December 1983 talks with Prime Minister Shamir and Defense Minister Moshe Arens, the Reagan administration agreed to increase U.S. military grants to Israel to US$1.4 billion in FY 1984. The entire military program has been converted for the first time into outright grants, with no repayment necessary.

From 1949 to 1965, capital imports in the form of unilateral transfers and long-term capital exceeded US$6 billion, of which US$730 million came from the U.S. government in the form of loans, technical assistance, and grants. The bulk of Israel's capital inflow during this period came from the West German government and contributions from world Jewry, the latter accounting for about half of the total. West Germany provided substantial assistance through government grants and loans and direct payments to individuals. In recent years these restitution payments, though remaining at previous levels, have become a less significant source of funds.

Israel also has been successful in obtaining private funds through the sale of bonds abroad. These bonds, sold to foreign individuals and groups, have had rates extremely favorable to Israel and have provided it with a reliable source of funds without resort to banking institutions and government agencies with attendant higher interest rates. Contributions to Israeli charitable and philanthropic institutions by world, primarily American, Jewry are another significant source of capital inflow. In Israel's first two decades, Jewish assistance was a crucial factor aiding the new nation's economic growth, and unilateral transfers remain the primary component of world Jewry's contribution to Israel's capital imports, although purchases of Israel Bonds complement them. Private foreign investment, from Jewish and other sources, has remained at relatively low levels, even while Israel's economy has grown

TABLE 3.1
U.S. Aid to Israel, by U.S. Fiscal Years (million of U.S. dollars)

| | | | U.S. Overseas Loans and Grants: Obligations and Loan Authorizations | | | | | | | | |
| | Marshall Plan Period 1949–1952 | Mutual Security Act Period 1953–1961 | Foreign Assistance Act Period | | | | | | Total 1949–1983 | Repayments and Interest 1949–1983[a] | Total Less Repayments and Interest 1949–1983[a] |
			1962–1979	1980	1981	1982	1983	Total			
Economic Assistance	86.5	507.1	4,183.7	786.0	764.0	806.0	785.0	7,324.7	7,941.0	913.9	7,027.1
Loans	—	248.3	1,595.7	261.0	—	806.0	785.0	1,856.7	2,079.6	913.9	1,165.7
Grants	86.5	258.8	2,588.0	525.0	764.0	806.0	785.0	5,468.0	5,861.4	—	5,861.4
Aid and predecessor	63.7	311.5	3,720.4	785.0	764.0	806.0	785.0	6,860.4	7,276.8	403.5	6,873.3
Loans	—	96.0	1,160.5	260.0	—	—	—	1,420.5	1,509.3	403.5	1,105.8
Grants	63.7	215.5	2,559.9	525.0	764.0	806.0	785.0	5,439.9	5,767.5	—	5,767.5
(Security supporting assistance)	(—)	(—)	(3,554.5)	(785.0)	(764.0)	(806.0)	(785.0)	(6,694.5)	(6,694.5)		
Food for peace	22.7	195.6	463.3	1.0	—	—	—	464.3	664.1	510.4	153.7
Loans	—	152.3	435.2	1.0	—	—	—	436.2	570.3	510.4	59.9
Grants	22.7	43.3	28.1	—	—	—	—	28.1	93.8	—	93.8
Title I	—	165.1	453.7	1.0	—	—	—	454.7	601.7	510.4	91.3
Repayment in $—loans	—	—	340.2	1.0	—	—	—	341.2	323.1	239.1	84.0
Payment in foreign currency	—	165.1	113.5	—	—	—	—	113.5	278.6	271.3	7.3
Title II	22.7	30.5	9.6	—	—	—	—	9.6	62.4	—	62.4
Emergency relief, economic development, and World Food Program	—	—	2.2	—	—	—	—	2.2	2.2	—	2.2

Voluntary relief agency	22.7	30.5	7.4	—	—	—	—	7.4	60.2	—	60.2
Other economic assistance	0.1	—	—	—	—	—	—	—	0.1	—	0.1
Loans	—	—	—	—	—	—	—	—	—	—	—
Grants	0.1	—	—	—	—	—	—	—	0.1	—	0.1
Other	0.1	—	—	—	—	—	—	—	0.1	—	0.1
Military assistance	—	0.9	11,911.6	1,000.0	1,400.0	1,400.0	1,700.0	17,411.6	17,404.2	4,137.4	13,266.8
Loans	—	0.9	7,161.6	500.0	900.0	850.0	950.0	10,361.6	10,354.2	4,137.4	6,216.8
Grants	—	—	4,750.0	500.0	500.0	550.0	750.0	7,050.0	7,050.0	—	7,050.0
Credit financing	—	0.9	7,161.6	500.0	900.0	850.0	950.0	10,361.6	10,354.2	4,137.4	6,216.8
Other grants	—	—	4,750.0	500.0	500.0	550.0	750.0	7,050.0	7,050.0	—	7,050.0
Total economic and military assistance	86.5	508.0	16,095.3	1,786.0	2,164.0	2,206.0	2,485.0	24,736.3	25,345.2	5,051.3	20,293.9
Loans	—	249.2	8,757.3	761.0	900.0	850.0	950.0	12,218.3	12,433.8	5,051.3	7,382.5
Grants	86.5	258.8	7,338.0	1,025.0	1,264.0	1,356.0	1,535.0	12,518.0	12,911.4	—	12,911.4
Other U.S. loans	135.0	57.5	481.2	305.9	217.4	24.0	—	1,028.5	1,135.9	733.5	402.4
Export-Import Bank	135.0	57.5	481.2	305.9	217.4	6.5	—	1,011.0	1,118.4	728.1	390.3
All other	—	—	—	—	—	17.5	—	17.5	17.5	5.4	12.1

^aValues in these columns are net of deobligations.

Source: Agency for International Development, *U.S. Overseas Loans and Grants and Assistance from International Organizations, July 1, 1945–September 30, 1983* (Washington, D.C., 1984), p. 18.

in diversity, in development of high-technology industries, and in government incentives conducive to foreign investment.

The various methods of raising capital have permitted Israel to pursue a policy of rapid economic and demographic expansion despite the lack of natural resources. Israel has maintained growth rates in real Gross National Product (GNP) exceeding 9 percent for prolonged periods. From 1950 to 1972, real output grew at an average annual rate of nearly 10 percent, and output per worker more than tripled.

The rapid increase in population and economic output has been accompanied by significant increases in the standard of living. Real per capita income has increased steadily since 1948, and in 1984 was equivalent to approximately US$5,500. Government expenditures have consumed a large portion of the GNP, and in 1978 the government received in taxes nearly one-half of the total GNP. Even this high level of tax revenue was insufficient to fund the budget, requiring the government to finance the deficit by borrowing from Israel's central bank, in effect printing money, an inflationary activity. Israel has had double-digit inflation since at least the 1970s, and triple-digit inflation began in 1979. In 1980 inflation was 131 percent; in 1982, 120.4 percent; and in 1983, 145.6 percent. At the time of the July 1984 Knesset elections, the inflation level was estimated at a 400 percent annual rate (see Table 3.2).

Government-sector demand has been high in recent years, despite attempts by a succession of finance ministers to implement austerity plans, and private demand has also been substantial. The result is high inflation, large deficits in the current account with Israel importing more goods and services than it exports, and constant devaluations of the local currency (originally the pound, or lira, and now the shekel). All in all foreign capital inflows have allowed Israel to "live beyond its means."

The pattern of imports exceeding exports has had an adverse effect on Israel's foreign debt position, as Israel has borrowed abroad to finance its propensity to consume more than it produces. The foreign debt service obligation is increasingly burdensome. Total long- and short-term obligations of Israel abroad, including liabilities of the banking system

TABLE 3.2
Israel's Economy: Selected Indicators (in percentage)

	Inflation Rate	Rate of Change of Real Wages	Rate of Growth of GNP	Unemployment Rate
1970	6.1			3.8
1971	12.0	3.0	11.0	3.5
1972	12.9	1.0	12.0	2.8
1973	20.0	6.0	4.0	2.6
1974	39.7	−2.5	4.6	3.0
1975	39.3	−2.0	3.0	3.1
1976	31.3	1.5	1.2	3.6
1977	34.6	10.3	1.1	3.9
1978	50.6	2.0	4.0	3.4
1979	78.3	9.5	3.5	3.0
1980	131.0	−3.0	2.5	4.8
1981	116.8	10.4	4.2	5.1
1982	120.4	−0.9		
1983	145.6			

Derived from *The Economic Quarterly*, December 1982, January 1984, April 1984, and *Monthly Bulletin of Statistics* (Supplement), April 1984

to foreign banks, amounted to US$21.5 billion as of the first half of 1983. Debt service to the U.S. government alone for 1983 was US$1.05 billion and is expected to reach approximately US$1.155 billion by 1985. Most of Israel's external debt is a liability of the government, and a very large proportion (over 85 percent) is in the form of loans from foreign governments and publicly placed bonds, both of which have interest rates well below the prevailing market rates.

Originally the structure of Israel's debt was extremely favorable; however, the policy of indebtedness has been pursued over a long period and various fifteen- and twenty-year bonds will be coming due in the near future. Also, because of the grace periods on repayment of the principal owed, Israel faces an accumulation of maturities in the latter half of the 1980s that will place serious strains on its ability to meet its obligations. Even if Israel is able to roll over this debt, current interest rates are substantially higher than those prevailing when the loans were first secured, and even the concessionary intergovernmental rates can be expected to increase.

Even though the United States has forgiven all debt-service obligations on US$500 million of FMS credits each year and despite grants by the United States and the concessionary rates applicable to most of Israel's foreign debt, debt service still consumes well over US$2 billion annually—an amount equivalent to about one-quarter of the value of Israel's total exports. Moreover, Israel has become dependent on these annual inflows of fresh capital and thus dependent on economic conditions in the United States and, to a lesser extent, Europe.

As already pointed out, Israelis have become accustomed to very high rates of inflation. Normally, inflation acts as a tax, reducing the value of wages, savings, and other monetary assets and transferring this wealth to the government that prints the currency. Israel's economy has developed various institutions that insulate most individuals from the effects usually associated with such inflationary conditions, thus helping to perpetuate inflation. The key to understanding the effect of inflation on the average Israeli is to be found in linkage, or indexing. Virtually all aspects of financial life in Israel are linked (indexed) to the domestic consumer price index (CPI). Those who deposit money in banks receive a return that includes a positive real rate of interest and an amount to account for the linkage to the consumer price index, so savings rates have remained high in spite of inflation. The banking system permits accounts to be held domestically, denominated in various foreign currencies, or indexed directly to the domestic price index. Similar linkages affect borrowers' interest rates, wages, Israel government bonds, insurance, pensions, and so on. Most Israelis' assets and wages have risen to keep pace with prices, and this makes them much less willing to undertake sacrifices to bring the inflationary spiral under control.

ECONOMIC DEVELOPMENT

Over the initial two and one-half decades of independence, the Israeli economy expanded at a continuing rate, except for 1966–1967. Its rapid and sustained growth over

such a lengthy period was truly phenomenal. Israel began
with a relatively underdeveloped economy but substantially
increased its per capita income. During the initial twenty-
five years, the state and its citizens undertook massive housing
construction, built new towns, established new agricultural
settlements, developed a modern agricultural system, mod-
ernized industry, constructed a national road network, and
created a new economic and social infrastructure. A social-
welfare system to include government aid for the disadvantaged and education and health schemes were created. This
development occurred despite substantial resources being
allocated to defense.

During Israel's first thirty-three years, the GNP increased
more than ninefold, and the standard of living more than
tripled. The average annual growth rate of real GDP (Gross
Domestic Product) was 9.9 percent from 1953 to 1973, 3.4
percent from 1973 to 1979, and 2.3 percent from 1979 to
1982. At the same time the average annual rate of inflation
(CPI) was 7.1 percent from 1953 to 1973, 44.9 percent from
1973 to 1979, and 122.7 percent from 1979 to 1982. While
the GDP was increasing, Israel's economy also underwent
structural changes. At independence the economic resources
of the new state were committed to the military effort to
defeat the attacking Arab armies; later Israel increasingly
turned to the problems of building the country and settling
the new immigrant populations. As already discussed, these
immigrants more than doubled the population of the state
within some three years, burdening the economy with the
problems of food, shelter, integration, and employment. There
was a requirement for investment in infrastructure, agriculture,
and industry as well as for housing construction; to help
meet these needs the government established a regime of
austerity, rationing, and price control. But the problems
mounted, and the government was forced to modify its
approaches. By the end of 1953 a degree of normalization
was achieved, and at the same time new sources of capital
became available for the expansion of economic activity.

During the first ten years agricultural production had a
high priority, and output increased rapidly until land and

water resources were fully utilized and the growth rate slowed. By the mid-1950s manufacturing industry began to secure a greater share of investment and increased its role in and contribution to the economy. In 1954 a period of rapid and sustained economic growth at rates of between 10 and 12 percent per year began. In agriculture there was an effort to utilize all available land and water, and industrial development continued at a rapid pace. Housing construction allowed new housing to replace the transition camps to which Israel's immigrants had gone in the earlier years, and development towns were founded. As time went on the standard of living increased rapidly. However, by the mid-1960s inflation and the balance-of-payments deficit worsened, and the government sought to reduce public and private expenditures.

The deflationary policy of the government, begun in 1964, consisted primarily of a reduction in government expenditure for investment and for housing. At the same time, immigration also declined. By the middle of 1966 Israel was in a severe recession; construction declined sharply, investment was reduced, unemployment spread, economic growth slowed considerably, and prices continued to rise. At the beginning of 1967 unemployment reached high levels that were socially and politically unacceptable, and the government began to reflate the economy.

Its efforts were soon overshadowed by the Six Day War of 1967, which wrought dramatic and important changes in Israel's circumstances and affected its economic situation significantly.[1] Defense expenditure rose sharply, as did investment. Unemployment declined rapidly and disappeared by 1969. There were increased expenditures for development, a higher standard of living and associated consumption, and a revival of immigration. The economy resumed its growth at about 8 to 9 percent per year. The occupied territories had a negligible effect on the economy, although they provided a portion of Israel's labor force, about 5 percent by 1971. Taxation increased, but expenditure grew at a greater rate; the government resorted to deficit financing, and the balance-of-payments deficit began to grow. The recession that had characterized Israel's economy immediately before the 1967 war became an economic boom, with full employment. Building construction developed rapidly, including development of new towns, and exports grew. A tourist influx, accompanied by increased contributions from world Jewry, contributed to the improved conditions. By the time of the Yom Kippur War of 1973 the Israeli economy was enjoying full employment and continuous growth. At the same time there were significant inflationary pressures, including rapid real wage increases, an increasing balance-of-payments deficit, and a rapid rise in foreign debt.

Israel's economic situation deteriorated after the Yom Kippur War. The outbreak of the war exacerbated the economic problems, and after the hostilities defense expenditures grew and reached a high level, equivalent to about 40 percent of GNP in 1974. There was also a sharp increase in the balance-of-payments deficit, and inflationary pressures grew. To help deal with the problems, the government instituted policies to slow economic growth. Soon growth slowed to below 5 percent, inflation soared, the current-account deficit grew dramatically, and the foreign debt increased. Taxes were increased, other war-related levies were introduced, and a rate of inflation exceeding 40 percent began to have its effect. As already mentioned, agricultural and industrial production was dislocated by the mobilization of many of the able-bodied workers during the war and by the increased reserve duty required after the hostilities ended, and at the same time tourism and other sources of foreign exchange fell in earnings, and the port of Eilat was cut off by blockade. Replacing military equipment lost in battle, servicing the prewar debt, and acquiring new matériel to meet current and future defense needs added to the burden.

The post–Yom Kippur War redeployment of Israeli forces in Sinai was costly. Subsequently, the Israeli decision to return all of Sinai to Egypt as part of the Camp David process necessitated a further redeployment of Israeli forces from Sinai to the Negev. That redeployment in the late 1970s and early 1980s was a multibillion-dollar project with attendant ramifications for the Israeli economy, as only a portion of that expenditure was covered by U.S. aid. Approximately

US$3.2 billion of the estimated US$5 billion necessary for the redeployment was financed with U.S. government assistance.

During the Labor party's domination of Israel's political life from independence until 1977, socialist and economic policies, pursued in a mixed economy, were adapted to the special circumstances of Israel. The government played a central and decisive role in the economy, aided by semigovernmental institutions such as the Jewish Agency, the United Israel Appeal, the Jewish National Fund, and the Histadrut. The government owned and operated the railroads, postal service, and the telephone, telegraph, and broadcasting facilities in addition to the usual government public works such as road and irrigation projects, and there was also substantial government investment in public corporations in areas such as oil, electricity, and fertilizer.

In 1977 the system was altered when the Likud government came to power. By October of that year that government was ready to inaugurate its new economic plan that sought to modify substantially the existing socialist system and to replace it with a free-enterprise approach. Finance Minister Simcha Ehrlich declared that the program would check inflation, cut the foreign trade deficit, raise the growth rate, and promote foreign investment. The new economic policy would also remove some of the vast bureaucratic holds on the economy and some of the government-imposed controls instituted over the previous three decades. Virtually all foreign currency regulations were eliminated, and arbitrary exchange rates for the Israeli pound were abandoned, leaving it to find its own level on international exchanges. The pound continued to depreciate, and its devaluation was expected to promote a flow of dollars and other foreign currency into the country. A new value-added tax of 12 percent was also imposed. It was hoped that these new policies would increase exports by making Israeli products less expensive and would decrease imports (and consumption generally) by making imports more expensive, by leaving less money in the hands of the Israeli consumer, and by encouraging greater productivity. The overall goal was to eliminate the government from the economy and to apply free market principles.

Yigal Hurvitz of La'am replaced Ehrlich in 1979. He advocated hard-line economic policies, promoted austerity, and sought sharp cuts in subsidies, a reduction in civil service employment, some wage freezes, and other measures to reduce government expenditure. The Israeli pound was replaced by the shekel (the term drawn from the Bible), worth ten Israeli pounds.

Late in 1979 the government announced a program of economic austerity designed to restrain domestic demand, stimulate exports, decrease imports, and curb inflation. The program, accompanied by an increased pace of depreciating the currency against the dollar, improved Israel's balance of payments, although inflation continued—and indeed worsened—after 1979. This was primarily because the government was unable to implement plans to cut the budget as a result of the pressures of coalition politics and the approaching election. The main features of the austerity program were (1) fiscal restraint, to be achieved by sharp reductions in development expenditures, a freeze on public-sector employment, reductions in subsidies to both capital and consumption, and a cutback in social services; (2) a tight monetary policy, with positive real interest rates to be implemented by the central bank; (3) an import deposit scheme designed to increase the price of imported goods; (4) more efficient collection of taxes; (5) a shift from the general price subsidy programs to direct aid to individuals in need; and (6) wage agreements between government, industry, and the unions that mandated that real wages be held constant through 1980 (later extended through 1981).

Israel, like many developing nations, relies heavily on import duties and value-added taxes as a source of government revenues. Direct taxes, such as income tax, are less important than they are in the United States. Thus by reducing the demand for imports, the government also reduced tax revenues. In addition, the elimination of subsidies, although it initially reduced government expenditures, resulted in increases in the consumer price index. Since real wages were held constant, this initiated wage increases for all workers, both in the government and private sectors, thus increasing the price of domestically produced goods and again raising the consumer price index.

This inflationary spiral, along with the relative reduction in government revenues, caused an unforeseen increase in the deficit. To finance this deficit in a noninflationary way the government needed to either increase taxes or increase private borrowing from individuals. A tax increase was not seriously considered, and efforts to sell government bonds were also unsuccessful, thus forcing the government to finance the deficit by selling its bonds to the central bank. The result was an increase in the money supply, which made the central bank's efforts to restrict money growth and maintain a tight monetary policy more difficult. This also tended to place upward pressure on the price level. Thus, for a variety of reasons, the austerity program was unsuccessful in controlling inflation, although it was helpful for the balance of payments. Hurvitz's unpopular austerity measures were not fully implemented, and he left office in 1981, prior to the elections.

Yoram Aridor came to office in 1981 with a program of measures that, in the face of the upcoming elections, had more political than economic validity. He reduced taxes on various luxury items and other consumer goods, the most prominent being the taxes on color television sets and cars, which led to buying surges and increased consumer satisfaction prior to the elections. Although there was an economic rationale, the program became better known for its election effects—adding votes to the Likud column from a more contented population.

Following the resignation of Yoram Aridor in the fall of 1983, the new finance minister, Yigal Cohen-Orgad, introduced austerity measures and sought to strengthen the balance of payments through export-led growth and a cut in imports. In order to promote this growth, public and private consumption had to be restricted, and he sought to promote those sectors focusing on production and export. Attempts to limit private consumption included the rapid depreciation of the shekel (making imports more expensive), major cuts in consumer subsidies, and attempts to reduce the cost-of-living adjustment system. A variety of budget cuts, including the slashed subsidies, were aimed at reducing government expenditure. New measures for raising revenue included education fees, taxes on early pensions, higher income tax in the higher brackets, and a cut in fringe benefits for civil servants and public-sector workers. Cohen-Orgad's tenure was terminated by the accession to power of a national unity government in 1984.

The 1984 Knesset election campaign focused substantial attention on Israel's economic situation, and the economy became an early priority for the national unity government installed in September 1984. In its basic guidelines presented to and approved by the parliament, the new government pledged to reduce the balance-of-payments deficit, check inflation, renew economic growth while maintaining full employment, strengthen the export and productive sectors of the economy, and reduce the proportion of public and administrative services. To achieve these goals the government noted that it would reduce public, civilian, and defense expenditure and consumption and would curb private consumption. It would also seek a variety of other objectives, including increased national saving and taxation system reform. It pledged itself to expand the infrastructure for technological services and to promote high-technology enterprises; to bolster agriculture and agricultural exports; to encourage tourism; and to provide housing for new immigrants, younger Israelis, and large families.

In keeping with its stated policies the government soon instituted an austerity plan that included cuts in military expenditure, increases in taxes, charges for public services, and reductions in food subsidies. Arrangements were also concluded for initial freezes in wages and prices, and a temporary ban on imports of luxury products was instituted. The new government has taken the problem seriously and has launched a series of steps to respond to the economy's various problem areas.

ECONOMIC PROBLEMS AND FUTURE PROSPECTS

Israel continues to face balance-of-payments, inflation, and debt management difficulties in its economy, largely as a result of the country's strong commitment to security. The demands of Israel's defense sector are a major element in its economic concerns. The continuation of the Arab-Israeli conflict and the consequent security requirements imposed by Arab hostility have necessitated large and continuous defense expenditures that have imposed a substantial burden. Judged purely on the basis of efficiency, certain security-related policies have clashed with more rational economics. For example, the deliberate effort by the government to disperse the population throughout the country and to develop outlying areas has generated high economic costs. Israel has been forced to divert scarce resources to defense. The cost of maintaining an army and diverting manpower to military service has grown as enemy states have acquired substantial arsenals for their wars with Israel. In recent years, the Arab states have purchased increasing amounts of military hardware, thus requiring Israel to continuously upgrade and improve its military capability to maintain its qualitative edge.

The result is an increasing arms race. For example, Israel's Foreign Military Sales purchases from the United States, its major supplier, increased 21 percent from the 1982 amount to US$1.7 billion in FY 1983. More than half, US$950 million, was in loans that Israel must repay with interest. In 1982, Israel's total military spending, including that funded by U.S. government loans, amounted to US$8.24 billion, representing approximately US$2,060 per Israeli. During the period 1974–1980, the average annual rate of defense spending as a percentage of GNP was approximately 30 percent in Israel, as opposed to about 5 percent in the United States.

Factors relating to the Arab-Israeli hostilities, in addition to direct military costs, include the economic embargo of Israel by the Arab countries that has cut Israel's economy off from markets for exports as well as from nearby sources for raw materials. Israel has thus built its industrial base with Europe and the United States as its export markets. There has been, too, a boycott by countries and companies interested in dealing with the Arab world who have been offered a choice of trade with the Arabs or with Israel. Arab hostility also has reduced investor interest in Israel's economy.

Israel's defense posture places other strains on the economy. Mobilization is economically costly, since more than 25 percent of the work force could be called up for a major mobilization. Such a loss of personnel seriously strains productive capacity, exacerbates balance-of-payments problems, and drains needed foreign reserves. The requirement of active reserve service each year further reduces the available work force for the civilian sector. Peace and the reduction of regional tension would help to achieve a measure of economic stability.

Over 60 percent of all governmental expenditures are devoted to the two areas of defense expenditures and debt service, placing much of the allocations beyond the reach of austerity measures and requiring that the remaining 40 percent (such as social programs, government housing schemes, and so on) carry most of the burden. This makes any austerity program difficult to pursue, since vital services must be continued, and many other governmental programs are politically or ideologically difficult to cut.

Consistent implementation of austerity measures, especially those designed to restrain domestic consumption while encouraging exports and a reduction in real government expenditures, should result in improvement in Israel's balance of payments and in a moderation of inflationary pressures over time. Attracting private capital through the sale of bonds to foreign nationals at concessionary rates is helpful in sustaining economic growth and in meeting international obligations. Over the long term Israel is heavily dependent on actions outside the government's direct control, meaning that domestic consumption must be reduced. Large increases in oil prices would place additional strains on the balance of payments and necessitate even more stringent measures. Similarly, added defense expenditures could be achieved only by reducing the standard of living below existing levels or by further increasing external debt.

TABLE 3.3
Israel's Foreign Trade (millions of U.S. dollars)

	1982		1983	
	Exports	Imports	Exports	Imports
Africa	190.2	191.8	158.3	186.0
Asia	528.9	301.4	505.2	405.0
Canada	33.1	112.4	42.6	104.7
Central and South America	121.9	153.8	82.6	139.3
Europe	1,823.2	3,235.3	2,225.9	4,478.5
United Kingdom	404.1	618.8	412.9	667.3
United States	1,119.2	1,342.0	1,329.2	1,650.0
Other	1,060.9	1,960.6	712.7	1,574.7

Source: Israel, Central Bureau of Statistics, *Monthly Bulletin of Statistics*, April 1983, p. 32, and May 1984, p. 32.

TABLE 3.4
Foreign Exports by Sector (millions of U.S. dollars)

	1982	1983
Diamonds	1,157.7	1,207.7
Chemicals	647.7	644.4
Agriculture	553.0	507.5
Textiles, clothing, and leather	354.4	344.0
Food and tobacco products	348.7	316.1
Ore	189.1	216.6
Rubber and plastic	107.2	117.8
Other industrial products	1,923.7	1,757.6

Source: Israel, Central Bureau of Statistics, *Monthly Bulletin of Statistics*, April 1983, p. 31, and May 1984, p. 31.

As noted previously, Israel's balance-of-payments deficits often reflect the very high rates of imports in the defense sector and Israel's continuous need to import oil. Israel's exports have continued to grow in value and to involve a wide range of items (see Tables 3.3 and 3.4). Industrial exports include minerals (potash, phosphates, and bromine), chemicals, textiles, and fashion products. Metal, machinery, and electronics have in recent years increased their share of the export sector. Diamonds continue to be an important export. Agricultural exports have declined in volume in recent years, but price rises have provided for modest growth in export value. High-technology industries have become a new focus of Israeli efforts; income from tourism remains an important source of revenue. Israel's exports are primarily directed at Western Europe, with the United States accounting for about 15 percent of all Israeli exports. Overall, imports continue to exceed exports.

The decision by the U.S. Congress in October 1984 to authorize the president to negotiate a free trade area with Israel may prove to be a major milestone in Israel's economic future. The idea was broached during the meeting between President Ronald Reagan and Prime Minister Yitzhak Shamir in November 1983, and subsequently the president sought the requisite congressional approval to negotiate such an agreement. Under the arrangement, Israel would become the only country in the world that enjoys a bilateral free trade arrangement with the United States. It would allow Israel access to its largest trading partner on substantially improved terms, thereby improving its export capability. The potential benefit to Israel's economy is considerable.

The question continues to be whether the government of Israel can reverse the negative economic trends (inflation and stagnation) of the later 1970s, given defense and other burdens. Israel lives beyond its means and is dependent on outside assistance, a dependence that Israelis would like to see reduced. Israel must also devote resources to future growth. It spends significant portions of its resources on providing public services (such as education, health care, and housing), and there is also a high level of private consumption.

Although the magnitude of Israel's external debt and its servicing are troublesome, the significance of the burden depends upon a number of factors, including how the deficit in the balance of payments is financed. Because assistance given in grant form imposes no addition to the burden of debt repayment, Israeli officials increasingly have requested more U.S. assistance in the form of grants rather than loans, and the future composition of U.S. aid appears likely to meet that request.

Although the manner in which the debt-service burden is financed is important, the strength of the economy is the most essential factor in determining Israel's ability to meet

its debt obligations in the long run. In 1983, the Israeli
economy was buffeted by a series of economic shocks. In
the first five months of that year, Israel's trade deficit was
31 percent higher than it was for the same period in 1982.
The trade gap for May was US$389 million, a 26 percent
rise over the US$309 million recorded in May 1982, and it
was the eighth consecutive month in which the excess of
imports over exports increased. Inflation was rampant and
rising. In the fall the finance minister resigned over the
controversy surrounding his proposal to link the Israeli shekel
to the dollar, and government actions designed to restrict
private consumption caused adverse reactions in the economy—the stock market survived a near crash and prices
soared.

A large reduction in public expenditure is seen by many
economists as the solution to the debt problem and to Israel's
broader economic difficulties. The government, however, has
encountered stiff opposition in its attempts to restrict consumption. Many in political life insist that indexation cannot
be abolished, and the government appears unable to restrict
wage increases, though modifications in the cost-of-living
adjustment system have been instituted. In order to implement
further restrictive measures, the government needs to win the
approval of the powerful Histadrut. In the past, the labor
union's ability to extract real wage gains (despite the inflationary spiral) has stimulated domestic demand, thereby ex-
acerbating the balance-of-payments problems.

The support of the Israeli public is also essential if the
austerity measures are to succeed. Periodically the government
has issued admonitions to the public concerning the high
level of private consumption. It is unlikely that such entreaties
will convince members of the Israeli public to "tighten their
belts." What is certain, however, is that Israelis must realize
that, ultimately, there will be little choice.

Whether or not Israel is able to strengthen its economy
will also depend on the amount of public consumption. The
negative public reaction to the government's proposed (and
partially implemented) austerity measures exposes a deeper

conflict within the Israeli system. Zionist ideology places a strong emphasis on stable economic growth and development and an equally strong emphasis on social welfare; often, however, the economic policies promoting welfare directly contradict those policies necessary for growth. The social-welfare ideology has a direct effect on consumption levels, both public and private. The government's desire to maximize social welfare has resulted in Israel's high level of government expenditures and great reluctance to restrict consumption. The government's dominant role in the Israeli economy had led to an extensive social-welfare system that has done everything from subsidizing bus tickets and bread to adjusting salaries to compensate for inflation. However, the pressing problems of the Israeli economy have necessitated restrictive policy measures. The success of Israel's long-run objectives for a strong and stable economy will largely depend on the willingness of Israelis (both the government and general public) to endure and accept a short-run reduction in their standard of living.

In recent years Israelis have become more aware of economic issues and more concerned about the failure of the government to deal effectively with them. There seemed to be little confidence that the government, or its potential successors, could deal with the crucial economic issues facing the country. At the same time, because the average Israeli was well insulated from the effects of poor economic management, inflation, unemployment, and trade deficits were subjects for academic discussion rather than everyday concerns of the population. The Israeli economy has been in trouble, but the Israelis' economic well-being was barely affected, as they perceived it. Many Israelis did not see much difference in the economic policies and programs of Labor (socialism) and Likud (capitalism), despite the ideological differences each sought to portray. A major test for future Israeli governments will be their ability to create public awareness of the issues and to gain public confidence in their ability to deal effectively with the salient economic issues facing the country.

NOTES

1. During the 1967 war Israel occupied the densely populated Gaza Strip and the West Bank, which together had about 1.3 million inhabitants by 1985. Although the economies of these areas interact with that of Israel in important ways, the discussion focuses on the economy of Israel within its 1949–1967 frontiers. The West Bank and Gaza Strip are underdeveloped areas relative to Israel's industrial economy. The 1967 war disrupted production, caused destruction, led a portion of the population to leave the area for Jordan, and caused widespread unemployment for a short while, but the economy soon surpassed its prewar levels. Between the Six Day and Yom Kippur wars the economies of the West Bank and Gaza Strip grew at an unprecedented pace because of increased employment opportunities, including those in Israel itself, and increased productivity (especially in the agricultural sector). The territories benefited from their close links to Israel—the latter providing markets for the increased output of the territories and jobs for Arab employees. At the same time Arab employees provided a relatively cheap source of labor for Israel.

Fish ponds in northern Israel (*top*). Modern agriculture—growing crops under plastic (*center*). Packing oranges for export (*bottom*).

Solar energy for heating water—a common site on Israeli rooftops (*top*). Elscint Ltd. develops nuclear electronic medical equipment (*center*). Assembling electronic products (*bottom*).

4

Politics

The provisional government of Israel, formed at independence and recognized by the major powers, was new in name only. It had begun to function *de facto* following adoption of the United Nations partition resolution in November 1947 and it drew on the experience gained by the Yishuv during the mandatory period. In the fall of 1947, when the United Nations was considering the future of the Palestine mandate, the Jewish Agency Executive and the Vaad Leumi (the National Council of the Yishuv) formed a Joint Emergency Committee to prepare and arrange for the transfer of power from the British mandatory administration to the government of the proposed Jewish state. Among other activities, that committee drafted a legal code and a proposed constitution, developed a roster of experienced civil servants willing to serve the future government, and instituted recruitment for the Hagana to preserve the security of the Jewish community. The scope of the advance planning was broad and included many of the tasks of the new state, such as blueprints for the proposed ministries and their personnel, as well as substantial consideration of the policies to be pursued.

Shortly after the partition vote, the United Nations established a Palestine Commission to effect the transfer from the mandatory power to the proposed Arab and Jewish states. Lacking cooperation from the Arabs and the British, that body worked almost exclusively with the Jewish community. In March 1948 a temporary National Council of State, chosen from the National Council and Jewish Agency Executive, assumed control in many areas of Palestine. On May 14, the

105

provisional government proclaimed Israel's independence, repealed the British mandatory restrictions on immigration and the sale of land, and converted the Hagana into the Defense Army of Israel.

The provisional government had three elements: a state council that acted as parliament, a cabinet elected by the state council from among its members, and a president elected by the state council. The National Council of the mandate period formed the basis of the state council; the executive committee of the National Council became the cabinet; the presidency was new. David Ben-Gurion, chairman of the Jewish Agency and leader of the dominant political party, Mapai (Israel Workers' party), was chosen prime minister and minister of defense, and Chaim Weizmann was elected president.

The provisional government directed the war with the Arab states, levied taxes, established administrative agencies, and conducted essential public services. It functioned from May 14, 1948, until early 1949. At its session just prior to the national election of January 25, 1949, the state council adopted a transition ordinance transferring its authority to a Constituent Assembly that convened on February 14, 1949. That assembly, which later declared itself the First Knesset, was a unicameral chamber composed of 120 members representing twelve of the twenty-four parties that contested the January 1949 election.

CONSTITUTIONAL CONSENSUS

Israel's system of government, as already noted, is based on an unwritten constitution. The first legislative act of the Constituent Assembly in February 1949 was to enact a Transition Law, often referred to as the Small Constitution, that became the basis of constitutional life in the state. Administrative and executive procedures were based on a combination of past experience in self-government, elements adapted from the former mandatory structure, and new legislation. According to the Small Constitution, Israel was established as a republic with a weak president and a strong cabinet and parliament. It was anticipated that this document would be replaced in due course by a more extensive and permanent one.

The First Knesset devoted much time to a profound discussion of the constitutional issue. The major debate was between those who favored a written document and those who believed that the time was not appropriate for imposing rigid constitutional limitations. The latter group argued that a written constitution could not be framed because of constantly changing social conditions, primarily the result of mass immigration and a lack of experience with independent governmental institutions. There was also concern about the relationship between state and religion and the method of incorporating the precepts and ideals of Judaism into the proposed document.

The discussion of these issues continued for over a year, and on June 13, 1950, the Knesset adopted a compromise that has postponed the real issue indefinitely. It was decided in principle that a written constitution would ultimately be adopted, but that for the time being there would be no formal and comprehensive document. Instead, a number of fundamental, or basic, laws would be passed dealing with specific subjects, which might in time form chapters in a consolidated constitution. By the end of 1984 Israel had adopted eight Basic Laws dealing with various subjects: The Knesset (1958), The Lands of Israel (1960), The President (1964), The Government (1968), The State Economy (1975), The Army (1976), Jerusalem, The Capital of Israel (1980), and The Judiciary (1984). The Basic Laws thereby provide a definitive perspective of the formal requirements of the system in specific areas of activity, a "written" framework, in a sense, for governmental activity.

Several areas of consensus, together with the extant fundamental laws, define the parameters of Israel's political system. Israel's self-definition as a Jewish state is perhaps the most significant area of agreement, although there is a divergence of views on some of its tenets and their interpretation. Accord centers on the goals or purposes of Israel, such as the "ingathering of the exiles"—the return of the Jewish people from the Diaspora to their ancient homeland in Eretz Israel (the Land of Israel)—and the establishment of a state based on "Jewish" principles. Those disavowing allegiance to these Jewish-Zionist ideals, or at least those (such as the Communists and the ultra-Orthodox Neturei Karta) dissociating themselves from the immediate manifestations of these ideals, serve as little more than protest groups, although the Communists have elected members to the Knesset and are active at the local political level.

There is also consensus that Israel should be a social-welfare state, in which all share in the benefits of society and have access to essential social, health, and similar services, although there are conflicting views regarding the specific scope and method of implementation of this principle. Foreign and security policy constitutes another area enjoying wide consensus because of its overriding importance in light of continuing Arab hostility and the resultant conflict, although there is discord concerning methods and techniques of implementation of the agreed goals. The Israel Defense Forces enjoys an enviable military reputation that was enhanced by the 1967 war and was refurbished following the initial reverses in the 1973 war. The IDF remains outside politics and under civilian control and is identified with the state rather than with any particular group or party. This status is partly because of virtually universal citizen participation in the military for national service and, subsequently, in the reserves. Despite these broad areas of consensus, there are divergences concerning specifics and the means of interpreting and implementing these ideals.

POLITICAL INSTITUTIONS

The president, the government (cabinet), and the Knesset (parliament) perform the basic political functions of the state within the framework provided by Israel's constitutional consensus.

The President

The president (*nasi*) is elected by the Knesset for a five-year term and may be reelected for no more than two consecutive terms. The president is head of state and has powers that are essentially of a representative character. In the sphere of foreign affairs these functions include signing instruments that relate to treaties ratified by the Knesset, appointing diplomatic and consular representatives, receiving foreign diplomatic representatives, and issuing consular exequaturs. In the domestic sphere, the president has the power to grant pardons and reprieves and to commute sentences. Subsequent to nomination by the appropriate body, the head of state appoints judges, *dayanim* (judges of the Jewish religious courts), *kadis* (judges of Muslim religious courts), the state comptroller, the president of the Magen David Adom Association (Red Shield of David—Israel's equivalent of the Red Cross), and the governor of the Bank of Israel, as well as other officials as determined by law. The president signs all laws passed by the Knesset, with the exception of those relating to presidential powers, and all documents to which the state seal is affixed. Official documents signed by the president require the countersignature of the prime minister or other duly authorized minister, with the exception of those where another procedure is laid down, as in the case of the judges.

The president's powers and functions relating to the formation of the government fall into a different category. After elections, or the resignation or death of the prime minister, the president consults with representatives of the parties in parliament and selects a member of the Knesset to form a government. Although anyone may be chosen, traditionally the member has been the leader of the largest party in the Knesset. Until 1984, this formal discretion had not been accompanied by any real choice because the political composition of the Knesset had determined the selection. Nevertheless, situations are conceivable in which different party combinations might gain the support of the Knesset, and in such instances the president would fulfill a crucial political role in determining the person chosen to form a cabinet. In 1984 President Chaim Herzog, a Labor party stalwart, chose to give Labor party chairman Shimon Peres, the head of the largest party in the Knesset, the mandate to form the government, although it was conceivable that Yitzhak Shamir of Likud might have had a similarly good opportunity to succeed at forming the government.

The president also receives the resignation of the government. Another aspect of the presidential role that could have political significance is the public position and prestige—visits throughout the country, speeches, and the formal opening of the first session of each Knesset. Generally, however, these activities have been ceremonial in nature.

The Cabinet

The member of parliament entrusted by the president with the task of forming the government establishes a cabinet, with himself or herself as prime minister and a number of ministers who are usually, but not necessarily, members of the Knesset. The prime minister may appoint any number of ministers, and there is no formal requirement regarding the size of the cabinet or the distribution of portfolios. The government is constituted upon obtaining a vote of confidence from the parliament, which must approve the composition of the government, the distribution of functions among the ministers, and the basic lines of its policy. The cabinet is collectively responsible to the Knesset, reports to it, and remains in office as long as it enjoys the confidence of that body. There has never been a successful motion of no confidence by the Knesset causing the ouster of a government. A government's tenure may also be terminated by ending the Knesset's tenure and scheduling new elections, by the resignation of the government on its own initiative, or by the resignation or death of the prime minister.

After obtaining the confidence of the parliament, the cabinet decides Israel's policies in all spheres, subject to Knesset approval, and generally initiates the largest portion of leg-

POLITICS   111

islation. Increasingly much of the work of the cabinet has been conducted by a small and select group of ministers meeting informally in "kitchen" cabinets (for example, under Golda Meir) or in ministerial committees on such issues as security and defense. Ministries are divided among the parties forming the coalition in accordance with the agreement reached by the parties and generally reflect their size and influence. The prime minister may select a replacement, subject to Knesset confirmation, for a minister who resigns or dies in office.

The Parliament

The Knesset is the supreme authority in the state, and its laws are theoretically the source of all power and authority, although in reality decisions are made by the prime minister and the Government and ratified. The Knesset's name is derived from the Knesset Hagedola (Great Assembly), the supreme legislative body of the Jewish people after the Biblical period and prior to the Maccabean Revolt. The modern body is based, to a large extent, on the British model, adapted to Israel's needs and special requirements. It is a unicameral body of 120 members elected for four-year terms by general, national, direct, equal, secret, and proportional suffrage in accordance with the Knesset Elections Law. The entire country elects all members; there are no separate constituencies. This system derives from that used by the World Zionist Organization (WZO) and the Histadrut and other elements in the Yishuv prior to Israel's independence. All Israeli citizens over eighteen may vote in Knesset elections without regard to sex, religion, or other factors, unless deprived of that right by a court of law. Voters cast their ballots for individual parties, each with rival lists of candidates, rather than for individual candidates. Each party may present the voter with a list of up to 120 names—its choices for Knesset seats.

Numerous parties contest the election, and the creation of a new list is a relatively simple matter. In the 1984 election it required securing twenty-five hundred signatures and posting a deposit of 500,000 Israeli shekels (then worth about US$2,000), which was forfeited if the group did not secure at least 1 percent of the valid votes cast in the election. A party represented in the outgoing Knesset may contest the election without meeting these requirements. Each party utilizes an alphabetical symbol as a means of party identification to achieve voter recognition. The voter chooses a party list as constructed and may not change it in any way.

The lists usually are prepared by the party's leadership acting informally or organized in a central committee or some other body. The names highest on the list usually represent party leaders who will become members of the government and the number-one position, at the head of the list, is reserved for the party's candidate for prime minister. The construction of the list is a major political act involving substantial intraparty discussion and political trading. Candidates seek high positions on the list to be assured of a "safe" (or "realistic") seat and thus election to the Knesset, rather than lower positions that are doubtful or "honorary" in nature. Election campaigns have been financed by the government since 1969, although private funds are also raised.

After ballots are cast, seats in parliament are determined. Only those party lists that have received at least 1 percent of the total number of valid votes cast are represented in the Knesset. Any list failing to obtain this minimum does not share in the distribution of mandates, and its votes are not taken into account when determining the composition of the Knesset. The number of valid votes cast for all the lists that obtained the minimum percentage is divided by the number of Knesset members, and the result is the quotient for each Knesset seat. The distribution of seats among the party lists is finally determined by dividing the number of votes each list received by the quotient.

The remaining seats are allocated by a complicated formula (known as the Bader-Ofer process for the two parliamentarians who proposed the law) that generally benefits the larger parties. The actual seats in the Knesset are allocated to individuals in the order in which they appeared on their party's list. Should a member of parliament die or resign prior to the next election, a successor is designated by the party from the election lists, thus precluding the need for special elections (by-elections) between general elections.

Candidates for the Knesset must be Israeli citizens at least twenty-one years old. Some individuals are not eligible because of positions they occupy: the president, the chief rabbis, judges, the state comptroller, the chief of staff of the IDF, senior officers of the IDF, senior civil servants who had not resigned by a specified date prior to the election, and rabbis and clerics of other religions while holding office for remuneration. Generally all others, except those deprived of that right by a court acting under the law, may contest the available seats.

The main functions of the Knesset are similar to those of most modern parliaments. They include expressing a vote of confidence or no confidence in the government, legislating, participating in the formation of national policy, and supervising the activities of the governmental administration. The Knesset must also approve the budget and taxes, elect the president of the state, recommend the appointment of the state comptroller, and participate in the appointment of judges. Members of the Knesset may debate issues and question ministers, but when votes are taken, party discipline demands they support their party's position for or against the government's stand. In so doing they demonstrate their loyalty to the party, a process that helps to guarantee support for themselves and their views in the party (including placement in a "safe seat" on the party's next election list).

Many of the Knesset's activities are performed in committees, each responsible for specific areas of legislation, that meet in closed session. With some minor exceptions (for example, the Communists are traditionally excluded from the Foreign Affairs and Security Committee), the ratio of committee memberships is generally proportional to that of the party's representation in the Knesset as a whole. The legislative process is lengthy, as in most other parliamentary systems.

The Judicial System

Judicial authority is vested in religious as well as civil courts. The latter include municipal and magistrates' courts for civil and criminal actions, district courts for appeals from the lower tribunals and matters not triable by a magistrate, and a supreme court. The supreme court, known as the High Court of Justice, cannot review legislation passed by the Knesset, but it has the power to invalidate administrative actions and to interpret statutes it regards as contrary to the rule of law.

Each major community has its own religious courts that deal with matters of personal status. Rabbinical courts have exclusive jurisdiction over Jews in marriage and divorce, and they may act on alimony, probate, succession, and other similar questions with the parties' consent. The Christian ecclesiastical courts have exclusive authority over Christians in marriage, divorce, alimony, and confirmation of wills, and they may judge other similar matters if the parties agree. The Muslim courts have exclusive jurisdiction for Muslims in all matters of personal status. The judicial appointment procedure seeks to discourage political influence, and judges enjoy tenure subject only to good behavior.

Nongovernmental Institutions

Two other institutions unique to the Israeli system are notable elements of the political structure. The Histadrut and the Jewish Agency/World Zionist Organization, even though nongovernmental, perform functions instrumental to Zionism and important to the government's activities; their personnel often move to positions of responsibility within the government. During the mandatory period, these organizations served as part of the governing structure of the Yishuv. They promoted Zionism, encouraged and facilitated immigration, raised funds, engaged in social-welfare activities, promoted Jewish culture, developed economic enterprises, and formulated domestic and external policies for the Jewish community. Upon independence the government of Israel began to assume many of the functions previously performed by these institutions and formalized its relationship with them through legislation and administrative decisions.

The Histadrut, Israel's trade-union federation, is of greater significance than the usual trade-union organization in that it combines trade unionism, economic enterprise, cultural and social activities, and social welfare. It is one of the largest employers in Israel and has engaged in overseas projects in support of Israel's foreign policy.

The Jewish Agency today is responsible for the organization of Jewish immigration to Israel; the reception, assistance, and settlement of immigrants; care of children; and aid to cultural projects and institutions of higher learning. It fosters Hebrew education and culture in the Diaspora, guides and assists Zionist youth movements, and organizes the work of the Jewish people in support of Israel.

POLITICS AND PARTIES

Political parties play a central role in the social and economic, as well as political, life of the country. Many of Israel's parties had their origins in the mandate period when the political parties and movements competed with each other for control of the institutions and political life of the Zionist organizations and of the Yishuv. After independence they continued their activity with little change.

Political parties tend to be involved in all aspects of life—they publish newspapers, sponsor social and athletic events, and run medical facilities and youth and athletic organizations. Some schools are affiliated with the parties. But it is in the political realm that parties are overwhelming in their presence: Virtually all political life is organized in and through the parties and they are crucial for the political socialization of Israelis as well as for the policymaking of the state. Because Israelis vote not for individuals but for parties, it is the party that determines where individuals will be placed on the election lists and thus who will represent it in parliament and in government. Individuals or groups of individuals, no matter how prominent, have not done well when divested of the support of established parties. In the several instances in which there has been notable success (the Democratic Movement for Change—DMC—in 1977), it has tended to be emphemeral in nature. The party list system is also utilized in the Histadrut, and there, too, individual positions are determined by the parties. Election campaigns are controlled by the parties who make the decisions, wage the campaigns, and spend the money. In the final analysis the voter focuses on the party, the party member looks to it for fulfillment of his or her needs, and the politician needs its leaders and machinery to assure a political future.

Israel's political system is characterized by a wide range and intensity of political and social viewpoints that are given expression not only in political parties but also in newspapers and a host of social, religious, cultural, and other organizations. Numerous minority and splinter factions freely criticize the government. This diversity has been most apparent in the existence of multiple parties contesting parliamentary elections (and in the factions within most of the major parties) and in the various coalition governments that have been characteristic of Israel since its inception (see Tables 4.1 and 4.2).

Israel's political parties (and the blocs they have formed) have gone through substantial numbers of mergers and splits, disagreements and reconciliations as a result of ideological differences, policy disagreements, and personality clashes. Large numbers of parties have contested the 120 seats in parliament, and many have been successful in winning representation in it. For example, in 1977 twenty-three parties sought parliamentary representation, and thirteen were successful. In 1981, thirty-one parties sought seats, and initially ten were represented. In 1984, twenty-six political parties sought Knesset mandates, and fifteen were successful. The large number of parties, reflecting Israel's political fragmentation, is a result of the proportional representation system compounded by personal and ideological differences and the intensity of views held by segments of Israel's polity on numerous issues.

The electoral system that has perpetuated party proliferation and necessitated coalition governments has been subject to debate virtually since its inception. It has been suggested that the lack of individual constituencies has led members to be less responsive to citizens' requirements and less knowledgeable concerning their views and perspectives. Over the years there have been numerous suggestions for electoral reform in an effort to reduce the number of parties that contest the elections and are represented in the Knesset. The larger parties seek to move closer to systems used elsewhere that preclude the confusing array of parties in the Israeli system. The smaller parties, recognizing their probable fate should there be substantial electoral reform, generally have opposed changes in the proportional representation system. Although there have been various compromise proposals and suggestions, electoral reform has made no significant headway. Israelis have not been especially concerned about these issues, although the matter was a subject of substantial discussion in the 1977 election and in subsequent votes. The DMC, newly created for the 1977 election, emphasized the need for electoral reform and put this at the heart of its electoral platform and campaign. Ultimately its insistence on the need for reform became inconsequential when it joined the coalition without exacting concessions in this arena. Subsequent efforts similarly have failed. In the wake of the 1984 election, numerous calls for a change in the electoral system were again made.

Israel's complex party structure demonstrates various dimensions of cleavage, but socioeconomic, religious-secular, and foreign policy–national security issue areas tend to be the most significant. Israel's parties have economic views ranging from Marxism through liberal socialism to free enterprise. There are also different views concerning the role of government in economic (and consequently social) policy. The role of religion has differentiated those who seek to make Jewish religious law a central factor in state activity from others who have sought to enhance the secular nature of the system and those who have worked to eliminate virtually all vestiges of religious influence. Some have opposed Zionism and the authority of the state. Views of the ultimate extent of the state and the role of Zionism have divided groups (for example, the Communists) that oppose the concept of a Zionist state from others that have supported the notion of a binational entity or a truncated Jewish state, and from others that favor an exclusively Jewish-Zionist state in the whole of Palestine—

TABLE 4.1
Political Parties and Knesset Election Results (1949–1961)

Party	1949		1951		1955		1959		1961	
	%	Seats	%	Seats	%	Seats	%	Seats	%	Seats
Mapai (Israel Workers)	35.7	46	37.3	45	32.2	40	38.2	47	34.7	42
Mapam (United Workers)[a]	14.7	19	12.5	15	7.3	9	7.2	9	7.5	9
Ahdut Haavoda (Unity of Labor)[b]	—	—	—	—	8.2	10	6.0	7	6.6	8
Herut (Freedom)	11.5	14	6.6	8	12.6	15	13.6	17	13.8	17
General Zionists	5.2	7	16.2	20	10.2	13	6.2	8	—	—
Progressives	4.1	5	3.2	4	4.4	5	4.6	6	—	—
Liberal[c]	—	—	—	—	—	—	—	—	13.6	17
United Religious Front[d]	12.2	16	—	—	—	—	—	—	—	—
Mizrahi (Merkaz Ruchani—Spiritual Center)	—	—	1.5	2	—	—	—	—	—	—
Hapoel Hamizrahi (Workers of the Spiritual Center)	—	—	6.7	8	—	—	—	—	—	—
National Religious (Mafdal)[e]	—	—	—	—	9.1	11	9.9	12	9.8	12
Agudat Israel (Association of Israel)[f]	—	—	—	—	—	—	—	—	3.7	4
Poalei Agudat Israel (Workers of the Association of Israel)[f]	—	—	—	—	—	—	—	—	1.9	2
Torah Religious Front[g]	—	—	3.6	5	4.7	6	4.7	6	—	—

Arab Democratic List	1.7	2	2.4	3	1.8	2	—	—	—	2
Arab Progress and Work	—	—	1.2	1	1.5	2	1.3	2	1.6	2
Arab Farmers and Development	—	—	1.1	1	1.2	1	1.1	1	—	—
Arab Cooperation and Brotherhood	—	—	—	—	—	—	1.2	2	1.9	2
Communist	3.5	4	4.0	5	4.5	6	2.8	3	4.2	5
Sephardim	3.5	4	1.8	2	—	—	—	—	—	—
Fighters List	2.1	1	—	—	—	—	—	—	—	—
Women's International Zionist Organization (WIZO)	1.2	1	—	—	—	—	—	—	—	—
Yemenites	1.0	1	1.2	1	—	—	—	—	—	—

[a] Formed 1948—Hashomer Hatzair, Ahdut Haavoda, Poalei Zion.

[b] Formed by merger of Poalei Zion (Workers of Zion) and smaller socialist Zionist groups. Included in Mapam 1949 and 1951.

[c] Formed 1961—merger of General Zionists and Progressives.

[d] Elected as follows: Hapoel Hamizrahi, 6; Mizrahi, 4; Agudat Israel, 3; Poalei Agudat Israel, 3.

[e] Merger—Mizrahi and Hapoel Hamizrahi.

[f] In Torah Religious Front until 1961 elections and again in 1973 elections.

[g] Joint list Agudat Israel and Poalei Agudat Israel.

TABLE 4.2
Political Parties and Knesset Election Results (1965–1984)

Party	1965 %	1965 Seats	1969 %	1969 Seats	1973 %	1973 Seats	1977 %	1977 Seats	1981 %	1981 Seats	1984 %	1984 Seats
Mapai (Israel Workers)	IA		IA	IA	IA	IA	IA	IA	IA	IA	IA	IA
Mapam (United Workers)[a]	6.6	8	IA	IA	IA	IA	IA	IA	IA	IA	IA	IA
Ahdut Haavoda (Unity of Labor)[b]	IA		IA	IA	IA	IA	IA	IA	IA	IA	IA	IA
Alignment (Mapai and Ahdut Haavoda)	36.7	45	—									
Rafi (Israel Labor List) (Reshimat Poalei Israel)[c]	7.9	10	IA	IA	IA	IA	—		IA	IA	IA	IA
Israel Labor[d]	—		IA	IA	IA	IA	IA	IA	IA	IA	IA	IA
Maarach (Alignment of Israel Labor and Mapam)	—		46.2	56	39.7	51	24.6	32	36.6	47	34.9	44
State List[e]	—		3.1	4	—		—		—		—	
Gahal (Gush Herut Liberalim)[f]	21.3	26	21.7	26	—		—		—		—	
Independent Liberals[g]	3.8	5	3.2	4	3.6	4	1.2	1	—		—	
Shlomzion[h]	—		—		—		1.9	2	—		—	
Free Center[i]	—		1.2	2	—		—		—		—	
Likud[j]	—		—		30.2	39	33.4	43	37.1	48	31.9	41
National Religious (Mafdal)[k]	9.0	11	9.7	12	8.3	10	9.2	12	4.9	6	3.5	4
Agudat Israel (Association of Israel)[l]	3.3	4	3.2	4	—		3.4	4	3.7	4	1.7	2
Poalei Agudat Israel (Workers of the Association of Israel)	1.8	2	1.8	2	—		—		—		—	
Torah Religious Front[m]	—		—		3.8	5	1.4	1	—		—	
Tami	—		—		—		—		2.3	3	1.5	1
Morasha (Heritage)[n]	—		—		—		—		—		1.6	2
Shas (Sephardi Torah Guardians)[o]	—		—		—		—		—		3.1	4
Arab Progress and Work	2.0	2	—		—		—		—		—	
Arab Cooperation and Brotherhood	1.4	2	—		—		—		—		—	
Alignment-affiliated Arab and Druze lists	—		3.5	4	2.4	3	—		—		—	
United Arab List	—		—		—		1.4	1	—		—	

New Communists (Rakah) (Reshima Komunistit Chadasha)[p]	2.3	3	2.8	3	3.4	4	—	—	—	—	—	—	—	—	—
Israel Communists (Maki) (Miflaga Komunistit Israelit)[p]	1.1	1	1.2	1	—	1	—	—	—	—	—	—	—	—	—
Democratic Front for Peace and Equality (Hadash)[q]	—	—	—	—	1.4	1	4.6	5	3.4	4	3.4	4	—	—	—
Moked[r]	—	—	—	—	—	—	—	—	—	—	—	—	—	—	—
Flatto-Sharon	—	—	—	—	—	—	2.0	1	—	—	—	—	—	—	—
Citizens' Rights Movement (Ratz)	—	—	—	—	2.2	3	1.2	1	1.4	1	2.4	1	2.4	—	3
Democratic Movement for Change (DMC) (Dash)[s]	—	—	—	—	—	—	11.6	15	—	—	—	—	2.6	2	3
Shinui	—	—	—	—	—	—	—	—	1.5	2	—	—	—	—	—
Haolam Hazeh	1.2	1	1.2	2	—	—	—	—	—	—	—	—	—	—	—
Shelli (Shalom Lemaan Israel—Peace for Israel)[t]	—	—	—	—	1.6	2	1.6	2	—	—	—	—	1.8	—	2
Progressive List for Peace	—	—	—	—	—	—	—	—	—	—	—	—	—	—	—
Telem[u]	—	—	—	—	—	—	1.6	2	—	2	—	—	—	2	—
Ometz (Courage to Cure the Economy)	—	—	—	—	—	—	—	—	—	—	—	—	1.2	—	3
Yahad[v]	—	—	—	—	—	—	—	—	—	—	—	—	2.2	—	1
Kach[w]	—	—	—	—	—	—	—	—	—	—	—	—	1.2	—	1
Tehiya[x]	—	—	—	—	—	—	—	—	2.3	3	—	—	4.0	3	5

IA: In Alignment

[a] Formed 1948—Hashomer Hatzair, Ahdut Haavoda, Poalei Zion.

[b] Formed by merger of Poalei Zion (Workers of Zion) and smaller socialist Zionist groups.

[c] Formed 1965—Ben Gurion splinter group from Mapai.

[d] Formed 1968—merger of Mapai, Rafi, Ahdut Haavoda.

[e] Ben Gurion splinter group from Israel Labor. Later part of Likud (in 1977 as part of La'am).

[f] Formed 1965—merger of Herut and majority of Liberal party.

[g] Minority of Liberal party not joining in merger with Herut.

[h] Joined Likud after 1977 election.

[i] Formed 1968—splinter group from Herut.

TABLE 4.2 (*cont.*)

[j] Formed 1973—merger of Gahal, State List, Free Center, Greater Israel Movement. La'am—formed within Likud 1976—part of Free Center (Merkaz Hofshi), State List (Reshima Mamlachtit), Greater Israel Movement (Hatnuah Leeretz Israel Hashlemah).

[k] Merger—Mizrahi and Hapoel Hamizrahi. Elected as follows: Hapoel Hamizrahi, 6; Mizrahi, 4; Agudat Israel, 3; Poalei Agudat Israel, 3.

[l] In Torah Religious Front until 1961 elections and again in 1973 elections.

[m] Joint list Agudat Israel and Poalei Agudat Israel.

[n] Splinter from NRP and Poalei Agudat Israel.

[o] Sephardi split from Agudat Israel.

[p] Split of Communist party in 1965 resulted in formation of Rakah and Maki.

[q] Formed 1977—Rakah and some Israel Black Panthers.

[r] Israel Communist party and Tchelet Adom (Blue-Red) Movement.

[s] Formed 1976—Shinui (Change), Democratic Movement, Free Center, Zionist Panthers, various individuals. Led by Yigael Yadin. Split September 1978.

[t] Formed 1977—merger of Moked, Haolam Hazeh, independent socialists, and some Black Panthers.

[u] Led by Moshe Dayan.

[v] Led by Ezer Weizman.

[w] Led by Rabbi Meir Kahane.

[x] In 1984 Tehiya-Tzomet.

both east and west of the Jordan River. Foreign policy issues have been less divisive than in the early days of the state. When the Soviet Union was an ardent suitor of the new Jewish state, it facilitated the adoption of pro-Soviet foreign policy stances by political groups with a Marxist orientation, such as Mapam. At the same time, parties of the right (such as the General Zionists and Herut) advocated a Western orientation. Soon, however, the choice was unrealistic, and since the early 1950s a pro-Western orientation has dominated Israeli thinking.

Particular or special interest groups have created parties to represent their views and to secure their interests more effectively. These parties have reflected a wide spectrum of perspectives and concerns, ranging from the ethnic and social goals of the Arab parties and parties seeking to represent Yemenites and Sephardim to the more practical attempts of some groups to promote more narrow goals such as revocation of income tax. Individual and personal factors have also played a role in party formation. Individuals with ambitions or personal concerns, ranging from animosity to other political figures or a desire to achieve a particular status, have established their own parties to contest Knesset elections; this was the case with Shmuel Flatto-Sharon in 1977, who sought election and the accompanying parliamentary immunity as a means of avoiding extradition for trial in France. Historical developments, mostly during the preindependence period, and personal differences among the political elite have been important elements in fostering party proliferation.

Despite such proliferation, political life has been shaped by the views of a few leading parties and individuals. The parties themselves tend to be tightly organized and highly centralized, with party authority exercised over members' activities in virtually all areas of political concern.

POLITICAL PARTIES

Israel's political parties may be categorized into three groupings: parties of the left, parties of the center right, and

the religious parties. There are also various particularistic
parties that tend on the whole to be small and short-lived.

The Left

On the left are the socialist parties, of which the major
element is the Israel Labor party (Mifleget Haavoda Haisraelit).
It formally came into being in 1968 as a result of the merger
of three labor parties: Mapai, Ahdut Haavoda, and Rafi.
Mapai (acronym for Mifleget Poalei Eretz Israel—Workers
Party of the Land of Israel), the Labor party's major component, was founded in 1930 by a merger of Ahdut Haavoda
and Hapoel Hatzair. Under the leadership of David Ben-
Gurion it became the most prominent and important party
in the Yishuv and, later, in independent Israel.

Prior to statehood Mapai's role virtually was unchallenged. It controlled the Assembly of the Elected and the
National Council in the semiautonomous Jewish government
in Palestine. In the 1931 elections it received 43.7 percent of
the vote for the Assembly of the Elected and gained control
of the National Council, which it maintained until 1948.
Mapai continued its dominant role after statehood, and in
elections for the Knesset it consistently obtained the largest
single percentage of votes until the 1977 election. It was the
dominant member of all government coalitions, and ordinarily
its members held the important portfolios of prime minister,
defense minister, foreign minister, and finance minister. Its
role in the Jewish Agency was also significant. Although the
agency was governed by a coalition of parties, Mapai had
the largest representation on the executive board and usually
held the chairmanship and other major posts. Mapai also
frequently won the largest bloc of representation in the
Histadrut election, in which political parties compete against
each other as in the Knesset election; it often won a majority
and was the controlling party on the executive board.

The continuing role of Mapai as the most important
member of the parliament and of the cabinet, and its status
in the Jewish Agency and Histadrut, were the basis for its
unique position in the Israeli system. The party was one of

the political institutions of the country and was identified with the state in the minds of many voters. Also, because of its long tenure of office, it permeated the governmental, administrative, economic, and other institutions of Israel.

On January 21, 1968, Mapai merged with two other labor parties—Ahdut Haavoda–Poalei Zion (Unity of Labor–Workers of Zion) and Rafi (Israel Labor List)—to form Mifleget Haavoda Haisraelit (Israel Labor party). Together with the Mapai-affiliated Arab parties, the new party held 59 out of the 120 votes in the Knesset, only two short of an absolute majority. The June 1967 war was the catalyst that precipitated the trend toward the merger of the labor parties. The Arab threat led to the establishment of a broadly based government of national unity. When the termination of the war did not bring peace, and the continuation of the conflict with an accelerated tempo became evident, prudence dictated the maintenance of the broader coalition to present a solid front in international negotiations. The need for cooperation for reasons of security contributed to the creation of a climate suitable to the consummation of the merger.

Beginning with the 1969 Knesset elections, the Israel Labor party was joined in an election Alignment (Maarach) by Mapam (acronym for Mifleget Poalim Hameuhedet—United Workers party), although each maintained its own organizational structure and ideological posture. Mapam was formed in 1948 as a coalition of groups believing in socialism and Zionism—primarily members of Ahdut Haavoda–Poalei Zion and Hashomer Hatzair. It adopted a pro-Soviet orientation that it maintained until the mid-1950s, when the party split on this question. In 1954 Ahdut Haavoda left Mapam. Mapam has adopted a position championing the cause of Israel's Arab population and promoting a solution to the Arab-Israeli conflict.

The Labor party was dominant and remained the single most important factor in Israeli politics until the 1977 parliamentary elections. The merger of the labor parties did not eliminate the differences between the coalition's components but rather shifted the quarrels from the interparty to the intraparty sphere. It was within the Israel Labor party that the problems of leadership and succession were resolved. However, the Labor party began to lose support in the 1970s. Disillusionment with its weakening leadership, particularly at the time of the Yom Kippur War of 1973 and in subsequent negotiations for an Arab-Israeli settlement, combined with scandals and with economic and social problems to raise significant doubts about the efficacy of its governmental role. Labor lost its dominance in 1977 and failed to regain it in the 1981 and 1984 elections.

On the extreme left of the political spectrum is the Communist party, which has gone through a number of permutations over the years since its founding in the mandate period. The party's membership and voting support is overwhelmingly Arab, but its leadership has become increasingly divided between Jews and Arabs. The party, known as Rakah (Reshima Kommunistit Chadasha—New Communist List), is pro-Moscow and strongly anti-Zionist. It is legal, competes in the political system, and wins seats in parliament, but it is isolated in Israeli political life—it does not join the government and is seen as a perennial and reflexive opponent of government policy.

The Right

On the right of the political spectrum are a number of parties at whose core lies Herut (Freedom), formed by Menachem Begin as an independent political party in 1948. Herut's origins go back to the 1920s and Vladimir Zeev Jabotinsky's establishment of the Zionist Revisionist movement, whose views Herut reflects. The Revisionist movement undertook numerous activities during the mandate, including the organization of illegal immigration to Palestine and the establishment of the Irgun. When the Israeli government forced the Irgun to dissolve, the action served also as the rallying point for the creation of a new political party. Menachem Begin created the Herut party to carry on the work of the Irgun and of the Jabotinsky-Revisionist ideology, and Herut became the representative of the Revisionist movement in Israel. Begin remained the leader of the party and the Likud bloc that it dominated until his retirement from public life in 1983.

After independence Herut deemphasized its claims to the territory of Jordan, but retained its interest in the West Bank and other portions of historic Eretz Israel. Ideologically, Herut remained faithful to the Revisionist program. Originally, it insisted on an end to Histadrut power, Israel's socialist orientation, and the primacy of Labor in the government's policies and institutions. Since Mapai was the primary architect of government policies, Herut's attacks were directed mostly against it, and since it was Ben-Gurion who destroyed the Irgun, the attacks had a vengeful aspect. Mapai viewed Herut in similar terms as an irresponsible political party that left the World Zionist Organization and organized terrorist activities. Mapai saw Herut as irresponsible in both the substance and the style of its parliamentary opposition. Much of the bitterness between Herut and Mapai stemmed from the personal and ideological animosity of Begin and Ben-Gurion, and each readily denounced the other, in public and in private.

In 1965 Herut was joined by the former General Zionists in the Liberal party to form the parliamentary bloc Gahal (acronym for Gush Herut Liberalim—bloc of Herut and the Liberals). Likud (Unity) was formed in 1973 as a parliamentary bloc by the combination of Gahal and La'am (Toward the People), and Begin retained his dominant role.

On the extreme right are two parties formed in recent years. Tehiya (Renaissance) was created in response to the Camp David Accords and the Egypt-Israel Treaty, which its founders saw as inimical to Israel's interests in that they relinquished territories important for Israel's security and made other concessions deleterious to Israel's future. Kach, headed by Rabbi Meir Kahane, focuses on the need to make Israel Jewish by ousting the Arabs from both Israel and the West Bank and the Gaza.

The Religious Parties

Parties with a religious orientation have played a major role in Israel's political life. At the core are the National

Religious party and Agudat Yisrael (or Agudat Israel), although
their centrality increasingly has been challenged in recent
years. The National Religious party (NRP or Mafdal—Miflaga
Datit Leumit) was founded in 1956 by Mizrahi (Spiritual
Center) and Hapoel Hamizrahi (Workers of the Spiritual
Center) as a religious party seeking to combine religious
concerns and a moderate socialist orientation in economic
matters within a Zionist framework. Agudat Israel (Association
of Israel) is an ultra-Orthodox party focusing its attention
on the religious nature of the state and seeking to have Israel
function in accordance with the principles of the Torah.

Israel's religious political parties are a direct response to
the emergence of political Zionism at the end of the nineteenth
century, and a point of difference among them has been their
perspectives on Zionism. In the ultra-Orthodox camp were
those who denied the basic validity of the Zionist idea on
the grounds that it contradicted the traditional conception of
divine redemption. Nevertheless, some who opposed Zionism
as a secular nationalism encouraged Jews to settle in Israel
as a means of fulfilling a religious obligation. As historical
developments made the idea of a Jewish state more logical
(such positive pronouncements as the Balfour Declaration and
such negative developments as the Holocaust, growing anti-
Semitism, and assimilation that threatened many of the great
centers and institutions for the study of the Torah), many of
the ultra-Orthodox who continued to oppose Zionism began
to recognize the importance of Jewish settlement in Israel
and of the State of Israel itself to the survival of the Jewish
people. The religious Zionists took an alternative approach.
Although there were and are exceptions, they tended to see
Zionism as a solution to the problems faced by Jews in the
Diaspora but also as a first stage in the messianic process.
Thus Israel's independence was, in their view, the beginning
of redemption, and the process became of religious significance.
This approach was reinforced by Israel's victories in the Six
Day War of 1967 and spawned movements such as Gush
Emunim (Bloc of the Faithful), which linked Israel's accom-
plishments with both religious concepts and Zionist ideals.

Agudat Israel (the Aguda) is a religiously oriented political party representing the interests of a section of Orthodox Jewry living both in the Jewish state and outside it. The Aguda formally was established and its policies and programs delineated in Kattowitz (Katowice), Poland, in 1912 during a conference of the major East European and German–Austro-Hungarian Orthodox rabbis. It was formed, to a significant extent, in reaction to the growth of Zionism, with its secular majority. The Aguda was to be a Torah movement directed by a Council of Torah Sages (Moetzet Gedolei Hatorah), which was to be the supreme authority in all matters. The council, instituted in the 1920s, is a group of rabbinical scholars who represent the various factions of the Aguda movement and are chosen for their scholarly merit and prestige in the realm of Orthodox Jewry. The Council of Torah Sages continues to be the supreme decision-making body for Aguda adherents, and its decisions are sovereign in all questions affecting the membership, including religious and political matters such as joining or remaining in a government coalition. This authority derives from the personal standing and reputation of its members, who have achieved recognition as qualified inter-preters of the *halachah* and are viewed with high esteem by members of Aguda.

Initially the Aguda opposed Zionism as religiously un-acceptable (a position similar to that of Neturei Karta today), although even in the 1930s and 1940s Agudat Israel cooperated with the Jewish Agency and other bodies of the Yishuv in several clearly and specifically defined areas. This stemmed from purely pragmatic considerations based on the reality of the prevailing situation, particularly the rise of Nazi Germany and widespread European anti-Semitism, and the understand-ing that the Holocaust required some mechanism to save the persecuted and threatened Jews of Europe. Ultimately, Aguda gave partial backing to the Zionist endeavor when it supported the establishment of Israel and participated in the institutions of the new state. It joined the provisional Council of State and was represented in Israel's first cabinet. The decision to move into the mainstream of Israeli politics led to a split within the Aguda, with its more conservative elements rallying around the perspective of the Satmar Rebbe who opposed Zionism and formed the Neturei Karta.

Agudat Israel did not participate in any government from 1952, when it resigned from the coalition, until 1977, when it joined the government formed by Begin. During that period, it did not display hostility to Israel, nor did it consistently oppose its actions, although it generally did not concur with the government. There were elements within the Aguda whose attitudes were similar to those of the Neturei Karta and who refused to cooperate in any way or to engage in dialogue with other groups in Israeli society. The Aguda still does not belong to the Zionist organization, but this is primarily a voice against that organization's secular bias, not opposition to Israel. The Aguda supports the state and participates in its institutions without necessarily accepting all of its policies or particular ideologies. It does not link Israel with the biblical promise of redemption; rather it supports Israel because of a pragmatic perspective that sees the state as vitally important to the survival of the Jewish people because of worldwide conditions. Opposition to and complaints about the secular nature of Israel's political and social system remain a very significant part of the Aguda approach, even while it supports the state as a necessity. At the same time *aliyah* must be encouraged for religious and practical reasons, although no "holy" role is assigned to the state.

Throughout, Aguda has been motivated by its desire to ensure that no legislation would harm Orthodox interests and that its religious and educational institutions would receive maximum support from the government. Aguda has sought to secure expansion of Torah institutions and Jewish law within the political system. It has focused its attention on such issues as financial support for various religious institutions, education, and the schools and the extension of the religious perspective into essentially secular realms, such as the military service of females, and the question of "who is a Jew," which get to the core of the Orthodox viewpoint and perspective. To achieve its goals, Aguda was prepared to support the governing coalitions despite oftentimes uneasy alliances. Finally in 1977, with the coming to power of Likud, it found a less uneasy partner than the Labor governments that had previously governed. As its price for supporting the 1977 Begin government, Aguda sought a number of concessions. With the 1977 coalition agreement, Aguda was able to gain more from the government than was possible under Labor.

The National Religious party, by contrast, has participated within the mainstream of Jewish life and the activities of the state of Israel. Mafdal has been a central figure on Israel's political scene since independence and consequently has wielded substantial political power. Mafdal's origins lie in the prestate period. Mizrahi came into being in 1902, although its central concept can be identified as early as the 1880s. The founders of the movement did not see a necessary contradiction between Judaism and Zionism. In contrast with Aguda, Mizrahi and its labor offshoot, Hapoel Hamizrahi (founded in 1922), functioned as a part of the World Zionist Organization and the Yishuv institutions in Palestine virtually from the outset. After independence Mafdal became a significant partner in Israel's governments. Prime Minister Ben-Gurion soon realized that he was unable to secure an absolute majority in Israel's parliamentary elections, and in his search for government coalition partners, it was often easier and more productive to work with NRP than with the political parties of the right or of the left who often had demands in areas he considered crucial. Thus, in exchange for concessions in the religious area, which mattered relatively little to Ben-Gurion, he was able to secure a free hand to deal with matters of greater consequence to him, such as foreign policy and defense matters.

NRP found the marriage of convenience equally beneficial, and as a consequence it has been a member of virtually every government coalition. Its main concerns and *raison d'être* were in the religious realm, even though it had views on most of the issues facing the state. It seemed to believe that in foreign policy and economics it had little to offer that was unique and that it was established to focus on religious and related issues. The political platforms for the various elections have focused on religious questions such as Sabbath observance, religious education, dietary laws, autopsies, and general support for religious institutions and activities. NRP has been pragmatic in its actions, thereby securing many of its objectives in the give-and-take of Israel's parliamentary maneuvering.

There are several differences between Aguda and the NRP. Many observers stress the fact that NRP members tend to be more modern than Aguda members. That distinction, which others question, is overshadowed by their differences in perspective concerning the relationship between Zionism and a secular society. Aguda focuses more on the rejection of modern secular culture or its acceptance only within the closed framework of Jewish life and society. NRP adherents accept modernization and participation in broader aspects of Jewish society and culture. Aguda has been relatively cohesive in nature, whereas NRP has been consistently characterized by internal factionalism.

Divisions within the ranks of the religious movements have become more pronounced in recent years, eclipsing the NRP-Aguda split. Within each party are differences over issues and leadership, but broader discord within the Orthodox religious community has led to new religiously based parties, some of which were offshoots of existing ones. Numerous factions, each with its own leadership and agendas, compete to secure loyalty and votes and to secure program goals and political patronage. In the 1981 election this led to the creation of Tami and in 1984 to the formation of new parties that also were successful in securing seats in the Knesset: Morasha (Heritage) was created by a splinter group from NRP that joined with Poalei Agudat Israel; Shas (Sephardi Torah Guardians) was a Sephardi split from Agudat Israel.

Notwithstanding these and other areas of discord, the religious parties have a major common denominator—their effort to represent the interests of Israel's Orthodox community. They share a loyalty to traditional religious Judaism and realize the need to organize and mobilize the religious community to prevent secular intrusion in the religious domain and to ensure perpetuation of religious values and life-styles. In part because of these concerns, the parties have created communal and educational frameworks to draw together those Jews who are faithful to the Orthodox perspective. They may differ in their approaches to secular society and in their views of Zionism, but they agree that there must be no contradiction of *halachah* and that Orthodox religious interests must be preserved and enhanced.

Nonmainline Parties

Over the years a number of political parties have been created with focuses and concerns not readily categorized into right, left, and religious groupings. Some have been of consequence; others have had fleeting roles. The more significant of these parties have been near the center of the political spectrum. The Liberal party (Hamiflaga Haliberalit) was established during the Fifth Knesset by a merger of the General Zionist party (Hatzionim Haklaliyim) and the Progressive party (Hamiflaga Haprogressivit). The Independent Liberal party (Haliberalim Haatzmaim) was formed in 1965 by the Progressive faction in the Liberal party. The Citizens' Rights Movement (CRM—Hatnuah Lezhuiot Haezrach) was founded in 1973.

The Democratic Movement for Change (DMC—Hatnuah Hademocratit Leshinui) was formed in 1976, under the leadership of Yigael Yadin, to contest the 1977 election. It was not a typical political party: Its membership cut across the spectrum of political ideologies and party affiliations, and its main theme was electoral reform and the revitalization of Israel's political system. It focused on the mismanagement and corruption of the Labor-led coalitions of Israel. Yadin brought to the party a reputation based on a "nonpolitical" (and hence "clean") past; he had been chief of staff of the army as well as a distinguished professor and archaeologist popularly known for his work at Masada.

A number of smaller parties do not fit into the three main groups. These include the Yemenite lists, the WIZO (Women's International Zionist Organization), and the Black Panthers—groups that lasted for a brief period and focused on specific issues and concerns.

THE DYNAMICS OF GOVERNMENT

Coalitions

The multiplicity of parties, the diversity of views they represent, and the proportional representation electoral system have resulted in the failure of any one party to win a majority of Knesset seats in any of the eleven elections between 1949 and 1984, thus necessitating the formation of coalition governments. Prior to the national unity government formed in 1984, only twice have the coalitions been truly broad based— the provisional government formed on independence and the government of national unity formed during the crisis preceding the 1967 war and maintained following the 1969 election until the summer of 1970. The latter two were unusual in that they were established in times of national stress. The 1984 national unity government was unique in that it was based on a principle of power sharing between Labor and Likud, the two major political blocs.

Notwithstanding these factors, all of the coalitions have proved remarkably stable, due to a number of factors. Israel had only six prime ministers during its first three decades of independence: David Ben-Gurion (1948–1953, 1955–1963), Moshe Sharett (1954–1955), Levi Eshkol (1963–1969), Golda Meir (1969–1974), Yitzhak Rabin (1974–1977), and Menachem Begin (1977–1983). Yitzhak Shamir (1983–1984) and Shimon Peres (1984–) came to office following Begin's resignation and the Knesset election of 1984, respectively. Although there have been a number of cabinet changes, most have been essentially formal. They occurred following the election of a new Knesset, the choice of a president, the retirement of David Ben-Gurion, his return to public life, his second retirement, the 1967 crisis and war, the death of Levi Eshkol, the retirement of Golda Meir, the retirement of Menachem Begin, and so forth. The personal stabilizing influence of Ben-Gurion, Moshe Sharett, Levi Eshkol, and Golda Meir during their respective tenures as prime minister and the preponderant strength of Mapai and the Labor party were important factors in maintaining stability. After the 1977 election Menachem

Begin played a similar stabilizing role in the governments he headed, until his resignation in 1983. The rigorous discipline of Israel's parties has curbed irresponsible action by individual Knesset members. Continuity of policy also has been enhanced by the reappointment of many ministers in reshuffled cabinets and the continuity of bureaucratic officeholders.

The formation of a governing coalition is an arduous and complex task involving numerous factions and individuals in tough bargaining for political power and prestige. Coalition partners understand their political value and exact high political prices (usually measured in power to secure policies and patronage) for their participation in a government coalition. Thus, all governments and their programs have been compromises in terms of personnel, positions, and policies.

The coalitions constructed since independence have involved a multiplicity of parties, with Labor as the dominant party between 1949 and 1977, and Likud dominant between 1977 and 1984. Nevertheless, despite the clear supremacy of one coalition member, the smaller parties often tend to be powerful because of their importance to the government's continuation in office. The divergent views represented in each cabinet often have had the effect of mutual cancellation and a resultant lowest-common-denominator policy for the government. Dramatic moves are thus unlikely to result—and have not. At the same time, the need to accommodate the several coalition parties has often led to the creation of needless or redundant ministries and governmental positions, at best a wasteful procedure. Although this process has led to numerous coalition participants, the major portfolios have always been retained by the dominant coalition party. Thus Mapai/Labor and Likud held the portfolios of prime minister, defense minister, foreign minister, and finance minister while allocating less central positions to the other parties in the coalition.

The requirements of coalition government have placed limitations on the prime minister's ability to control fully the cabinet and its actions. The prime minister does not appoint ministers; he or she reaches accord with the other parties, and they select the occupants of the several portfolios who share in the cabinet's collective responsibility for governing Israel. Similarly the prime minister cannot dismiss any of the ministers. At the same time the prime minister possesses substantial powers that enable him or her to "influence" the process by which ministers are selected and removed. Cabinets may often contain individuals selected because of party loyalty—not qualification, who may well be divided in regard to perspectives and quarrelsome in regard to procedures.

The bargaining resulting from the coalition system has permitted the religious parties—Mafdal, Agudat Israel, Poalei Agudat Israel, and, more recently, Tami, Morasha, and Shas— to gain considerable policy concessions and to play strong roles in government decision making because they were essential to secure a majority in the Knesset. This was particularly apparent in the wake of the 1981 Knesset elections. The inevitable clash of interests and the persistence of partisan loyalties implicit in this procedure limited governmental flexibility and, to an extent, reduced the efficiency of the administrative machinery. Since members of the Knesset do not represent any specific constituency and depend on party backing for election and reelection, their attitudes and actions have frequently been motivated more by party considerations than by the general will.

The Political Elite

Despite party proliferation and general political diversity, Israel's political life has been dominated by a relatively small and cohesive elite. During the initial three decades, this group maintained its positions in the major state institutions (especially the cabinet and the Knesset), had substantial political experience, and was characterized by a relatively high average age. Israel's elite group was Jewish and tended to be mostly homogeneous in background, despite ideological diversity. Most of the leaders were European (especially East European) in origin and most were personally acquainted, if not intimate. Many members of the elite, especially in the first two decades of independence, owed their origins to the Second Aliyah (1904–1914)—including Prime Ministers Ben-Gurion, Sharett, and Eshkol. But many others, arriving later, possessed similar characteristics. The power of the Second Aliyah derived from a number of significant factors. These were the individuals who controlled the state institutions at the time of independence, and it was their ideology and values (pioneering, labor ideology, and so on) that became the objectives of the state. Moreover, these were the founding fathers and the heroes of the struggle for independence. Their centrality lasted for more than two decades and only began to decline in the late 1960s as age and death reduced their ranks and as their association in the minds of many Israelis with the institutions and values of the state became less clear.

The political elite has been predominantly civilian in character and background. The military generally is not regarded as part of the political elite, although it is consulted on matters relating to national defense and plays a role in the decision-making process on security-related issues. The armed forces are generally excluded from politics, although retired senior military officers (including generals and chiefs of staff) have increasingly been coopted into the political elite and included in the cabinet and other key posts. In addition, they have formed political movements and parties to pursue their goals. Their involvement has been the result not of military action or influence but rather of the decision of the political parties to include highly visible and publicly acclaimed figures in their ranks or individuals seeking to build second careers while taking advantage of existing reputations.

Religious elements have had a somewhat similar position. They have exerted strong influence in the cabinet and Knesset as political parties because of their role in coalition formation. The rabbinate is not considered part of the political elite, and the religious establishment generally does not intervene in politics.

Role of the Military in Politics

The IDF is virtually unique in the Middle East in that it does not, as an entity, play a role in politics, despite its size, budget, and importance. Individual officers and senior commanders have secured important positions, but they have done so as individuals, when not on active service and without the backing of the military as an institution. Active duty officers are prohibited from engaging in political activities. The IDF performs the tasks of the traditional army—defense of the state—and does so in an apolitical fashion. It has not been seen as a threat to the regime, and there has never been consideration of a military coup. The elite of the Israel Defense Forces has shown a continued confidence in the political system, although there are occasional complaints about some of the individuals who run it and their political views and perspectives. Civilians continue to control the military and do so by virtue of their dominant positions within the Israeli system, not because they control the military itself.

The officer corps has not, and probably could not, become closely aligned with one political faction or party. The highly developed and sophisticated nature of the political system and its institutions, and the complex and often bewildering array of political and quasipolitical institutions, make it extremely difficult for the army to play an independent political role and to seek to seize power through political means and institutions and procedures. The close identification of Israel's leadership with the development of the state would significantly reduce the ability of the army, even if cohesive, to claim that the political leaders had betrayed the state and therefore had to be replaced by military coup or similar device.

The political ambitions of senior Israeli officers have been restricted, and relatively few senior officers joined political parties in Israel's first three decades, although there was a growing tendency for postcareer political roles among senior officers in the period following the 1967 and 1973 wars. Those who have become involved in politics often take advantage of their military accomplishments, "charismatic" appeal, or established prestige and join parties representing diverse political views and ideologies. Retiring military officers often concentrate their talents in other realms, particularly business and industry, and some have become a part of the state bureaucracy. The system has been able to absorb, with relatively little disruption, virtually all of the retiring senior officers, in most cases into positions of some responsibility that take advantage of their talents and skills, particularly those of an administrative and organizational nature.

It has only been after their retirement that such military men as Generals Moshe Dayan, Yigal Allon, Yitzhak Rabin, Yigael Yadin, Ezer Weizman, Haim Bar Lev, and Ariel Sharon have played a key role in political life. They have attained position and power by working within the bounds of the political system and by joining political parties, not by their utilization of the military in opposition to the system. Their military reputations and popular prestige enhanced their chances for, but did not ensure, significant political careers.

Contributing to the limited role of the IDF in politics is its nature. It is a small standing force with a sizable reserve. Its officer corps and its personnel reserve are integrated into society, and there is little in the way of a separate barracks mentality. Permanent service is limited to a relatively small group of men and women, and no separate ideology or political life can be easily created. Israel's army is part of its society—its personnel and political concepts and its ideology are a part of the Israeli national life-style. It is not an independent unit seeing itself in opposition to the civilians who control it. Thus, despite the extraordinary role and performance of the military in Israel, there has been a consistent persistence of civilian rule over the military, and civil-military relations have not been a problem. This pattern was established at independence when Prime Minister David Ben-Gurion assumed the defense portfolio. He asserted the authority of the government and assured the consolidation of the several underground military forces under the IDF and, ultimately, the Minister of Defense. He saw the army as a nation-building instrument through education, integration, agricultural activity, and youth activity.

Today, despite a strong military and its participation in Israeli life, decisions are still made at the political level. The Minister of Defense controls the defense establishment, usually with a firm hand. Of those who have served in that capacity only Moshe Dayan, Ezer Weizman, Ariel Sharon, and Yitzhak

Rabin were senior military officers. On the other hand the chief of staff (and often, too, the DMI—director of military intelligence, sometimes accompanied by other officers) has participated in cabinet meetings and meetings of such bodies as the Ministerial Committee on Security Affairs. The advice of senior military officers is sought on all security-related matters. It is the DMI who provides the government with political-military intelligence. The criterion of loyalty to the regime or to the leader has not been central to the decision-making process by which senior military positions are filled or retained, rather, competence and skill have been the major factors involved in the determinations of senior positions in the IDF. To a great extent the military has been insulated from politics in Israel.

NEW DIMENSIONS FOR ISRAEL

Politics After the Yom Kippur War

The turmoil in the political process and political life of Israel at the time of the Yom Kippur War set in motion forces that subsequently affected the political process. The change from euphoria before the war to uncertainty after it accelerated political change and facilitated the replacement of personalities and the alteration of policies. The effect was not obvious in the elections for the Eighth Knesset and local authorities, held at the end of December 1973. Although about a third of the members were new and the party composition of the Knesset was modified, the profile of the new parliament was not substantially different from that of its predecessor. Golda Meir was charged with creating a new government and did so in early 1974, only to resign a month later, primarily because of dissension within the Labor party that centered on the question of political responsibility for lapses at the outset of the war.

This set the stage for the selection of a new prime minister and the formation of a new coalition. Yitzhak Rabin, former chief of staff and a hero of the 1967 war and former ambassador to the United States, as well as a scion of a prominent labor-movement family, was chosen prime minister. The choice of Rabin was important in that he was relatively young (in his fifties) and of a new generation—not of the group of pioneers who came to Israel at the beginning of the twentieth century and who had controlled the situation since. He was, however, the choice of the Mapai establishment and had the support of both Golda Meir and Pinchas Sapir, leading members of the old guard.

Rabin's government represented a departure from the past and ushered in a new era in which some of Israel's most well known names and personalities moved from the focus of power. The coalition was constructed initially with a different structure, as the National Religious party was replaced by the Citizens' Rights Movement (although this was reversed within a matter of months). Leadership had begun to be transferred from the immigrant-founder generation to the native-born sons. The policy process also underwent some change as the kitchen cabinet of Golda Meir and her strength of leadership was replaced by a cabinet with more diverse views and with an increased role in the policy process. Golda Meir's singular role gave way to the representation of diverse views in Israel's three-man shuttle-diplomacy negotiating team (Rabin, Yigal Allon, and Shimon Peres) and in their coterie of advisers. Although comprising the leadership of the government and the party, they, and especially Rabin and Peres, were constantly seeking to ensure their individual preeminence. Peres and Rabin each sought to gain advantage over the other in the struggle to lead the party and the government.

The protest movements and new political parties resulting from the Yom Kippur War have had varying degrees of success in establishing themselves in the political structure. They developed initially in response to perceived mismanagement during the war and focused on the need for political reform. Among the resultant parties was the DMC, which secured sizable representation in the Knesset in 1977 and joined the Likud-led coalition in the fall of that year. It later split into several smaller groups and disintegrated by the time of the 1981 Knesset elections. Yigael Yadin, its founder and titular head, retired from politics to return to academic-scholarly pursuits.

The Political "Earthquake"

In a more general sense, many of the forces set in motion by the Yom Kippur War and its aftermath seemed to coalesce to affect the situation in a tangible way when Israel's electorate went to the polls in May 1977. They gave the largest number of votes to the Likud, led by Menachem Begin, and Labor lost a substantial number of seats compared to its showing in 1973. Many of Labor's lost mandates went to the newly established DMC, but Likud also gained additional members. This ended the Labor dominance of Israeli politics that had begun in the Yishuv period. Israel thus chose a new regime, and the Likud, under Begin's leadership, emerged as the leading political force.

To a substantial degree, the results suggest that Labor lost more than Likud won. Likud did not dominate the results and the system as Labor and Mapai had done previously. Voters were concerned with the lack of leadership and the weakness of the government in dealing with a wide variety of issues ranging from labor unrest to broader social problems. Government vacillation in response to challenges seemed to confirm general impressions of weakness, and several major scandals prior to the election contributed to the negative image. The emergence of the DMC allowed voters to shift their support from Labor and to choose a somewhat similar and respected new alternative rather than being forced to cast their ballots for Menachem Begin and Likud.

The loss of identification of Mapai with the state and demographic changes, especially the growth of the Oriental population, further contributed to Mapai's decline and Likud's growth. The Oriental community began to resent the treatment it had received under the Labor establishment and found in Menachem Begin a figure of authority to whom it could relate, despite his European demeanor, as it sought to manifest its resentment. Many of these elements contributed to Likud's new status as Israel's leading political grouping after the 1977

election. The dominant party system that had characterized
the pre-1977 period was replaced by the more typical gov-
ernment-versus-opposition system, and the two major parties
increased their joint share of the seats in the Knesset at the
expense of the smaller parties. But, like the Labor party, Likud
did not capture a majority of seats in parliament, and a
coalition government was required.

Israel's 1977 elections were seen as a new political
"earthquake" reflecting and foreshadowing substantial change.
Menachem Begin and the Likud now formed the government
and took control of Israel's bureaucracy. The parties comprising
the Likud bloc (especially Begin's Herut) had been serving
as the opposition since independence, with the exception of
their joining the "wall-to-wall" government of national unity
during the 1967 war crisis and remaining in it until their
withdrawal in 1970, when they vocally opposed the government and criticized its programs, politics, and leadership. As
a consequence of the 1977 election, Likud became the ruling
coalition responsible for establishing and implementing programs and policies for Israel. It sought to implement its own
program within the broad ideology developed decades before
by Vladimir Jabotinsky. Once in power as prime minister,
Begin found in Jabotinsky a source of inspiration and a guide
for concrete policy and worked toward the implementation
of Jabotinsky's vision.

The 1981 Knesset election was not conclusive in identifying a popular preference for Likud or Labor. The electorate
virtually divided its votes between the two blocs but awarded
neither a majority of votes or seats in parliament, and coalition
politics continued to characterize the system. President Yitzhak
Navon granted the mandate to form the new government to
Begin, and he succeeded in forming a Likud-led coalition that
subsequently received the endorsement of the Knesset. The
election highlighted the political dimension of the ethnic issue
when Likud secured the majority (probably some 70 percent)
of the Oriental Jewish vote, following a pattern foreshadowed
in the 1977 election.

Extensive Oriental support for Begin and the Likud in
1981 must be seen as a desire to achieve change through

support of a party and government perceived as sympathetic to the Oriental plight. Begin's popularity in the Oriental community was a direct result of previous Oriental failures, his courting of the community even as opposition leader, and his responsiveness during his first administration. This support of Begin and Likud, an apparent identification of a political "home," to a significant degree came in lieu of an effective independent Oriental political organization that had not arisen and remained successful in previous years, although both Tami (in 1981 and 1984) and Shas (in 1984) were able to draw some voters to their Oriental-based political movements. Likud was widely seen as the party to assist the Oriental community to emerge from its second-class status.

The second Begin government (1981–1983) came to office with a narrow margin in parliament, but the prime minister was able to maintain that control despite the traumatic events associated with the war in Lebanon and major economic problems. Begin, personally, was a popular politician with strong charismatic appeal to broad sections of the populace, and he was an able and skilled political leader, in much the same manner as Ben-Gurion and Meir. He remained popular and powerful until his resignation from office in the fall of 1983. His foreign minister, Yitzhak Shamir, a relative newcomer to politics, replaced him. The short-lived Shamir government, officially endorsed by the Knesset in October 1983, was virtually the same as its predecessor in personalities and policies. Shamir pursued a policy of continuity to the extent possible.

The 1984 Election

In the spring of 1984 parliament called for new elections, and in July the Eleventh Knesset was chosen. A new phase of leadership by more conventional individuals was launched— a phase of "politics without charisma." The 1984 campaign lacked a sense of vibrancy created by a figure able to generate interest in the election process and in the issues facing Israel. Begin's refusal to emerge from his self-imposed retirement brought to an end the period of "father figures." It was thus left to Yitzhak Shamir (Likud) and Shimon Peres (Labor Alignment) to lead the lackluster politicians who vied for the voters' approval, and the results, in part, reflected their inability to entice the noncommitted voter to full participation. Labor was unable to capitalize on Likud's misfortunes, including the retirement of Begin (and his remaining in seclusion throughout the campaign), the Lebanese quagmire, and the economic problems (reflected in the oft-quoted figure of 400 percent inflation). Shamir proved able to retain much of Likud's electoral support, avoiding what many thought (and the polls earlier predicted) would be a Labor victory by a substantial margin.

Fifteen of the twenty-six political parties that contested the 1984 election secured the necessary 1 percent of the valid votes cast to obtain a seat in parliament. The two major blocs were relatively close—the Labor Alignment secured 724,074 votes (44 seats), while the Likud secured 661,302 votes (41 seats). The remaining parliamentary seats were not distributed in any clear pattern that would facilitate the forming of a new government. Following the prescribed procedure, President Chaim Herzog consulted with the leaders of the parties and eventually designated Shimon Peres as the member of the Knesset who should try to form a government, following the maneuvering of the two major parties to induce the smaller parties to join with them to form a majority in parliament. The designation of Peres followed the tradition of granting the mandate to form the government to the head of the largest party in the Knesset and reflected the president's assessment, probably tempered by his own long-time membership in the Labor party, that Peres had the better chance to form a government given the complicated configuration of the party structure in the newly-elected Knesset.

Herzog sought to promote the idea of a national unity government as the most appropriate and efficacious means of governing Israel in the ensuing period. His views, and those of many others, were conditioned by the perspective that it would be difficult for either major party to form a government on any but a narrow, and therefore fragile, coalition base involving numerous small parties each pursuing its own program. This would make important decision making on crucial issues such as the economy, the presence in Lebanon, and the peace process extremely difficult, if not impossible.

The election had a number of other results of note including the success, after failure in previous elections, of Rabbi Meir Kahane and his Kach party in gaining nearly twenty-six thousand votes and a seat in the Knesset. Kahane had campaigned on a theme of "making Israel Jewish again" by seeking the expulsion of the Arabs from Israel, as well as from the West Bank and Gaza. Initially, the party was banned from participation in the election by the Central Elections Committee, but its ruling was reversed by the supreme court—a move that gained the party additional publicity and probably facilitated its effort to secure a Knesset seat. Despite Kahane's success he is considered an extremist, even by many on the right, and his political ideology and programs remain marginal in Israel and are considered by the majority of Israelis in that vein. He was ruled out as a political ally and coalition partner by all the major factions in the Knesset, including Tehiya.

The 1984 election results seemed partly to reflect a small but perceptible shift to the right in the electorate as a whole. The Labor Alignment and its closest parliamentary allies secured about the same number of seats they had in the outgoing parliament. Although Likud appeared to lose some of its mandates, Tehiya gained seats, and Kach's mandate resulted from a move to the right of enough of the voters to gain the minimum percentage required for a seat. The vote of the Oriental Jewish community seemed to play a role in Kahane's victory, as well as in the move to the right of the soliders' vote and in securing the four seats gained by the Sephardi Torah Guardians, apparently at the expense of the more European-dominated "establishment" Agudat Israel (which lost half of its seats) and Tami. The Oriental vote could, once again, be associated with Likud and its allies to the right.

In a major sense the results of the election were inconclusive. No party secured a majority, but none ever had in previous elections. This time, however, no party or grouping became the obvious choice to form the next government. Each had natural allies and opponents, but there was little room for maneuver in forming a coalition. Every significant perspective seemed to secure a place in parliament, and most were represented at about the same level as their ideological opposite numbers. Israelis appeared to be divided on many of the key issues facing the country, whether in the foreign policy, political, economic, social, or religious arenas; between those who supported Likud and those who supported Labor; and among a host of smaller parties with their own particular agendas and conceptions of Israel's future.

This division in the Israeli body politic proved to be the main factor that led to, and complicated the formation of, a government of national unity that was approved by the Knesset in September 1984. The negotiations leading to the formation of the government were lengthy and complex, and the basis for the new government was a complicated series of compromises and concessions. It inaugurated a new experiment in Israeli politics.

148

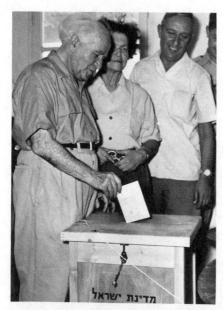

Prime Minister David Ben-Gurion casts his ballot at Kibutz Sde Boker for the Fourth Knesset election, November 1959 (*left*). Jerusalem (*below*): In the background is the Knesset. The curvilinear building (Shrine of the Book) houses the Dead Sea scrolls.

5

The Quest for Peace and Security

Israel recognizes that peace and cooperation with the neighboring Arab states is vital for the long-term survival and development of the Jewish state, and this remains a cornerstone of its foreign policy. In its Declaration of Independence Israel proclaimed: "We extend our hand to all neighbouring states and their peoples in an offer of peace and good neighbourliness. . . ." Successive governments have included these concepts in their official programs and have sought their attainment. At the same time, the refusal of the Arab states to enter into negotiations for peace fosters Israel's focus on security.

The preoccupation and preeminent concern of Israelis and of Israeli policymakers with peace, national survival, and security is a consequence of Israel's geostrategic situation, particularly the conflict with its Arab neighbors. During its first thirty-four years of existence it fought six wars with the Arab states and the PLO, and it remains at war with all of the Arab states but Egypt. Israel spends, on a continuing basis, a major portion of its budget and GNP on defense and defense-related items and has, by regional standards, a sizable standing army and reserve force. Its military power is substantial but not unlimited, constrained by its own demography and economy as well as by international factors. Virtually all aspects of foreign policy are skewed toward the Arab-Israeli question and are overshadowed by the focus on the security and survival of the state. Nevertheless, Israel remains concerned with its international position and has sought to establish and maintain positive relations with as many states as possible.

In its first statement of principles, on March 8, 1949, the Government of Israel announced that its foreign policy would be guided by "loyalty to the fundamental principles of the United Nations' Charter and friendship with all peace-loving states especially with the United States of America and the Union of Soviet Socialist Republics." The pursuit of peace through negotiations with the Arab states, the assurance of security in a region of hostility through an effective defense capability, and the attainment of international support continue to be the central and dominating elements in Israel's political life and in its foreign and security policy. At the outset it also held a strongly positive view of the United Nations, fostered by that organization's role in the creation of the state. With the increasingly large anti-Israel majority in the United Nations and with its virtually automatic support for Palestinian and Arab perspectives, Israel's views have changed markedly, and the United Nations is regarded as an unhelpful factor in the quest for peace and security.

THE CENTRALITY OF THE ARAB THREAT

Israel is perhaps unique among states in having hostile neighbors on all of its borders, with the exception, since 1979, of Eygpt. This dominates all aspects of Israeli life and has done so since 1948, when Israel's Declaration of Independence was greeted by an invasion of hostile Arab armies dedicated to the destruction of the fledgling state. Six wars, countless skirmishes and terrorist attacks, and incessant, vituperative rhetoric, as well as the Holocaust and Arab hostility during the mandatory period, have all left their mark on Israel's national consciousness. Israelis have a clear view of Arab hostility, which has been modified significantly only by the actions of President Anwar Sadat of Eygpt and, for a brief period, by the relationship with Lebanon after the 1982 war. This hostility is seen in the Arab unwillingness to join in the process initiated by Sadat, in the condemnation of the peace process at the Baghdad Arab Summit meetings of 1978 and 1979, and in the reiteration and amplification of the negative Khartoum Arab Summit (1967) formula.

The Arab threat is perceived not as an aberration of history, but rather as its latest manifestation. Israel's independence is the most recent phase of four thousand years of Jewish history, replete with episodes of persecution and conquest. Israelis recall clashes with outside military forces seeking to overrun their country and enslave their people, and they recollect the exile of the Jews from their homeland and the creation of the Diaspora. Nineteenth-century anti-Semitism, which made Jews the scapegoats for the failings of society (primarily in European countries but also in Muslim and Arab societies), is a particularly vivid memory, as is the Holocaust, which originated in a highly developed twentieth-century European country and was not thwarted by the civilized world. The Holocaust reconfirms the perspective that there are those who seek the destruction of the Jews and that Jewish survival should not depend on the guarantees or efforts of others. Thus, Israel sees that it must rely on its own defense capability to ensure its survival and protect its people.

Israel's perspective is further influenced by the experience during the British mandate, when Arab hostility to the Yishuv initially emanated from a small section of the Arab community but soon spread, and tension, periodically punctuated by disturbances and massacres between the communities, became a permanent feature of life. For more than half a century Arabs opposed the establishment of an independent Jewish state, and after its independence continued to act in this vein. During his 1977 address to the Knesset, President Sadat noted that for thirty years there was a wall between Israel and the Arab states who isolated and rejected the Jewish state. Despite the beginnings of change associated with his initiative, Israel's perspective remains conditioned by a vivid view of Arab hostility as the latest manifestation of centuries of historical experience.

Israel's position is also affected by its isolation. Israelis are not permitted to enter or cross the territory of neighboring states, with the exception, now, of Egypt. This geographical isolation is compounded by the lack of an alliance system and the fact that no state is formally committed to come to its defense in the event of war. In none of the six wars it fought between 1948 and 1982 was Israel joined in combat by any other state (with the exception of the British and French action in 1956, which took place after Israel's effort in Sinai was completed and did not affect its success). At the same time, Israel's diplomatic relationships have declined since the Six Day War, especially as a result of the substantial ruptures with the African states at the time of the Yom Kippur War. It has been increasingly isolated in, and condemned by, the United Nations and other international forums by overwhelming votes.

Israel's geographical vulnerability has been a continuing source of concern. The frontiers that existed prior to the Six Day War were vulnerable to enemy attack and made the defense of population centers difficult. The distance between Israel's Mediterranean coast and enemy military installations in the Jordanian-occupied West Bank, which included the coastal corridor between the port city of Haifa and the commercial center of Tel Aviv, was less than 10 miles (16 kilometers) in places. At its widest point, near the Negev town of Dimona, the country was only 65 miles (105 kilometers) across. In most locations there were no natural defense barriers to the advance of enemy forces, and Israel's population centers and major military installations were within a few hours advance by enemy ground forces, many being within enemy artillery range. This contributed to a perception of vulnerability that helped to shape Israel's view of the significance of the territories it occupied in the 1967 war and its policy that it would not return to the perilous situation that existed within the pre–Six Day War armistice lines.

In its assessment of the threat, Israel relates its survival to a broader self-identity and ultimate purpose. It sees itself as having a number of interrelated missions: the prevention of threats to its independence and territorial integrity, the need to preserve its Jewish character and its links to Jews throughout the world, and the requirement to serve as protector of persecuted Jews everywhere. There is also a belief that if Israel loses this opportunity, no Jewish state will ever again exist, with all that implies for the survival of world Jewry.

Although Israel sees the enemy threat as having broad consequences, it sees the source of the threat as more limited in scope and essentially confined to the Arab world. Although the definition has varied over time, in a narrow military sense the focal point is the "confrontation" Arab states—those sharing a common frontier with Israel—and the PLO as well as Iraq (and, since 1973, Saudi Arabia—because of its oil reserves and production, its substantial earnings of petro-dollars, its growing military capability and acquisition of sophisticated military equipment, and its increasingly important regional and international political roles). The other Arab states are included in the conception of the enemy because they have been allied with the confrontation states in the Arab League and other institutions, have participated in Arab summit decisions against Israel, have joined in the chorus of anti-Israel rhetoric, and have provided some of the wherewithal for wars, terrorist acts, and other anti-Israel military and paramilitary actions, occasionally sending troops as participants.

Even though Israel has been concerned about Soviet actions and potential roles, neither the Soviet Union nor other Soviet-bloc states have been at the center of Israel's planning or conceptions, and a potential Soviet threat is seen as something to be dealt with by the United States and the West. Nevertheless, in November 1981, Israel and the United States negotiated and signed a Memorandum of Understanding (MOU) on Strategic Cooperation in which it was agreed that U.S.-Israeli strategic cooperation "is designed against the threat to peace and security of the region caused by the Soviet Union or Soviet-controlled forces from outside the region introduced into the region." This phraseology reflected the Reagan administration's strong anti-Soviet attitude and also Israel's perception of the Soviet Union's role as an ally of the Arabs and as a hostile critic of Israel.

For Israel, this combination of its historical-psychological perspective, anti-Semitism, geographic and political-military isolation, and vulnerability to enemy attack has conditioned the formulation of its security and foreign policies.

THE QUEST FOR PEACE WITH THE ARABS

The armistice agreements of 1949 were to facilitate a transition to "permanent peace in Palestine" in the early years after independence. Israelis tended to be hopeful about achieving peace, but negotiations were not begun, and Israel was soon convinced of the implacable hostility of the Arab states and thus became preoccupied with the need for security. Israel sought to achieve acceptance within its territorial boundaries and to acquire aid from foreign sources to improve its economic situation, deal with the Arab boycott, and provide for Jewish immigration. Israel also sought to limit the number of returning Arab refugees (primarily because of fear of subversion), to gain access to the waterways of the region, and to guarantee its ability to defend itself militarily. Israel focused on the goal of peace, survival, and security within the armistice lines of 1949, but the refusal of the Arab states to accept Israel's existence within either the borders delineated by the 1947 partition plan or the 1949 armistice lines precluded achievement of those goals.

The Sinai War of 1956 was one consequence of the failure to settle the conflict, although Israel's fear of Egypt's growing military capability and concern about the Czech-Egyptian arms deal of 1955 were factors contributing to the conflict. Israel sought to use its occupation of the Sinai Peninsula as a means to secure negotiations for a peace settlement or to secure geographic changes that would enhance its security. However, as already noted, intense U.S. pressure forced Israel to withdraw in return for only minor alterations in the prewar situation. The United States sought to reassure Israel concerning its shipping in the Gulf of Aqaba, which had been prevented by Egypt, and the UNEF patrolled the Egyptian side of the Egypt-Israel armistice line from 1957 to 1967.

A Quiet Decade: 1957–1967

After the Sinai War, Israel had ten years of relative tranquility insofar as major military operations were concerned. Quiet prevailed on the frontier between Israel and Egypt, and although there were episodes of terrorist action on the other frontiers, they did not pose an intolerable threat to Israel's security. There was no progress toward resolution of the Arab-Israeli conflict, and the Arab world remained unwilling to accept Israel's existence. Between 1957 and 1967 there was no major debate within Israel on either the premises or the content of its policy relating to the Arab-Israeli conflict. Israel did not see peace as a viable policy, and it concentrated on internal development. Its foreign policy focused on securing arms and support for the security of the state and on issues such as the relationship with the Soviet Union and with the United States and the question of establishing relations with West Germany.

The Six Day War (1967)

The Six Day War of June 1967 modified the content of the issues central to the Arab-Israeli conflict as the realities of Arab hostility, the nature of the Arab threat, and the difficulties of achieving a settlement were reinforced. Israel's significant victory and subsequent control of substantial amounts of territory dramatically altered the regional and domestic situation and generated discussion concerning appropriate policies. Between 1949 and 1967 Israel was prepared for peace with the Arab states on the basis of the 1949 armistice lines with minor modifications, but after the events of May and June 1967, the stark reality of "politicide" began to enter into these considerations, and many argued for a need to change the security situation. Religious and ideological-historical claims to territory reinforced that view.

Israel's primary goals in the 1967 war were tactical: first, to relieve the blockade of the port of Eilat resulting from President Nasser's announced closing of the Strait of Tiran to Israeli shipping and to strategic cargoes bound for Eilat and, second, to relieve the pressure imposed by the massing of Egyptian forces along Israel's southwestern frontiers. However, once the scope of Israel's success was seen, it was hoped that the military achievements could be carried over into a full-scale settlement with the Arab states. Israel saw the inability of the Soviet Union and the Arab states to secure adoption of anti-Israel United Nations resolutions in the summer of 1967 in a positive light. U.S. support and the creation of a national unity coalition government contributed to Israel's confidence, and Israel adopted the view that negotiations with the Arab states for peace would have to precede the return of territories, which would serve as security frontiers in the interim.

Israel's position did not strike a responsive chord in the Arab world. The Arab states argued that negotiations were impossible and that recognition of and peace with Israel could not occur. The three no's of the Khartoum Arab Summit of 1967—no peace, no recognition, and no negotiations with Israel—became the centerpiece of the Arab position, which was diametrically opposed to that of Israel. The Arab leadership at Khartoum pledged joint military, political, and diplomatic activity to achieve Israel's withdrawal from occupied Arab territory.

Within Israel, between the Six Day and Yom Kippur wars, two alternatives to the official position developed that focused on the occupied territories and their disposition. The Land of Israel Movement, which began its efforts shortly after the Six Day War, argued that Israel should retain the territories occupied in 1967 and establish settlements there. The peace movement, which was composed of a number of small groups on the left, took much longer to become established, in part because the official position preempted the movement's main arguments by making overtures to the Arab states that indicated Israel was prepared to return territory for peace and to be magnanimous in victory. When it became clear that Israel's insistence on direct negotiations for peace was unsuccessful in achieving its objective and when the government began to show an interest in establishing settlements and retaining territories, the peace movement became more prominent. It argued that the failure of the peace process could be attributed to the government of Israel for not taking greater initiatives.

Paralleling the positions of these interest groups were those of established political parties. The Land of Israel Movement had a like-minded, but not totally identical, group in Herut (now joined with the Liberals in Gahal), which sought Israel's control over all of mandatory Palestine. Paralleling the peace movement were the positions of a number of political parties such as Mapam, which believed that the answer lay in greater Israeli overtures to the Arabs. Of the minor parties on the extreme left, the Communist parties (Maki and Rakah) argued that Israel's overall position was untenable, and Haolam Hazeh pressed for greater government action. Israelis generally rejected the premises and policies of the peace and the annexationist groups, and the majority of Israel's population supported the government position.

Between 1967 and 1973 the focus of Israel's foreign policy was the effort to secure a just and lasting Arab-Israeli peace and to ensure its security. The regional states, the superpowers and lesser powers, and the main instrumentalities of the international system were engaged in peace efforts based on United Nations Security Council Resolution 242 of November 22, 1967. Although some of the interwar efforts were promising, peace was not achieved, and there was little movement in that direction. The Egyptian-initiated War of Attrition (1969–1970) along the Suez Canal did not meaningfully alter the prospects for peace.

The Yom Kippur War (1973)

The Yom Kippur War of 1973, launched by Egypt and Syria against Israel, created a new environment. Israel's international position had been declining prior to the hostilities—it was losing world sympathy, partly as a consequence of its continued refusal to withdraw from occupied Arab territories without peace, and its responses to Arab terrorism increasingly were condemned by the international community. After the break in relations with Uganda in the spring of 1972, several other African states severed relations, and in September 1973

Cuba took similar action. Immediately prior to the outbreak of hostilities, Israel became involved in a dispute with Austria over the latter's refusal to provide facilities for Russian emigrants on their way to Israel. There was increasing international sentiment, and resolutions of various international and regional organizations, calling for Israel to withdraw from the occupied territories.

During the course of the war and immediately afterward, virtually all of the states of black Africa broke relations with Israel and linked the rupture to Israel's refusal to withdraw from the occupied territories. To most Israelis this not only symbolized the injustice of the international community but also the success of Arab oil blackmail and the failure of Israel's program of international cooperation that had provided many of the African states with technical assistance, previously lauded for promoting African development. In November 1973 the Organization of African Unity Ministerial Council noted the "expansionist designs of belligerent Israel" and denounced it.

The ruptures with Africa were a disappointment, but a shift in the attitudes and policies of the European states was perhaps more significant. Israel's international isolation was compounded by the unwillingness of the United States' European allies (with the exception of Portugal, which permitted the use of the Azores) to allow the use of their facilities and/or airspace for the shipment and transfer of supplies to Israel during the war. The Europeans were reluctant to be associated with the U.S. resupply effort and were concerned about the possible reduction of Arab oil shipments to them. In a move designed to placate the Arabs, the European Economic Community adopted a joint communiqué on November 6, 1973, that called on Israel to end the "territorial occupation" it had maintained since 1967 and to recognize the "legitimate rights" of the Palestinians. Japan, also heavily dependent on Arab oil, began to modify its posture from that of neutrality to a more pronounced pro-Arab position. Japan called for implementation of United Nations Security Council Resolution 242 and stressed the Arab interpretation of the resolution, which required Israel to withdraw from all the territories; increased its contributions to the United Nations for aid to Palestinian refugees; and offered development loans to several Arab states.

Israel's dependence on the United States increased after the war. President Richard Nixon asked Congress to authorize $2.2 billion in emergency security assistance for Israel in response to a large-scale resupply of Syria and Egypt by the Soviet Union and alerted U.S. armed forces when there were indications that the Soviet Union might become involved militarily. The United States reacted to the Arab oil embargo by stressing that it would seek to become independent of those supplies and that its energy requirements would not cause a change in its Middle East policies.

Despite these reassuring signs there was concern in Israel that the United States might shift away from its support of Israel and use its leverage to effect changes in Israel's position. This anxiousness derived from U.S. actions relating to peace negotiations and to the terms of a Middle East settlement as well as from U.S. pressures on Israel to accept the initial cease-fire and to permit a relief convoy to resupply the Egyptian Third Army located on the east bank of the Suez Canal. Some Israelis were concerned by an apparent U.S. courting of the Arabs, including the restoration of formal diplomatic relations between the United States and Egypt; by the visits by Secretary of State Kissinger to Arab capitals (Rabat, Tunis, Cairo, Amman, and Riyadh); and by the possibility that Israel might be sacrificed by the United States in an effort to further détente. The oil factor and its potential effect on U.S. policy became a matter of public discussion. The central role assumed by the United States in the peace process, the energy crisis in the United States and the increased dependence of Israel on the United States combined to stress the importance of the U.S. relationship with Israel and suggested that this would be a major focus of Israel's foreign policy during the postwar period.

The so-called political earthquake that accompanied the Yom Kippur War reaffirmed some Israeli perceptions and caused substantial questioning of others. The war was perceived as a military victory, which could have been greater had the cease-fire not intervened, and as a vindication of

Israel's strategic concepts. At the same time, the view that Israel required secure and defensible borders and an assured supply of modern and sophisticated military equipment was reinforced. The psychological-political changes were more complex, as the complacency of the prewar period was replaced by substantial questioning of attitudes and policy and criticism of the system and its decision makers.

Modifications in Israel's policy were relatively minor immediately after the Yom Kippur War. Israel recognized the dangers inherent in its isolation in the international community and in its dependence on the United States. It attempted to reaffirm and reestablish the ties that had been disrupted, and an intensive effort was launched to restore Israel's traditionally close relations with the European states. In connection with the Arab-Israeli conflict, Israel was faced with the need to respond to situations relating to the cease-fire and to the disengagement of forces rather than formulating broad policy positions. U.S. Secretary of State Henry Kissinger's approach focused on "step-by-step" agreements rather than on an effort to achieve comprehensive peace. Kissinger's shuttle diplomacy that achieved the Israel-Egypt and Israel-Syria military disengagement agreements preempted the formulation of an overarching policy. Nevertheless, a mainstream position, articulated by the government, emerged in the period between the Yom Kippur War and the 1977 election.

The policies adopted by the Meir (1974) and Rabin (1974–1977) governments were not dissimilar from those adopted by the Eshkol and Meir governments between the 1967 and 1973 wars. In *U.S. News and World Report* (June 23, 1975), Prime Minister Yitzhak Rabin expressed the goal in these terms:

> Israel's position is we want peace, a real one. We want boundaries of peace that will make Israel capable of defending itself by itself. We do not want a peace agreement that ends up as peace on a piece of paper. We want peace based on the realities of relations between the peoples of all the countries involved in the area.

The objective was a peace of reconciliation that included an end to hostilities and open borders across which goods and services could move freely. The extent of Israel's withdrawal from occupied territories and the borders of the state would depend on the extent of concessions made by the Arab negotiators and by the situation at the bargaining table, but Israel would not return to the armistice lines that existed on June 4, 1967. Israel continued to stress the need for defensible borders that would allow it to defend itself by itself without the need for external assistance; its position was that it would not retain or return *all* of the occupied territories. Partly indicative of Israel's intentions was the establishment of settlements in the areas occupied in the Six Day War, although the settlements did not necessarily determine Israel's final position.

United Jerusalem was not considered occupied territory: It was the eternal capital of Israel and discussions concerning its status were limited to the administration of the holy places and to accommodating the religious sensibilities of other faiths. This view was reflected in several actions after 1967, but capped in the Basic Law "Jerusalem, The Capital of Israel" adopted by the Knesset in 1980. It provided: "Jerusalem united in its entirety is the capital of Israel," but said "the Holy Places shall be protected from desecration and any other violation and from anything likely to violate the freedom of access of the members of the different religions to the places sacred to them or their feelings with regard to those places."

The Palestinian issue became more intense but also evoked a precise official position. Palestinian terrorists were to be dealt with by Israel's security forces as a security problem. The issue of Palestinian refugees was seen as a humanitarian one to be treated within the context of the appropriate United Nations resolutions that called for "justice for the refugees" and provided for repatriation or resettlement with compensation for the Arab refugees and appropriate consideration of the Jewish refugees who fled Arab lands to come to Israel. The political future of the Palestinians was a more complex matter. After the Six Day War, Israel's reaction was expressed by Prime Minister Golda Meir, who commented that there was no separate Palestinian people. She noted that the Palestinians were part of the West Bank population then under Israel's control but also were a substantial portion of the population of Jordan on the east bank of the river and that the distinction between them was artificial.

Subsequently, Israel recognized that, as expressed by then Prime Minister Rabin on "Issues and Answers" on July 14, 1974, "in the settlement the Palestinian problem has to be solved because without its solution, there will be no durable peace in the Middle East," yet it insisted that a settlement must be between Israel and the Arab states, since the "key to peace, as well as to war, lies in the relations between the Arab countries and Israel. . . . The only solution . . . is to make peace between the Arab countries and Israel." Israel continued to believe that the creation of a third state in the area between the Mediterranean Sea and Iraq was unnecessary for Palestinian self-identity, would not be viable, and would be a threat to Israel. The "Jordanian option"— that Israel and Jordan would determine the future of the area since Jordan is the government of most of the Palestinians— was Israel's preferred position. Israel continued to refuse to negotiate with the PLO and other terrorist organizations whose declared purpose, as articulated in the Palestine National Covenant and elsewhere, was the destruction of Israel. It viewed the PLO's formula of a democratic, secular state of Palestine as fatal to Israel and pointed out that no PLO spokesman had ever accepted Israel's existence. However, Israel was prepared to negotiate with Palestinian Arabs committed to peaceful coexistence with a Jewish state of Israel.

Renewed Peace Efforts

The policies to achieve peace adopted by the Rabin government after the Yom Kippur War were similar to those of its predecessor Labor governments. The 1977 elections that brought Begin and Likud to power brought changes in some policy sectors and reconfirmed others.

The Begin government maintained Israel's focus on the goal of establishing peace that would include the end of war, full reconciliation and normalization, and an open border over which people and goods could cross without hindrance. On the question of occupied territories, the new government could rely on a general consensus opposing a return to the armistice lines of 1949, thus ruling out total withdrawal, although there was disagreement concerning the final lines to be established and the extent of compromise on territorial retention. The focus of territorial disagreement was the West Bank. In regard to that territory there was a substantial difference between the Begin-Likud view, which opposed relinquishing any territory, and the compromise views articulated by Labor and others to Likud's left. Begin's position, as stated on "Issues and Answers" on May 22, 1977, was rather specific:

> I believe that Judea and Samaria are an integral part of our sovereignty. It's our land. It was occupied by Abdullah [King of Jordan] against international law, against our inherent right. It was liberated during the 6-day war when we used our right of national self-defense, and so it should be. . . . You annex foreign land. You don't annex your own country. It is our land. You don't annex it.

In the presentation of its policy to the Knesset on June 21, 1977, the new government noted: "The Jewish people has an eternal historic right to the Land of Israel. The inalienable legacy of our Forefathers. The Government shall plan, create and encourage urban and rural settlements on the soil of the homeland." The Labor governments between 1967 and 1977 had generally tried to limit settlements to those that could serve a security function and had sought to avoid conflict between the settlements and the local Arab populations. Thus, settlements generally were established in areas with relatively small Arab populations, although there were exceptions, such as Kiryat Arba at Hebron, that were established for a combination of ideological, religious, traditional, and historical reasons. The Begin government altered that policy. Rather than restricting settlements in Judea and Samaria to those that were primarily security oriented, it supported settlement as a natural and inalienable Jewish right in that area.

The broadest and most articulate consensus continued to revolve around the question of a Palestinian state and the PLO—Israel's refusal to negotiate with the PLO and its opposition to the establishment of an independent Palestinian state on the West Bank and in the Gaza Strip was reaffirmed. Israel's national consensus focused on the need for peace, and the main obstacle appeared to be the continuing Arab unwillingness to accept Israel and to negotiate with it. This was modified as a result of the November 1977 initiative of President Anwar Sadat of Egypt that led to his visit to Israel and to the inauguration of direct negotiations between Israel and Egypt. The prospect of direct negotiations with its most populous and powerful Arab adversary led to extensive debate concerning Israel's policy, which had not been tested previously in negotiations. Israel's ability to avoid detailed and specific policy positions, because of the refusal of the Arab states to negotiate directly, was altered. Nonetheless, despite Sadat's visit and his speech to the Knesset and subsequent statements, and despite the direct discussions between Israel and Egypt in Jerusalem, Cairo, and Ismailia, Israelis continued to hold a deep mistrust of Arab intentions. Sadat did not alter the basic Arab position, and he argued that to move toward a settlement Israel would have to conform to the Arab conception of peace. Israel's continued doubt was influenced by the fact that no other Arab leader joined Sadat in Jerusalem, no other Arab state participated in the Cairo conference or subsequent negotiations, and no major Arab state provided substantial support for Egypt's position. At the same time, the PLO refused to accept the fact that Israel should exist in the Middle East.

The negotiations following Sadat's visit to Jerusalem culminated in the Camp David summit meeting of September 1978 at which Israel, Egypt, and the United States agreed to two frameworks for continued negotiations. The primary objective of post–Camp David negotiations was to convert the frameworks into peace treaties. Despite substantial U.S. efforts to secure the involvement of other Arab states, especially Jordan and Saudi Arabia, none agreed to participate in the negotiations or to encourage the peace process. The parties concentrated their initial efforts on the Egypt-Israel Peace Treaty, and after substantial negotiations and the personal intervention of President Carter, a treaty was concluded and signed at the White House on March 26, 1979.

Egypt-Israel Peace Treaty

The Egypt-Israel Peace Treaty was a significant accomplishment that implemented one of the two Camp David frameworks and represented a first step toward a comprehensive Arab-Israeli settlement and regional stability. A long and complex process was necessary to resolve fully the Arab-Israeli conflict, and negotiations to that end could involve only Egypt and Israel since the other Arab states and the Palestinians refused to participate. In a letter accompanying the treaty of peace, Begin and Sadat noted that "for the purpose of achieving a comprehensive peace settlement . . . they have agreed to start negotiations . . . [for] the establishment of the self-governing authority in the West Bank and Gaza in order to provide full autonomy to the inhabitants." They established the goal of completing the negotiations within one year, and it was understood that the United States would be a "full partner" in the negotiations. On May 25, 1979, in keeping with the previously agreed-upon timetable, Egypt and Israel opened negotiations in Beersheba, Israel. Over the following year, representatives of the parties met at several locations to continue the discussions. Various expressions of optimism, pessimism, and skepticism continued to characterize the effort, and the talks were suspended (by Egypt) and restarted on a number of occasions.

The failure of Israel and Egypt to reach agreement concerning the West Bank and Gaza by the self-imposed May 1980 deadline and the subsequent suspensions of the negotiations reflected the wide divergence of the parties with regard to the translation of the concept of "full autonomy" from paper to reality. On peripheral and essentially technical matters substantial agreement was reached, but central problems remained unresolved. Much of the discussion focused on the problem of how to divide responsibility for internal and external security. Israel's security had to be assured by the IDF, and the strong local police force of the self-governing authority had to have a role in internal security to ensure public order. Israel and Egypt could not agree on the extent of powers of the self-governing authority, since Israel clearly was concerned that the Egyptian proposals would lead to a Palestinian state, which it opposed. Israel argued that there should be "full autonomy to the inhabitants" as stipulated in the accords and saw the self-governing authority as an administrative council with limited powers derived from the military government. Egypt believed that autonomy should extend also to the land and that the self-governing authority should have full legislative and executive authority as well as control of the administration of justice. Egypt therefore sought a self-generating authority and the transfer to it of all powers from the military government.

There was also discord on such issues as the sharing of the scarce water resources of the West Bank, the right of the Arabs of East Jerusalem to participate in the vote on questions relating to the self-governing authority, the status and use of private and public lands, and the question of Jerusalem's final status. Israel saw agreement on autonomy as a practical solution to the status of the Palestinian Arabs, since such agreement would be responsive to Israel's need for security, Egypt's wish to adhere to the Arab cause, and the Palestinian Arabs' desire to govern their own affairs. Israel's proposed autonomy plan would allow the Arab inhabitants to manage what it saw as "areas of legitimate internal administration," while Israel would "retain those powers and functions which are essential to her defense and security."

Parallel to the autonomy talks, the process of normalization of relations between Egypt and Israel moved ahead on schedule and without major disturbances. "Normal relations" between Egypt and Israel began officially on January 26, 1980. By that date Israel had completed its withdrawal from two-thirds of Sinai, as called for in the peace treaty, and land, air, and sea borders between the two states were opened. Holders of valid visas were able to travel from one country to the other through air and sea ports as well as at the Sinai crossing point at El Arish. Direct communications links by telephone, telex, and post were inaugurated. In late February embassies were opened in Cairo and Tel Aviv, and on February 26 Ambassadors Eliahu Ben-Elisar of Israel and Saad Mortada of Egypt presented their credentials.

In the government program approved by the Knesset on August 5, 1981 (after the 1981 Knesset election returned Begin to office), the peace treaty between Israel and Egypt was hailed as a historic turning point. The government also committed itself to observe the Camp David agreements diligently and to work for the renewal of negotiations on the implementation of the agreement on full autonomy for the Arab residents of Judea, Samaria, and the Gaza District, but noted that it would reassert its claim to sovereignty over those territories. It also noted that, in the interim, Israel's settlement efforts would continue as a "right" and as an integral part of Israel's security. The Golan Heights and Jerusalem received particular attention. "Israel will not descend from the Golan Heights, nor will it remove any settlement established there. It is the Government that will decide on the appropriate timing for the application of Israeli law, jurisdiction, and administration to the Golan Heights." Finally, the program provided, "Jerusalem is the eternal capital of Israel, indivisible, entirely under Israeli sovereignty. Free access to their holy places has been and will be guaranteed to followers of all faiths."

Initially, the new Begin government concentrated on the relationship with Egypt, including normalization, the withdrawal from Sinai, and the autonomy talks. The position became more complex with the assassination of Anwar Sadat in early October 1981 and the succession of Hosni Mubarak to the presidency of Egypt. After Sadat's assassination Israel closely watched and carefully gauged Egypt's position and its capacity to remain on the course Sadat had set. Some Israelis sought to modify Israel's policy on the assumption or hope of change in Egypt, and militant Jewish settlers in northern Sinai accelerated their campaign to force the Israeli government to abrogate the Egypt-Israel Treaty and to cancel the scheduled withdrawal. Begin provided reassurances that

Israel's commitment was firm, and ultimately the obligations concerning Sinai were fulfilled. The autonomy talks were resumed, but the complexity of the issues and the positions of Israel and Egypt precluded agreement.

The Lebanon War

The peace process was soon overshadowed by the sixth Arab-Israeli war—the war in Lebanon in 1982. The continued presence in Lebanon of missiles that had been moved there by Syria in the spring of 1981 remained an Israeli concern despite the cease-fire secured by U.S. envoy Philip Habib later that summer. Israel made clear its view that the presence of the missiles and continued PLO attacks against Israeli and Jewish targets worldwide would not be tolerated indefinitely. On June 6, 1982, Israel launched a major military action against the PLO in Lebanon. In some respects this represented a "second round" against PLO positions in Lebanon; it followed Operation Litani, in the spring of 1978, in which Israel launched an invasion of southern Lebanon to drive the Palestinians from their positions close to the Israeli border from which they had been launching attacks against Israel since before the 1973 war. Although Israeli forces were withdrawn and the UNIFIL (United Nations Interim Force in Lebanon) entered the sector to replace the departing Israeli troops and to help prevent infiltration into Israel, the area soon became a more active base for actions against northern Israel.

Operation Peace for Galilee in 1982 sought to remove the PLO military and terrorist threat to Israel and to reduce the PLO's political capability. The war had both military and political objectives. The military objectives were to achieve security for northern Israel; to destroy the PLO infrastructure that had established a state within a state in Lebanon; to eliminate a center of international terrorism; and to eliminate the PLO from Lebanon so that its territory would not serve as a base of operations from which Israel could be threatened. The political objectives were not as precise—primarily there was the goal of weakening the PLO politically so that its influence would no longer be as significant, but there was also the hope that a new political order in Lebanon. might lead it to consider becoming the second Arab state to make peace with Israel.

In many respects the results were ambiguous. Israel's northern border was more secure, but Israeli troops who remained in Lebanon became targets of terrorists and others, and numerous casualties resulted. The costs of the war, no matter how measured, were high. Externally, Israel's military actions caused concern and dismay in many quarters, including the United States, and its international isolation was increased. The achievements were primarily in the military realm—the PLO was defeated, and its military and terrorist infrastructure was destroyed, thereby eliminating the threat to northern Israel. The political achievements were less tangible or obvious. Although the PLO's positions were severely damaged and there were questions about Yasser Arafat's continued leadership of the organization, the PLO remained the primary spokesman for the Palestinians, and Arafat soon rebounded to his preeminent position in the organization.

Subsequently, Israel engaged in negotiations with Lebanon, under U.S. auspices, concerning the withdrawal of foreign forces from Lebanon and related arrangements. An agreement was concluded in May 1983, under the auspices of U.S. Secretary of State George Shultz, that secured Israel's northern frontier and removed the PLO presence from southern Lebanon. Under the terms of the agreement, Israel committed itself to withdraw from southern Lebanon in return for specific security arrangements in the south and some elements of normalization approaching but not quite becoming a peace treaty. The May 1983 agreement was an important milestone in Israel's relations with the Arabs, for it represented a second arrangement for the "normalization" of Israel's relations with an Arab neighbor. It also was thought, at the time, to provide the basis for subsequent arrangements to secure the removal of Syrian and PLO forces from Lebanon. However, Syria refused to withdraw its forces from Lebanon and opposed the May 1983 agreement. Eventually the Lebanese government, under pressure from Syria, unilaterally abrogated the agreement and forced Israel to close its liaison office near Beirut that had been established to help carry out the terms of the accord.

By the time of the 1984 Knesset elections, Israeli forces were still in Lebanon and were subjected to daily attacks that contributed to the growing casualty tolls despite redeployments of forces designed to reduce the number of casualties. The tangible gains from Operation Peace for Galilee seemed to be less apparent as Syria remained in Lebanon, a weakened PLO returned, and the Lebanese government appeared no more stable and willing to maintain a positive relationship with Israel than were its predecessors. Two years after the start of Operation Peace for Galilee, Israel was debating the war as an election issue, and many Israelis were disillusioned concerning the prospects for a significant improvement in the situation.

Menachem Begin's tenure as prime minister brought peace with Egypt and reduced, significantly, the military danger to the existence of Israel by neutralizing the largest Arab army with whom it had fought five wars. Operation Peace for Galilee led to debate and demonstration within Israel but did not expand the peace domain for the Jewish state. The government of Prime Minister Yitzhak Shamir, endorsed by the Knesset in October 1983, proposed continuity in principles and policy, but its brief tenure was not highlighted by major developments in the quest for peace. The national unity government installed in September 1984 highlighted the importance of peace in its government program. It restated the elements of Israel's national consensus on the elements of peace and identified its objectives as "continuing and extending the peace process in the region and consolidating the peace with Egypt." It called on Jordan to begin peace negotiations.

PLANNING FOR SECURITY

The failure to achieve peace and the continuation of Arab hostility has fostered Israel's focus on security. Israel's response to the Arab military threat has taken the form of an effective military capability and a carefully constructed military doctrine. The Israel Defense Forces is central to Israel's security policy. The IDF has its roots not only in the security forces of the Yishuv but in Jewish history, particularly Jewish defense units established in Eastern Europe and Russia. The Hagana (Defense) was established in the 1920s as an underground defense organization in the Yishuv. In 1941 it created a commando or "striking" force, the Palmach (a full-time military force of volunteers, something of a professional and elite unit), which later provided a large proportion of the senior officers of the IDF. Alternative military bodies were created under the mandate, especially Irgun and LEHI or LHY (Lohamei Herut Yisrael, or Fighters for the Freedom of Israel, also known as the Stern Group). After independence the various military groups were brought together as the IDF.

The prime minister and the cabinet exercise ultimate control over the IDF, and the minister of defense is the cabinet officer charged with responsibility for security. The Defense Forces of Israel are unified and presided over by the chief of the general staff (who is also commander of the army). The general staff directs the activities and operations of the various commands of the IDF.

Security Policy

Israel has developed an impressive body of fundamental principles and political-military concepts on which it bases its security policy. Given its assumptions concerning its broad purpose for Jewish survival, the Arab call for the destruction of the state, and unremitting Arab hostility, it must take into account the "asymmetry" of its situation as compared with the Arabs—its numerical inferiority ("few against many"), the territorial and resource disparity, and the political influence of its enemy. It therefore plans for the "worst case" scenario of a combined and coordinated Arab attack. Recognizing that it cannot achieve quantitative superiority, Israel seeks to ensure a qualitative edge over its rivals. Highly trained and motivated personnel, equipped with the most sophisticated and advanced weapons systems, are the core of Israel's response to the overwhelming superiority of Arab numbers.

Israel also seeks to minimize losses and reduce expenditures in all encounters in order to decrease the personal and financial drains of warfare. To accomplish this, principles such as short wars and extensive use of advanced weaponry are employed. Israel believes that any Arab victory would be "final" and would result in the destruction of the state with all that that implies for Israel and world Jewry. Should Israel win additional victories they, like past achievements, could never be "final and definite" given Arab numerical superiority. But it must win wars and battles, destroy enemy forces, and inflict heavy losses on the Arabs, and it believes that such decisive, temporary victories might have a deterrent effect.

In building its military power Israel must exploit fully all its national resources (personnel, equipment, and vehicles) in time of war, and there is a constant need for readiness and alert. Because of its small population Israel relies on a relatively small standing force and a large number of reserve units that can be mobilized quickly and yet fight with a high level of efficiency. But this creates an additional burden. In personal terms the contribution is virtually universal; young men and women (with some exemptions for religious and other reasons) serve in the IDF upon reaching the required age, and most former male soldiers (and some females in special areas) are called to fulfill reserve obligations each year.

Israel's security posture is aided by the existence of a high-quality intelligence service. The importance of an "early warning system" (intelligence concerning enemy intentions and actions) is clear in a system that must mobilize its forces to meet a military threat. Intelligence must be prepared for all eventualities at all times and must provide sufficient warning time to permit efficient and rapid mobilization of Israel's reserve forces. Despite the "failure" of Israeli intelligence at the time of the Yom Kippur War (1973), its capabilities are significant and its results have been remarkable. It has benefited from the high level of education and diverse backgrounds of its people, including substantial immigration from the Arab world. In addition to its own capabilities, Israel has had close and beneficial links with the intelligence operations of other states, particularly France and the United States. But, unlike many developing states, Israel is not dependent on the data (except, perhaps, in particular instances, for specialized information from electronics and satellite sources) or analysis of these other services but rather relies on its own gathering and analysis activities.

Since Israel, in its pre-1967 frontiers, had no strategic depth, artificial depth was created by means of area defense, including the use of settlements as fighting positions in wartime, and by carrying the war to enemy territory as quickly as possible. In combat the IDF must deal with the most dangerous enemy and strongest opponent first. This typically led to a focus on Egypt and the southern front, although in the 1973 war the strategic depth of the Sinai Peninsula and concerns about a Syrian breakthrough on the Golan Heights dictated a modification of this approach. Israel must strike the first blow as a preemptive strike (as in 1967) or a preventive war (1956), take and keep the initiative, and dictate the terms of battle. In 1973, the problem of transferring combat operations to enemy territory was obviated partly by the fact that Israel occupied substantial amounts of enemy territory, which provided a strategic advantage since the fighting could take place in those territories rather than in pre-1967 Israel or in the remaining territory of the Arab enemy. Israel must stress and utilize fast, mobile attacks, and thus substantial flexibility granted to field commanders in direct combat with the enemy permits innovation. The need to achieve a quick victory results, in part, from the anticipated intervention of the great powers and/or the United Nations, the need to avoid high levels of casualties, and the economic costs of maintaining mobilization of the civilian sector over an extended period.

The problems of strategic depth and long borders were altered with the acquisition of Arab territory during the Six Day War of 1967. As a result of these changes and alterations in weaponry and costs, there were modifications in Israel's doctrine and growing acceptance of a "defensive" approach. Although other factors were involved, the strategic depth and alternative options available helped to form Prime Minister

Golda Meir's decision in 1973 not to launch a preemptive strike against Egypt and Syria but to absorb the first blow. After 1967 the concept of "defensible" borders became an element in Israel's political-military planning. Between 1967 and 1977 the government approached the issue of settlements in the West Bank, and elsewhere, primarily in terms of the concepts and phraseology of security needs. The Labor-dominated governments seemed to believe that settlements established in strategically important areas essentially devoid of Arab inhabitants, such as along the Jordan River, would help to ensure security.

Military Establishment and Capability

In its response to the Arab threat, Israel has created an impressive military establishment relative to its population, size, and resources, although not all elements have been equally developed, and, at different times, different components have been given priority for funding and weapons systems. Generally, considerations of short wars and the need for decisive action, flexibility, and mobility in combat have led Israel to focus on its air force and armored corps. Israel's air force has been seen from abroad as its most colorful and effective fighting element. Despite its inferiority in numbers to the forces of the Arab states, the Israeli air force has been indisputably superior, at least since the 1967 war when it virtually eliminated the Egyptian air force in the first few hours of combat, assuring Israeli air superiority and decisively influencing the pace and nature of the ground conflict in Sinai.

During the War of Attrition (1969–1970), Israeli air superiority became more obvious in both air-to-air combat and in its unique function as "flying artillery" (partly to offset the superior firepower of Egypt) against Egyptian installations on the west bank of the Suez Canal. In the later phases of that conflict it took on the task of "deep penetration" raids into the heartland of Egypt that brought Israeli airmen into direct conflict with Soviet pilots who were flying air defense missions for Egypt.

Israel's ground forces are the largest and most central elements of the IDF. Although its roles have varied with modifications in Israel's military doctrine, the armored corps has received much attention for its highly flexible, and ultimately decisive, operations in Sinai in 1956, 1967, and 1973.

The IDF, and Hagana before independence, sought to achieve the essential military strength and to acquire the wherewithal to meet the identified threat and to provide for the defense of the state. As a consequence, a major proportion of GNP and budget has been allocated to defense and defense-related expenditures and the development of a substantial defense production capability. The equipment available to the IDF is of various types, quality, and generations. At the beginning it was little more than a motley assortment drawn from any available source for a force with multiple backgrounds and little formal training. The escalation of the conflict after Israel's War of Independence and the increasing sophistication of weapons systems led to growing weapons expenditures. Subsequently, equipment has come from several foreign suppliers including, most prominently, the United States, France, and England. Israel also has a significant quantity of Soviet equipment, primarily that captured in combat in 1967 and 1973 and subsequently refurbished.

Arms acquisition has involved purchases from foreign sources and production by Israel. Although these purchases have the benefit of providing access to modern and sophisticated equipment of all types, including those that Israel cannot produce, these purchases have increased Israel's debt and its dependence. At the same time, Israel has increasingly sought to produce and coproduce (and sometimes develop) equipment on its own, in part as a means to guarantee supply, reduce defense costs and external debt, and earn foreign exchange through sales.

An indigenous military industry has been an element of security planning since independence, and considerable resources have been invested in it with uneven results. Its basic shortcoming has been natural and financial resources. There is also the problem of economies of scale and the difficulties posed by the enormous start-up costs involved in the development and production of a sophisticated weapons system. Israel seems to have overcome many of the technological problems that plagued the industry in earlier years. Its infrastructure has been relatively well suited to the advanced technology of a sophisticated armaments industry, and despite the constraints, there have been important accomplishments. Israel produces a wide range of high-quality and advanced weapons and related defense items and is an exporter ranking only after the major powers.

Israel Aircraft Industry (IAI) is the centerpiece of the armaments industry. It has grown rapidly, from a company of less than a hundred employees when founded to more than twenty thousand by 1984. IAI produces a wide range of items, some under license, including aircraft (such as the Fouga-Magister), ammunition, armor, radar/sonar, and gyroscopes. Israel's indigenous defense manufacturing capability includes civil and military aircraft, such as the Kfir jet aircraft, surface-to-surface antishipping missiles such as the sea-to-sea Gabriel missile, air-to-air missiles, patrol boats, combat vehicles, tanks, howitzers, mortars, grenades, radar systems, communication and navigation systems, industrial and shipborne monitoring and control systems, medical electronic and microelectronic products, computers and computerized communications systems, fire control systems, security systems, air and ground crew equipment, ground support equipment, microwave components, and small arms.

A major challenge appears to be limited export capability. Israel has sold a variety of products to a number of customers, ranging from small Third World countries to West European NATO (North Atlantic Treaty Organization) allies of the United States and including Latin America and the United States. Israel has been constrained by U.S. limitations placed on products (such as the Kfir jet) that have U.S. components, by a self-imposed limitation arising out of the political ideology of some prospective customers, by the Arab-imposed boycott that threatens states that deal with Israel, and by the technical limitations of some of Israel's products. Israel's military exports have earned a substantial amount of foreign exchange, although the precise levels are classified. Export sales of the

Gabriel surface-to-surface missile, the first operational sea-to-sea missile in the Western world, have earned hundreds of millions of dollars, and it has been purchased by South Africa and Argentina, among others. Despite its significant accomplishments in this area, Israel remains dependent on the United States for many sophisticated weapons systems and for some of the advanced components of its indigenous products—a condition not likely to be altered in the near future. And Israel remains dependent on other states for critical raw materials.

Israel's desire to acquire conventional weapons for its defense and security is affected by its views concerning nuclear proliferation. Israel's official position continues to be that it will not be the first to introduce nuclear weapons into the region, but it has continually refused to sign the nuclear nonproliferation treaty. It has supported a nuclear free zone, and in 1980 it proposed at the United Nations a conference of Middle Eastern states to write a treaty barring the production and use of nuclear weapons in the region. The general consensus of knowledgeable analysts is that Israel has the ingredients to produce and deliver a nuclear weapon, and some believe it has nuclear devices "on the shelf." Israel's nuclear ambiguity is regarded as a strategic asset, serving as a deterrent to Arab adventurism while not goading Arab nuclear development. Israel might decide to take its bomb "out of the basement" should it deem that necessary to maintain or rectify the regional balance of power or to increase its deterrent strength in relation to the Arab states. This would be a distinct possibility if an Arab state acquired an overt nuclear weapons capability. The Israeli bombing of Iraq's nuclear reactor in 1981 reflected Israel's concern about that possibility.

The real or supposed existence of an Israeli nuclear capability apparently has not affected conventional military doctrine or force structure and deployment. If Israel has assigned a role to such a nuclear capability, it must be seen in terms of an ultimate "doomsday" weapon—that is, a weapon to be used in the event of the possible or prospective downfall of the state due to hostile enemy actions. The possibility of use of tactical nuclear weapons should not be ruled out, however. The imminent destruction of the state might generate a threat to strike at major Arab population or resource centers. Short of that form of speculation, there is no identified role for nuclear weaponry in the openly expressed Israeli military doctrine, except insofar as the uncertainty of such weaponry's existence has a deterrent effect on Arab military-political action and behavior.

Despite the development of a substantial military establishment with much of the latest and most sophisticated military equipment, the IDF has primarily limited its actions to responses to specific threats from the Arab world. It has projected its power into Jordan and, in battle, has struck in Egypt, Syria, and Lebanon, and at Iraq in 1981 to eliminate a perceived nuclear threat. But, other than the July 1976 raid on Entebbe, Uganda, to secure the release of hostages, the IDF has not employed force beyond its own limited geographic area. This restraint has resulted more from political decisions than from inherent limits in forces or equipment.

Israel's military assistance programs have involved limited training of foreign personnel, mostly in Israel, and some advisers have served abroad on a very limited scale, primarily in connection with specific and limited tasks such as military sales. Other than the sale of military equipment and the transfer to third parties of some materiel acquired from other powers, including Soviet military and ancillary equipment captured from the Arab states, Israel's ability to influence worldwide military or security developments is limited. It has not been able to help finance other states' military acquisitions, it has not supported terrorist or similar operations abroad, and it has not had long-range military action or shows of force or other symbolic uses of power beyond its immediate area. But there are substantial rumors concerning Israel's support of various minority groups in neighboring states and beyond, in part to reduce those states' ability to join in the Arab effort against Israel and in part to make a point concerning survival of beleaguered minorities. Israel was involved with the Biafran revolt in Nigeria and supported the Christian elements of Major Saad Haddad in South

Lebanon as well as the Christian militias in the north. It reportedly has also helped the Kurds in Iraq and the southern Sudanese against the Arab-Muslim dominated northern-based government. It has also been involved in counterterrorist actions in Europe and elsewhere.

THE SEARCH FOR FRIENDS AND ALLIES

Israel's approach to foreign policy began to take shape once it became clear that peace would not follow the armistice accords that marked the end of its War of Independence. Israel directed its attention beyond the circle of neighboring Arab states to the broader international community in an effort to establish friendly relations with the states of Europe and the developing world, as well as with the superpowers. These relationships were seen as having a positive effect on the Arab-Israeli conflict and as having bilateral political and economic advantages that would help to ensure Israel's deterrent strength through national armed power and through increased international support for its position. Israel has seen Europe and the developing world, especially Africa and Latin America, as important components of its overall policy. It has sought to maintain positive relations with Europe based on the commonality of the Judeo-Christian heritage and democratic tradition and the memories of the Holocaust; its approach to the developing world, which began in earnest in the late 1950s, has focused on Israel's ability to provide technical assistance in the development process. Despite substantial effort in these sectors, the centrality of the Arab-Israeli conflict has enlarged and enhanced the role of the superpowers, particularly the United States, in Israeli eyes.

The Arab threat and Israel's isolation has suggested a need for positive relationships with other states, but from the outset, Israel's approach to "alliances" with other states has been marked by an ambivalence. Israel sees itself compelled to elicit the support of at least one major Western power for weapons supply and for deterrence of Soviet participation in conflict on the side of the Arabs, as well as for political and diplomatic support. Since 1967 the United

States increasingly has been identified as that power. But Israel believes in self-reliance and has demonstrated wariness of dependence on others and skepticism regarding the security value of international or great power guarantees. Israel's policy has been that it does not want any foreign power to fight on its behalf.

Israel's leaders early recognized the crucial role that the great powers would play in ensuring the country's defense and integrity. In the euphoric days following independence it was believed that nonalignment in the cold war was possible and that Israel could establish and maintain friendly relations with, and secure support from, both East and West (the Soviet Union and the United States), although most realized that Israel's long-term interests lay in the West. Nonalignment was in accord with Israel's perception of its national interest and seemed to be a realistic assessment in light of the policies and activities of both powers in the period immediately following World War II, when Soviet and U.S. support for Israel and the competition between them was seen as auguring well for the new state.

Upon attainment of statehood Israel's government proclaimed a policy of noncommitment (nonidentification) in the East-West conflict. Foreign Minister Moshe Sharett said, in July 1950, that Israel was not neutral and that in the ideological struggle between the democratic and communist social orders it had chosen democracy, but that it was nonaligned and not identified with any bloc in the cold war. The principles of Israel's policy were defined as the "pursuit of peace, support of the United Nations as the main instrument of peace, and non-identification with either of the large blocs against its rival." It was the preferred policy alternative and was facilitated by Israel's relations with both superpowers immediately following independence, when it received political support and financial and military assistance from sources in both blocs. The Soviet Union voted for the partition plan of November 1947, accorded *de jure* recognition to Israel shortly after its independence, and supported its applications for membership in the United Nations. In addition, the Soviet Union gave moral, political, and material support to the new state during its War of Independence, and Czechoslovakia was an important source of arms and materiel. In these instances, and others, the Soviet Union appeared to be competing with the United States to achieve a closer relationship with the new state.

With the termination of Israel's War of Independence in 1949, a distinct trend developed in Israeli-Soviet relations. Various factors contributed to Israel's shift to a pro-Western orientation, including ideological sympathies with Western democracy and the large size and importance of Western, especially American, Jewry. Soviet abandonment of a policy of support for Israel and denial of loan requests, coupled with a relatively constant flow of economic aid from the U.S. government and from American Jewry, contributed to Israel's moving closer to the Western bloc. Israel supported the United Nations Security Council's resolution of June 25, 1950, that, in effect, labeled North Korea an aggressor and recommended that United Nations' members join in the effort to repel the attack and restore peace. Israel emphasized that it considered this a United Nations matter, rather than an episode in the cold war, and that its support of the United Nations should not be interpreted as a stand with the West against the East but rather as a stand against any threat to world peace no matter what its origin. The decision was seen in other terms in the Soviet bloc.

During the 1947–1949 honeymoon period, Israel held out hopes for friendship, support, and aid from the Soviet bloc as well as for emigration to Israel of Soviet Jewry. Israel's political parties were divided among those favoring a pro-Western foreign policy and those favoring a Soviet orientation. With the deterioration of relations between the two states in the period from 1949 to 1953—climaxed by the anti-Jewish and anti-Israel Slansky trial in Czechoslovakia, the Soviet discovery of a "doctors' plot" in Moscow (of primarily Jews accused of being agents of the Zionists and the United States who sought to liquidate Soviet political and military leaders), and the severance for a brief period of diplomatic relations— Israel's foreign policy relinquished belief in Soviet friendship and support as a realistic alternative. With the exception of incurable optimists (who thought that a complete metamorphosis in Soviet policy was possible) and the Israeli Communist party and fellow travelers who were committed to belief in the ultimate victory of the communist system, Israelis were convinced of the unlikelihood of Israeli-Soviet friendship and cooperation. Political parties that had advocated a pro-Soviet policy alignment shifted to a call for nonalignment or neutrality. Soviet support for, and expanded relations with, the Arab states by the mid-1950s tended to confirm this perspective. Soviet economic and military assistance to the Arab world and the Soviet bloc's rupture of relations with Israel in 1967 (and the continuation of that break) have led Israel farther into the Western camp, although it continues to seek the restoration of ties to the Soviet Union and its allies.

Israel has not been a major regional military factor, nor has it been involved in a central way in the functions of international organizations or blocs. It does not belong to any regional organization or to any voting bloc in the United Nations or informal grouping of states in the international arena. This status is a result of its relations with the Arab states, their boycott of Israel, and their influence in the international system. Furthermore, Israel is not a party to any formal mutual-security pact or to any Soviet-style "treaty of friendship and cooperation." There have been implicit or quasi alliances—first with France and then with the United States and, in the instance of the Sinai War of 1956, a temporary alignment with Britain and France. These relationships have been seen as valuable and useful but all have been viewed as having limitations.

The credibility of the ally and of the "alliance" has been viewed differently at various times. The arrangement with Britain and France was for a short duration and had a particular and limited set of objectives: the reduction of Egyptian power, the removal of Nasser as a credible force affecting the revolts against France in North Africa, the security of the Suez Canal, and the threat to Israel of newly acquired Egyptian military capability. But it failed to change the regional or international structure. Nasser emerged from the encounter with increased prestige, if not power, and the British and French roles in the region were substantially reduced, if not formally terminated. Israel gained a respite from Arab threats and a reputation as a military force that had a deterrent value over the ensuing decade. The "tacit alliance" with France that lasted from the mid-1950s until the Six Day War, although its quality suffered after Algeria's independence in 1962, was more a marriage of convenience, with mutual benefits derived by the participants, than a full-fledged alliance. It provided Israel with substantial military equipment and technological (including nuclear) assistance. But the decline of the relationship under de Gaulle in the period 1967–1969 contributed to Israel's negative perceptions concerning the reliability of allies.

As the foreign policy of Israel became Western oriented, France and, to a lesser extent, Britain and Germany became important friends for Israel in the 1950s and into the 1960s. During the 1950s the U.S. relationship with Israel remained proper, and even positive, but had not achieved the level that was to develop following the Six Day War of 1967. The West provided Israel with the political and moral support and the arms and economic assistance essential for its survival and defense, while the Soviet Union increasingly identified itself with the Arab cause. Ultimately, the relationship with the United States became the most significant.

Peace with Egypt: (*upper left*) President Anwar Sadat (center) visits
Israel in November 1977 and is met at Ben-Gurion airport by
Prime Minister Begin (left) and President Katzir (right): (*lower left*);
Begin (saluting) visits Egypt in January 1978 to continue the peace

negotiations; (*upper right*) signing the peace treaty at the White
House, Washington, D.C., March 26, 1979 (left to right at table:
Sadat, U.S. President Jimmy Carter, and Begin); (*lower right*) Israel's
first ambassador to Egypt presents his credentials to President
Sadat in February 1980.

Mirage and Phantom jets in Israel's air force (*top and center*). Israel's upper Galilee as seen from Tel Faher, a pre-1967 Syrian military stronghold on the Golan Heights (*bottom*).

6

Israel and the United States

The United States and Israel have been linked in a complex and multifaceted "special relationship" that had its origins prior to the establishment of the Jewish state in 1948. The relationship has focused on the continuing U.S. support for the survival, security, and well-being of Israel.

POLITICAL AND STRATEGIC CONSIDERATIONS

At the outset U.S. policy was based on humanitarian considerations associated with the plight of European Jewry, but by the 1970s political and strategic considerations were dominant. U.S. policy on arms supply evolved from "embargo" to "principal supplier," and arms became an important tool of U.S. policy to reassure Israel and to achieve policy modification. The two states developed a diplomatic-political relationship that focused on the need to resolve the Arab-Israeli dispute, but while they agreed on the general concept, they often differed on the precise means of achieving the desired result. The relationship became especially close after the Six Day War, when a congruence of policy prevailed on many of their salient concerns. Nevertheless, the two states often held differing perspectives on regional developments and on the dangers and opportunities they presented. No major ruptures took place, although significant tensions were generated at various junctures.

The accession to office of Jimmy Carter in Washington and of Menachem Begin in Jerusalem in 1977 inaugurated a new period in the relationship characterized by increased public tension and recrimination. The two leaders focused on the desire to terminate the Arab-Israeli conflict. Nevertheless, they often disagreed on the modalities of the peace process, and there were significant personality clashes between senior U.S. and Israeli figures. There was also a reduced exclusivity in the relationship, especially after the Sadat visit to Jerusalem in November 1977.

The relationship during the administrations of Begin and Ronald Reagan was characterized by close positive ties, but there were clashes over divergent interpretations of the regional situation, of the peace process, and of Israel's security needs. Israel struck at the Iraqi nuclear reactor near Baghdad and at PLO positions in Beirut during the summer of 1981 and took action on other issues when it believed its national interest was at stake, even when it understood this would lead to clashes with the United States. The United States strongly opposed the raid on the Iraqi reactor, questioned the Beirut bombings, and postponed the delivery of previously contracted F-16 aircraft to Israel. Various substantive issues emerged, including disputes about settlements in the occupied territories and Israel's concern about a perceived pro-Saudi tendency in U.S. policy. The latter was manifested, in part, by arms supply to Saudi Arabia, including F-15 enhancements and Airborne Warning and Control System (AWACS). Israeli anxiety was heightened when the Reagan administration found some merit in a proposal put forward by then Crown Prince Fahd of Saudi Arabia in August 1981, which Israel had rejected.

Reagan sought to reassure Israel that the United States remained committed to help it retain its military and technological advantage in relation to the Arab states. Israel was drawn to a Reagan administration proposal of strategic cooperation, and in the November 30, 1981 Memorandum of Understanding (MOU), Israel recognized the need to enhance strategic cooperation to deter threats from the Soviet Union to the region. For the Begin government it represented an important achievement, suggesting an improved relationship with the United States and some mitigation of the negative effects of the U.S. sale of AWACS and other advanced weapons systems to Saudi Arabia.

The positive aura resulting from the strategic cooperation accord was dissipated when the government of Israel, in keeping with its perspectives and official program, decided in December 1981 to alter the status of the Golan Heights by extending the law, jurisdiction, and administration of Israel to that area. The rationales were many but centered on historical and security factors and on the refusal of Syria to recognize Israel's existence and to negotiate with it for peace. The action generated a swift negative reaction in Washington, where spokespersons stressed that there had been no advance warning and that the United States opposed any unilateral change in the status of the Golan Heights. These statements were accompanied by U.S. support for a United Nations resolution of condemnation and by suspension of the MOU. Israel was stunned by the extent of the U.S. response; its strongly negative reaction included Begin's castigation of the U.S. ambassador.

Although the Golan decision exacerbated tensions, the main watershed was the war in Lebanon, which called into question various aspects of the links between the two states and led to clashes over the nature and extent of Israel's military actions and the U.S. effort to ensure the PLO's evacuation from Beirut. U.S. forces, which had been withdrawn from Beirut following the PLO's evacuation, returned there after the massacres at the Shatila and Sabra refugee camps, leading to the burdensome involvement of the marines in the turmoil of Lebanon.

The war also precipitated the Reagan "fresh start" initiative of September 1, 1982, which sought to reinvigorate the Arab-Israeli peace process by taking advantage of the opportunities presented by the new situation in Lebanon. Israel, which was not consulted in advance, saw the various proposals as detrimental because they departed from the conceptual framework of Camp David and seemed prematurely to determine the outcome of negotiations on several points, including the status of Jerusalem and the future of the West Bank and Gaza. There were other concerns as well, and these led Israel to reject the initiative. That action, coupled with the refugee camp massacres, resulted in a sharp deterioration in Israel's standing in U.S. public opinion and in further disagreements with the Reagan administration, resulting in months of rancor.

POSITIVE RELATIONS

By the summer of 1983, however, the U.S.-Israel relationship reverted to positive levels as a consequence of the Kahan Commission report, the failure of King Hussein to join the peace process, the increase in the Soviet involvement in Syria, the signing of the U.S.-promoted Lebanon-Israel agreement of May 1983, and the Syrian-Soviet opposition to it. The United States and Israel appeared linked by a congruence of policy that included recognition of Israel's strategic anti-Soviet value and its desire for peaceful resolution of the Arab-Israeli conflict, as well as a parallelism concerning Lebanon and its future. This comported well with Reagan's initial perceptions of Israel and presaged a period of positive relations between the two states that was given tangible expression at the end of November 1983 when President Reagan and Prime Minister Yitzhak Shamir reached agreement on closer strategic cooperation. During the visit of Shamir and Defense Minister Moshe Arens to Washington, D.C., the major foreign policy problems were addressed, although not all the differences were resolved. The reportedly "positive" visit focused on the areas of current mutual concern of the two states, primarily the question of Lebanon, and demonstrated the extent to which the concerns and policies of the two states had become congruent.

The involvement of the United States in Lebanon and the attacks on U.S. forces and positions in Lebanon and elsewhere in the region provided the context for the improved situation. The need to reinforce the Gemayel government and to rebuild Lebanon as a free, independent, and sovereign state, with the reconstruction of its economic infrastructure and the withdrawal of all foreign forces, and with an army capable of supporting the government's position, seemed to be parallel goals of the two leaders. Syria and the Soviet Union were viewed as the forces promoting instability and seeking to prevent or obstruct reaching these goals, and both were identified as threats to peace and stability. This coincidence of perspective and objective led the Israeli and U.S. governments to achieve wide-ranging agreement on closer coordination and policy. At the same time the major issues of discord in the relationship, which centered on the West Bank and Gaza and the Reagan "fresh start" initiative, were not addressed in any meaningful way.

The quadrennial U.S. presidential election season was characterized by a hiatus in the peace process and a positive aura for the special relationship. This mimicked past patterns but also reflected the reality of the situation in 1984, when there was no clear and obvious mechanism for a breakthrough in the peace process. But the process will resume, given its centrality to both the United States and Israel, and the issues will be contentious, given the positions of the parties. Periodic crises will emerge, and there will be clashes between the United States and Israel that will no doubt be characterized, as their predecessors have been, as "the worst ever" and reflective of "the nadir" of the relationship. However, given the strong ties linking the United States and Israel in the special relationship, the storms of the future will be weathered as those of the past have been.

THE U.S. COMMITMENT TO ISRAEL

In a press conference on May 12, 1977, President Jimmy Carter said:

> We have a special relationship with Israel. It's absolutely crucial that no one in our country or around the world ever doubt that our No. 1 commitment in the Middle East is to protect the right of Israel to exist, to exist permanently, and to exist in peace. It's a special relationship.

Israel's special relationship with the United States—which revolves around a broadly conceived ideological factor and is based on substantial positive perception and sentiment evident in public opinion and official statements and manifest in political-diplomatic support and in military and economic assistance—has not been enshrined in a legally binding document joining the two states in a formal alliance. Despite the extensive links that have developed, the widespread belief in the existence of the commitment, and the assurances contained in various specific agreements, the exact nature and extent of the U.S. commitment to Israel remains imprecise.

Israel has no mutual-security treaty with the United States, nor is it a member of any alliance system requiring the United States to take up arms automatically on its behalf. It has been assumed that the United States would come to Israel's assistance should it be gravely threatened, and this perception has become particularly apparent during times of crisis. Despite this perception and the general "feeling" in Washington and elsewhere that the United States would take action if required, there is no assurance that this would be the case. The exact role of the United States in support of Israel, beyond diplomatic and political action and military and economic assistance, is unclear.

The commitment has taken the rather generalized form of presidential statements rather than formal documents. U.S. statements of policy have reaffirmed the U.S. interest in supporting the political independence and territorial integrity of Middle Eastern states, including Israel. They do not, however, commit the United States to specific actions in particular circumstances. In more recent years, the arrangement has been codified in the Sinai II accords of 1975 and the MOU of 1981. Although commitments made in the Egypt-Israel peace process and other memoranda have been significant, they do not provide a formal and legally binding commitment for U.S. military action. Israeli leaders continue to be interested in military and economic assistance as the primary tangible expression of the U.S. commitment and have been particularly cautious about potential U.S. participation in conflict, fearing that U.S. combat losses might lead to questioning of the relationship and concerns about a situation analogous to that in Vietnam.

Although the United States has incurred no legally binding commitment requiring it to come to Israel's assistance in the event of conflict, general support for such a posture is clearly reflected in public statements, polls, and the election of those espousing such views. This tends to render a formal document superfluous and perhaps undesirable, as the critical factor is not a formal requirement but the perception of one and the willingness to act in support of perceived obligations. The conclusion is that the commitment of the United States to Israel reflects the nature of the relationship at any particular time.

The United States is today an indispensable, if not fully dependable, ally. It provides Israel, through one form or another, with economic (governmental and private), technical, military, political, diplomatic, and moral support. It is seen as the ultimate resource against the Soviet Union; it is the source of Israel's sophisticated military hardware; it is central to the Arab-Israeli peace process. But although there is this positive relationship, there is also the Israeli reluctance, bred of history, to abdicate security to another party's judgment and action. Israel will continue to consider its perceptions of threat and security as decisive.

Over nearly four decades the United States and Israel have established a special relationship replete with broad areas of agreement and numerous examples of discord. Broad agreement and understanding and a generalized commitment to peace exist, and specific questions and issues have been approached within that framework. It is with regard to the specifics, especially the tactics and techniques to be employed in efforts to achieve the broad objectives, that the relationship has often had its episodes of disagreement. Such agreement on broad goals and discord on specifics is likely to characterize the relationship in the future.

The two states maintain a remarkable degree of parallelism and congruence on broad policy goals. The policy consensus includes the need to prevent war, both regional and that involving the superpowers, the need to resolve the Arab-Israeli conflict, and the need to maintain Israel's existence and security and to help provide for its economic well-being.

At the same time there was, is, and will be a divergence that derives from a difference of perspective and overall policy environment. The United States has broader concerns resulting from its global obligations; Israel's perspective is conditioned by its more restricted environment and lesser responsibilities. Israel's horizon is more narrowly defined and is essentially limited to the survival of the state and a concern for Jewish communities and individuals that goes beyond the frontiers of the Jewish state.

Despite the generally positive nature of the relationship since 1948, Israelis tend to recall a series of negative episodes as well. They highlight the 1947 arms embargo preventing the shipment of arms to the Jews in Palestine and, later, to Israel as well as to neighboring states; the subsequent refusal to provide military equipment or other assistance during the War of Independence and much of the subsequent period; John Foster Dulles's aid suspensions and general unfriendliness; U.S. actions in connection with the Sinai War of 1956 and Israel's subsequent withdrawal from Sinai and the Gaza Strip; and the disappointing lack of action by the United States just prior to the Six Day War in support of its 1957 pledge concerning freedom of passage for Israeli shipping in the Strait of Tiran. In 1967, Israel ultimately decided that the United States would not act unilaterally and that multilateral action would not succeed. Israel determined its need to act alone and estimated that the United States would not object to or seek to prevent its action, and when Israel decided to go to war, it did not consult or inform the United States.

There has been a divergence on methods and techniques to be employed as well as discord on specific issues. During the 1967 war there was a clash over Israel's mistaken attack on the U.S. intelligence ship *Liberty*, with the consequent casualties. In May 1968 there was disagreement over Israel's control of the islands of Tiran and Sanafir. The United States and Israel have disagreed on the matter of reprisals by Israel in response to Arab *fedayeen* actions and on the limits placed on the refugees from the West Bank in the wake of the Six Day War. They have come into major disagreement concerning the value of great power efforts to resolve the conflict, Israel's need for military supplies, and the status of the occupied territories and Israel's role with respect to them, including the building of settlements. The two nations have differed over the construction of settlements in the territories and over whether they are legal and/or are obstacles to peace. They have argued over Israel's desire for significant changes in the pre–Six Day War armistice lines as contrasted with the U.S. perspective that there be "insubstantial alterations" or "minor modifications." The two states will continue to hold divergent views on the several elements of the Palestinian issue, particularly the West Bank's future, the rights of the Palestinians, and the potential creation of a Palestinian homeland, entity, or state. These differences have become increasingly obvious in the Carter and Reagan administrations.

In many respects the issue of Jerusalem has highlighted the areas of discord. The United States has supported the partition plan designation of Jerusalem as a separate entity and has stressed the international character of the city while refusing to recognize unilateral actions by any state affecting its future. The United States refuses to move its embassy to Jerusalem and maintains it in Tel Aviv, thus illustrating the differing perspectives of the two states. These perspectives have placed the two states in conflicting positions virtually continuously from 1947 to the present, especially since the Israeli declarations of Jerusalem as the capital of the state and the reunification of the city during the 1967 war. The increase in Israel's dependence on the United States and the areas of policy discord suggest possible reemployment of various forms of pressure previously utilized by the United States, including the withholding of economic aid as in the mid-1950s, military aid decision and delivery slowdowns since 1967 (such as the slow response to Israeli requests during the 1973 war), joining in United Nations censures, moral suasion, private and open presidential letters, and similar devices.

The general consensus on major issues does not ensure agreement on all aspects or specifics of each problem. As the dialogue has increasingly focused on details, rather than broad areas of agreement, there have been disturbances in the relationship. Israel and the United States understand that this is inevitable, but seek to minimize the areas of discord. Strains in the relationships are probably inevitable given the extensive nature of the issues that will be considered in the dialogue. Foreign Minister Yitzhak Shamir described the situation in these terms to the Knesset in September 1982:

> Our relations with the United States are of a special character. Between our two nations there is a deep friendship, based on common values and identical interests. At the same time, differences between our two countries crop up occasionally, chiefly on the subject of our borders and how to defend our security. These differences of opinion are natural; they stem from changing conditions, and they express our independence and our separate needs. . . . Israel is a difficult ally, but a faithful and reliable one. We are certain that what we have in common with the United States is permanent and deep, while our disagreements are ephemeral. The permanent will overcome the ephemeral.

The special relationship will continue with its particular patterns of intercourse unique to the links between the United States and Israel.

U.S.-Israel consultations: A working meeting in Jerusalem, March 1979. The president of the United States, Jimmy Carter, and the prime minister of Israel, Menachem Begin, meet, with their aides, to discuss issues of mutual interest.

Chronology of Major Events

B.C.E.

c. 17th Century	The period of the Patriarchs of Judaism: Abraham, Isaac, Jacob.
c. 1250–1210	The Exodus of the Jews from Egypt; wandering in the desert of Sinai and the conquest of Canaan under Joshua.
c. 1020–1004	King Saul. Establishment of the kingdom.
c. 1004–965	King David. Consolidation and expansion of the kingdom.
c. 965–928	King Solomon. The Temple is built in Jerusalem.
c. 928	Division of the state and the establishment of Kingdoms of Judah and Israel.
c. 722	Assyrian conquest of Samaria, Kingdom of Israel; large number of Jews exiled.
c. 586	Jerusalem conquered and the Temple is destroyed. Mass deportation of Jews in the Babylonian Captivity.
c. 520–515	Temple rebuilt.
c. 167–160	Hasmonean rebellion under Judah Maccabee.

164	Jerusalem is liberated and the Temple is rededicated.
37–4	Reign of Herod.
c. 19	Temple rebuilt.

A.D. 1 to 1878

66	Revolt against Rome.
70	Siege of Jerusalem; destruction of the Temple by Romans. Direct Roman rule is imposed (until 395).
73	Fall of Massada.
132–135	Bar Kochba War.
395–638	Byzantine rule.
638	Arab Muslim armies conquer Jerusalem.
c. 636–1072	Arab rule.
1072–1099	Seljuk rule.
1099	Jerusalem captured by the Crusaders.
1099–1291	Crusader rule (with interruptions).
1187	Jerusalem captured by Saladin.
1291–1516	Mameluke rule.
1517–1917	Ottoman Turkish rule.

1878 to 1947

1878	Petah Tikva founded.
1882–1903	First Aliyah.
1882	Rishon Le-Zion founded.
1894	Dreyfus trial in France.

1896	Publication of *Der Judenstaat* by Theodor Herzl.
1897	First Zionist Congress held in Basel, Switzerland. World Zionist Organization established.
1904–1914	Second Aliyah.
1909	Kibbutz Degania founded.
1917	British capture Jerusalem. *November 2:* Balfour Declaration issued.
1919–1923	Third Aliyah.
1920	British mandate over Palestine begun although not formalized until 1922–1923. Histadrut and Hagana founded.
1921	Moshav Nahalal founded.
1924–1928	Fourth Aliyah.
1929	Arab riots in Jerusalem and massacres in Hebron and Safed.
1929–1939	Fifth Aliyah.
1947	Great Britain turns the Palestine issue over to the United Nations. United Nations Special Committee on Palestine examines the problem and recommends solutions. *November 29:* Partition Plan for Palestine adopted by United Nations General Assembly.

1948 to 1977

1948	*May 14:* Proclamation of the independence of the State of Israel. *May 15:* Arab armies invade and first Arab-Israeli war (Israel's War of Independence) officially begins.

1949   *January.* First Knesset election.
        Chaim Weizmann becomes first president;
            David Ben-Gurion becomes first prime
            minister. Armistice Agreements signed
            with Egypt, Lebanon, Syria, and Jordan.
            Israel becomes a member of the United
            Nations.

1950   *July:* Law of the Return.

1951   Second Knesset election.

1952   Chaim Weizmann dies; Itzhak Ben-Zvi
            becomes second president.

1954   Moshe Sharett becomes prime minister.

1955   Election for Third Knesset.
        David Ben-Gurion becomes prime minister.

1956   Sinai War.

1957   Israel evacuates Sinai and Gaza Strip;
            United Nations Emergency Force
            established.

1959   Election for Fourth Knesset.

1961   Fifth Knesset election.

1963   Itzhak Ben-Zvi dies; Zalman Shazar
            becomes third president; Levi Eshkol
            becomes prime minister.

1965   Sixth Knesset election.

1967   *June:* Third Arab-Israeli (Six Day) war.
        November 22: UN Security Council adopts
            Resolution 242.

1969   War of Attrition begins along the Suez
            Canal. Levi Eshkol dies; Golda Meir
            becomes prime minister.

1969   Seventh Knesset election.

1970   *August:* War of Attrition ended by cease-
                fire.

1973   *April:* Ephraim (Katchalski) Katzir elected
                president.
                October: Arab-Israeli (Yom Kippur) war.
                November: Agranat Commission established.
                December: Election for Eighth Knesset.

1974   *January:* Egypt-Israel Disengagement of
                Forces Agreement signed.

                April: Golda Meir resigns: Yitzhak Rabin
                becomes prime minister.
                May: Israel and Syria conclude
                disengagement agreement.

1975   Egypt and Israel sign disengagement (Sinai
                II) agreement.

1976   *July:* Israeli commandos free hostages at
                Entebbe Airport, Uganda.

1977 to 1984

1977   *April:* Yitzhak Rabin resigns as prime
                minister. Shimon Peres is selected as
                Labor party leader.
                May: Election for Ninth Knesset. Likud,
                under leadership of Menachem Begin,
                emerges as largest party.
                June: Begin forms government coalition
                with himself as prime minister.
                November: President Anwar Sadat of Egypt
                announces to Egyptian National
                Assembly his willingness to visit Israel to
                discuss peace; Israeli Knesset
                overwhelmingly approves invitation to
                Sadat. Sadat arrives in Jerusalem and
                addresses the Israeli Knesset.
                Negotiations begin.

1978   Yitzhak Navon elected president.
                       March: Following an attack on an Israeli
                           bus, Israel launches Operation Litani
                           against Palestinian bases in Lebanon.
                       May: U.S. Congress approves weapons
                           package for Israel, Egypt, and Saudi
                           Arabia.
                       June: Israel completes the withdrawal of its
                           armed forces and UNIFIL takes up
                           positions in southern Lebanon.
                       September: Anwar Sadat, Menachem Begin,
                           and Jimmy Carter meet at the summit at
                           Camp David, Maryland. Camp David
                           Accords are signed on the seventeenth.
                       October: Egypt and Israel begin peace
                           negotiations in Washington, D.C., to
                           implement Camp David Accords.

1979   *March 26:* Egypt-Israel Peace Treaty signed
                           in Washington, D.C.
                       May 25: Israel begins withdrawal from the
                           Sinai Peninsula; Egypt and Israel begin
                           discussion of autonomy issues.

1980   *February:* Egypt and Israel exchange
                           ambassadors.
                       July 30: Knesset adopts Basic Law
                           reaffirming united Jerusalem as Israel's
                           capital.

1981   *June:* Israel destroys Osirak nuclear reactor
                           near Baghdad.
                       June: Knesset election. Likud secures largest
                           number of seats. Begin coalition
                           government secures vote of confidence
                           from the Knesset in August.
                       December: Israel extends its "law and
                           jurisdiction" to the Golan Heights.

1982   *April:* Israel completes its withdrawal from
                the Sinai Peninsula and returns it to
                Egypt.
                June: Arab-Israeli war (Operation Peace for
                Galilee).
                September 1: President Ronald Reagan
                outlines his fresh start initiative for
                peace in the Middle East.
                September: Massacre at Sabra and Shatila
                refugee camps. Establishment of Kahan
                Commission to inquire into the
                massacres.

1983   *February:* Kahan Commission reports its
                findings. Ariel Sharon resigns as defense
                minister and is replaced by Moshe Arens.
                March: Chaim Herzog is elected president.
                May 17: Israel and Lebanon sign an
                agreement concluded with the assistance
                of U.S. Secretary of State George Shultz.
                Lebanon abrogates the agreement in
                March 1984.
                September: Menachem Begin resigns as
                prime minister.
                October: Yitzhak Shamir forms a new
                government and takes office as prime
                minister.

1984   *July:* Knesset election.
                September: Government of national unity is
                formed with Shimon Peres as prime
                minister and Yitzhak Shamir as alternate
                prime minister.
                Mass immigration of Ethiopian Jews
                (Falashas) to Israel in Operation Moses.

Suggested Readings

The amount of material available on Israel is so vast that a reader is faced with a bewildering choice even though much of the literature is oriented toward the Arab-Israeli conflict. The following listing is highly selective and designed to suggest a number of English-language books that elaborate on the themes discussed in this volume.

Howard M. Sachar's *A History of Israel: From the Rise of Zionism to Our Time* (New York: Alfred A. Knopf, 1976) and Noah Lucas's *The Modern History of Israel* (New York and Washington, D.C.: Praeger Publishers, 1975) provide histories of Israel that antedate independence. The mandate period is discussed in J. C. Hurewitz's *The Struggle for Palestine* (New York: W. W. Norton, 1950) and Christopher Syke's *Crossroads to Israel* (Cleveland and New York: World Publishing, 1965). Shlomo Avineri's *The Making of Modern Zionism: The Intellectual Origins of the Jewish State* (New York: Basic Books, 1981) and Walter Laqueur's *A History of Zionism* (New York: Holt, Rinehart and Winston, 1972) provide a comprehensive history and examination of the Zionist movement, its origins, and diverse ideological trends. Amos Elon's *Herzl* (New York: Holt, Rinehart and Winston, 1975) is a biography of the Zionist movement's founder, and Ben Halpern's *The Idea of the Jewish State*, 2d ed. (Cambridge: Harvard University Press, 1970) is a sympathetic study of the origins and development of the Zionist idea.

A brief introduction to various aspects of Israeli society and to Jewish history and values may be found in the Israel

Pocket Library (Jerusalem: Keter Books, 1973 and 1974), a series of fifteen paperback volumes containing material from the *Encyclopedia Judaica*. The titles are *Anti-Semitism, Archaeology, Democracy, Economy, Education and Science, Geography, History from 1880, History Until 1880, Holocaust, Immigration and Settlement, Jerusalem, Jewish Values, Religious Life and Communities, Society,* and *Zionism*. The series also has a *Cumulative Index*. Efraim Orni and Elisha Efrat, in *Geography of Israel*, 3d rev. ed. (Jerusalem: Israel Universities Press, 1971), provide a detailed examination of all facets of Israel's geography.

The constitutional and legal parameters of the political system are considered in Emanuel Rackman's *Israel's Emerging Constitution, 1948–51* (New York: Columbia University Press, 1955), which deals with the problems involved in the development of a constitution; in Henry E. Baker's *The Legal System of Israel* (Jerusalem: Israel Universities Press, 1968); and in *Fundamental Laws of the State of Israel* (New York: Twayne Publishers, 1961), edited by Joseph Badi. An important study of the parliament is Asher Zidon's *Knesset: The Parliament of Israel* (New York: Herzl Press, 1967), which is complemented by Eliahu S. Likhovski's *Israel's Parliament: The Law of the Knesset* (Oxford: Oxford University Press, 1971).

The basic features and issues of the political system are described and analyzed in the following works: Joseph Badi, *The Government of the State of Israel: A Critical Account of Its Parliament, Executive, and Judiciary* (New York: Twayne Publishers, 1963); Marver H. Bernstein, *The Politics of Israel: The First Decade of Statehood* (Princeton, N.J.: Princeton University Press, 1957); Leonard J. Fein, *Israel: Politics and People* (Boston: Little, Brown & Co., 1968); Yehoshua Freudenheim, *Government in Israel* (Dobbs Ferry, N.Y.: Oceana Publications, 1967); and Oscar Kraines, *Government and Politics in Israel* (Boston: Houghton Mifflin Co., 1961). Gad Yaacobi's *The Government of Israel* (New York: Praeger, 1982) provides unique insight into the political process by a leader of the Israel Labor party who has served as a member of the Knesset and as a cabinet minister. In *Israeli Democracy: The Middle of the Journey* (New York: The Free Press and London: Collier Macmillan, 1982),

Daniel Shimshoni examines the ways in which public policies were formed in Israel until 1977.

Various aspects of Israeli politics are discussed in the following more specialized studies: Alan Arian, *The Choosing People: Voting Behavior in Israel* (Cleveland and London: Case Western Reserve University Press, 1973); Alan Arian, ed., *The Elections in Israel—1969* (Israel: Jerusalem Academic Press, 1972); Howard R. Penniman, ed., *Israel at the Polls: The Knesset Elections of 1977* (Washington, D.C.: American Enterprise Institute for Public Policy Research, 1979); Dan Caspi, Abraham Diskin, and Emanuel Gutmann, eds., *The Roots of Begin's Success: The 1981 Israeli Elections* (London and Canberra: Croom Helm and New York: St. Martin's Press, 1984); Yuval Elizur and Eliahu Salpeter, *Who Rules Israel?* (New York: Harper & Row, 1973); Eva Etzioni-Halevy, *Political Culture in Israel: Cleavage and Integration Among Israeli Jews* (New York and London: Praeger Publishers, 1977); Peter Y. Medding, *Mapai in Israel: Political Organization and Government in a New Society* (Cambridge: Cambridge University Press, 1972); Lester G. Seligman, *Leadership in a New Nation: Political Development in Israel* (New York: Atherton Press, 1964); and David M. Zohar, *Political Parties in Israel: The Evolution of Israeli Democracy* (New York, Washington, D.C., and London: Praeger Publishers, 1974).

Studies of the salient domestic political and social issues tend to be relatively few in number. Among the more reliable are S. N. Eisenstadt's *Israeli Society* (New York: Basic Books, 1967); Judith T. Shuval's *Immigrants on the Threshold* (New York: Atherton Press, 1963); and Alex Weingrod's *Israel: Group Relations in a New Society* (New York: Frederick A. Praeger Publishers for the Institute of Race Relations, 1965). Israel's economy is examined by David Horowitz in *The Economics of Israel* (Oxford: Pergamon Press, 1967). The relationship of religion and the state is discussed in the following: Joseph Badi, *Religion in Israel Today: The Relationship Between State and Religion* (New York: Bookman Associates, 1959); Gary S. Schiff, *Tradition and Politics: The Religious Parties of Israel* (Detroit: Wayne State University Press, 1977); Charles S. Liebman and Eliezer Don-Yehiya, *Civil Religion in Israel:*

Traditional Judaism and Political Culture in the Jewish State (Berkeley, Los Angeles, London: University of California Press, 1983); and Oscar Kraines, *The Impossible Dilemma: Who Is a Jew in the State of Israel?* (New York: Bloch Publishing Co., 1976). Yigal Allon's *The Making of Israel's Army* (New York: Bantam Books, 1971) and Amos Perlmutter's *Military and Politics in Israel: Nation-Building and Role Expansion* (London: Frank Cass and Co., 1969) consider the role of the military. For a general overview of the IDF, its background and development, see Edward Luttwak and Dan Horowitz's *The Israeli Army* (New York: Harper & Row, 1975). Jacob M. Landau, in *The Arabs in Israel: A Political Study* (London: Oxford University Press, 1969), presents a comprehensive survey and analysis of the role of the Arabs in Israel. An alternative perspective is provided by Sabri Jiryis's *The Arabs in Israel* (New York and London: Monthly Review Press, 1976).

Israel's international relations are discussed in Theodore Draper's *Israel and World Politics: Roots of the Third Arab-Israeli War* (New York: The Viking Press, 1968) and in *Israel and the United Nations*, the report of a study group set up by the Hebrew University of Jerusalem (New York: Manhattan Publishing Company, 1956). Ernest Stock's *Israel on the Road to Sinai, 1949–1956* (Ithaca, N.Y.: Cornell University Press, 1967) is an incisive study of Israel's foreign policy from 1948 to the Sinai campaign, with a sequel on the June 1967 war. Walter Eytan, a ranking Israeli diplomat, has written *The First Ten Years: A Diplomatic History of Israel* (New York: Simon and Schuster, 1958). Israel's international cooperation program is discussed in these books: Leopold Laufer, *Israel and the Developing Countries: New Approaches to Cooperation* (New York: The Twentieth Century Fund, 1967); Shimeon Amir, *Israel's Development Cooperation with Africa, Asia, and Latin America* (New York: Praeger Publishers, 1974); and Michael Curtis and Susan Aurelia Gitelson, eds., *Israel in the Third World* (New Brunswick, N.J.: Transaction Books, 1974). Michael Brecher's *Decisions in Israel's Foreign Policy* (New Haven: Yale University Press, 1975) and *The Foreign Policy System of Israel: Setting, Images, Processes* (New Haven: Yale University Press, 1972) provide a comprehensive approach to Israel's foreign policy process and examine some major decisions. Meron Medzini, editor of *Israel's Foreign Relations: Selected Documents, 1947-1979,* 5 vols. (Jerusalem: Ministry for Foreign Affairs, 1976-1982), provides the major documents of Israel's foreign policy from its inception through 1979.

Nadav Safran, in *Israel: The Embattled Ally* (Cambridge: Belknap Press of Harvard University Press, 1981), provides coverage of Israel's domestic scene as it affects foreign policy. Yehoshafat Harkabi, in *Arab Strategies and Israel's Response* (New York: The Free Press, 1977), and Gabriel Sheffer, ed., in *Dynamics of a Conflict: A Re-examination of the Arab-Israeli Conflict* (Atlantic Highlands, N.J.: Humanities Press, 1975), deal with aspects of the Arab-Israeli conflict and Israel's position and perspective. Bernard Reich's *Israel and Occupied Territories* (Washington, D.C.: U.S. Department of State, 1973), focuses on the problem of the territories occupied by Israel in the 1967 war, and Gershon R. Kieval's *Party Politics in Israel and the Occupied Territories* (Westport, Conn.: Greenwood Press, 1983) provides a more detailed analysis of Israel's policy. Bernard Reich, in *Quest for Peace: United States–Israel Relations and the Arab-Israeli Conflict* (New Brunswick, N.J.: Transaction Books, 1977), deals with Israel's relations with the United States in the context of the efforts to resolve the Arab-Israeli conflict. Bernard Reich's *The United States and Israel: Influence in the Special Relationship* (New York: Praeger, 1984) examines Israel's crucial links with the United States.

Books by and about senior Israeli policy and decision makers offer valuable insights into the past and present of Israel. Among the numerous works of this genre, the following are of particular interest: Menachem Begin, *The Revolt* (New York: Nash, 1981); Eitan Haber, *Menachem Begin: The Legend and the Man* (New York: Delacorte Press, 1978); David Ben-Gurion, *Israel: A Personal History* (New York: Funk and Wagnalls; New York and Tel Aviv: Sabra Books, 1971); David Ben-Gurion, *Rebirth and Destiny of Israel* (New York: Philosophical Library, 1954); David Ben-Gurion, *My Talks with Arab Leaders* (Jerusalem: Keter, 1972); Michael Bar-Zohar, *Ben-Gurion: The Armed Prophet* (Englewood Cliffs, N.J.: Prentice-Hall, 1968); Moshe Dayan, *Story of My Life: An Autobiography*

(New York: William Morrow, 1976); Moshe Dayan, *Breakthrough: A Personal Account of the Egypt-Israel Peace Negotiations* (New York: Alfred A. Knopf, 1981); Abba Eban, *Autobiography* (New York: Random House, 1977); Terence Prittie, *Eshkol: The Man and the Nation* (New York: Pitman, 1969); Teddy Kolleck and Amos Killeck, *For Jerusalem—A Life* (New York: Random House, 1978); Golda Meir, *My Life* (New York: G. P. Putnam's Sons, 1975); Shimon Peres, *David's Sling: The Arming of Israel* (London: Weidenfeld & Nicolson, 1970); Matti Golan, *Shimon Peres: A Biography* (New York: St. Martin's Press, 1982); Yitzhak Rabin, *The Rabin Memoirs* (Boston: Little, Brown & Co., 1979); Ezer Weizman, *On Eagles' Wings* (New York: Macmillan, 1979); Ezer Weizman, *The Battle for Peace* (Toronto, New York, London: Bantam Books, 1981); and Chaim Weizmann, *Trial and Error* (New York: Schocken, 1966).

The government of Israel is a prolific publisher of high-quality materials that would serve the interested reader well. Among these, the *Israel Government Year Book* and *Statistical Abstract of Israel,* both issued annually, are particularly valuable.

About the Book and Author

The modern state of Israel is a product of centuries of Jewish history that affect all aspects of Israel's society and culture, its politics, and its policies. Professor Reich introduces us to a nation seeking to maintain and enhance its traditions while struggling to deal with present domestic and foreign challenges. He examines the land and people of Israel, the division between Jews of Oriental and Ashkenazi backgrounds as well as the division between Jewish and Arab citizens, before turning to the economic concerns facing a country virtually devoid of natural resources. His discussion of Israel's history provides the background for a detailed consideration of the dynamics of its political system and the implications of the 1984 election and its resulting government of national unity. Finally, Professor Reich addresses Israel's foreign and security policies, focusing on the problems created by the continuing Arab-Israeli conflict. He also analyzes Israel's special relationship with the United States within the broader context of Israel's foreign relations.

Bernard Reich is professor of political science and international affairs and former chairman of the Department of Political Science at George Washington University in Washington, D.C. He is the author of *Quest for Peace: United States–Israel Relations and the Arab-Israeli Conflict* (1977) and *The United States and Israel: Influence in the Special Relationship* (1981) and other books and coeditor (with David E. Long) of *The Government and Politics of the Middle East and North Africa* (Westview, 1980).

Index

215